a special gift

presented to:

_____

from:

_____

date:

_____

"For the LORD your God is living among you.
He is a mighty savior.
He will take delight in you with gladness.
With his love, he will calm all your fears.
He will rejoice over you with joyful songs."
—*Zephaniah 3:17, NLT*

The Women's Devotional Series

Notes of Joy

Carolyn Rathbun Sutton

EDITOR

Pacific Press®
Publishing Association

Nampa, Idaho | Oshawa, Ontario, Canada
www.pacificpress.com

You can obtain additional copies of this book by calling toll-free 1-800-765-6955 or by visiting http://www.adventistbookcenter.com.

Library of Congress Cataloging-in-Publication Data
Names: Sutton, Carolyn, 1944- editor.
Title: Notes of joy / Carolyn Rathbun Sutton, editor.
Description: Nampa : Pacific Press Publishing Association, 2017.
Identifiers: LCCN 2017030143 | ISBN 978-0-8163-6326-1 (hardcover : alk. paper)
Subjects: LCSH: Devotional calendars. | Devotional calendars—Seventh-Day
   Adventists. | Christian women—Religious life.
Classification: LCC BV4810 .N68 2017 | DDC 242/.2—dc23 LC record available at
https://lccn.loc.gov/2017030143

July 2017

About the Editor

Carolyn Rathbun Sutton finds great joy in "being there" for other women, especially those struggling to find renewed purpose after a major life setback. She particularly enjoys helping women share with others their own personal stories of God's faithfulness.

Scholarshipping Our Sisters
Women Helping Women

There is an aspect of this book that is unique . . .

None of these contributors has been paid—each has shared freely so that all profits go to scholarships for women. As this book goes to press, approximately 2,200 scholarships have been given to women in 127 countries.

For more current information, or to contribute to these scholarships, please go to http://adventistwomensministries.org/index.php?id=52. In this way you too can help fulfill the dream of some woman—or even yourself—to attend college or university.

General Conference Women's Ministries Scholarship Fund

The General Conference Women's Ministries scholarship program supports higher education for Adventist women globally. Recipients are talented women of vision who are committed to serving the mission of the Seventh-day Adventist Church.

Among Friends, published in 1992, was the first annual women's devotional book. Since then, proceeds from 22 of these devotional books have funded scholarships for Adventist women seeking to obtain higher education. However, as tuition costs have risen and more women have applied for assistance, funding has not kept pace with the need. Many dedicated women who apply must be turned down.

Recognizing the importance of educating women—to build stronger families, stronger communities, and a stronger church—each of us can help. Together we can change lives!

There are many ways to support our sisters, such as . . .

- praying for women worldwide who are struggling to get an education;
- telling others about the Women's Ministries scholarship program (Materials are available to share.);
- writing for the women's devotional book (Guidelines are available.); and
- your gift or pledge to support women's education.

To make a gift or receive materials, send us a postcard with the following information. (Our address is on page 8.)

Name _____

Street _____

City _____ State/Province _____

Postal Code_____ Country _____

E-mail _____

To contact us:

Women's Ministries Department
General Conference of Seventh-day Adventists
12501 Old Columbia Pike
Silver Spring, MD 20904

Phone: 301-680-6636
Fax: 301-680-6600
E-mail: womensministries@gc.adventist.org
Web site: http://adventistwomensministries.org
Scholarship application and devotional book writers' guidelines are available at our Web site.

My Silk Dress

"Choose for yourselves this day whom you will serve. . . .
But as for me and my household, we will serve the LORD."
—*Joshua 24:15, NIV*

Years ago, I wanted to have a silk dress but didn't have money for the expensive fabric. Much later, I bought soft, shiny, silver-gray material for the beautiful dress that I wore to my wedding. It felt like a second skin on my body—elegant, light, and *so* good! This was a dress for only special occasions, so I rarely wore it and washed it only one or two times. One day, deciding to wear it to the wedding celebration of a close friend, I took my silk dress from the closet to put on. But I could not zip it up. I held my breath, tucked my tummy, and let my husband struggle with the zipper. It didn't look nice on me any more, so I had to say goodbye to it. The dress had not changed size, but I had. It was painful to have to give it away—a sad ending to my silk dress story.

Yet this happens elsewhere, does it not? A table we keep only for special occasions. A keepsake book that never gets read. A visit we postpone until it's too late. Or we suffer from the past, fear for the future, but forget to live for, and enjoy, the present. What we have saved can lose its value over time. So, at the start of this new year, we need to think about the word *now*.

"*Now* is the appointed time." The Israelites had to decide whether to go back to what they knew and disliked or to go forward into the unknown. And they needed to decide *now*.

In John 12:3–9 we read the story of Mary Magdalene, who in the past had felt dirty, abused, denied, and unworthy. But she did what her heart, impressed by God's Spirit, told her to do *now*—anoint the feet of Jesus with expensive oil. Though criticized by the men, she gave her *now* to Jesus. *Now* was her time—and it was also His time to give her back her God-given worth.

We women can do things that men cannot; men can do things that women cannot do. Let us recognize our true God-given worth and do what He asks us to do. Let us change our habits *now*. So let us not wait until the dress doesn't fit any more or until it is too late for that visit. Let us not wait until the marriage is in pieces. Let us not wait until we have forgotten what we liked—or until we have lost ourselves. Let us be salt and light! Let us remember the past and count our present blessings. Let's be courageous. Now!

Denise Hochstrasser

The Year I Will Never Forget

Cast all your anxiety on him because he cares for you.
—*1 Peter 5:7, NIV*

"For I know the plans I have for you," declares the LORD,
"plans to prosper you and not to harm you,
plans to give you hope and a future."
—*Jeremiah 29:11, NIV*

Have you ever had a really rough year? A year when everything seemed to go wrong?

In the wee hours of January 1, the sound of exploding fireworks filled the air. Residents and visitors alike filled the streets to celebrate the incoming new year. As I listened to the merriment, my thoughts drifted back to events that had happened the previous year.

Oh, Lord, I prayed, *thank You for sparing my life to see this new year, but, oh, what a year the last one was!*

Have you ever had one of those years when your challenges assailed your family from all sides? Was it the difficulty you faced meeting your financial demands? Could it have been that terrible car accident that has left you paralyzed? Oh, it must have been that medical diagnosis—a diagnosis that included many tests, many doctors, and few answers. A diagnosis that had you wondering where the Great Physician was in all of this; then you watched the medical bills pile up and grasped for solutions that could bring about relief and healing.

But every so often you began to find some comfort in God and His words and in the words of those who love you. These words, in hours of despair, reminded you not to be fearful because, as with the wayward Samson, God is still involved in your life.

Whatever it is that might have happened in your life this past year, no matter how challenging, remember that our heavenly Father asks us to cast all our cares on Him.

He reminds us that He will never leave us nor forsake us.

As we begin this new year, let's remember that our heavenly Father loves and cares for us.

Let's ask God to give us the strength we need to face whatever challenges come our way. No matter how difficult life may be, He has our backs.

Won't you allow Him to lead you along the path of trust and righteousness as you commence this year? He will be glad to walk it with you.

Taniesha Robertson-Brown

Brighten Your Corner

"Before they call I will answer."
—Isaiah 65:24, NIV

I t was time to leave for Wednesday night prayer meeting. Miguel, my husband, rushed me out of the house because he'd promised to pick up a neighbor on the way. I suggested that we take my van because I needed to fill up the gas tank. I'd gone to the gas station after work, but there had been a line of cars waiting, so I'd come on home. Miguel quietly grumbled that I always wait until the gas tank indicator light on the dashboard goes on before I fill up, so I agreed to get gas on the way to church.

Miguel did not take our usual route. I squinted in the sunset glare across the windshield and couldn't help but comment that "we" had made a mistake going down Yellowhead Trail. Traffic was backed up, with only one lane moving. As we inched along, we realized that there'd been an accident ahead. We could see an ambulance, a fire truck, and several cars pulled over on the shoulder of the road. Suddenly I recognized a couple from our church standing beside the road. *And* beside their smashed truck! Unfortunately, they had rear-ended another vehicle that, in turn, had hit a third vehicle. Miguel quickly pulled over. We jumped out of the van and ran toward our friends.

These church members, a senior couple, were visibly shaken by the accident but not hurt. First responders placed a woman from one of the involved vehicles into a neck brace and then onto a stretcher. "She doesn't have life-threatening injuries," they assured us. The third driver, after exchanging contact information, drove off, praise God! I could not bring myself to continue on to church and leave our friends waiting alone for a tow truck. So I phoned the church and informed someone about what had happened and received their assurance of prayer.

Since we could not go to church, we did the next best thing. The Bible says to give thanks in all things (1 Thessalonians 5:18). So, right there, we began singing and praising God for His watch care over everyone involved in the accident. We recited Psalm 100 and shared stories about God's goodness until the tow truck arrived. In the process, we witnessed to the ambulance attendants, tow truck driver, and police officers who were still on the scene.

Brighten whatever dark corner in which you find yourself.

Sharon Long (Brown)

Much More Than What We Asked or Dreamed

"For I know the plans I have for you," declares the LORD,
"plans to prosper you and not to harm you,
plans to give you hope and a future."
—Jeremiah 29:11, NIV

Some time ago, my husband and I decided to submit applications for job openings in a small town. We decided to pray about it and asked God to show us where we should go. We agreed to take the qualifying exams. If one of us passed the exam and was offered a position, we would sell our house and move to that town.

The prospective employer informed me I was selected as the top applicant. I took the job. God had worked out everything. There was only one problem: The houses in the new town were much more expensive than where we had previously lived. Even with money from the sale of our home, it would be impossible for us to afford a house there. We prayed to God about this problem.

We looked at several houses during this time. Everything seemed to go wrong. I began to claim the promises of our heavenly Father; after all, we believed our move was His will. My husband told me about a house he had seen along a dirt road, but I was not interested. At night, before I went to bed, I prayed to God.

That night I dreamed that I had arrived at a house resembling one that our friends lived in. In my dream, the front door was on the opposite side from our friends' actual home. In the dream, I asked my friend why she had moved the door. She had smiled and said, "This isn't my house. It's yours."

The next day we went house hunting. As we neared the house that my husband had already seen, I said I'd be willing to take a look at it. To my surprise, it looked the same as the house in my dream! "This is our house," I said to my husband. He looked at me, scared. I explained that I believed God had shown me this very house in my dream the night before.

We called the real estate agent and closed the deal that had been made possible only by the grace of God.

To this day, I am touched every time I remember how God can give us so much more than we ask for or dream. *Thank you, Lord.*

Nilva de F. Oliveira da Boa Morte

I Will Save Your Children

Shall the prey be taken from the mighty,
or the captives of the righteous be delivered? But thus says the LORD:
"Even the captives of the mighty shall be taken away,
and the prey of the terrible be delivered; for I will contend with him
who contends with you, and I will save your children."
—Isaiah 49:24, 25, NKJV

The sun had barely set Friday evening as I eagerly ushered my four children to their beds. My heart was heavy. Too heavy to enjoy their noise and activity a moment longer!

As quiet descended, I plunked myself down on the couch and burst into tears. My husband was away on a seven-week trip, and parenting without his help had taken its toll on me. As the end of week six rolled around, discouragement settled on me like a heavy blanket. All I could see were my kids' faults—fighting, crying, teasing each other, and not obeying quickly—they were so naughty! Now, with tears rolling down my face, I begged God to talk to me.

Look at my kids, Lord! They'll never go to heaven like this! They're hopeless! And I am too! Look at me! I'm a failure of a mother, and I can't even save myself, much less my children!

I hugged my Bible for dear life. *You have to talk to me! Please, talk to me! We're all hopeless, and I need to hear Your voice!*

I opened the Bible, looking for . . . I don't know what. But my eyes fell immediately on these words: "Shall the prey be taken from the mighty, or the captives of the righteous be delivered? But thus says the LORD: 'Even the captives of the mighty shall be taken away, and the prey of the terrible shall be delivered; for I will contend with him that contends with you, and I will save your children' " (Isaiah 49:24, 25, NKJV).

I will save your children. The very words my heart most craved to hear! The answer to the heaviest burden on my heart! Peace stole over me. He will save my children! He promised! It's His job, not mine. It never was mine. Of course, I can't save my children, or myself. We're all completely dependent on Him, and He has promised to save us!

Joy filled my heart, and I wanted to shout, laugh, and sing! God had talked to me! He heard my cries! He answered me! He knows the anguish of my heart! He listened to me, and He replied! He really does love me, He really does. We can trust our children to Him.

Patsy Arrabito

Insight From a "Web Site"

"Behold, I make all things new."
—Revelation 21:5, NKJV

Of all the marvelous things I look forward to seeing in heaven, spiders are not on my list. I know there are people who are fascinated by them and the good they do. Each spider consumes about two thousand insects per year, and I applaud them for their part in keeping these bugs from taking over the world. It's all right with me if these arachnids live in my yard. I just don't like them camping out in my house.

In spite of my aversion to spiders, I must admit that God has a special purpose for them, as He does for all His creatures. In watching them I have learned something that has helped me through some difficult times—times when I just wanted to give up.

If you've ever seen a spider building a web, you can't help but notice the persistence it employs. It builds that piece of architecture as if its life depends on it—because it does; without that web, there is no dinner. With precision and patience, that little creature keeps at the task until it's finished.

If a heavy rain destroys the web, the spider waits out the storm. Then, no matter how tired it may be, it starts rebuilding.

Like most people, I've experienced storms in my life. When they are short, like thundershowers, I simply do the best I can and rearrange my day. But when the storm is more like a hurricane, it washes away my plans, my hopes, and my dreams. It's then I remember the lowly spider, waiting for the tempest to pass so it can begin to build its web again.

It's tempting to think that the spider can simply build a new web, while for me starting over is a lot more complicated. That may be true. The difference is that the spider doesn't give up. It never quits until it has a new web.

Have you had any storms lately? Whatever damage they have caused, God doesn't want you to give up either. He's always near. But He is especially close to us during the storms of life.

If the Lord can equip the lowly spider with the strength and motivation to rebuild after it has lost everything, just imagine what wonderful things He can do for you and me when a crisis overwhelms us like a flood. All we need to do is ask.

Marcia Mollenkopf

God Moves in a Mysterious Way

He leads me beside the still waters.
—*Psalm 23:2, NKJV*

I looked forward to joining my husband, who was serving as a missionary in Liberia. But the people he arranged for me to travel with left without informing me. As I waited for the Lord to work things out, I dreamt about flying to somewhere with rubber plantations. I also dreamt about having a son in a land with many flowers. At work I was asked to travel with other ladies to cook for our soldiers. I was impressed, "Do not accept." So I declined. Upon arriving home that afternoon, a voice said to me, "Go fetch water." I did. Again the voice said, "Lie down." I lay down, and about an hour later, the voice told me, "Go take a bath." Carrying the bucket of water toward the bathroom, I saw a man in the hallway with luggage. To my surprise, it was my husband, who had come from Liberia to get me so I could join him in mission service.

"The vehicle that dropped me at your house vanished after I got my luggage," he told me. "It had traveled over four hundred miles without stopping." My dad had mixed feelings about our leaving; however, he said he would pray for our safety. We boarded a vessel at the same seaport where the mystery vehicle had picked up my husband earlier.

While we were on the high seas, an enemy warship sighted us. Then suddenly, the tides made it impossible for the larger ship to overtake us. Our small vessel escaped and made it to the last seaport in Biafra. Passengers on the next boat to arrive told us that the warship that had missed us had caught them. Because of the many foreigners aboard the smaller vessel, however, the crew of the larger ship spared everyone on the overtaken boat. At our seaport stopover, the soldiers who searched our luggage gave us permission to sail away. Again, this was by God's grace, for within two hours the same warship arrived at this very port!

We were able to board a plane in Douala, Cameroon. Then, arriving at Robertsfield Airport in Liberia, I saw rubber plantations looking like those in my earlier dream. In less than one year, we traveled to the United States of America. I loved the beautiful flowers there, and that is where my son was born. The Lord is faithful.

Do you have a mountain in your life? Just remember that God is able to remove it.

Margaret Obiocha

Divine Interruptions

For I know the plans I have for you, says the Lord.
They are plans for good and not for evil,
to give you a future and a hope.
—*Jeremiah 29:11, TLB*

I had plans. I would finish grad school by a certain time. Then I would travel to Europe as a reward for all the hard work and sacrifice I had put into making it through school. Finally, I would seek out my dream job. I was on course . . . until I no longer was. One after the other, interruptions came. My heart was broken. I was no longer going to proceed through my graduate program at the pace I had anticipated. I would not be graduating at the time I told my friends and family I would be. I wasn't even sure what my dream job looked like anymore.

The Bible gives accounts of times in people's lives when they undoubtedly felt "interrupted" too. Yet often in those moments of apparent interruption, God was up to something—big! Take Simon Peter, for example. He was out doing his thing—washing his net after fishing. Then, along comes Jesus: "Launch out into the deep and let down your nets for a catch" (Luke 5:4, NKJV). Peter had toiled all night and caught nothing. However, he obeyed Jesus' command and caught a great multitude of fish, so much so that the nets began to break! Then Jesus introduced the beginning of the rest of Peter's life: "Do not be afraid. From now on you will catch men" (verse 10, NKJV).

Ask the woman at the well (John 4) about her interruption. She was merely about her usual business of fetching water. But there sat Jesus—a Jew asking a Samaritan for a drink. A conversation ensued. She left her water jar and returned to the village saying, "Come, see a man. . . . Could this be the Messiah?" (John 4:29, NIV).

God shows up in the midst of our mundane or adrenaline-charged tasks with a divine interruption that changes the course of our lives in significant ways—and forever. Those interruptions may come in the form of a major disruption or a quiet conviction. In those moments, as difficult as they may seem, we must simply trust and obey, knowing that God is up to something! He has thoughts of peace toward us and not evil.

May we be open to embracing the divine interruptions as God seeks to prosper us (whatever that looks like for each of us) and also to use us to further the cause of His kingdom.

Stacey A. Nicely

Depending on God!

"But blessed is the one who trusts in the LORD,
whose confidence is in him."
—*Jeremiah 17:7, NIV*

The young girl's heart fluttered with excitement! Her sparkling brown eyes could hardly take in the beauty and opulence of the royal palace. She had grown up with unimaginable pain, losing both parents when she was very young. All known security was suddenly ripped from her until the warm hand of her cousin reached through her grief and offered her a place in his home.

Cousin Mordecai cared for young Esther with respect and love. He gave her the best he had. Nourishing food promoted her radiant complexion. He taught her to love and trust God with her life. This gave her an inner peace that could be seen in her soft eyes and quick, genuine smile.

Now, some years later, Esther had matured into a beautiful, poised, and shapely young lady. And it was in this stage of life that her beauty caught the attention of the king's scouts. She was brought to the buildings of the royal residence, where she would enter the competition to be the new queen.

Esther's appearance and pleasant disposition did not go unnoticed. The keeper of the women was so attracted to Esther that soon he couldn't hide his partiality. He directed her to the very best part of the house for her year of preparation. Now, can you imagine a whole year of being pampered with oil massages and milk baths, or whatever skin and muscle treatments the Persian royals used?

It all worked! Esther was crowned the new queen of Persia.

As time passed, her cousin Mordecai's life of honor to God deeply irritated the head prince, Haman. Haman schemed to have all the Jews killed. Mordecai laid the burden of saving her people on Esther's shoulders. What did this young queen do? She prayed! She fasted! She got friends to fast and pray with her. She totally depended on God for wisdom to put together a plan. And He did.

Whatever our life story and whatever challenges we face, the Problem Solver is still on the throne with solutions we can't even imagine. The story of Esther helps us realize that God gives opportunities to us—even to unlikely women in unlikely places—to see His deliverance as we depend on Him for wisdom and demonstrate a living faith in Him!

Roxy Hoehn

Safari

"Fear not, for I am with you; be not dismayed,
for I am your God. I will strengthen you, yes, I will help you,
I will uphold you with My righteous right hand."
—Isaiah 41:10, NKJV

It was 1977. Together with two other missionary families and friends from Kenya, we went on a safari that included a boat ride on the Victoria Nile River in northwestern Uganda. Murchison Falls National Park, also called Kabalega Falls National Park, is the largest park in Uganda. It was a perfect day for a cruise. The scenery was beautiful. Crocodiles lay on the riverbank basking in the sunshine. As the boat drew closer to shore, some of these magnificent creatures slowly slid into the water, their eyes watching our every move while others remained, their massive mouths open to cool off as birds cleaned their teeth.

The hippos grazing nearby ran toward the murky depths of the Nile, only to emerge with their huge bodies making waves that rocked our small boat. On the other side of the river, a lone water buffalo stood watching us.

Suddenly the motor of our boat sputtered and then . . . silence. The captain tried to start the engine, but it was a futile attempt. There we were, drifting downstream among the huge creatures of the river.

Then, in a heroic act, the captain steered the boat toward the shallow part of the river. In spite of the danger around, he waded to shore and ran for help. It seemed like forever, but he eventually came back and repaired the engine. Then we were on our way to see Murchison Falls.

The falls proved to be a breathtaking display of power. At the top of the falls, the 164-feet-wide (fifty-meter-wide) river squeezes its way with tremendous force through a twenty- to twenty-three-foot (six- to seven-meter) gap in the rocks as it tumbles into a pool below. From there it continues its flow, bisecting the African savannah on its way to the Mediterranean Sea.

I came out of this experience knowing that, in my own Christian life, the Captain of my boat will never leave me drifting helplessly among the huge "creatures" of this uncertain world and future. He won't abandon me to riverbank dangers that wait to destroy me.

Evelyn Porteza-Tabingo

Secretary

For I know the thoughts that I think toward you, says the Lord,
thoughts of peace and not of evil, to give you a future and a hope.
—Jeremiah 29:11, NKJV

G rowing up during the late 1950s in southern Oregon was a challenge for my siblings and me. Our parents owned a wholesale gladiola business, and their "booming" business was not booming anymore! They were committed to providing a Christian education for us. Yet even though we all worked hard, it became more increasingly difficult to pay our tuition.

I had always planned to get a college education, but during my sophomore year of college, I met and fell in love with a young man who was ready to begin his career. The financial security was very appealing to me. So I dropped out of college, and we were married that summer. Even though I completed several college courses, taught home economics one year, and owned my own business, I never obtained the college degree that had always been a longing in my heart! Yet God had other plans.

Fast-forward to the 1980s. We moved our family to the foothills of central California. I kept busy raising our family, directing the Pathfinder club, and working as secretary and bookkeeper of the nearby junior academy. I was employed there for fourteen years to ensure that our children could have a Christian education. I loved the students at school. During those years I became like a second mom to many of them. Recently April, whose father was a teacher at the school, told me that because I had made such an impact on her life during her growing up years, her greatest ambition and passion had grown into the desire to become a school secretary just like me. She had already taken a bookkeeping class to become better qualified. Though April felt the timing wasn't yet right, she wanted to share her dream with me so I could keep it in prayer.

Not long after, I shed grateful tears upon learning that April was just hired to be the school secretary in the very secretarial office where my presence had inspired her so many years earlier. It amazes me that God used me, even though I didn't feel qualified at the time. God showed me I didn't need a degree in order to be able to touch others for Him. He just needs a heart willing to do the very best we can wherever He has placed us.

May God use each of us to make a difference for His kingdom.

Nadine Parker Proctor

What a Friend We Have in Jesus

"I no longer call you slaves,
because a master doesn't confide in his slaves.
Now you are my friends,
since I have told you everything the Father told me."
—*John 15:15, NLT*

Throughout my life I've had many friends: childhood friends, school friends, college friends, work friends, best friends, and the list goes on. For most of us, friends come and go. Life's circumstances can rob us of good friends.

The persons I count as my best friends do not live close to me. I can always call them, but sometimes they are not available or are facing their own troubles. Then I find myself isolated from the emotional and spiritual support I need.

The hymn says, "What a friend we have in Jesus, all our sins and griefs to bear; what a privilege to carry everything to God in prayer!"* This is undergirded by our text today, which tells us that Jesus calls us friends—which makes Him our Friend. Proverbs 18:24 reminds us that we have a friend "who sticks closer than a brother" (NIV). That friend is Jesus.

There are times when my Friend Jesus ministers to me through an earthly friend—a hug, words of encouragement, and love. But there are times when He ministers to me directly: through His Word, a hymn or song, or the comforting presence of the Holy Spirit. At times of loss in my life, when no one understood, my Friend Jesus did and ministered to my heart.

The hymn goes on to say, "O what peace we often forfeit, O what needless pain we bear, all because we do not carry everything to God in prayer."† How many times have I struggled with problems? Struggled and lost? How many times have I felt I could handle a situation and then failed? Yet we have a Friend who is always near and willing to take our problems and give us sweet peace, to face life's trials. He calls us friend. What a privilege to call the Son of God our Friend!

Today you may be facing a trial and feel you are alone. Take a moment to reach out to Jesus, the Friend who is closer than any other friend you may have. The one Friend who never fails, never leaves, but is always, always ready to help.

Heather-Dawn Small

---

* Joseph M. Scriven, "What a Friend We Have in Jesus," 1855.
† Ibid.

He Leadeth Me!

The Lord heareth your murmurings
which ye murmur against him.
—*Exodus 16:8*

Every day I travel about seventy miles for work. On a fair-weather day in Michigan, that's about a forty-five-minute to one-hour commute. On a snowy or foggy day, however, my commute can take anywhere from an hour and fifteen minutes to almost two hours. I usually have to wake up at four-fifteen each morning. In wintry weather, I would frequently whine to the Lord, *I'm not sure how much longer I can do this!*

Over time I realized that I was leaving home every morning with an almost angry disposition. I would pull out of the driveway at six-thirty only to realize that my neighbors were still cozied up in their warm beds. Having to dig my car out from under several inches of snow while everyone slept also upset me. I was impatient with my colleagues who lived only ten or fifteen minutes from work yet still complained about being tired in the morning.

I remembered the Bible story of Hezekiah, who asked for a longer life. I also recalled the parable of the prodigal son, who demanded his inheritance. God granted both requests, although the impatience of these men ultimately led to pain. So I pleaded with the Father not to leave me to my own devices and attitudes. I meditated on 1 Corinthians 3:19, which says that "the wisdom of this world is foolishness with God." I pled with the Spirit of God to help me honor His Word so that I would not be defrauded by the enemy because of my own selfish desires. I could not trust my life to my own hands.

I claimed Psalm 23:3, "He leads me in the paths of righteousness for His name's sake" (NKJV), and envisioned myself as a little girl walking hand in hand with my Savior. Surely I would not be deceived. I trusted His leading. He leads me in the paths of righteousness.

Murmuring is a form of disregard for the power of God. I had essentially been denying my belief in His guidance and His power to sustain me on the road where He had led me. I had grumbled at the Giver of my wonderful gift—a job.

Father, I surrender to You today my affair with the spirit of complaint and disgruntlement. Forgive me for showing ingratitude for the blessings you have given me.

Shanter H. Alexander

His Unfailing Love

The LORD has appeared of old to me, saying:
"Yes, I have loved you with an everlasting love;
Therefore with lovingkindness I have drawn you."
—Jeremiah 31:3, NKJV

I was going through a very difficult season in my life. Here I was, a forty-two-year-old widow, with a ten-year-old son. My husband, with no chronic health condition, went to sleep and just did not wake up. I was devastated. I could not stop the tears from falling. It seemed I was always crying. *Where was God? Why did He allow this to happen?* I was very angry with God.

Even though I was going through the motions of going to church, reading my Bible, and praying, my heart wasn't in any of it. My heart was in turmoil. How could a loving God do this to my family?

One night as I was going around the living room putting things in place and turning off lights, my heart cried out, *Does God really love me?* I had doubts. *Where is God in all of this pain?* As I climbed the stairs, I heard an audible voice, "Open the front door." I stopped and looked around! I was the only one on the stairs. I took another step. "Open the front door," the voice said again.

This time I stopped, and loudly I said, "Yeah, right. Why should I listen to You? You don't love me. You don't care about me. If you did, why did You take my husband?" Defiantly, I took another step.

This time the voice was more urgent, "Open the front door!"

"OK, Lord," I said. "If You want me to open the door, I will." I went back downstairs, marched to the front door, and yanked it open. Looking down as I did so, I saw my keys—still in the outside of the door. I had left my keys outside! I stood there shaking.

"Lord!" I cried, "You *do* love me. You really *do* care for me!" What if I had gone to bed with the keys in the front door outside? I shudder to think what could have happened! I bowed my head and asked God to forgive me for doubting His love for me and to please help me trust in Him. Thus began my healing!

I rejoice to know that Jesus will always be with me. He will always protect and keep me safe in His love. We can each trust Him to do the same in our lives.

Jannett Maurine Myrie

The Good Samaritan and the Jew: After the Parable

"But a Samaritan, as he traveled, came where the man was;
and when he saw him, he took pity on him. He went to him and
bandaged his wounds, pouring on oil and wine. Then he put the man
on his own donkey, brought him to an inn and took care of him."
—Luke 10:33, 34, NIV

Have you ever thought about what happened in the story of the good Samaritan—*after* the parable? Have you ever wondered how the Samaritan's unselfishness and kindness might have changed the life of the wounded man? Unless the wounded man was changed by grace, he would have turned away in shame and embarrassment the next time he encountered the Samaritan in public. Not because he didn't appreciate what the Samaritan had done, but rather because he was too filled with the pride of life to risk the loss of face that public acknowledgement might bring.

I've realized that it's possible to be touched by grace but not changed by it. The injured Jew was touched, literally, by the care that came straight from the heart of the good Samaritan. But the Jew did not have to sacrifice any pride to receive the care. It was freely bestowed while he was too wounded to accept or reject it. However, once he recovered, the Jew was able to choose how to respond to the Samaritan's kindness. If his heart was not changed by grace, there's a good chance that he did not acknowledge his benefactor—at least, not publicly.

I can even imagine that, over time, the Jew may have become hardened enough in pride to reason that, in a way, the incident had actually done the Samaritan a favor by allowing him to help one of God's chosen. He may have rationalized away the entire incident so that he was left with no sense of obligation to one who had risked his life to save another who despised him.

Think you would never be guilty of such a thing? Take a closer look inside, and you might think differently. The pride of life rests in all of us, and, barring the miracle of grace, at one time or another it can cause us to turn away in shame, perhaps even from someone who has helped us to become who we are. That's because being the recipient of grace doesn't automatically change you. You have to *choose* to be changed. So next time you find yourself feeling ashamed of someone, just remember the story that might have followed the parable of the good Samaritan: the recovered Jew and rejected Samaritan.

Rachel Williams-Smith

Pictures

And the appearance of the glory of Jehovah was like devouring fire
on the top of the mount in the eyes of the children of Israel.
—*Exodus 24:17, ASV*

The sun was just coming up that cold January day as my daughter and I drove down the mountain. The sky held bright shades of pink, violet, orange, lavender, and purple. The clouds were feathery as if an artist had painted them. Though we stopped to take pictures of this breathtaking artistry, our pictures were a sad reflection of the beauty we were really seeing. The clarity and intensity of the colors lasted so long that, further down the mountain, we stopped again, trying to capture the beauty of the moment. Our pictures were a little better this time but still didn't begin to reflect what we were actually seeing.

This experience started us talking about our great Lord and Savior, Jesus. How we are supposed to be pictures of Him here on this planet? Yet so often the reflection of Him that we present to the world is dingy and dull, not manifesting the complete radiance of His glory.

How can I, a sinner, reflect my Savior in my life so that others might glimpse Him? When I prayed and asked the Lord about it, my mind was taken to Moses. He spent forty days and nights with God up on Mount Sinai. When he came down, his face glowed so much that the people were afraid of him. "And it came to pass, when Moses came down from mount Sinai with the two tables of the testimony in Moses' hand, when he came down from the mount, that Moses knew not that the skin of his face shone by reason of his speaking with him. And when Aaron and all the children of Israel saw Moses, behold, the skin of his face shone; and they were afraid to come nigh him" (Exodus 34:29, 30, ASV).

That is the secret to reflecting Jesus to others—spending quality time with Him. Oh, how I want to be a better picture and reflect the One who gave everything for me. Imagine the beauty in this world if we were pictures of Jesus and reflected just a tiny bit of His glory. Wow!

"Arise, shine; for thy light is come, and the glory of Jehovah is risen upon thee. For, behold, darkness shall cover the earth, and gross darkness the peoples; but Jehovah will arise upon thee, and his glory shall be seen upon thee. And nations shall come to thy light, and kings to the brightness of thy rising" (Isaiah 60:1–3, ASV).

Mona Fellers

A Hole in My Heart

Therefore, my brothers and sisters, you whom I love and long for,
my joy and crown, stand firm in the Lord in this way, dear friends!
—*Philippians 4:1, NIV*

After working as missionaries in Africa for six years, it was time for us to return to our homeland in Germany. It had been a wonderful experience even though it was sometimes very hard. We had learned a lot. We were looking forward to seeing family and friends, but it was hard to leave Africa and our African friends.

I directed the church's young people's choir. I showed the women of the church how to sew clothes for their babies. And I brought recorders and taught the children to play on these musical instruments. We had a mission in common with our coworkers with whom we wanted to proclaim the gospel to the people of central Africa. And now we were packing up our belongings and returning to our home country!

We spent the last few nights in the guesthouse of the mission, as our replacement had already moved into our former house. On our last morning in Bangui, church members came to the guesthouse to say farewell. The young people who had sung in my choir came to see me off. We hugged each other and cried. It was as if a piece had been ripped out of my heart. We had an overnight layover in Paris, and I could hardly sleep because the hole in my heart was bleeding. I heard their tearful voices again and again, and I longed to take them into my arms.

A few years later, a mission spotlight from Africa was shown in church. A choir was singing. As I heard the African voices singing to God's glory, my heart started bleeding again. Tears came into my eyes as I remembered my friends. The hole in my heart is still there today.

The apostle Paul also seems to have had a hole in his heart. Writing to the church in Philippi, he said that he longed for his brothers and sisters in the faith. He called them his crown and joy. They were his recompense for all his hard work. He encouraged them to stand firm in the Lord. He didn't expect to ever see them again (he was writing from prison in Rome), but he knew that there would be a great reunion at Christ's return if all stayed faithful to God.

When Jesus comes again, we will have a big celebration, and our bleeding hearts will be healed. Then the hole in my heart will also be closed forever. I am looking forward to that day.

Hannele Ottschofski

Heating the Heater

I am the vine, ye are the branches: He that abideth in me,
and I in him, the same bringeth forth much fruit:
for without me ye can do nothing.
—John 15:5

When my husband, Al, is working, he stays in a trailer near his work. During the winter he uses portable heaters to heat his living space. He has had many different kinds of heaters, but there is one that has been his faithful little heat source. One winter he got a second, more efficient, heater to help. One morning he noticed the older heater was not heating as it usually did. He checked to see whether it was beginning to give out from old age and much use. During his inspection he discovered that the heaters were close to each other. The newer heater was blowing in the direction of the older heater. Therefore, the older heater did not have to work as much to keep things warm because its sensor was "reading" the heat put out by the second heater. The older heater was working just fine and putting out just the amount of heat that was required.

In today's verse Jesus tells us that if we are a branch on His vine, we can be assured of a life-giving source from the main vine in order to grow and function. If we are cut off, we are just that—cut off. We no longer have a connection to help us to grow and develop. Let's look at the last six words of Jesus in this text: "without me ye can do nothing." So many times we want to be able to do things ourselves, much like a child learning something new. Yet looking to someone who can help us along our journey is a better way to learn what we need to know. Being plugged in to a pure power source does have advantages!

Just as the second heater was providing a source of heat, the first heater put out what its sensors "told" it to. Are we fully connected and then cooperating together with Christ as the older heater was doing with the newer one? If so, we are receiving the life-giving love of Jesus to spread to those around us.

Every day I want to start by plugging in to the pure power source, Jesus. I want to work with Him, living in His presence and fully learning the lessons He has for me. When I invite Him into my day, He will guide me, teach me, and be with me, so I will not fail. And if, by some chance, I do fail but confess and turn back to Him, He will find ways to heal, comfort, and teach me. For without Him, I can do nothing. What a blessing to be plugged in to heaven's power source!

Mary E. Dunkin

Unconditional Love

The LORD has appeared of old to me, saying:
"Yes, I have loved you with an everlasting love."
—Jeremiah 31:3, NKJV

I met my maternal grandmother only once, when I was only four years old. I traveled with my mother and four of my five siblings from Barbados to Dominica to meet her. My mother and grandmother had been estranged for many reasons, including my mom's dark complexion, which was vastly different from that of her siblings and her mother. However, the greatest reason for the separation was my dad's economic status. His lack of wealth did not meet my grandmother's standard. He was from the "wrong side of the tracks." After several months in Dominica, we returned to Barbados. Grandmother disowned my mother, her eldest child, and we never saw or heard from my grandmother again.

About ten years later, my mom heard through the grapevine that her mother had died, leaving one penny for her in the will, the final signal she had been disowned.

Twenty-four years after my mother's death, I sit and reflect how deeply she loved her children and the pain she must have suffered from being disowned, abandoned, and separated from her own mother's love. In this quiet moment, Jeremiah 31:3 comes to mind, "I have loved you with an everlasting love." And also Romans 8:38, 39, "For I am persuaded that neither death nor life, nor angels nor principalities nor powers, nor things present nor things to come, nor height nor depth, nor any other created thing, shall be able to separate us from the love of God" (NKJV).

How comforting to know that, regardless of what I do, God loves me. Nothing separates me from that love: not my skin color, or my educational or financial status, or the economic status of my spouse. Nothing causes God to disown me.

What unconditional love! My acceptance of His love entitles me to an inexhaustible inheritance. "Blessed be the God and Father of our Lord Jesus Christ, who according to His abundant mercy has begotten us again to a living hope through the resurrection of Jesus Christ from the dead, to an inheritance incorruptible and undefiled and that does not fade away, reserved in heaven for you" (1 Peter 1:3, 4, NKJV).

My desire is to live a life whose reward is eternity with a God of unconditional love.

Terry Roselmond-Moore

A Bad Word

Suffer little children, and forbid them not, to come unto me:
for of such is the kingdom of heaven.
—*Matthew 19:14*

It was a very pleasant day. I was delighted and happy to be in the school where I was substitute teaching. Everyone was enjoying the lessons the regular classroom teacher had left for me to follow. As the students completed their work, I took a five-minute break from circulating the room and sat down. Within minutes a student approached, complaining that another student had said a bad word to her. I asked her what the bad word was. She answered, "He said the word *God* to me." I was very surprised and sad. For a moment, I could not say anything. At first, I was a bit fearful to mention the word *God*—afraid I might lose my job. Then I conquered my fear.

"*God* is not a bad word," I told her. "It's a good word."

"It *is* a bad word," she insisted, "because my mom said no one should say it."

I tried my best to convince her that *God* is a good word. "I talk to God all the time," I explained. "He is good." I told her that He lives in heaven but can see and hear us. Toward the end of our discussion, most of her anger was gone. She wasn't as upset as she had been earlier when coming to complain to me about the incident.

As I reflected on the event of that day, I knew I would never forget it. I felt a deep pity for that student, knowing that there are many who believe *God* is a bad word—or a bad being. I wish that I had been able to tell her more about our kind, loving, merciful, and wonderful God. Some Christian teachers in public schools are restricted from using the name of God. As a Christian teacher, I believe that I have a duty to the children to tell them, as I can, about God. The Lord promised that He will take care of His saints. And I recall the words of Joshua: "Choose you this day whom ye will serve . . . : but as for me and my house, we will serve the LORD" (Joshua 24:15). The choice to serve God is up to us.

Many individuals in my country do not have a clue about who God is or what He is like.

I pray each day that the students will see something different in me. May my life be a reflection of Christ, and may others see the image of God displayed in me. Then perhaps they will know who He is.

Patricia Hines

Improving With Age

Though our outer man is decaying,
yet our inner man is being renewed day by day.
—*2 Corinthians 4:16, NASB*

don't like getting old, but I refuse to pretend it's not happening. Besides, my life doesn't begin and end with temporal existence. In the above Bible verse, God—through Paul—doesn't deny the sad facts of aging and death. In fact, He puts them in the most graphic and despairing of terms. Can you imagine if the United States Special Commission on Aging changed its name to the Special Commission on Decaying? Senior citizens would storm the White House en masse, flailing walkers and canes, demanding a less derogatory label. But along with its realism, the verse places the unavoidable negatives of our death-bound existence in the context of a powerful spiritual hope. "Our inner man is being renewed day by day." What? You mean something about me is getting better instead of worse? In Jesus I actually improve with age, as does the time-mellowed wood of a Martin guitar, giving it better resonance. I improve as does an old, beat-up towel that actually absorbs more water. I improve like a fifty-seven-year-old woman who is becoming more like Jesus each day through an ongoing inner renewal.

What is this "inner man" that is "being renewed day by day"? This *esothen* (in the Greek) refers to the inner life of a human being. Jesus said, "For from *esothen*, out of the heart of men, proceed evil thoughts" (Mark 7:21, NASB). The renewal of the *esothen*, then, is the rebirth experience Jesus put forth to Nicodemus in hushed tones one moonlit night. In order to improve "characterologically," we need direct, divine, and dramatic intervention. We must be born again.

My greatest fear in aging is not losing my memory or my wit, but becoming grouchy, grumpy, unloving, and unlovable. Cognitive decline can rob an individual of the ability to "put on" a good personality, but character resides at a more foundational level. You can't fake a good character. But a heart transformed day after day by the Holy Spirit can stay soft with love and grace long after the mind has decayed. I want that transformation.

And when I'm not fifty-seven, but eighty-seven (if I live that long), perhaps in the late stages of dementia, I want to be like the sweet old lady who kissed her daughter and said, "I don't know who you are, but I love you."

Jennifer Jill Schwirzer

January 22

The Prayer of Faith

Wait for the LORD;
be strong and take heart
and wait for the LORD.
—*Psalm 27:14, NIV*

The faith of four Hebrew youths speaks to us in the time of crisis. The three worthies, Shadrach, Meshach, and Abednego, stated their faith in God's power and providence (Daniel 3:16–18). And then the persecuting king saw a fourth Person, the Son of God, in the fiery furnace with the three young men whom he had thrown in for their refusal to bow to another god. The story of Daniel in the lions' den also inspires faith.

I have been wanting to understand what faith means in my life as a Christian. At times, I pray and nothing seems to happen. When I read Christ's comment about mustard seed faith being able to move mountains (Matthew 17:20), I yearn to have that kind of faith. I need faith! I need it to open the doors of heaven as well as doors at my workplace, in my family, in my studies, and in every decision I make.

I keep on praying daily to have the faith that Daniel, Shadrach, Meshach, and Abednego had. I need the fourth Person wherever I go. I need His help both for myself and as I extend my hand to help others have faith in Him.

If we can have faith and walk with God, we will be changed. God will use us to draw many broken hearts to Himself. By faith we can win battles because He arms us with strength for every battle against the enemy. Our battlefields will be changed into fields of blessings.

By faith we will see stumbling blocks turned into stepping-stones. These things happen when we know who we are and who holds us in the palm of His hand. None other than *Jesus*.

Another reason we need faith is so that we can wait patiently for the answers to our prayers. I like what David said to King Saul before the young man went to fight the giant, Goliath: "Let no one lose heart on account of this Philistine; your servant will go and fight him. . . . All those gathered here will know that it is not by sword or spear that the LORD saves; for the battle is the LORD's" (1 Samuel 17:32, 47, NIV).

For these praying Bible characters, faith was the hand on the key that opened doors for them. But prayer without faith is like a key without a hand to turn it.

Let's pray with faith as did these Bible characters, and God will open doors for us as well.

Pauline Gesare Okemwa

The Blessings in My Life

For the LORD God is a sun and shield: the LORD will give grace and glory: no good thing will he withhold from them that walk uprightly.
—*Psalm 84:11*

Morning after morning, over a period of months, I sat and wondered whether I had made the right decision. After finishing my doctoral program almost a year earlier, I had chosen not to go the expected route for someone with my degree. Instead, I was working on a voluntary basis with a ministry. Though the work was not hard, the decision itself had been. I was not fully utilizing my knowledge or gifts, or even getting to exercise my passion. Granted, helping to plan and prepare strategic documents coincided with my studies, but I had a general sense of dissatisfaction.

Furthermore, I had to make many adjustments to my normal level of physical comfort. I was sure there were many more to make, causing me to question again the decision I had made. I daily comforted myself with one thought: *It is not about me, it is about Him.* Though that thought carried me through some days, it did not fill the void when I faced situations of great discomfort. Simple pleasures and luxuries I once embraced were distant. Simple social circles I had once enjoyed were now nonexistent. I had no opportunity even to make friends. My life seemed surrounded by what I was doing, and apart from that, I felt empty to a large extent.

One memorable morning, I woke up around five o'clock, as had become the usual in recent weeks. I wanted to go to a gym to exercise and desired to be able to speak to someone and do something outside of my current norm. During my devotional time, tears flowed because I was sensing a lack of purpose. As I bowed my head to pray, tears hit the sofa. I opened my mouth to pray, and the words that came out shocked me. They did not reflect the thoughts I was harboring: "Thank You, Lord, for the blessings in my life." The moment was surreal. I thanked God that for almost ten years, since I'd been in college, I had trained myself to thank Him when things were not going right. Now the apostle Paul's words flowed naturally: "In every thing give thanks: for this is the will of God in Christ Jesus concerning you" (1 Thessalonians 5:18).

Today thank God for your blessings—even for the things that seem to be working against you. For, in the end, He has your best interest at heart!

Nadine A. Joseph

31

Don't Leave

And let us not be weary in well doing:
for in due season we shall reap, if we faint not.
—Galatians 6:9

Come on, let's just be truthful with each other for a minute. Sometimes we just feel like giving up. At times I want to stop having faith in God. Stop hoping. Stop believing the Bible or God's personal promises to me. Stop helping others when they use my kindness as permission to stamp *Welcome* across my forehead and clean their feet. I get tired of being conscious of my witness or fasting and prayer for others who don't fast and pray for themselves. And the big one: I sometimes give up on the promise that "he that shall come will come" (Hebrews 10:37). I realize you aren't my priest, but "they say" confession is good for the soul. Yet what is funny—and great—about spiritual weariness is that when I am at my lowest, the very thing that causes my frustration is the one thing that stops me from giving up. Yes, you guessed it, the Bible.

When I read about Anna, the prophetess, she gives me a whole new perspective. She knew a thing or two about wrestling with God. Anna became widowed after only seven years of marriage. She was eighty-four, with no sons to take care of her, no home, and no Social Security or Medicare. She had reason to give up. Instead, our sister Anna worshiped God despite her circumstances. She was faithful in her lifestyle witness. She knew that no matter how she felt, fasting and prayer still produced results. No matter what the day brought, she remained grateful for God's provision. She accepted God's call to be a prophetess, which took great courage. Yes, Anna has taught me a lot. I don't go off the deep end nearly as fast as I used to. I now push through a bit longer with my fasting and praying. I now understand better that I need to maintain my lifestyle witness for my Savior, no matter what kind of day I am having. But the most valuable lesson from our sister is she *never* left the temple (Luke 2:37). She waited expectantly for God to rescue Jerusalem.

Help me, Lord, to always remember to wait expectantly for You to come to the rescue, no matter how long it takes. Don't leave! Then, Lord, help me to rejoice while I wait.

D. Reneé Mobley

Love Remains

And now abide faith, hope, love, these three;
but the greatest of these is love.
—*1 Corinthians 13:13, NKJV*

My daughter and son are six and four years of age. They affectionately call my parents "Oma" and "Opa." Our family recently went on a Caribbean cruise with Oma and Opa. The cruise ship had five waterslides that sent swimmers plunging into pools below. My daughter watched others go down the slides, and she too wanted to try them out. She barely made the height requirement to go down the slide but still begged to go. After going down one of the slides myself, I decided that she was a strong enough swimmer to try the slides. Her first trip down brought a big smile to her face.

As she emerged from the water, my father leaped from his chair, walked over to her, took her face in his hands, and said, "I am so proud of you!" My daughter beamed from ear to ear. It was a beautiful and loving moment between a grandfather and his granddaughter.

Sadly, my father passed away unexpectedly three months after our trip. After his death, my mother came to live near us. She attended a fundraising event at my daughter's school. Part of the fundraising event included my daughter taking part in running a relay of thirty-five laps within a certain time period. My daughter ran thirty-nine laps!

As my daughter crossed the finish line, my mother made a beeline to her. She placed my daughter's face in her hands and said, "I am so proud of you!" My daughter beamed from ear to ear. My eyes filled with tears at that moment. I missed my father, but I felt as if the love my father had always shown my children was going to live on in the love that my mother continues to show them.

Since my father's death, we sense a loss that won't be filled by any other person. However, the love shown by my father over many years continues to live on in our memories and in our ability to continue to show love to one another. As a family, we also draw close to our heavenly Father, and we are thankful for the tremendous love He bestows on us.

"And we have known and believed the love that God has for us. God is love, and he who abides in love abides in God, and God in him" (1 John 4:16, NKJV).

Beatrice Tauber Prior

Ignorance May Be Fatal

Study to shew thyself approved unto God, a workman that needeth
not to be ashamed, rightly dividing the word of truth.
—*2 Timothy 2:15*

This world is full of problems and difficulties. Everybody has his or her own share of burdens to bear, but the burdens become more difficult when we are ignorant of the things we should know from the Word of God. This is especially true for women who have many responsibilities: children to raise, household chores to finish, a husband to provide for, and even income-generating activities to help support the family. The list is long. Thus, many women do not take time to cultivate the habits of studying, learning, and being informed.

An inspired writer counsels, "Instead of sinking into a mere household drudge, let the wife and mother take time to read, to keep herself well informed, to be a companion to her husband, and to keep in touch with the developing minds of her children. . . . Let her take time for the study of His word, take time to go with the children into the fields and learn of God through the beauty of His works."*

The Bible is the library that contains instruction on how to experience joy and peace, as well as suggestions for solving daily problems and overcoming temptation. It guides us to a healthier relationship with God and our fellow human beings.

We read in today's theme text where the apostle Paul admonishes us, "Study to shew thyself approved unto God, a workman that needeth not to be ashamed, rightly dividing the word of truth." This admonition is especially true for us women who have the responsibility of educating our children. Right understanding may save from problems later in life. After all, ignorance may be fatal. Jesus' disciples went through unspeakable agony during His crucifixion because of ignorance. They might have been saved much sorrow and grief had they "rightly [divided] the word of truth." In fact, for Judas, ignorance proved to be fatal.

Dear reader, maybe your present suffering and sorrow will be alleviated by knowing and believing the promises of God. Maybe you will find a solution to your problems. Why not take time to invite the Holy Spirit to teach you God's Word? After all, Jesus "opened" the disciples' minds "that they might understand the scriptures" (Luke 24:45). He will do the same for you.

Omobonike Adeola Sessou

* Ellen G. White, *The Adventist Home* (Hagerstown, MD: Review and Herald®, 1980), 110.

God Won't Give Up

"Never will I leave you; never will I forsake you."
—Hebrews 13:5, NIV

Twenty-eight years ago, I foolishly allowed my relationship with God to falter. Raised by loving Christian parents, I still believed in God, but due to circumstances in my life, I failed to maintain a daily walk with Him. I stopped reading His Word, and my prayer life also ceased. My parents and church members continued to pray for me.

I was unresponsive.

One day, while listening to the news and contemplating the world's situation, my mind was led to consider spiritual things. The seriousness of my previous actions suddenly hit me.

I fell to my knees in desperation, crying out to God to forgive me. Satan, however, who is always quick to attack us when we are down, told me that I had pushed God away. Perhaps I might have committed the unpardonable sin of ignoring the Holy Spirit, and God could no longer hear me. I pleaded with the Lord to show me whether there was still a chance for me and whether His grace could still reach me. I asked Him for a specific response. *God, I know there is a new pastor at my parents' church. Please have him call me.*

The next day, while having a day off from work as a nurse, my telephone rang. I answered it and heard a voice saying, "Hello. I am Pastor Jonathan Gallagher. I have had your phone number for a while but just now I felt that I should contact you. Would you like me to visit you?" I could hardly believe my ears! This was the pastor from my parents' church! How wrong I had been in thinking that I had pushed God away and that He would no longer hear my prayers.

God does not give up on us that easily! He directly answered my prayer and gave me the reassurance I needed. In His grace and mercy, He had not left my side. He was just waiting there for me to realize my need of Him.

God has gone to such lengths to save us. He is determined to give us His gift of salvation if we will only accept it.

His gentle, loving voice is calling out to you today. Don't put off turning to Him. He will welcome you with open arms as did the father of the prodigal in Christ's parable. The heavenly Father loves you so much, and He will never leave you.

Karen Richards

God Does Provide

My God shall supply all your need
according to his riches in glory by Christ Jesus.
—*Philippians 4:19*

Our 2005 Chrysler Town and Country Stow and Go vehicle was accumulating a lot of miles. We knew that it could not keep running well forever, so we started saving as much as we could each month in order to purchase a newer vehicle. We have always tried to avoid car payments by saving ahead and buying when we had enough. We are snowbirds, so we put a lot of extra miles on our vehicle when traveling from north to south and back again each year. We also make a lot of side trips out from our southern location. Our car had not had any problems, and we wanted to keep it that way. Very slowly, the savings added up. Then in January the mobile home insurance bill arrived. It totaled more than a thousand dollars. We were going to have to dip into our savings in order to cover the payment. I was bemoaning that fact because I really hated to take anything out of savings. Yet the insurance had to be paid. I decided to talk to the Lord about this little problem but didn't have much faith that anything would change. When you are retired and living on a fixed income, there is not much chance of extra money showing up.

Just a few days before I had to write the insurance check—while I was still praying but disbelieving—we received an unexpected check in the mail. It was made out for just a few dollars less than the insurance bill.

Once again, God had come through, even when I couldn't see how He would. The difference between the unexpected check and our insurance bill I took from our regular bank account without any problem—and paid the insurance bill. This left the savings account intact.

I was so ashamed of myself. Why had I disbelieved?

When we are faithful in our tithes and offerings, God has promised to take care of our needs. It wasn't that we did not have the money to pay the insurance at all, it was just that our savings account was earmarked for something else.

God knew that was important to us.

Oh, dear Father, forgive my doubts, and help me to always remember that You are in control and that You will take care of our needs.

Anna May Radke Waters

Jesus—the Trustworthy One

Trust in the LORD with all your heart,
and lean not on your own understanding.
—*Proverbs 3:5, NKJV*

My heart breaks whenever someone I trust betrays my confidence. It happens often—especially in the workplace, where honesty and transparency are sometimes missing in my daily interactions with the various entities. It's the nature of being an administrator, I conclude. People seem to forget that I'm human. Words are spoken in my absence that undermine my work and promote a spirit of discord. Worst though are the kind words spoken in my presence by the same people who are not pure in their motives. This is what causes the heartbreak and confusion because I tend to take people at their word.

One morning as I drove to work, I hurt deeply and lamented the fact that I'm so very unsure about whom to trust besides my immediate family. I stood on slipping sand and felt lost and vulnerable. Then the Spirit of God began to speak to me. I had a sudden thought: *What if I didn't trust anyone but God? That would be crazy!* I reasoned. Again the same thought lingered. *What if I didn't trust anyone but still committed myself to loving everyone, no matter what? What if I just trusted God to keep me true and left Him to do the same for others?*

Knowing that God can, and will, change the hearts of men and women helps me be free to just love them, just as I pray that they would love me should I prove to be disloyal.

The Bible is full of people who trusted in their chariots and their horses, but they failed (Psalm 20:7). Some trusted in themselves. Some had confidence in other gods, power, or riches. Yet they all failed. But God's love never fails. It is no wonder that the command to love God is the greatest commandment, and loving our neighbors as our selves is only second to that.

On the drive to work that morning, my heart settled and rested on the pressing call to trust God above all else and also to love others. I felt reassured and ready to face my tasks knowing that God is in control. I can rely on God to give me a pure heart, selfless motives, and the grace to simply love my fellow men and women. I can accept people who smile in front of me—and sneer behind me—without falling apart. Why? Because my complete confidence is in the Lord.

And you? What is it that causes your heart to break? Why not trust God to take care of it?

Rose Joseph Thomas

Fearfully and Wonderfully Made

I praise you, for I am fearfully and wonderfully made.
Wonderful are your works; that I know very well.
—*Psalm 139:14, NRSV.*

So God created humankind in his image, in the image of God
he created them; male and female he created them.
—*Genesis 1:27, NRSV*

Have you ever stood before the mirror and been unhappy with the way you looked? I know there have been times I have avoided looking in the mirror altogether, not wanting to see the parts of me that I have felt are too big, too long, and too bumpy. I have looked in the mirror and felt myself lacking in some way. Maybe you have too. We are critical of our own appearance—every time we turn on the television or the radio, or open a magazine, we are bombarded with society's picture of beauty. As a mother of two girls, I do not want my daughters to look at themselves the way society teaches them to look at themselves.

Recently I was reflecting on Psalm 139, one of my absolute favorite psalms. After spending some time thinking about how God knows everything about us—what we think, where we go, what we say, and what we need (verses 1–5)—I paused at verse 14 and read this: "I praise you, for I am fearfully and wonderfully made. Wonderful are your works; that I know very well" (NRSV). David's words cut straight to my heart of fears about how I look. They make me pause and I am reminded that I am fearfully and wonderfully made. Another word for *fearfully* in this context is "awesomely." So I am awesomely and wonderfully made.

Taking this a step further, Genesis 1:27 says, "So God created humankind in his image, in the image of God he created them; male and female he created them" (NRSV).

Think about these truths for a moment, and let them penetrate your heart. You are fearfully and wonderfully made *in the image of God*. He made you especially as you are, and His works are wonderful. When we believe we are lacking or that if we wear that or that if we nip and tuck here and there—what we are really saying is that we are not happy with God's workmanship.

Today I choose to believe the truth about myself. I hope you will believe the same truth about yourself. We are fearfully and wonderfully made . . . in the image of God.

Sylvia Mendez

God's Great Playground

How clearly the sky reveals God's glory! How plainly it shows
what He has done! Each day announces it to the following day;
each night repeats it to the next. No speech or words are used,
no sound is heard; yet their message goes out to all the world
and is heard to the ends of the earth.
—*Psalm 19:1–4, GNT*

I grew up on a farm on the East Coast. It was nestled on a point with the ocean only a quarter of a mile away—on three sides of us. At times, during winter, we would be snowed in for weeks waiting for a plow to clear the road. In winter my brother and I would also wait for ice storms so that we could climb to the top of evergreens and slide down the branches into the fluffy snow piles below. We would dig elaborate forts into the sides of six- to nine-foot (two- to three-meter) snowdrifts. At night we would follow the footpath between the high snowbanks leading from our house to the barns, where we would get a warm welcome from the animals, especially the cats playing on the beams and hay piles. In summer we played hide and seek in the tall grass fields, lay in the sun finding shapes in the clouds, and watched the ants carry loads three times their size to their queen. We rode our dirt bikes to the beach, where we built castles and forts and played with minnows and sea creatures in the tide pools. It was essentially our private beach, our paradise, as we had no care in the world as we played and roamed the rocks, beaches, and woods so close to home.

Oftentimes I wish I could return to the simplicity, purity, and peace of those days. Now life is so busy: bills to pay, errands to run, obligations to fulfill. The news is depressing, good health is nothing short of a blessing, and, at times, I don't know whether I'm coming or going.

What has changed? Not the fields or clouds or ocean or anthills or falling snow. It's not God's nature or His simplicity that has changed—rather, my priorities have. I've become consumed with what adults grow to care about and have lost what children see and experience: God's great playground and the ability to bask in His love with those I care about. I may not be able to play full time anymore, but, if I take the time, I can still see shapes in the sky and butterflies on flower beds. And, if I really wanted to, I probably could even build a snow fort.

Take a moment today to enjoy what money can't buy and poverty can't take away—God's great playground.

Naomi Striemer

February 1

The Yellow Dress Moment

*Don't worry about anything; instead, pray about everything.
Tell God what you need, and thank Him for all He has done.
—Philippians 4:6, NLT*

Every time I see a yellow cotton dress, it takes me back to that dreary February morning when I stumbled into a situation that would change my life and deepen my trust in God.

She was standing on the sidewalk, her back turned toward me, the skirt of her yellow dress swaying in the light breeze. I didn't even see her until I'd almost reached her. I was mesmerized by that lovely shade of yellow on this gray day, a day filled with destruction from the recent devastating hurricane. When I reached where she was standing, she smiled warmly. I commented on her fabulous yellow dress. That encounter immediately began my friendship with Connie. We spoke for quite a while. Then she offered me a job, a direct answer to a prayer I'd sent up not even two days prior. Talk about my faith being strengthened!

I was amazed at how quickly God was coming to my aid yet again! He knew I had a job I didn't like and that I needed to earn more money to provide for my family's needs. He also knew I was dealing with a difficult divorce, a transition back to my parents' home with my two small children, and a bout of depression. The new job was a lifesaver! It gave me a purpose as well as an opportunity to learn and grow.

Connie taught me all she knew and helped me find my strength and voice as a woman. I know that God had her wear that eye-catching yellow dress and placed her on that particular sidewalk to lead me to find peace—and Him.

I thank the Lord today for His intervention in my life so many years ago—and praise Him for always directing my path even when I have doubts. I smile when I realize how the simple moments are often the ones that He uses to bolster our faith and help us to take notice that we are not on this voyage alone. All He asks in return is our trust in Him.

Today I ask you to search your heart and find one of your "yellow dress moments." Thank God again for it. Then share it with a friend.

Simonette Appleton

Out of Chaos, Redemption and Peace

"Then your light will break forth like the dawn,
and your healing will quickly appear."
—Isaiah 58:8, NIV

Recently I watched a video filmed at a women's prison, portraying the everyday lives of women who had committed crimes and were incarcerated—some for life—as punishment for their deeds. The film showed the loneliness, despair, and hopelessness of their everyday existence. Many felt that God had abandoned them. The film delved into their formative years in an attempt to discover how their journeys had led them to prison.

Professional Christian counselors volunteered to work with the prisoners. To start the healing process, counselors asked the prisoners to write about their backgrounds, their family connections, and how they had reached this point in their lives. Then they shared their stories with each other as tears flowed. In this process, the women soon experienced the dissolving of their inner chaos.

These women gradually discovered that the human mind, with negative memories locked within, can become the worst prison of all. Writing about their earlier negative memories became the key to the women's freedom of mind. Sharing their stories brought freedom as they felt released from negative happenings in the past. Conversely, they learned that if they allowed negative memories to control them, they would be chained to them. These memories would act as a deterrent to their healing. The regrets, guilt, and what-ifs would clamor for their attention and their very souls. In the writing and sharing process, the inmates soon realized they could choose whether or not to spend the balance of their days looking back, grieving, and asking *why.*

The Christian counselors helped these broken women assess what was left. They helped these women move forward by focusing on strengths newly discovered and dormant talents newly resurfaced. As a result, the women came to believe they *were* strong and *did have* worth. They saw that God *did* love them and would forgive and sustain them. Education and training at the facility followed, giving them the ability to hold positions of responsibility within the facility. Though they were still incarcerated, their lives were changed for the better, and healing began.

What memories from your past can you share with God in order to experience healing?

Peggy Miles Snow

Learn to Endure

We can rejoice, too, when we run into problems and trials,
for we know that they help us develop endurance.
And endurance develops strength of character,
and character strengthens our confident hope of salvation.
—Romans 5:3, 4, NLT

After flying for more than fifteen years, I have learned that storms up in the air are frequent, unexpected, and often frightening.

When I left Johannesburg on my way to Mauritius, the weather was perfect. I thanked God for the beautiful day as the plane took off. After two hours, I noticed heavy dark clouds outside. Although the pilot said nothing, we were facing a cyclone. The plane started losing altitude in the heavy turbulence. In a situation like this, there is nothing you can do except pray and trust that God is in control. I prayed for a safe landing, for my life, and for endurance during the long minutes of the flight, minutes that seemed to stretch into an eternity. All the passengers were silent. Time passed. Then came the pilot's voice: "Prepare for landing." We were safe!

Life is filled with storms of one kind or another. In the midst of those storms, we tend to respond as if God has somehow been caught off guard. We can't explain why terminal illness strikes godly people. The anguish of a broken marriage or the overwhelming heartbreak of a prodigal child drives us to doubt God's purpose, plan, and provision. The fear of financial ruin paralyzes us. God understands. Why? Because he knows us (Psalm 139). Also, He uses our trials and storms as tools of refinement to build endurance in us. The word *endure* comes from two Greek words that, when combined, give the meaning "to remain under." It is the capacity to stay under the load, to remain in the circumstances without running away or looking for the easy way out. God can help us develop endurance through trust. "Be still, I am God. Trust."

When I landed in Port Louis that night amid a heavy rain, I learned anew a wonderful lesson: God is more powerful than the storms. No matter what storm rages in your life today—where you are is no surprise to God. Heaven is not in a panic. Keep your *gaze* on Him and your *glance* on the raging waters. Trust in His leading, and He will supply everything you need to stand firm in the storm. Do not be afraid. Storms are not forever. They pass, and soon you will have a safe landing. Trust. Endure. God is with you today and always.

Raquel Queiroz da Costa Arrais

God's Protection

And my God shall supply all your need
according to His riches in glory by Christ Jesus.
—*Philippians 4:19, NKJV*

had just finished a busy day as a nursing instructor with my students at the hospital. I was anxious to get home, though my drive between work and home was a distance of forty miles. Since it was late afternoon, the traffic was heavy even on the county road I needed to travel. As was my custom when getting behind the wheel of my car, I first paused to pray for God's care and protection on my journey. I also prayed the same for those who would be in vehicles around me on my way home.

As I came around the sharp curve in the road about one and a half miles from my home, the tire on my right back wheel suddenly blew out, sending me toward oncoming traffic.

Help, Lord! was all I could think. I jerked the steering wheel so my vehicle would land in the roadside ditch, thus avoiding a collision. As I came to a stop, the dust flew and then started to settle.

Tears filled my eyes. Joy filled my heart as I realized the nearness of God at that moment.

The Bible is full of promises. God tells us in Titus 1:2 that He cannot lie. Therefore, we have the assurance that He keeps His promises to protect, guide, and bless us. God wants us to put our trust in His promises yet be willing to accept whatever the outcome may be. In so doing, we learn to trust Him for all He does for us. Through His promises, we come closer to Him in faith. He is truly our awesome Father. He gave His promises to bless those who accept Him and are faithful to Him.

After my tire blowout, I realized I was safe, and no one had been injured by my car. I bowed my head and thanked my heavenly Father for His love and protection. Then I called my husband on my car phone and asked him to come and help me with the car. He arrived quickly to comfort me and take care of the car. Drivers of other cars around me also stopped to make sure I was OK. One man said to me, "God must surely love you. Your angel was working overtime today." God is always with us even when we don't realize His presence.

Carolyn Voss

Moved by a Tornado

The Lord will keep you safe. . . . He will spread his wings over you
and keep you secure. His faithfulness is like a shield or a city wall.
—*Psalm 91:3, 4, CEV*

Our house in the highlands of Tennessee was built on a concrete crawl space that is about eighteen inches high on one side and five feet high on the other side. The taller side has a wooden door so one can go under the house. The crawl space also houses air-conditioning ducts, electricity, and lights. We can use it as a safe place during severe weather.

One very rainy day, the TV weather forecaster said our area would have a chance of tornadoes that day. We began making plans to go under the house . . . just in case. My grandson and I got our folding lawn chairs, a lantern, and a flashlight. We put them under the house during a break in the rain. We also brought in things that were outside so they wouldn't be blown away. We gathered a gallon jug of water, cups, sleeping bags, and the dogs' cage. Those we also put under the house. While we were waiting to see what the weather would do, we continued doing things in the house. It was Friday, and I still had to finish cooking for Sabbath and get the house cleaned.

About thirty minutes before sundown, my sister called to tell me a tornado was headed straight toward us. We quickly called our two dogs and headed under the house. We prayed for God's protection over us and over our neighbors . . . and waited some more. A few minutes went by, and then we could hear the wind picking up outside. The noise of the wind got stronger for a few seconds and then stopped.

My husband was the first one to step outside to see whether there was any damage. It was already dark, but everything seemed OK. Our house and garage didn't appear to be damaged. We thanked God for keeping us safe and went inside the house to retire for the night.

Sabbath morning, as we got ready for church, we looked at our neighbor's house about seven hundred yards down the valley. We could see that most of it was gone! The field was covered with debris. We drove over to see whether we could be of help. Thankfully, no one had been hurt. Friends and family were already there assessing the damage and salvaging what they could.

What a wonderful Father we have who protected lives in our neighborhood that day!

Celia Mejia Cruz

What Will Our Answer Be?

"When the Son of Man comes,
will He really find faith on the earth?"
—Luke 18:8, NKJV

As we see the signs of the last days around us, we believe Jesus is coming soon. Jesus is the One who asked the question in today's text, "Will He really find faith on the earth?" I'd like to suggest that components of an acrostic will demonstrate our F-A-I-T-H in God.

F in my acrostic stands for *Father*. If we believe God is our Father, that means we are His children. Jesus taught His disciples to address God as "our Father in heaven" (Matthew 6:9, NKJV). Also Paul wrote that "we cry, Abba, Father. The Spirit itself beareth witness with our spirit, that we are the children of God" (Romans 8:15, 16).

A in my acrostic stands for *affection*. When the lawyer asked Jesus what he should do to inherit eternal life, Christ told him to love God with all his heart, soul, strength, and mind, and his neighbor as himself (Luke 10:27). Do we love God and others as Christ asked us to? Jesus also said we should love even our enemies. God, through Paul, tells his children to set their "affection on things above" (Colossians 3:2).

I in the acrostic stands for *influence*. Do we influence others for good? Jesus said, "Let your light so shine before men, that they may see your good works, and glorify your Father which is in heaven" (Matthew 5:16). When we use our influence on God's behalf, others see Jesus reflected in us and often want to know more about Him.

T in my acrostic stands for *trust*. Where there is love for God, there is also trust. Since we are human, weak, and easily inclined to sin, we need to trust in divine power for victory over sin. Proverbs 3:5, 6 counsels us to "trust in the LORD with all your heart, and lean not on your own understanding; in all your ways acknowledge Him, and He shall direct your paths" (NKJV). If we trust God fully and accept His guidance, then surely we will be ready to go to heaven.

Finally, *H* in my acrostic stands for *happiness*. Psalm 144:15 states, "Happy are the people who are in such a state; happy are the people whose God is the LORD!" (NKJV).

Our solid F-A-I-T-H in God will be manifested by our affection for the heavenly Father, trust in Him, and right use of our influence for Him. These will result in unquenchable happiness that we will freely share with others, along with the reason for our faith: Jesus.

Birdie Poddar

I Am Not Spam!—Part 1

But GOD told Samuel, "Looks aren't everything.
Don't be impressed with his looks and stature. I've already
eliminated him. GOD judges persons differently than humans do.
Men and women look at the face; GOD looks into the heart."
—1 Samuel 16:7, The Message

Recently I sent an e-mail to a friend who said she had not received it. My e-mail said, "Delivered," so she checked her e-mail again. My message to her had gone into the spam folder. I laughed and told her, "I am *not* spam!" In today's technological environment, no one wants spam. In case you don't know, *spam* is unsolicited, undesired e-mail messages. You know, *those* messages—the ones you don't want or need—that perhaps have a familiar sender's name, but nothing else matches. Spam is frustrating and annoying.

Yet we allow spam into our lives when we listen to all the "voices" around us to determine who and what we are and can become! As women, we often listen to "voices" that tell us the four following untruths about ourselves.

1. *Our self-worth is based on how others see us and on our accomplishments.* This is not true. Besides, if we are living to make sure that others love us, we give them permission to evaluate us based on what we do. We give people the power to determine *our* self-worth.

2. *We should be feeling shame from our past.* Absolutely false! We need to believe the Lord when He says, "I have forgiven you and will remember your sins no more!" (See 1 John 1:9 and Isaiah 43:25.)

3. *Our value is based on our looks.* How sad that we buy into the beauty myth, thinking that our appearance is our number one asset and that it is what will bring us acceptance and the approval of others!

4. *We should set high standards for ourselves, even if they are unrealistic.* Doing so, however, sets us up for excessive stress and failure. Therefore, we have to work at changing our thinking in order to cut ourselves some slack. We need to humble ourselves to accept God's grace and give grace to ourselves when we don't "measure up." Start taking notice of all the spam messages you receive everywhere and all the time—including some you send yourself!

Ask God to help you identify spam. He can help "delete" it, but only if you request it.

Wilma Kirk Lee

I Am Not Spam!—Part 2

But now, GOD's Message, the God who made you in the first place,
Jacob, the One who got you started, Israel: "Don't be afraid,
I've redeemed you. I've called your name. You're mine."
—Isaiah 43:1, The Message

It's easy to become discouraged if all you hear is spam. *You're never good enough. You're never beautiful enough. Think of all the wrong you've done during your life.* And tell me, who *can* be perfect?

I want you to get a spam blocker! Did you know you have a no-fail spam blocker? Well, you do—it's Jesus. He says, "But now, GOD's Message, the God who made you in the first place . . . the One who got you started . . . : 'Don't be afraid, I've redeemed you. I've called your *name.* You're mine' " (Isaiah 43:1, *The Message*, emphasis added).

Wow! God has called you by your name! That's exciting. If God has created you and called you by name, then *all* the other messages don't count. Just listen to the messages God has for you. Sometimes it's difficult to hear God's voice because He does not shout! He speaks in the stillness and the quiet. So if you want to block spam, you have to stop the other noise!

You can't be constantly distracted by your phone, iPad, computer, or text messages. Too often, these only increase the spam in our minds. God says that if you listen to Him, He will bring you peace.

When you listen to God's message about who you are, you will begin to develop all the gifts and talents He has given you. You won't look around to see what others are doing because you will have enough to do with yourself. God's plans for your life are far greater than any you may ever have considered.

Moreover, since He is the supreme spam blocker, He also looks at your heart, calls you by name, and reminds you that He has created you to be His masterpiece.

The advice of Galatians is so important: "Make a careful exploration of who you are and the work you have been given, and then sink yourself into that. Don't be impressed with yourself. Don't compare yourself with others. Each of you must take responsibility for doing the creative best you can with your own life" (Galatians 6:4, 5, *The Message*).

Remember that, rather than being spam, "we are God's masterpiece" (Ephesians 2:10, NLT).

Wilma Kirk Lee

The Bonds of Illness

Trust in the LORD with all thine heart;
and lean not unto thine own understanding.
In all thy ways acknowledge him, and he shall direct thy paths.
—*Proverbs 3:5, 6*

I smile this morning as I think of a particular incident that occurred some time ago. It was exam time at a north Caribbean university when a young lady came to me with tears in her eyes. She pleaded, "Dean, I have chicken pox. Can you believe it? It is exam time, and if I miss my exams, it is going to push me far behind. I will not be able to graduate on time." Knowing this young lady's background and financial constraints, I immediately set about seeking an alternative for her. My efforts proved to be unsuccessful, and I was at a loss as to what to do. I went to my apartment and thought about the situation and made further inquiries regarding the examination process. Then I went back to the worried student.

"Why don't you stay in my spare room for now?" I suggested. "The examination personnel say they would grant permission for you to take your exams in seclusion."

"Oh, Dean Cain, that will be great!" she said.

I cared for her and extended motherly and sisterly love to her during her illness while she took her time and did her exams. Those few days of caring for this young lady, along with my other responsibilities as residence hall dean, formed a bond between us, a bond that is not likely to be broken, though we may not see each other on this earth again, as our lives have taken us in different geographic directions since that time.

Extending a hand to another in dire circumstances, such as illness, suffering, and death, allows us to form bonds with them. Perhaps we do not consider a simple act of help as forming a bond. But it often does, and those whom we have helped will probably stand by our sides when we need *their* help. I like to think that we live in a world of people who not only need the help of others but who are also willing to help in return. I like to think that, in a sense, when we help others, we help ourselves. Daily prayer for God's guidance will certainly lead us to make the right decisions when it comes to helping others.

From my experience with the young lady suffering from chicken pox, I know that the "bonds of illness" can be a blessing to all involved when we extend the hand of love and care.

Elizabeth Ida Cain

The Bed

Delight yourself also in the LORD,
and He shall give you the desires of your heart.
—*Psalm 37:4, NKJV*

A furniture advertisement arrived in the mail just when I decided I needed a new mattress. I searched online to compare prices. I also looked at reclining chairs and electric beds, knowing I could not afford either one. I suspected the store owners might be people I used to know.

I went into town, ran some errands, and decided to go look at the mattresses. As I entered the store, I discovered that I did know the owners. I also saw reclining chairs—which had *not* been advertised on the flier. The store had no twin mattresses, but the owners could order one. I tried out a queen-size mattress that would be comparable to the twin that I needed, and then I looked at the reclining chairs. I began to talk with the lady, telling her why I needed a new mattress. She looked at me very strangely and said, "We have something in the back room that you might like to look at." I followed her to the back room. She told me about their purchase from a few weeks before. They had purchased a showroom full of mattresses, reclining chairs, and one other item—an electric bed, brand-new and complete with a mattress!

I was shocked when she told me. I had been in the hospital earlier, and due to medical conditions, I had to elevate my head with three pillows and one pillow under my knees in order to sleep at night. With this electric bed, I could use one pillow under my head and none under my knees because I would be able to raise the bed electrically.

But could I afford it? The woman told me the rest of the story. Their store sold a certain brand of mattresses and chairs, so their dealership would not let them put the other bed in the showroom because it was of a different brand. The store owners had no idea why that bed and mattress had been included with the rest of the items they had purchased. The bed and mattress were of the brands I had looked at the day before on the Internet. The bed cost more than I had planned to spend, yet, as the woman pointed out, it was less expensive than the mattress and chair together and a very fair price. The price she quoted was one I could afford.

Who could have guessed my needs would be met by those improbable circumstances? Many would say it was a coincidence—but *I know* God was providing.

Loraine F. Sweetland

February 11

Send Down Your "Happy," Lord

Now the God of hope fill you
with all joy and peace.
—*Romans 15:13*

I was born with a mouth that points down at both sides and a heart that tends toward negative thinking. Even though God has wrought wonderful things for me and through me, I can't seem to shake off this bulldog hold on a negative nature.

On my early morning walks in our beautiful countryside, I hear the birds of "pray" singing and am awed by the gorgeous colors flung across the sky as the sun climbs the back side of our mountain. I call out to my Abba. I cry and plead for God to work a miracle, and I am encouraged. Yet as soon as I step back into my world, this bulldog nature grabs me again, shaking me from top to bottom.

I have a prayer tree—my "tri-tree"—toward the last part of my walk. Beside a gurgling stream with the persistent sounds of nature's sacred music, my prayer tree reaches for refreshment with its massive roots.

This is definitely a God place—my sanctuary.

I kneel at its knees. On my right is the biggest trunk. On my left, connected by an overlapping base, is a somewhat smaller one. Another branch, low to the water at the base of this triple tree, is separate yet connected in the hollow where they overlap. At this point grows a tiny wild violet plant with a few heart-shaped leaves. My eyes light on them; my heart breaks out into a song God gave me years ago: "Lord, take my heart; for I cannot give it. . . . Keep it pure, for I cannot keep it for Thee."* All the while I am singing, the "gurgling stream" assures me that my Abba is loving, long-suffering, and merciful.

Yesterday, at a memorial service, I heard spoken memories of a smiling disposition even through three years of fighting cancer. One called it "putting her smile on," a smile well known during her lifetime of service but especially during her last painful days on this earth. Those who came to cheer her during those last months left being cheered by her.

I asked God why I couldn't have that type of personality. He sent me a new prayer: *Send down Your "happy," Lord. Fit it onto my face today, so heart and home will hear me sing Your melody of grace.*

Jodi Eulene Owens Patterson (Dodson)

* Ellen G. White, *Christ's Object Lessons* (Hagerstown, MD: Review and Herald®, 2003), 159.

Blessed Assurance

The Lord gave, and the Lord hath taken away;
blessed be the name of the Lord.
—Job 1:21

Life is a journey filled with sweet and bitter experiences. Yet I thank God for all the trials in my life because without trials I would not have known how wonderful God's love is. Yes, it is painful to have something in life that we value and then lose it. However, I have learned that there is life after loss. God allows things to happen to us for a reason. But we must stay focused on worshiping the Giver of blessings rather than on His gifts. Sometimes we lose spiritual focus too easily when we have so much.

Job was a righteous man who had everything, but he lost it all in the blink of an eye. As a man of God, however, he stood firm. Spiritually, he proved to stand as strong in time of devastation as he had in time of prosperity. Like Job, we need to learn to trust God more. Do we not serve the Master of the universe who promises to supply the needs of those who trust Him?

Once while I was trying to survive the best I could, I spent lonely nights crying, asking why I had so many problems. But the next day I would dry my tears and walk tall. I know in my heart God is busy preparing something for me.

I am grateful for my job and for my health. When I gaze at all that is around me, I realize that I should indeed count my blessings. Having a car became a necessity. After struggling for years, I was blessed to be able to secure a car. When I bought it, though, it was a bit challenging financially because I was still busy with my studies. I had to sacrifice a lot in order to survive. Now I have completed my studies in labor law.

Dear friend, all I can say is this: *God is alive!* He will never leave you nor forsake you. If you accept and trust Him with your life at all times, He will never disappoint you. Friends and family members may disappoint, but God never will. You may never live up to some people's expectations of you. Yet in God's eyes, you are the best. Believe it! What a foretaste of glory divine! Even if you are feeling alone in the world right now, please know that you definitely are not. When it seems the world is conspiring against you, your character, or your integrity, remember that the fact you are still breathing is a testament of God's favor resting upon you.

You are His child—the beloved child of the King.

Deborah Matshaya

God's Gift Cards

The gift of God is eternal life
through Jesus Christ our Lord.
—*Romans 6:23*

Many gift cards go unspent each year. Perhaps some recipients of gift cards forget about their gift card or think the giver could better use their money elsewhere. However, once a gift card is purchased, the giver's money has been spent. If the gift card is lost or not used, it's like losing or not spending cash. The only winner is the retailer, who then has both the money and the unpurchased products.

We have a generous heavenly Father who gives us gift cards for every conceivable occasion. What can we buy with these cards?

Well, His gift card for light secures for us brilliant sunshine, silver moonbeams, and lightning. His gift card for groceries covers succulent mangos, tangy lemons, sweet beets, buttery avocados, hearty potatoes, and leafy greens. His gift card to the symphony brings the trill of the mockingbird, the crashing of waves, the crackling of fire, and the laughter of children. His gift card to the art boutique ensures our enjoyment of sunsets, a red dotted ladybug on a deep green leaf, or white-capped mountains set against azure blue sky. The talent card brings us the ability to organize our lives, sing, sew, cook, care for our families, and bless others.

The most valuable gift card is the one that makes salvation available! Our Father purchased that gift for us with the shed, and priceless, blood of His only begotten Son. Ephesians 2:8 tells us how to exchange our card for the gift: "For by grace are ye saved through faith; and that not of yourselves: it is the gift of God." Salvation is a gift from God, which we claim by faith, counting on His grace to be sufficient (2 Corinthians 12:9).

What is faith? It is simply trusting in something, even though we cannot necessarily prove or understand it. For example, when we get on an airplane, we exhibit faith that the plane will take us to our destination. We exercise faith when we sit on a chair with assurance from past experience that it will hold us. To claim salvation by faith, we have to trust God's promises, just as we trust the chair that we sit on.

We especially trust that Christ's suffering on the cross has paid for our sins. Then, in the Shop of Grace, we accept by faith the "gift card" that guarantees our eternal life. Amen!

Elizabeth Versteegh Odiyar

Relationships

Seek your happiness in the LORD,
and he will give you your heart's desire.
—*Psalm 37:4, GNT*

Life is good. We can feel and see the goodness of the Lord around us. Simple things in nature remind us of God's abiding love: beautiful spring flowers, changing foliage during autumn, snowflakes in the winter, blue skies and white clouds in the summertime.

The year 2015 was a memorable year for our family. Our daughter and son decided to get married five weeks apart, each choosing life partners who shared their ideals and love for God. Family and friends from all across North America and the Philippines showed their support by coming to witness our children start this new chapter of their lives. We experienced a beautiful reunion of family and friends. Love was definitely in the air!

The same year, my husband and I also celebrated our thirtieth wedding anniversary. We thank the Lord for His guidance and leading all throughout the years. He has allowed us to grow as individuals and given us opportunities to serve Him. He has supplied all our needs as we learned to depend on Him. He has given us immeasurable blessings that we have shared with others along the way.

Throughout this journey, for example, we have learned to cultivate and nurture relationships. We realize that life is more meaningful when we surround ourselves with people who share our dreams and passions, people who encourage us when life is unfair, and people who will accept us just the way we are. In fact, we spend our whole lifetime cultivating friendships and relationships that we hope will last forever.

What about our relationship with our heavenly Father? Do we spend time getting to know Him better by reading His Word? Do we linger in His presence and talk with Him in prayer? Do we long to see Him or yearn for His soon return? Has life gotten so good that we do not have the desire, nor feel the need, to connect with Him? Yet God loves us so much that He wants to spend eternity with us.

Let us put Him first in our lives and make Him the center of our homes as we continue our earthly journey.

With Him beside us, we will surely succeed in our relationships with others.

Rhona Grace Magpayo

February 15

Stress Watch

I will sing unto the LORD as long as I live:
I will sing praise to my God while I have my being.
My meditation of him shall be sweet: I will be glad in the LORD.
—*Psalm 104:33, 34*

For quite some time now, people have been talking about stress. There is a lot of awareness regarding stress. According to *Oxford Advanced Learner's Dictionary*, stress (under mental pressure) is simply "pressure or worry caused by the problems in somebody's life."

Jose Carlos Rando, a theologian and family counselor, wrote in the prologue to the book *Less Stress*, by Dr. Julian Melgosa, that "we need to learn, not only how to control stress, but how to eliminate its source."[1]

In Dr. Melgosa's book he separates what is stress and what is not. Stress is the body's reaction to demand; a state of severe physiological and psychological tension; preparation for fight or flight; and the beginning of a number of diseases. On the other hand, stress is not necessarily bad since, at times, it helps the person reach desired goals.[2]

Psychologists Lazarus and Folkman (cited in the same book) concluded that people evaluate stress as (1) irreparable damage that has occurred or (2) as a danger or (3) as a challenge.

When people interpret problems according to conclusion number one, they engage in self-pity, which blocks "any chance of changing their circumstances."

When they view a problem according to conclusion number two, they see only negative consequences and view the future with trepidation.

Those who look at a problem according to conclusion number three realize that they cannot change the past and don't believe they will gain anything by punishing themselves. So they end up fortifying themselves in preparation for the future with their minds focused on achieving their goal.[3]

I would like to share an excellent antidote for stress that is found in today's theme text, Psalm 104:33, 34. "I will sing praise. . . . My meditation of him [the Lord] shall be sweet: I will be glad in the LORD." If we do what this verse says, it will help us manage our stress.

Rosenita Christo

---

1 Julian Melgosa, *Less Stress* (Thailand: Editorial Safeliz, 2009).
2 Ibid., 18.
3 Ibid., 24.

Surprise, Surprise!

Just then his disciples returned and were surprised to find him
talking with a woman. But no one asked, "What do you want?"
or "Why are you talking with her?"
—John 4:27, NIV

Since the beginning of time, God has surprised His people, not always operating as they had come to expect He would. I was just struck again with this idea in the story of Ruth. She was married to Mahlon, who died. Then she was married to Boaz in a levirate marriage, the purpose of which was to provide descendants and preserve the name of the dead husband. But in Ruth, the genealogy goes through Boaz, not Mahlon.

We are all familiar with the stories in which the younger son got the blessing rather than the expected elder: Abel, Isaac, Jacob, Joseph, Ephraim, David. King Solomon was not the next in line to be king—he was neither David's eldest nor the crown prince, but obviously chosen by God. And there were those barren women who had surprise babies: Sarah, Rebecca, Rachel, Hannah, and Elizabeth. To say nothing of the surprise Mary had when the angel visited her!

All through His short life, Jesus was surprising people. When He performed His first miracle, the master of the banquet was surprised at the improved quality of the wine (John 2). Very often after Jesus performed a miracle or answered His accusers and critics, the Bible says the people were amazed—that is, beyond surprised. In today's text the disciples were surprised that Jesus was carrying on a conversation with a woman! Proper Jewish men did not do that. And it was to this person—a foreigner, a woman, and a Samaritan!—that Jesus first clearly stated that He was the Messiah. And it was to a woman that Jesus first appeared after His resurrection and to whom He gave a message for His disciples and Peter. Of course, the men didn't believe the women at first. Surprise, surprise.

When Jesus met with Nicodemus at night, He told him, "You should not be surprised at my saying, 'You must be born again' " (John 3:7, NIV).

So what surprises has our Lord placed in your life lately? Perhaps the most amazing one of all is that while we are yet sinners, He loved and died for us (Romans 5:8). That is beyond surprising—amazing, unfathomable!

Ardis Dick Stenbakken

Choose the Good Part

But one thing is needful: and Mary hath chosen that good part,
which shall not be taken away from her.
—*Luke 10:42*

I believe each woman has both a Martha and Mary within. The Martha within is cumbered with stuff and doing things. Her mind is always racing. Martha is the one on the brink of insanity. She has hardly any time for personal worship or adequate sleep because she doesn't know how to "turn off." After work she cooks, washes dishes, gets the kids' things organized for the next day—and hasn't even begun to address her husband's needs. A workaholic, she begins to resent everyone around her. No one is helping her. Who is taking care of her?

The Mary within is calm. She chooses listening over ordering everyone around. She chooses character over strategy; purpose and mission over activity; sanity over her "to-do" list; quality time over getting things done. She chooses Jesus over the hustle and bustle of ministering. She chooses the good part!

The Bible says, "Martha received him [Jesus] into her house" (Luke 10:38). Immediately she went to work. Everything had to be just right. If I'm honest with myself, I would have been the exact same way, and so would you. However, she's doing so much—or if I could put it in urban vernacular, she was doing the most—she didn't realize how much actually needed to be done. Martha looks up and realizes her sister is just sitting. Can you believe Mary has the nerve to sit at Jesus' feet and listen to Him when so much work needs to be done? So she tattles on Mary.

"Martha," Jesus says. "Thou art careful [anxious] and troubled [distracted] about many things" (verse 41). There were so many things that she was anxious about, and, at the end of the day, it was all more of a distraction than anything. Jesus begins to explain to her that Mary has actually chosen the good part and He was not going to take that away from her.

There is a time and a place for everything. However, I would argue that the Martha within us tries to *make* a time and a place for everything. I hope you catch that subtle difference. I want to encourage you to speak lovingly to your Martha and tell her not to resent Mary or to feel guilty about choosing what Mary would choose. It's the good part!

Then let all your activity be birthed out, having been at Jesus' feet.

Rebecca Davis

The God of Music and Math

Praise ye the LORD. . . . Praise him with the sound of the trumpet:
praise him with the psaltery and harp.
—*Psalm 150:1, 3*

"For a ram you shall prepare as a grain offering, two-tenths of an
ephah of fine flour mixed with one-third of a hin* of oil."
—*Numbers 15:6, NKJV*

Have you ever wondered about all the numbers in the Bible and their important roles? God not only loves numbers, He also seems to have His favorites. Think of His use of seven, twelve, forty, and some of their multiples. Mathematics, the science that studies numbers, does not need any other science to be understood. Instead, math helps all the other sciences to be understood. Even music. God loves music, and I suspect He has His favorite pieces as well.

Bible authors have given us very specific numbers regarding measurements (even down to fractions) of capacity, length, width, volume, weight, population, age, increase, and interest rates. God the Holy Spirit certainly inspired the Bible writers to include all these numbers.

Whenever I am playing with numbers (even with Bible numbers), I can imagine my Abba Father smiling and saying: "My daughter, how you love numbers!" While reading my Bible, I like to underline, color, and write the number in digits beside each text. Obviously, reading the book of Numbers is fun for me! Try calculating and dividing the plunder as mentioned in Numbers 31:25–54. How precise the Bible is! As only numbers can be!

Numbers and music go together very well. Both express the grandeur and the greatness of God. Both math and music are helpful tools in our great need to create art or to discover more about science. Even when using exponential numbers, astronomers cannot calculate how vast this universe is! And the most sublime music can but only faintly express God's glory and splendor. When I drive around town to run errands, I sometimes like to sing hymns at the top of my lungs. Other times I sing softly or just in my heart. I sense my guardian angel watching over me and joining me as I sing.

Would you also like to join me in heaven to learn more about music and numbers? We can take part in the heavenly choir. We can also learn to calculate with exact precision the vastness of the our Father's universe. I hope to see you there!

Marli Elizete Ritter-Hein

_____

* One ephah = 19 dry quarts (~22 liters); one hin = 3.87 quarts (3.66 liters)

Footsteps

Whoever fears the Lord has a secure fortress,
and for their children it will be a refuge.
—*Proverbs 14:26, NIV*

The omnibus was so overloaded with people I could hardly find somewhere to stand without stepping on other people's toes. All of a sudden, a boy of about eight years old stood up and offered his seat to a girl who was about his age. She smiled, thanked him, and accepted his offer.

A long time ago, gentlemen gave their seats to ladies, and young people gave their seats to the elderly. But not today. Front seats in omnibuses are still designated as seats for seniors, the disabled, and nursing mothers. Yet many people do not care anymore and sit in them anyway.

Evidently that polite little boy had both a heart and good manners inherited in his upbringing at home. When he saw a need, he did what he could to meet it. His proud grandfather, sitting nearby, said, "That's my boy. He knows what to do at the right time." The little girl's mum also gave him a pat on his shoulder as a show of appreciation.

Seeing the politeness of that young man reminded me of Proverbs 22:6, which reads, "Train up a child in the way he should go, and when he is old he will not depart from it" (NKJV). I do not know what other people on the omnibus thought, but I was impressed. His actions gave me a mental picture of the kind of home he must come from. I believe that kindness and respect will follow him because he chooses to share those behaviors with others.

Children usually follow in the footsteps of adult role models. And we women—mothers, grandmothers, aunts—are the first teachers in the lives of children. Therefore, we need to be extra careful about what we say and do in the presence of our little ones. Surely, they are mentally "recording" every one of our words and actions, starting on their first day of life. Swiss psychologist Jean Piaget proposed that human beings go through four stages of mental development, observing that if we smile at a two-day-old baby, we will soon get a smile back.

Our children are often walking in our footsteps. Thus, we must do our best, with the help of our Lord and Master, Jesus, to set the right example for them.

One fine day, God will ask us whether we were good examples to the children with whom He entrusted us. After all, they are His children too. Let's lead them aright, shall we?

Mabel Kwei

Lost and Found

Now faith is confidence in what we hope for
and assurance about what we do not see.
—*Hebrews 11:1, NIV*

Last night, Sister Monica Joan (my favorite chicken, named for a character on the *Call the Midwife* television drama series) didn't turn up in the coop. We looked high and low but couldn't find her. I heard a noise in the garage, and thinking it was her, I figured I'd see her out and about at first light. At least, that's what I hoped.

During the night, I had a dream that she was alive and well. It was so vivid that I woke up thanking God for keeping her safe. Each time I woke up that night I remembered the dream and thanked God again.

In the morning, there was no Sister Monica Joan. But there were fox tracks in the snow. My husband and I searched everywhere. I scoured the garage again. As I finally gave up the search, I thought, *I don't understand. I thought God sent me that dream to tell me she was safe. I don't believe . . .*

I wasn't sure how to finish that sentence. *I don't believe . . . she's dead? I don't believe . . . God didn't follow through on what I felt sure He'd promised me?* I was stuck there on *I don't believe*, which, of course, was my problem. So I left it in His hands. I wasn't ready to give up on finding her, but I didn't know where else to look.

I started my chores, which that morning included scraping the pans in the rabbit hutches. The bucket I use is outside the door, tipped upside down, leaning against the house. When I picked it up to bring it inside, I found Sister Monica Joan underneath it. Apparently the chickens were using the spot to lay eggs. She must have squirmed underneath and then gotten stuck there.

It occurred to me, even while I was hugging her in glee, that faith believes God even when we don't have the visual evidence of our eyes to back it up . . . *especially* when we don't have the evidence of our eyes to back it up. Faith is believing God when He tells us something, and that can be harder than it sounds.

The good news is that the closer we are to God, the clearer we can hear Him when He speaks and the more confident we can be when acting in accordance to His message.

Céleste Perrino-Walker

I Will Help You!

Fear not, for I am with you; be not dismayed,
for I am your God; I will strengthen you, I will help you,
I will uphold you with my righteous right hand.
—*Isaiah 41:10, ESV*

My best friend called me a few days ago to tell me how grateful she was for God's everlasting love. One evening as she left work, she discovered that one of her tires had low air pressure. *Not a problem*, she thought. She had a solution. She drove to the nearest gas station and put more air in the tire. The next day, as she drove her son to school, she noticed the tire pressure was lower than the night before. *No problem*, she said to herself. She rationalized that the change in climate and environment had been factors that affected her tire pressure. As she did the night before, she drove to the gas station and put more air into the tire. That done, she drove herself to work. As she walked to her desk, she thought about taking her car to the mechanic on her lunch break. However, wrapped up in the day's chaos, she never got a chance to get her tire checked.

That evening, as she walked to her car, the tire was visibly deflated. She noted the time. The mechanic's shop was already closed, and she had to go get her son. She didn't have an alternative. She drove herself to the gas station, added air to her tire, and went to get her son. The next morning the tire was completely flat. What was she going to do? She said a quick prayer and then drove to the nearest gas station, again added air to the deflated tire, and drove her son to school. She then drove to the mechanic across the street from her job, forty-five minutes away from where she lived. While driving, she constantly checked the digital indicator and realized that the tire was quickly deflating. She was concerned, yet not afraid, because she believed God's promise to help her. The tire remained inflated until she got to the mechanic.

As my friend inquired about the cost of replacing her tire, the mechanic gave her an estimate. It seemed high, but what was she going to do? Her tire situation had to be fixed. After leaving work, she went to pick up her car. The cost of the work was about 85 percent less than the estimate, and the mechanic had been able to repair the tire instead of replacing it.

Isn't God amazing? He had her problem all worked out. He was there with her all along the way, a present help in the time of her need.

God's promise is very clear: "I am your God; I will strengthen you, I will help you" (Isaiah 41:10, ESV).

Diantha Hall-Smith

The Only Way

Seek ye first the kingdom of God, and his righteousness;
and all these things shall be added unto you.
—*Matthew 6:33*

Y ou've made *The Big Ten Winners List!*" declares the bold red-and-black lettering on the oversized envelope.

Printed instructions follow, advising the addressee to send in the grand prize winning number, which can be located somewhere in the maze of enclosed advertisements. Of course, this is a gimmick to lure the recipient into purchasing a magazine and hoping for the nearly impossible.

To those who have a steady income, this ad may seem amusing and be easily tossed away. To those who have all their wants and needs met, the ad may barely catch the eye. And to those who have a firm trust in God to provide all their needs, the ad holds no attraction.

However, there are many people who are not able to work; they are sick, crippled, blind, or disabled. They may have limited ability to learn, and their earning power is minimal. Many are perhaps not professional enough in appearance or adequately gifted at social skills so that someone would hire them even if those individuals are able to do the actual work. Sadly, everyone does not have the same advantages or opportunities.

An advertisement that invites one to pursue instant sweepstakes earnings may sound wonderfully attractive to someone who is disenfranchised or impoverished. How else could they not only obtain the barest essentials but also move from their level of desperate need to the necessities and even comforts of life they see portrayed in today's media? The lure of a magical path—such as winning a sweepstakes competition or state lottery—undoubtedly has definite appeal when the big brown envelope shows up in their mailbox.

Yet the Bible warns against misusing talents, including money, and coveting. So how do we overcome a desire for gain that is not earned? There is nothing magical to overcoming this temptation. We simply make the day-by-day choice to trust God to provide for our care. We seek His kingdom first, doing what we can to provide for ourselves. Then we trust Him to provide for the remaining needs. That is the only way, and He is faithful.

Elizabeth Darby Watson

Put Down Your Waterpot and Run

Wherefore . . . let us lay aside every weight,
and the sin which doth so easily beset us,
and let us run with patience the race that is set before us.
—Hebrews 12:1

Let's call her Rose, for truly she resembled a fading rose. It was noon when Rose wended her way to the reservoir outside the city to fetch water. Hastily she filled her bucket and was about to leave when a male voice said, "Give me a drink of water." She froze in her tracks as she quickly realized the man who spoke to her was an enemy of her people.

Surprised, she said, "You're not my friend; why are you asking me for water?"

He replied, "If only you knew who it is that is asking you for water, you would respond favorably, and I in turn would give you everything your heart desires." Rose was astounded by the stranger's words, for somehow his intentions seemed noble when compared with her previous male associates.

Hope welled up within her as she prolonged the conversation. During the ensuing dialogue, the stranger revealed to Rose that he had knowledge of her shameful past and her present adulterous life. By the time the conversation ended, Rose, whom you probably realize by now is the woman at the well, was fully convinced that this Man who could read her innermost thoughts was the promised Messiah!

The divine revelation struck Rose like a bolt of lightning, illuminating her soul. She dropped her waterpot, so as to be unencumbered, and hurried into the city to tell her fellow citizens the good news. Because of her witness, many of her fellow citizens believed in Jesus and accepted Him as the Messiah (John 4:39–42). Such, my sisters, is the power of the gospel!

Woman of God, what is *your* waterpot? What is weighing you down and preventing you from accomplishing the task God has designated for you? What is hindering you from realizing your full potential? What is restricting you from fulfilling God's purpose for your life? Is it pride and self-sufficiency? Is it fear and lack of self-confidence? Is it a besetting sin? Whatever it is, I admonish you to "lay aside every weight, and the sin which doth so easily beset" you and "run with patience the race that is set before" you (Hebrews 12:1), "looking unto Jesus, the author and finisher of our faith" (verse 2).

As did the woman at the well, put down your waterpot . . . and run!

Gerene I. Joseph

A Simple Smile

"May the LORD *bless you and protect you.*
May the LORD *smile on you and be gracious to you.*
May the LORD *show you his favor and give you his peace."*
—Numbers 6:24–26, NLT

How is my daughter's mother?" Mrs. B asked me on the phone one morning. I smiled at the memory of the precious incident we both shared. During freshman orientation week fifteen years earlier, students were rushing about in search of advisors, schedules, and friends. A sniffling freshman, Rebecca, had walked into my office with Mrs. B, her equally tearful mother. I had welcomed them both with a smile.

"No, Mamita, I'm staying," Rebecca insisted. "I've dreamed about coming to this university for years. You spent a lot of money for this, and I'm staying."

Her mother responded, "You can stay, but I'll fly you home immediately if that's what you decide to do." Mother and daughter both dissolved into a pool of even more tears at the mother's words. Then the mother turned to me with surprising candor and said, "I'm leaving my child with you."

It became clear, however, that Mrs. B did not intend for Rebecca to actually live with me. She knew her daughter needed the collegiate camaraderie of dormitory life. Months later, Mrs. B told me why she had made that choice. "I could see God's grace in you."

I enjoyed watching Rebecca mature into womanhood, graduate with honors, marry, and obtain a prestigious position. Rebecca, the child I never birthed, still functions as my daughter. We share a zillion love-laden, cross-country calls and birthday bouquets.

Last month when Mrs. B called to ask, "How is my daughter's mother?" I smiled at the medley of nostalgia, love, and connection in her greeting. Then she said, "I hear the smile in your voice." Wandering back in memory to those long-ago years, she noted, "My daughter learned so much from you during those four years. Now you both tilt your head and smile the same way. The Lord is looking on you both with favor." I was humbled yet gratified that she could read such depth into a simple smile.

Thank You, dear God, for the joy of smiles and the privilege of sharing them with others along the way. They bring us such peace and contentment.

Glenda-mae Greene

Bored to Tears

"What are you discussing together as you walk along?"
—Luke 24:17, NIV

W hat a boring guest speaker!" said Melissa, exploding into the room. "I nearly fell asleep twice—and would have if my teacher hadn't tapped me on the shoulder and let me stand at the back of the room with her. Actually, several of us did, and that kept us awake."

"Brilliant," I replied. "Your teacher must know about studies that showed fifty percent of students learn best when they were standing and moving."

"O-o-o-o, that is so me!" said Melissa. "I learn best when I'm moving around." How well I knew. "Christ taught people while they were standing around or walking. My teacher called that the Socrates method."

"John said, 'The truth will set you free' [John 8:32, NIV]," I said. "I think that means figuring out how our brains work most efficiently so that we can best use what has been built into them."

"So how come we always have to sit and sit and sit and be still, especially in church?" Before I could reply, Melissa added, "I'll bet kids who stand around in the lobby instead of sitting down have a brain that needs to move to learn."

When I had stopped laughing, I said, "I like the way your brain is thinking, Melissa. Churches in some parts of the world have relatively few chairs. Many attendees stand."

Aloud and earnestly, Melissa wondered whether we could do that in our church. "Someday we're going to stand on the sea of glass. I bet more kids would attend church if there were a place for them to stand." I suggested she talk to the pastor and thought, *Some churches have taken a few pews out at the back to make a place for people to stand.*

"I'm going to write him a letter," said Melissa. "Right now! Where's the reference for that study?"

"It's on my Web site," I replied. "I'll get it for you." As I was looking up the reference, I thought, *When will religion get up to speed with how differently brains function? Are we putting up unnecessary roadblocks, especially for young people, or are we making it easy for them to embrace corporate worship in a way that works well for their brains?*

"Do you have it?" Melissa called.

"Coming," I replied. I sensed that her letter was going to be quite the masterpiece.

Arlene R. Taylor

You Are My Witnesses!

"You are my witnesses," declares the LORD,
"and my servant whom I have chosen, so that you may know
and trust me and understand that I am the One.
Before me no God was formed, nor will there be one after me."
—*Isaiah 43:10, ISV*

Several months ago, my husband and I visited our daughter, Chioma, and her son, Nikolas, in California. She shared a devotional thought at vespers that deeply impacted me. The scripture reference was Isaiah 43:10: " 'You are my witnesses,' declares the LORD, 'and my servant whom I have chosen, so that you may know and trust me and understand that I am the One' " (ISV). She pointed out that God didn't say that we are His attorneys, prosecutors, or judges. An attorney serves as a legal representative to go between the accused and the judge; a prosecutor presents evidence to prove the accused is guilty of the crime committed. The judge listens to the evidence presented by both sides and pronounces a verdict—guilty or not guilty.

The Word of God says: "You are my witnesses." A witness can be defined as someone who provides vital information about an incident or possible crime. As a witness in the criminal system, you are expected to tell the truth about what you heard, saw, or experienced.

What kind of witness are you? A true witness or a false witness? Are you a witness of God's mercy and amazing grace? How He provided a way out of no way? How He rescued you from the pit of sin? How He touched and restored you when your body was ravaged by cancer? How He saved your beloved son or daughter from a debilitating drug addiction? How He comforted you in your time of deep personal loss and loneliness? God is looking for true witnesses to testify to the truth about His beloved Son, Jesus, and how He changes lives.

Will you be His witness for what He's done for you? Today I'll be a witness for my Lord. Yes, I can testify of His faithfulness and how He's been so good to me. How He rescued me from a tragic accident. How He saved me from the pangs of death twice in one week. O the joy that floods my soul; something happened, and I know without a doubt that He saved my soul. Has He touched you, your spouse, your son, daughter, loved one, a friend, your grandchild?

I pray that as we interact with others, wherever we are, we will be true and faithful witnesses of God's amazing grace. The time is now! Don't delay. Be a witness for Jesus today!

Shirley C. Iheanacho

The Source of Living Water

"But whoever drinks the water I give them will never thirst.
Indeed, the water I give them will become in them
a spring of water welling up to eternal life."
—*John 4:14, NIV*

Prior to our first trip to Israel, my husband and I had spent countless hours mapping out our itinerary. From the time we picked up our tiny rental car at the Tel Aviv airport, we were constantly moving. "We're actually here," we often repeated, "where Jesus walked." We explored so many places that had only been names before: Cana, Capernaum, Tiberias.

Jerusalem was our next stop.

Could we chance a trip to the West Bank and the city of Nablus, where Jacob's Well was located? "That can be dangerous," the bespeckled Jerusalem hotel clerk told us. "You'd better be careful." His comment only sparked more interest in my husband and teenage son! Soon we were off, stopping at checkpoints, only to be waved through. Arriving at the Bir Ya'qub monastery, we found the entrance door locked. Just as we were turning away, an elderly monk answered. In broken English he shared his delight at seeing us before beckoning us to follow him downstairs to a crypt where the well still stands, a small winch and bucket attached. The bucket descended, hit water, and, oh, so carefully, we pulled it upward. Nothing tasted better on a hot day in Israel than cool water from a deep well.

Oh, for the living water that lady in Samaria tasted over two thousand years ago! An encounter so profound. For Jesus knew all about her life of sin. Surprised, His disciples shuddered when they found their Master talking to this woman of mixed Jewish and Gentile blood. How could He? They still didn't understand, after years of being right there with Jesus, with that spiritual water available every day. Yet they still hadn't discovered the Source!

But wait! He is still the Source. He offers the water of life—to all of us, whether we are deserving or not! He's willing to accept us with all our flaws—just as with the Samaritan woman. He is waiting to throw His robe of righteousness around our shoulders—just for the asking.

What started as a routine trip to Jacob's Well forever changed the woman from Samaria. Reliving that long-ago encounter had a profound effect on me too!

Let's stay close to the Source.

Harryette Aitken

Angels and Hopscotch

When thou liest down, thou shalt not be afraid: yea,
thou shalt lie down, and thy sleep shall be sweet.
—Proverbs 3:24

While working as a chaplain in the pediatric oncology department, I have learned something very basic—their sleep is a luxury. As I turned into the hospital parking, I read the sign: Mercy Street. *Dear God, bring an abundance of mercy to this place tonight. It is the road we all seek for here.*

At eleven o'clock that night, Nurse Kate called me. One of her charges, Brandy, age seven, has not slept in two days. She is forcing herself to stay awake. For six weeks I have worked with her family as they went through a Bible study, all of them getting closer to God. Brandy was getting better. *There is hope for her. I believe she will be well.*

"I don't want to sleep," she whispered. I sat next to the bed and held her hand. "If I close my eyes, I may not wake up again." Her little hand was cold, and I knew she must be in pain. I asked her what she would rather do than sleep. She smiled and whispered: "Hopscotch."

An hour later, all permissions granted, Brandy and I stood in the hall next to the chapel. The tiles on the floor created the hopscotch model to use. We were figuring out the pattern when a booming voice stopped us. *Nurse Kate.* She looked at us and shook her head. "We are going to do this right. I played this as a child!" She tickled Brandy and helped us use red medical tape to create a pattern. Then she produced the grand prize: a bean-filled stuffed animal in the shape of a frog, just big enough to use in the game. Brandy laughed and named the stuffed animal Froggie.

Through the night, the three of us played. When Brandy won, Nurse Kate exaggerated her own loss, making us laugh. By six o'clock in the morning, Brandy was yawning. As the child finished her last win, she was ready to lie down. In the room Nurse Kate carefully placed her in bed and—just like that—Brandy fell asleep. Nurse Kate smiled at me and walked away. *Nurse Kate, she made this all happen.* As I heard Brandy breathing, I prayed that her sleep "shall be sweet."

I saw Nurse Kate at the desk and I was reminded that angels walk among us. How strong their influence, how strong the influence of the Holy Spirit. I walked out quietly to Nurse Kate's mailbox and placed Froggie in her box.

Heavenly Father, when another needs help, give me the strength to answer the call.

Dixil L. Rodríguez

What's in a Name?

Then Gideon built an altar there to God
and named it "God's Peace."
—*Judges 6:24*, The Message

The Bible gives us many names for God, but the one I love the most is Jehovah-Shalom, God of peace. I've been wondering what really is in a name, so I went to Google to check on my name. Here is what it told me: "Erna—is highly selective in friendship and in love. She seeks peace and harmony above all, and tends to avoid conflicts and any risk of getting hurt emotionally. Determined, demanding, and a perfectionist, she expects a lot from both her personal and professional lives, while she assumes her responsibilities in return." That's a mouthful, isn't it? Well, most of this description is right, I'd say. I don't like conflict and would much rather live in peace with everyone!

What's in a name? When I got married to Eddy, I became a "Johnson." No longer did I write my Icelandic last name, Gudsteinsdottir; now it was Johnson. The Johnson family is well respected in Mauritius, where my husband comes from, so it was an honor to carry that name.

When I was baptized at the age of twelve, I became a Christian, the daughter of the King of kings. That name means a lot to me, and I want to be worthy of carrying God's name. Jehovah-Shalom, God of peace, says something to me. If God is a God of peace, I should be associated with peace as well. Erna Peacemaker sounds good, doesn't it? Try doing the same with your name. Write or say your name:_____. Then add *Peacemaker*, and see what it says to you.

In the Bible, especially in the Old Testament, names were given to people that revealed something about them, their character, or where they were from. I'd love to have my name associated with peacemaking, wouldn't you? This world is suffering from so much conflict; it needs peacemakers. That could be you and I as we live our daily lives wherever God has placed us.

What's in a name? Jehovah-Shalom, God of peace. What a wonderful name! I believe our names, our characters, are everything! May all of us be known as peacemakers for God's kingdom. That is my prayer and wish for everyone!

Erna Johnson

Purple Balloon

If ye then, being evil, know how to give good gifts unto your children, how much more shall your Father which is in heaven give good things to them that ask him?
—*Matthew 7:11*

While I was walking on a treadmill at the local gym, I looked out a large window at the indoor walking track. A little girl, around two years old, wandered onto the track. She held a purple helium balloon, received at an event held in one of the conference rooms. As I exercised, I couldn't help but notice her happy smile as she skipped along.

Then the looped ribbon attached to the balloon slipped off her hand and floated up to the ceiling. She cried out, and her father appeared. The child pointed to the out-of-reach balloon and implored her father to get it for her. He shook his head and jumped with outstretched arms to show he could not reach the balloon. Then he disappeared from my view as he entered a hallway.

I know just how you feel, little girl, I thought as, through the window, I watched this grieving child staring upward. I was thinking of some of my prayer requests God had apparently not granted. Sometimes our hopes and dreams slip through our fingers, and our heavenly Father just doesn't get them back for us. I wondered what God was trying to teach me through this scenario. The little girl's father returned with a woman from the community center staff. She had a long pole but was not quite tall enough to reach the loop of the balloon ribbon. The father then took the pole and, after several attempts, successfully returned the balloon to his daughter. Happy once again, the little girl walked away holding her father's hand.

I pondered what I had just witnessed, sensing again that God intended for me to learn something. The balloon symbolized my desires. Then Matthew 7:11 came to my mind. God wants to give good gifts to me, His child. Yet I also remembered another story about a balloon and a young child that had been all over the news. The toddler had swallowed a piece of a popped balloon and ended up brain-dead from the lack of oxygen. In this case, the balloon was dangerous and not a source of happiness at all.

My heavenly Father, in His infinite wisdom, knows that what I want may not always be the best for me. These few moments on the treadmill, as I witnessed this purple balloon incident, served to renew my trust in the loving heavenly Father.

Marsha Hammond-Brummel

Radiant!

Those who look to him are radiant;
their faces are never covered with shame.
—*Psalm 34:5, NIV*

I grew up the third of six children. When you read about middle children, they tend to be the hardest to categorize. They can run the gamut of being very outgoing to painfully shy. I was very shy and had a tender conscience, the very opposite of my older sister (the second of six). I was the child that would burst into tears when Mom looked at me funny.

My people-pleaser personality was very strong. What resulted from all of this was a life of deeply held guilt and shame. By the age of twelve, I had developed a pre-ulcer. It was natural for me to blame myself for everything. I had convinced myself that I was very bad because I was keenly aware of my motives.

I became a spiritual perfectionist. I knew that God loved me. The Bible said so, and God wouldn't lie. But I was convinced He was disappointed in me. I had learned that God could read my mind and motives. He knew how wicked I was deep inside. And He knew that I knew better. But the more I tried and tried to become better, the more shame I felt. There was no relief.

I was on a destructive cycle of Satan's deception. He is the father of lies, and I believed him.

It was only when the Holy Spirit began to help me understand and internalize the true gospel that Satan's lies began to have less and less effect on me. The scales began to fall from my eyes, and I saw the true character of God—a God who not only loves me but likes me!

I slowly began to understand that He enjoys me not for what I do but because of who I am. Salvation is a Person, and His name is Jesus Christ.

I have learned that when I spend time getting to know Jesus, I am changed. I can wake up in the morning and know that when I look at my Savior, I am radiant to Him! I never need to cover myself with shame. "Therefore, there is now no condemnation for those who are in Christ Jesus" (Romans 8:1, NIV).

Allow the Holy Spirit to teach you and transform you to believe the truth, and the truth will set you free from destructive guilt and shame.

Lee Lee Dart

Just a Day Before

"I will repay you for the years the locusts have eaten."
—Joel 2:25, NIV

My brother, Sam, realized that his household was in dire financial trouble when he lost the family car. In an attempt to ease the worrisome situation, he decided to relocate his family next to his children's schools and other frequently used services. An ideal house was soon found. Sam notified the landlord that his family would be moving, so the landlord signed up a new tenant.

Just a week before the new tenant was to move in, Sam got word that the house he was planning to move into had been taken off the market. His family began a frantic search for another house, but most businesses were closed for the Christmas and New Year's holidays. Family and friends started praying. I claimed the promises, "You will have plenty to eat" (Joel 2:26, NIV) and "I was young and now I am old, yet I have never seen the righteous forsaken or their children begging bread" (Psalm 37:25, NIV).

Sam's feet were sore from days of walking along crowded streets in search for a house in one of the most notorious sections of Johannesburg. He was hungry, fearful, and frustrated. The day before his family was to be evicted, a stranger spoke to him, inquiring about his well-being. My brother, an introvert by nature, surprisingly poured out his heart to this total stranger. The stranger listened and then scribbled down a name, an address, and a phone number on a piece of paper. He told Sam to contact this individual, who had houses for rent. The stranger then wished Sam good luck before disappearing into the crowd.

In desperation, Sam made the call. A pleasant voice confirmed that a vacant house was available for rent. Sam rushed to sign the contract. At home later that day, Sam's former—and irate—landlord confronted him: "When are you vacating my property?"

"Tomorrow," Sam told him confidently. God spared his family the humiliation and dangers of living on the streets. Several months later, God truly restored the years eaten by the locusts when Sam got a promotion at work and a doubled salary, including benefits. The family moved into a more comfortable home, Sam was able to get another car, and the children continued their education.

Though Sam could not discern the future, Jesus sees the end from the beginning. Great is His faithfulness in responding to the prayers of His children!

Edith Kiggundu

Blessed to Be a Blessing!

*"I will bless you and make your name great;
and you shall be a blessing."*
—Genesis 12:2, NKJV

One cool Sunday morning at family camp, I was enjoying the beautiful natural scenery that God created for our enjoyment. Praise God, our Creator, that in a dark world of sin, He still allows us to enjoy His creative work! Look at the sky today and think of the Creator who delights in your enjoyment of what you see. If your morning sky is cloudy or rainy, simply enjoy it, knowing that it was created by God. Soon the sun will be shining again. He has a plan for your day. That morning at camp I met up with a friend in the cafeteria. She told me that, two days earlier, she'd had a dream concerning me. She had wanted to share her dream with me but had been unsuccessful in getting time to talk with me.

"In my dream," she said, "I was in a meeting where people were signing a large book. I did not know the reason for the meeting or why they were signing the book. When my turn came to sign, I picked up the pen but did not know what I needed to do. I approached the book and prepared to write on the last empty page. Out of curiosity, I turned to look at the pages that were already written on. My heartbeat quickened, my hand trembled, and my eyes opened wide in amazement when I saw your name written all over those pages! I did not understand what I was seeing. I woke up and asked the Lord to help me understand the meaning of the dream."

As my friend talked, someone came to announce that a meeting was being held after breakfast and all the women at camp were requested to attend the meeting. Upon arriving at the meeting room, we learned we were gathered for the purpose of choosing an Hispanic Women's Ministries director for that geographic area. Women from five different states were requested to nominate one person they would like to see as their new leader. The votes were tallied. To my surprise, I had been selected to assume that leadership position.

Dear sister, sometimes we cannot clearly see God's plans for us. We rush, and even push, to make things happen. It's much simpler to trust humbly in Jesus Christ, serving Him where we are and patiently waiting for His revealed will.

Just know that your life is in His divine calendar. He will bless you, and, in turn, you will be a blessing for Him, helping to make His name known throughout the world.

Bezaida (Betzy) Castro

The Black Suit

"So he said to him,
'Friend, how did you come in here
without a wedding garment?' "
—Matthew 22:12, NKJV

My son, Will, doesn't like dressing up in a suit. He never has. Will would not wear a suit—even to his graduation from high school. I offered to buy a suit for him, but he wasn't going to budge. He ended up wearing a Hawaiian shirt. He looked nice, but he wasn't dressed like most of his classmates. Years later, his friend, Daniel, asked Will to be a groomsman in his wedding party. When Will found out, it was but a few short weeks before the wedding. Daniel told Will that he would need a black suit and a white shirt. Daniel would provide the tie.

Will works at an academy in the small town of Lillooet, British Columbia, so shopping isn't easy. Just a few days before the wedding, Will still didn't have a suit. When I asked him about it, he told me that he would look in the thrift store on his way home to visit some of our relatives. I wasn't sure whether Will would even be able to find a black suit, let alone one that fit him. He really didn't want to buy a suit because, he told me, he wouldn't wear it again. I was concerned because Will had made a commitment to Daniel.

While praying during my morning devotions, I made a special plea to the Lord about the need of a black suit for Will that would work for the wedding. *We don't have much time, Lord, and it's important that he is properly dressed for the wedding!*

My husband also took this need to the Lord. When he was praying about it, he suddenly thought of his brother, John, who had a black suit. John is about the same size as Will. My husband phoned. Sure enough, John said he would loan Will his black suit. It was already at the dry cleaner's, ready to be picked up! John brought it with him the next day when he came to visit.

The suit worked very well for Will. He was properly dressed for the wedding. God had brought this about in answer to our need. Asking God for a black suit seemed like an almost impossible request, but He had the right solution. "And my God shall supply all your need according to His riches in glory by Christ Jesus" (Philippians 4:19, NKJV). You can trust Him too!

Martha (Marty) Cunnington

Never Abandon Ship

Noah was a just man and perfect in his generations,
and Noah walked with God.
—*Genesis 6:9*

So Noah walked with God as Enoch did, but for some reason, God did not take him to heaven as He took Enoch. Perhaps it was because Noah lived in momentous times, just before God destroyed the world with a terrible flood. God also knew that Noah's life would be an inspiration to us, living as we do under similar conditions immediately preceding the final destruction at Jesus' coming.

Noah was unquestioning in his obedience to God. One day, God said, "I want you to build a huge boat." A boat? On dry land? When rain was completely unknown? Without protest, Noah started to build. Then God said, "Warn those who come to watch you of this impending disaster." So Noah did, in spite of the mocking response. They rolled their eyes, tapped their foreheads, and made derisive remarks about his sanity. Then one cloudless day, God said, "Go into the ark with all the animals, and anyone else who wants to enter." Noah obeyed despite a crescendo of public derision that grew steadily as one beautiful day followed another. Then, true to His word, as He always is, God sent rain. Every living creature outside the ark died.

Conditions in the ark settled into routine. As the storm raged, Noah's family had to keep the windows shut until the rain abated. The stench from so many animals must have been overwhelming. Rough seas made their stomachs heave as they endlessly fed, watered, and cared for so many animals. Not much fun, but far better than the alternative. Noah certainly didn't think of abandoning ship.

As in the days of Noah, God has provided an "ark" for us today in the face of the coming tempest. We call it the church. When we give our lives to Jesus, He invites us to enter and asks us to work with Him for the happiness and salvation of our fellow travelers. That's not always an easy or pleasant task. Sometimes we become disillusioned, hurt, or angry with their responses to our efforts. But God says, "Stand firm. Continue to serve those who cause you heartaches, and forgive them for My sake." We live in critical times. Satan does his best to cause problems in the "ark." Yet however unpleasant life in the ark might get at times, leaving is not the solution.

Let's learn from the example of Noah and *never* abandon ship!

Revel Papaioannou

God Cares for You!

Fear thou not; for I am with thee:
be not dismayed; for I am thy God.
—*Isaiah 41:10*

When I was two years old, my family moved to California. My dad was a drafting engineer and was in defense work, so we got moved around a lot. Between the first and twelfth grades, I attended ten different schools. It was especially hard when we moved in the middle of the school year. My new classmates had already made friends for the year. The teachers usually weren't much help either. (When I started teaching years later, I made sure that any new students were included when they came into my class in the middle of the year.)

When I was seven, my family moved to Bakersfield, California, where the temperature sometimes reaches 130°F (54°C)! My mom was a nurse and worked each day, as did my dad. They left my thirteen-year-old sister, Priscilla, to take care of me. I was in the second grade, and it was in the middle of the year. However, my sister was more interested in a group of teenagers she hung out with than she was in taking care of me.

One day Priscilla decided we should walk down to the railroad yard and check out the trains. The yard was about three blocks from our house, and a lot of trains were parked there. Priscilla decided we should climb up on a caboose and pretend we were going somewhere. So we did. All of a sudden, the train we were on started to move forward slowly. Then it rolled along faster. "We've got to jump off!" Priscilla exclaimed.

I don't like heights, so when she tried to get me to jump, I told her, "You go first, and then I'll jump." Priscilla jumped to the ground and ran alongside the moving caboose, trying to get me to jump. Finally I jumped and rolled down the stone embankment along the side of the tracks. It was a wonder I didn't break a leg! My guardian angel was really with me.

God has promised to be with us always. "Fear thou not; for I am with thee: be not dismayed; for I am thy God: I will strengthen thee; yea, I will help thee; yea, I will uphold thee with the right hand of my righteousness" (Isaiah 41:10).

God has also said in Joshua 1:9, "Be strong and of a good courage; be not afraid, neither be thou dismayed: for the Lord thy God is with thee whithersoever thou goest."

Today He is with you too.

Anne Elaine Nelson

Four Casters

Casting all your care upon him;
for he careth for you.
—*1 Peter 5:7*

The bookcase was old, but I really liked it. It had been given to me, and I had decided to use it in one of our school classrooms. However, due to the fact that it had glass doors, we decided it would not be safe around the children. So I stored it in one of our school storage rooms until I was able to take it home to use.

When ready to take the bookcase home, I noticed that one of the rolling casters was missing. This would unbalance the legs, and the bookcase would not sit properly. I had one of the casters removed and placed it in my purse so that I would know exactly the size and type I needed. Since I needed an antique caster, which was hard to find, I prayed about it before beginning my search. I was soon convinced I would have no success, so I resolved in my mind that I would probably have to remove the other three and just let the bookcase set on its legs without any casters. However, God knows our needs and wants even after we have forgotten about them.

One day I drove by a furniture store that was having a going-out-of-business sale. I decided to stop in and look at bedroom nightstands. After talking to the sales lady, I started to leave the store. At that moment, my eyes spotted four casters nearby, lying on the floor. They were exactly like the type I needed for the antique bookcase and not associated with any of the furniture near them. I picked them up, compared them with the one in my purse, and saw that their size and type was exactly what I needed for my antique bookcase.

I asked the sales lady if she could sell me the four casters. She asked whether I was sure I could use them. I replied, "Yes." Taking them from my hand, she placed them in my purse, giving them to me free of charge.

I could very well have made that bookcase work without those casters, but God wanted me to learn that He is interested in even the small things we desire and that He is able to provide beyond our expectations.

Whatever it is that we need, let's just trust that God will provide according to His will and time schedule. If you are ever in a situation where you are tempted to doubt God's care for you, just remember the four casters and know that God really does care.

Beatrice Banks

Reverent, Submissive Service

Serve the LORD with reverent fear, and rejoice with trembling.
Submit to God's royal son, or he will become angry, and you will be
destroyed in the midst of all your activities—for his anger flares up
in an instant. But what joy for all who take refuge in him!
—*Psalm 2:11, 12, NLT*

In my discipleship walk and spiritual journey, I have chosen to add to my Google daily calendar "God Moments" at 6:30 A.M. As I have struggled through the years to have time with God, one skill that enhances my prayer life as well as my "God Moments" is journaling. Being in the Word and reading the Bible with prayer, while allowing the Holy Spirit's presence to impress my heart, are key factors that I have included in my devotional time. As the Holy Spirit reveals His topics and desires for me, journaling enriches my time with God and makes Him seem real.

Therefore, I want to challenge you: If you do not have a "prayer closet" or are rusty in your time with God, take your pen and paper and write down Scripture texts. Allow the Holy Spirit to impress upon your mind His thoughts and desires for your life. He will fill you to overflowing as you take time to meditate on Scripture. Pray for His Spirit to guide you in your precious moments with Him. This is a sample of my prayer journal.

"Dear Father God!

"I choose to serve You with reverent fear—show me how to serve You. I give You the reins of my life. Fill me to overflowing with Your Holy Spirit so I will know how to rejoice. I praise You for being my Father God—Abba Father! You are my Lord of lords, King of kings, Man of Sorrows! You are the Great I Am! The Beginning and the End. The Alpha and Omega. You are my Messiah—Christ Jesus! I bow before You as Your precious daughter whom You call Your beloved. I submit myself to You. Take away any sin that is ever before me and cleanse my heart, O God. Show me joy as I take refuge in You. God, Father, You have given me the gift of the Holy Spirit to convict me of my wrong. Operate on my soul and clean out any bitterness or harsh feelings within me. The Holy Spirit is given to work within my own heart, soul, and mind as You teach me how to submit to the Lord Jesus. I choose to take refuge in You. I choose to rejoice in the presence of the Almighty God. Blessed be the name of the Lord.

"Your precious daughter, Mary."

Mary L. Maxson

Childhood Dream

"For I know the plans I have for you," declares the LORD,
"plans to prosper you and not to harm you,
plans to give you hope and a future."
—*Jeremiah 29:11, NIV*

My childhood dream was to remain unmarried so that I could dedicate my life solely to the Lord. Every summer vacation, mother sewed white dresses for us five sisters to wear on Flores de Mayo. I gazed up at the paintings of Argao's old stone church as the *canturas* sang high-pitched Spanish songs for the worship service.

When I entered college, I attended church daily to quench the deep spiritual longing of my soul.

Unfortunately, I fell in love at the age of sixteen and got pregnant. My boyfriend's family would not consent to our marriage because he and I were of different religions.

In spite of the situation, I sensed a different perspective of the religion of my boyfriend. I could sense the holiness of the songs sung in his church as well as the sacredness of the Sabbath. Though he later left me and our daughter, I was baptized secretly into his church.

An unwed mother now, I continued my college education under my parents' care. Mom was a teacher in the same school I attended, so she discovered that I was absent every Friday night and on Saturdays. My parents forced me to promise to be in school on Saturdays, but doing so went against my conscience. I'd learned the Bible teaches that God designated the seventh day of the week as being holy. One night Dad got mad, and Mom pushed me out of the door. I pleaded because that meant I had to leave behind Ruvi, my one-year-old daughter. That midnight I was forced to walk away, though I heard, in my heart, an angelic choir singing, "Lord, lift me up."

I stayed with my new church friends. One night, while deeply longing for my child, I cried in my sleep. Then I dreamed Jesus was saying to me, "Don't cry. I will give your child to you." He pointed to a beautiful place filled with flowering shrubs lined up nicely on a green grass carpet. Then He lifted me up from a very dark hole to a luminously bright place. Today, as a mother of three and an active church member, I cling to the hope of heaven.

Jesus will bring you out of your dark places too.

Ruth Minoza-Gunida

Are You Thirsty?

Jesus answered and said to her, "Whoever drinks of this water will thirst again, but whoever drinks of the water that I shall give him will never thirst. But the water that I shall give him will become in him a fountain of water springing up into everlasting life."
—*John 4:13, 14, NKJV*

The first verse of the song "Fill My Cup, Lord," written by Richard Eugene Blanchard Sr., speaks of hearing God's voice—as did the Samaritan woman at the well—inviting us to draw from the well that never runs dry. Yet we often seek for satisfaction in things of this life; they bring only temporary gratification. No matter our backgrounds, many of us seem to have a sense of not being fulfilled in some area of life. So we seek fulfilment in love, acceptance, family, popularity, material things, or in some purpose—but we're still thirsty.

Are you thirsty today? The Samaritan woman was thirsty and seeking fulfilment in love, acceptance, and a desire to be treasured (John 4:10–15). She had already had five husbands. When Jesus met her, she was involved with a man who was not her husband (verse 18). Over the years, many women have been judged and labeled for having been involved with multiple partners. Yet their accusers often have no understanding of the circumstances that led these unfulfilled women to unfortunate choices and situations. After being rejected by someone, most of us, like the Samaritan woman, feel needy. Our thirst to address our neediness, whatever it may be, causes us to go after whatever we hope might satisfy it. We eventually learn, however, that most of these things satisfy only temporarily—and we are still left thirsty.

I have been thirsty and made choices I thought would quench my thirst, only to find myself being labeled and judged. I am happy, though, that, like the Samaritan woman, I found Jesus waiting for me with open arms, a loving heart, and nonjudgmental acceptance. He knew that I was seeking to be loved and accepted, and to belong. He knew that I worshiped "what [I did] not know" (verse 22, NKJV). He showed me that if I continued to thirst for temporary sexual gratification and temporary friendships and relationships, I would thirst again. Jesus offered me something better. He gave me everlasting life. He gave me unconditional love. He gave me purpose. He gave me acceptance. He even gave me what I did not know I needed.

Are you thirsty today? Let Jesus lead you to the fountain that will never run dry.

Charmaine N. Williams Tate

God Keeps His Promises

Bring ye all the tithes into the storehouse, that there may be meat
in mine house, and prove me now herewith, saith the Lord of hosts,
if I will not open you the windows of heaven, and pour you out a
blessing, that there shall not be room enough to receive it.
—Malachi 3:10

Once I fell behind in my mortgage payments but remained faithful in returning my tithes and offerings. I learned that a national organization that assists struggling homeowners was having a workshop in downtown Atlanta. This organization helps homeowners maintain ownership of their homes by asking lenders to reduce interest rates. After arriving downtown for the workshop, I had to wait longer than expected to receive help at the workshop. The money in my parking meter would expire. By the time I got to my car, I had already been booted! I had to pay fifty dollars to get the boot taken off. *God*, I cried, *I don't understand. I didn't have the money in the first place. And now this!*

I left the seminar without getting the necessary help that I needed. I was told I could go to the Web site and submit the necessary documents online. Each time I tried, I was unsuccessful. One day on my way home from work, I decided to stop by the local office in downtown Decatur. A gentleman listened as I explained my problem and then accepted a copy of my documents, telling me someone would contact me within a couple of weeks.

I finally received a call from a representative who asked me various questions about how much money I paid for certain things, including this question: "How much do you give in charitable donations?" When I told him how much, he said, "If you give that much in donations, you can also afford to pay your mortgage."

"Sir," I replied, "if your organization chooses not to help me because of my giving, it is OK because the same God that gave me my house can give me another one!" About a month later, my mortgage company alerted me they were sending me some papers to sign for financial aid that would come in the form of a fixed (not an adjustable) mortgage rate with a 5 percent drop in interest, and I would not have to pay on my mortgage for the next two months! I was overjoyed! God has made a promise to faithful tithe payers.

I know beyond a shadow of a doubt that God keeps His promises!

Deniece G. Anderson

Fear and Love

We need have no fear of someone who loves us perfectly.
. . . If we are afraid, it . . . shows that we are not fully convinced
that he really loves us.
—1 John 4:18, TLB

Many lives have interfaced with mine because I serve our community as a family therapist. Each person entering my door brings a new situation that illustrates the principles of God that determine the outcomes of our interactions. Today's text presents the best formula for the challenges of living with other human beings, for conflict, addictions, anxiety, depression, anorexia, parenting challenges, grief, phobias, and hopelessness all have a central thread—fear.

As life teaches principles to guide our choices and behaviors, one principle seems to be at the core. All behavior arises out of either fear or love. Like a seesaw, we may alternate between the two with frustrating regularity. Children operate from fear because they don't want to lose the secure relationship they experience from loving, consistent parents. Punishments, threats, being ignored, criticisms, deprivations, and abuse torture the child with hopelessness, helplessness, and fear. Thoughts of possible abandonment cause humans to act in scary ways. We become resistant, disobedient, and defiant, and we infect those around us with the poison of fear.

God's love is a perfect model for our dealings with each other. Our understanding of another's fear generates love. Fear is aborted. Behaviors of those around us begin to reflect love. It is that simple! The love of God is transforming! If we want to be surrounded with loving people, we simply seek to understand the fear underneath their actions and words. Expressing our new understanding begins to fill them with the love and confidence God offers. They find it easier to comprehend that God can love them. While this concept is so simple, it is at the center of God's plan of salvation. He understands our fear of separation from Him for eternity. He has provided a way of salvation for each of us. Our job is to "get it"—to sense His complete understanding and acceptance of us. Allowing God's love to preclude fear residing in our hearts allows us to experience the taste of heaven here on earth!

My prayer for you is that you may experience the peace and joy that come from knowing with assurance that you are understood and loved supremely. Wouldn't it be wonderful to infect the world with love and understanding, eliminating fear?

Arlene West McFarland

March 15

The Locked Room

Then [I] cried unto the LORD in [my] trouble,
and he delivered [me] out of [my] distresses.
—Psalm 107:6

On one of my annual mystery bus trips with about thirty colleagues, we ended up at The Locked Room in Calgary, Alberta. This place houses four locked rooms (each with a different theme) requiring teamwork in order for team members to escape the rooms. We were divided into four groups. With feelings of apprehension, we heard the door click behind us as we entered a windowless room full of pictures and gadgets. We were given one hour to solve a series of puzzles and codes so that we could attempt to find our way out. In case someone panicked or had a personal emergency prior to finding a way out of the room, there was a call button near the entry door that we could press for help. At this news, some breathed a sigh of relief.

Sharing ideas of how to solve this puzzle made our trapped situation more bearable. "Let me try." "I have an idea." "Maybe we need to assign letters to the numbers for a secret word." As we solved one part of the puzzle, we often found another code to decipher or a key that unlocked another section of the room. Whenever we came to a dead end, we could buzz for help from the front desk, receive more clues, and move forward.

As we were challenged to find release from a locked-in dilemma, I realized an analogy to real life experiences. Have you ever felt like you were trapped in a locked room with no escape? Perhaps you were short of money for the end-of-month bills, or perhaps your employment isn't secure. Perhaps there's a family crisis or, as a manager, you have to resolve an issue with an employee. Maybe you have health concerns with too many appointments and no answers.

When we feel trapped, we often have family and friends with whom we share our concerns. They offer suggestions and encouragement to help us get through our locked room experience. But above all, there is an emergency button within easy reach that we can press at any time to call on the One who does have the answers to all our problems. Release may not be immediate, but He will see us through our dilemma if we trust in Him with all our heart.

Along with King David, we have the assurance that "the LORD will hear when I call unto him" (Psalm 4:3).

Edith Fitch

Incredible Wonders

Praise be to the Lord, to God our Savior,
who daily bears our burdens. Our God is a God who saves;
from the Sovereign LORD comes escape from death.
—*Psalm 68:19, 20, NIV*

Sometimes things seem to happen unexpectedly and then stop without apparent cause. Often they demonstrate the incredible wonders of God and His love.

In 1976 my friend and her elder sister moved into their new home. Later that year the rest of the family moved into the same flat. There was peace and quiet.

One night, my friend's father thought a snake was under his bed as he felt the bed shake. The next day, however, he read in the newspaper about an earthquake in Indonesia.

On and off throughout the years, my friend has experienced mild earthquake tremors in her home. One particular evening, though, the residents of the whole housing estate experienced very strong tremors. They felt their individual units shake, while many of the residents ran to a big nearby field for refuge.

My friend and her family stayed in their home because her nephew was sound asleep. Yet she watched a plaque hanging on her door swing back and forth.

During the tremors she observed kitchen utensils moving about. Though it was shaking badly, my friend sat on the sofa while the whole flat moved and shook. She prayed until the tremors finally stopped.

Praise God Almighty for His incredible wonders and love!

Who can explain the ways, the love, and the wonders of God? On two occasions my friend believes that God sent bees to her flat as a warning. The day after one of these occurrences, a serious earthquake took place in Indonesia.

The Lord is indeed great to lead us as we bring our burdens to Him. He protects and guides us with His wisdom. We serve and worship a living God who loves His children. What a wonderful privilege to be able to testify how God performs wonders for His praying children!

Yan Siew Ghiang

God Is in Control

And it shall come to pass, that before they call,
I will answer; and while they are yet speaking, I will hear.
—*Isaiah 65:24*

Be still, and know that I am God:
I will be exalted among the heathen,
I will be exalted in the earth.
—*Psalm 46:10*

Transitioning from a developing country's nursing practice to a Western culture practice requires adaptation, learning, and unlearning. The learning and unlearning quickly took its toll on me, for critical care nursing requires quick, clinical decision-making, being on one's toes, and being on guard. Patient safety and quality of life are at the core of nursing. Though I loved fast-paced nursing, my heart's desire was to teach. The Lord knew that I needed to be well rooted in the dynamics of nursing practice and management to be equipped to teach. He led my path to a management position on a step-down pediatric unit, where my knowledge increased through extensive and challenging responsibilities.

Then in 1993 a global economic depression affected hospital operations and resulted in downsized management positions. I was among those laid off. Losing a job caused feelings of uncertainty regarding our family's financial survival and our ability to support our children's Christian education. I needed a job, but no one was hiring! I had only a part-time teaching position at the local community college. I placed my case in God's hands. In our family worship, I said to our children, "If the door closes, the Lord opens a window."

By this time our daughter was in college. Just as I mentioned the possibility of a second job to my husband, the telephone rang. The dean of a local college was calling: "Edna, you were recommended to us by another college dean. We need you." Awestruck, I did not know what to say! She asked, "Well, can you come now?" Of course, I could. When I arrived, the dean and her associate were waiting for me. Surely the Lord had opened a window.

Yes, God is in control! We experience troubles, but His promise in Isaiah 65:24 is sure. The God of heaven always proves His omnipotence and omnipresence. Job's faith in God affirms his words: "But he knoweth the way that I take: when he hath tried me, I shall come forth as gold" (Job 23:10).

Edna Bacate-Domingo

His Name

I will make Your name to be remembered in all generations;
therefore the people shall praise You forever and ever.
—*Psalm 45:17, NKJV*

had just safely passed through Canadian customs—or so I thought. Another security officer asked to see my customs forms. The interrogation began. "I see you're coming from Bermuda. How long will you be here in Ontario Province?" he first asked.

"Three days."

"Why are you here?"

"For my twentieth high school reunion."

"When did you go to high school here?"

"Twenty years ago."

"Who is meeting you here?" he continued.

"Pastor Millett," I said.

"How are you getting to Oshawa?"

"Pastor Millett," I responded again.

"OK. Have a good trip."

Although I found the interrogation a bit uncomfortable, I know that the customs official was just doing his job. But was I ever glad to know my pastor's name! In fact, I was going to be staying with him and his wife—friends from twenty years earlier—during my brief stay in Canada. Our longtime friendship began during my boarding school days. Now Pastor Millett was a church administer here in Canada.

I would like to think that Pastor Millett's name had some sort of influence or "power" on the airport security official's decision to end the interrogation. The names of well-known people, such as royalty, superstars, and politicians, pack a certain degree of influence, even "power," which may get them front row seats, flight upgrades, and other preferential treatment.

Yet there is one name whose power supersedes all others. The name of Jesus. The Bible tells us that at the name of Jesus, demons flee (Matthew 7:22). What power is in that name!

Do you personally and purposefully share His loving and powerful name with others?

Dana Bassett M. Bean

March 19

The Lost Dentures

And we know that in all things God works for the good
of those who love him.
—*Romans 8:28, NIV*

It was a beautiful Friday afternoon. I left at one o'clock for a doctor's appointment. I had just finished eating some fruit and nuts as I got into my Jeep. Since I wear partial dentures, I decided to take them out, put them in a napkin, and place them in the outside pocket of my handbag. This thought came to my mind: *You may lose them*. Yet I still left my dentures in the handbag pocket and drove off to my appointment.

It was necessary for me to stop at three places before returning home. When I arrived home, I discovered to my dismay that the napkin with the dentures was not in the handbag pocket. I searched the whole handbag and took out everything. My heart began to race. I recalled the *you may lose them* impression that I had not heeded earlier. I was so disappointed, especially thinking about the large sum of money it would cost to replace my dentures.

My husband arrived home after I did. He said that I should have gone back to look for the dentures where I had parked for my appointment. I wondered whether perhaps they had fallen from my purse and a vehicle had run over them.

On Sunday afternoon, on our way home from a birthday celebration, my husband drove on the street near where I had first parked on Friday. We decided to go look for the napkin with the dentures. I quickly found one denture piece on the road—and still in the napkin! We searched for the other piece. In a few minutes, my husband found the other piece. They were dusty, but no vehicle had run over them. I was so excited that God had protected them, despite the fact that I did not heed His warning. When we arrived home, my husband cleaned up the dentures, and they looked like new.

We can learn three lessons from this experience. First, when the Holy Spirit speaks to us, we should obey.

Second, the dust on the dentures can remind us that sin can make us dirty, but Jesus is able to clean us up.

Third, God cares for us even when we are disobedient.

Janice Fleming-Williams

I Am a Wonder

I am as a wonder unto many;
but thou art my strong refuge.
—*Psalm 71:7*

At first glance we could read this verse and think, *You go, girl! You are a wonder!* Yet in this case . . . not so much. The Hebrew word for "wonder" is *mopheth* (pronounced mofaith). It means that people gasp at you; you are conspicuous. Most of us would rather not be noticed, and especially not by people who have declared themselves to be our enemies or who speak against us (Psalm 71:10). Sometimes we become spiritually "old," not wanting to take chances.

Another sign of being spiritually "old" is that we get gun-shy. We have been burned a few times when sharing our faith, so we tuck our tails, put on a sheepish look, and no longer reach out to others for God. Or maybe we went way overboard when spiritually "young" and tried to share everything we knew with people who didn't want to hear even the basics. Yet those earlier choices or mistakes don't make it right for us to jump into the ditch, zip our lips, and live by the old rule, "Don't talk politics or religion."

God has called us to be His witnesses, and witnesses tell what they know. Keeping silent isn't an option if the love of God is burning a hole in our tongues.

Ask the prophet Jeremiah. He tried to keep silent when he believed doubting people were not going to listen to him or accept what God had instructed him to share. But Jeremiah could not keep silent. He would not become spiritually "old" even when suffering the persecution of his fellow countrymen for what he shared.

Sometimes when we experience resistance to our witnessing, it wears us down until we begin to let ourselves think it is OK to drift into carelessness and silence, OK to become status quo. The average "old age" Christian doesn't pray often, doesn't read the Bible regularly, and doesn't share their faith. Yet David said, "I am a wonder."

The other meaning of *mopheth* (mofaith) is to be a miracle! Psalm 71:14 says, "But I will hope continually, and will yet praise thee more and more." That makes me laugh! And cry.

That means the disbelief of others can just make us have *more* hope!

The evil speaking of others can drive us to praise God more. Even persecution by others can help us just hang on to our Savior more tightly and be a "wonder" for Him.

Angie Joseph

Prove Me Now

Bring ye all the tithes into the storehouse,
that there may be meat in mine house,
and prove me now herewith, saith the LORD of hosts,
if I will not open you the windows of heaven,
and pour you out a blessing.
—*Malachi 3:10*

Will a man—or woman—rob God? No! Not this woman. That would have been my first answer. Yet the economic recession of 2008 hit when I was teaching in South Korea, causing me financial difficulties, along with everyone else. The value of the Korean won dropped drastically, and by October and November things were even worse. Due to financial obligations in Korea (both expected and unexpected), I couldn't send home as much money as usual, especially when currency conversion rates and wiring fees were factored in.

I considered not paying my tithe and offerings one month in order to meet my financial obligations. As soon as that thought came into my head, I heard this: *Will a man rob God?* I knew then that I must be faithful in my giving. In worship that week, my students and I had been learning about God's provision, specifically the birds in the air being taken care of (Matthew 6:26). I also remembered that one of the members in my church, Mother Elliot, would always say, "Prove God." So right there in my classroom, I just stopped and prayed. I told God I trusted Him to stand behind His promise to be faithful to me to help me be faithful to Him.

When I checked my account the next day I had exactly $611.65 (after the wire fee). Once again I became discouraged over the low amount. Yet I paid my tithe and offering first and then added up my bills: tithe ($135.10), offering ($67.55), auto payment ($230), school loan ($65), and credit card bill payment ($114). After I added up all the numbers, I blinked and added up the bills again. They came to exactly $611.65! Isn't God wonderful?

When it came to finances, I had never put God to the test. If I had been home in the United States when this occurred, I would have tried to find a way to make extra money and handle the situation by myself. But being overseas forced me to rely on *God* to make the situation work.

Even today when I have moments of worry about my finances, I hear God whispering, "Prove Me now." I recall that His faithfulness is not a one-time occurrence. He says, "I am the LORD, I change not" (Malachi 3:6). God fulfills His promises over and over again.

Denise C. Braswell

The Peacemakers

Blessed are the peacemakers:
for they shall be called the children of God.
—*Matthew 5:9*

When I am at home, my gate is usually locked. After my morning walk one day, I decided to leave it open. My new neighbor, not knowing I was home, decided to help himself to water from my garden pipe. When I noticed his water hose stretching from my garden pipe to his house, I was not happy. I would have preferred his asking my permission first. I knew very little about him or his value system. Consequently, several unpleasant questions flooded my mind: *What should I do? What shall I say to him? How shall I approach him?* He needed to know how much I disapproved of his actions. I thought of turning off the water supply and disconnecting his hose. I was in a dilemma, but one thing *was* certain: I was very upset.

Then that "still, small voice" spoke to me: *Blessed are the peacemakers: for they shall be called the children of God.* The reminder was a timely one. I sat quietly on my patio. Suddenly a car drove up. It was my new neighbor. He had returned to complete his water project, but to his horror, he encountered me sitting on the patio. He was embarrassed! Apologizing profusely, he explained that his water supply was disconnected. When he saw my gate open, he thought I had gone to work and had decided to help himself.

"Since I did not have a telephone number to call and ask your permission," he explained, "I made my choice out of desperation for water." I readily accepted his apology and assured him it was all right, even expressing how happy I was to assist him. We exchanged telephone numbers, and I told him to call me if he needed my assistance at any time. We parted peacefully.

One month later, as I attempted to leave home for work, my car refused to move. I did all I could to start my faithful car, but it just would not go. I walked out into my yard, desperate to find anyone to help me. There he was, my neighbor, standing in his yard as if waiting to help! He quickly diagnosed the problem—and remedied the situation. Soon I was off to work and so grateful to him for his assistance. Of course, I remembered that day when he had needed my help. Under the guidance of the "still, small voice," we can be peacemakers by sharing one another's joys, griefs, and burdens.

Jacqueline Hope HoShing-Clarke

March 23

Thumbs Up

And how can they hear without someone preaching to them?
—Romans 10:14, NIV

The best stories need telling. As a believer, I consider all other Christians my teammates in the worldwide Christian church. We need to uplift and encourage one other to stay the course until Jesus comes. I'm always praying for new ways to share my love for Jesus as the Holy Spirit guides me. When I hear an excellent sermon, I'll spend my offering dollars to make CDs from the church's master copy so I can share it with friends. I had planned to get the master copy of the worship service held on March 16, 2013, and make several CDs to include in my annual Easter letter. However, the following Sabbath, March 23, I was terribly disappointed when told that the sound system had malfunctioned the week before, so there was no master copy CD of that service for sharing. Instantly I felt the Holy Spirit impress me to smile anyway, as these words came into my mind: *The Lord will have something much better for you to share!* And here it is, a priceless story . . .

My twenty-six-year-old autistic son, Sonny, was just beaming with happiness because he hadn't been to church for three weeks due to a nasty flu bug. Prayer and praise time is our favorite part of the service. The order of the service is usually always the same, unless there are time restrictions. On that day the announcements and children's story took up more time than usual. That day there was no time left for the congregation to share personal praises or prayer requests. Everyone was invited to come to the front of the sanctuary for the Garden of Prayer.

Sonny didn't understand the instructions. He sat in the second pew, waving his hands and pointing to himself in a vain attempt to attract the attention of the person holding the microphone. Now, Sonny loves to share his testimony, but it is spoken in Sonny language. I translate so that others will understand. *Bless his heart,* I thought. *Sonny isn't about to miss his turn to pray.* I followed him as he jumped from his seat and went up front. There he turned, smiled at the congregation, and gave everyone a thumbs up before we knelt for prayer. Many of our forever friends smiled as they bowed their heads. Sonny had connected with them on a spiritual level.

For more than twenty years I've known that two sermons are being preached in our home church on Sabbaths: one from the pulpit and the other from Sonny, who *is* a living sermon!

Deborah Sanders

Thank You for Giving to the Lord

Cast your bread upon the waters,
for you will find it after many days.
—*Ecclesiastes 11:1, ESV*

I was attending a morning service at my church in Canada. A first-year religious studies student was signing a song for special music. I was touched to the point of tears. It seemed odd that I would feel overcome like this because I had seen many people sign songs before. My mind took me back thirty-five years. My husband was a young pastor of three churches. An evangelist came and conducted an area-wide crusade. Two French Canadian families regularly attended the meetings. They readily accepted all the teachings. In the end, both couples were baptized, along with their children.

One couple had four of their six children living at home. Soon the two youngest ones were enrolled in the local Christian church school. My husband told them about a Christian boarding school in another province, thinking they might consider sending their teenage son there the following year. After some discussion, a decision was made to send him there. Upon arrival at school, he learned that the factory where he would be working to help pay for tuition was closed for two weeks. Discouraged, he was going to return home and give up the whole idea. However, my brother-in-law needed help with morning and evening milking. When offered that job, the young man accepted. He remained there until he completed high school, making this his home away from home.

After graduation, the young man returned to work with his father in his plumbing and heating business. He got married and became the father of twin girls. The girls, after finishing church school, made the same flight across Canada to attend the same Christian campus where their father had attended academy. My sister invited the twins and their father to spend the weekend with her before school started. In subsequent years, they enjoyed many of her home-cooked meals. She always remembered their birthdays as well.

Suddenly I realized the young lady signing was one of those twins! Many years ago, their grandparents had stepped out in faith, accepting Bible teachings about Jesus. Because they gave their lives to the Lord, this young lady and her twin sister were now enrolled at this university.

Vera Wiebe

Sweet Affirmation

It is more blessed to give than to receive.
—*Acts 20:35*

Ten years ago, my husband, Norman, and I made the decision to move our church membership from an eight hundred-member church to a smaller church of just fifty members in the North Carolina Smoky Mountains. We were not surprised when asked to take new church responsibilities. My new duties were to serve on the recreation, flower, and music committees. We had been there only a short time when I realized that the children's division (including children up to twelve years of age) was in need of reorganization. I felt impressed to start a class for the older children, who were overjoyed to have their own class and teacher. At present I teach three siblings, ages fourteen, fifteen, and sixteen, who are homeschooled by their grandmother.

The week before Easter, we decided to decorate the altar. I purchased five white Easter lilies in pots wrapped with lavender foil. We placed them in a semicircle at the back of the Communion table and decorated it with greenery and purple ribbon. It turned out to be an appropriate representation of the Lord's house. After the church service Easter weekend we usually give the lilies to different women in the congregation.

During our class, I told the kids we were going to do something different with the lilies this year. Two of them would be taken to church members who were in a nursing home, and then we could decide who would receive the others. I gave each of my students a piece of paper and asked them to jot down the names of three ladies who help our church run smoothly. My name appeared as one of the four names suggested. I quickly dismissed the idea of my receiving a potted lily, but the kids protested. I insisted the other ladies should receive them, though, and those women were pleased to be the recipients of the lovely, sweet-smelling flowers.

At prayer meeting the next week, I was already seated when my three students arrived. The older girl carried a beautiful orchid plant with six white blooms revealing purple centers. She proudly presented the plant to me and said, "This is for you, Miss Rose, for all you do for our church." A flood of joyous affirmation filled my heart and tears came to my eyes. I thanked them and felt humbled that the Lord had impressed them to affirm me in such a sweet way.

I learned it is blessed to receive as well as to give.

Rose Neff Sikora

My Miracle Mile

But those who hope in the LORD will renew their strength.
They will soar on wings like eagles;
they will run and not grow weary, they will walk and not be faint.
—Isaiah 40:31, NIV

That was a long walk!" As our taxi to Honolulu airport passed hotels, palm trees, and glimpses of the blue ocean along Ala Moana Boulevard, I realized how far we had walked to our hotel the previous night. My sister, Carol, and I hadn't been able to get a ride from the beach park, so we'd had to walk to our Waikiki hotel. The distance of one and a half miles would have been a breeze had I not sustained a bad sprain of my left ankle three weeks earlier. To Carol I said, "I'd consider it a miracle if that long walk doesn't aggravate my injury." Back in the hotel room and exhausted, I elevated my foot, said my prayers, and went to sleep. The next morning my feet were sore, but my ankle was fine.

On the airplane back to Los Angeles, I thoughtfully compared my "miracle mile" walk to a devastating storm that I recently encountered. Four months earlier, we had lost our dearly beloved mother to a stroke just days before her eighty-fifth birthday. My close-knit family was barely recovering from this loss when my brother-in-law passed away seven weeks later. The extreme sadness from missing my mother was compounded by grief over my sister's emotional pain. At that time, I could hardly apply the coping skills that I teach my patients at the psychiatric hospital. I struggled to alleviate my own anxiety and depression.

In times of paralyzing loss, we can be tempted to doubt God's faithfulness and mercy, so I held on to Isaiah 30:21, "This is the way; walk in it" (NIV). Overwhelmed by sorrow and helplessness, I prayed and surrendered my leftover strength to the Lord. I meditated on resting at the foot of the cross in the presence of the Holy Spirit and in a belief that a loving God gave His Son, Jesus, to die for us. Total surrender and the promise of eternal life brought comfort, thus enabling me to sleep in peace. "Come to me, all of you who are weary and burdened, and I will give you rest" (Matthew 11:28, NIV). As the days went by, my family was blessed with supportive friends and renewed joy and strength. The difficult journey drew us closer to God and fortified our trust and faith in Him. God's direction may not always be easy, but it gives us the opportunity to feel His love and allows us to have a closer look at the miracles along the way.

Clody Flores Dumaliang

Try Me

And God is able to provide you with blessing in abundance,
so that you may always have enough of everything
and may provide in abundance for every good work.
—2 Corinthians 9:8, RSV

Once in a sermon I was listening to on TV, the preacher shared his story and stated that the Lord had blessed him abundantly. His next question caught my attention: "Did you ever try the Lord?" This question continued ringing in my ears, especially when I would read stories of people who claimed and acted on God's promises and experienced more of His involvement in their lives.

I thought and prayed about that preacher's question. Then one day in 2009 I was impressed to start doing something in response to that question. I thought, *I don't have much, but I will try the Lord.* And as of this writing, I do not regret doing so. In fact, I wish I had started doing so much sooner because of the blessing and happiness I have experienced as a result.

That year, I began giving a second monthly tithe despite financial difficulties, as I was also sending financial support to my family. It was very hard at first. I was always tempted to break my vow to the Lord, yet through God's love and grace, He helped me to overcome all the trials and temptations I encountered. I separated my second tithe and saved it in an envelope. This sum I used for various ministries: the support of lay pastors, radio ministry, jail ministry, the feeding of street children, gifts for the less fortunate, and buying religious books to give away. And how God has blessed!

Though I did not add up prison ministry results between 2009 and 2012, others reported that more than 100 inmates had been baptized. By November 2013, 312 prisoners had given their hearts to the Lord. In November 2014, the prison ministry baptized 112 precious souls. The radio ministry now has a home church. I am amazed! I'm here in Germany, and our ministry is in the Philippines, yet the Lord has blessed it abundantly. And not only that . . . He has also blessed my financial status. Nothing is impossible for God. "The mind of man plans his way, but the LORD directs his steps" (Proverbs 16:9, NASB).

" 'Test Me now in this,' says the LORD of hosts, 'if I will not open for you the windows of heaven and pour out for you a blessing until it overflows' " (Malachi 3:10, NASB).

I challenge you, sisters in Christ, try the Lord and wait. He is faithful in His promises.

Loida Gulaja Lehmann

Heaven's Scent

> He [Christ] uses us . . . to spread the Gospel like a sweet perfume.
> —*2 Corinthians 2:14, TLB*

I f I were to write a script about an exchange that once occurred between my grandchildren and me, it would look and sound something like this:

Granddaughter (seven, and looking into my open suitcase on the bed): Grammy, what's this?

Me: It's my little travel pillow. It keeps my neck from hurting when I sleep on the airplane.

Granddaughter (burying her face into the pillow): Grammy! This pillow smells just like *you*!

Grandson (four years old; snatching the pillow from his sister): Let *me* see that! (putting pillow to face; inhaling deeply; looking up). It *does* smell just like you, Grammy. (pauses, thinking) Oh, Grammy! *Please*, can I sleep with your pillow tonight? It smells like being *with* you."

Fragrance lingers. Long ago a damaged but grateful woman broke an alabaster box of perfume over the head of Jesus. The aromatic liquid coursed through His hair and down his beard, emitting its fragrance throughout the room and arresting the attention of everyone present. When some started criticizing, Jesus cut them short by affirming Mary's forgiven state, her faith in Him, and the impact that her loving gesture would have on believers ever after.

Mere hours passed. Then blood, rather than perfume, ran rivulets through Christ's thorn-crowned head, onto His beard, and down His brutalized body. I sometimes wonder whether, during the crucifixion ordeal, Jesus didn't momentarily catch a whiff of the lingering scent from Mary's broken box. During His terrible suffering on our behalf, did that fleeting scent symbolize for Him how the Father's love—because of the Son's death—can now flow through one human vessel to another? Did that scent remind Jesus of why He'd come here in the first place? Did it recall to his anguished heart the miracles inherent in forgiveness—and impel Him to forgive those who knew not what they were doing, even as they killed Him? I suspect the fragrance—and the memory of Mary's tender, tearful gesture—reminded Jesus that, despite appearances and human emotions to the contrary, Someone still loved Him. The Father had not left Him alone.

Two grandchildren "sensed" my love for them through a worn travel pillow. May others sense God's love for them through us. And when they realize *they're* not alone, may the sweet scent of *their* praise waft outward and ascend upward, to cheer the heart of Jesus once again.

Carolyn Rathbun Sutton

Day and Night

"The sun will no more be your light by day,
nor will the brightness of the moon shine on you, for the LORD will be
your everlasting light, and your God will be your glory."
—Isaiah 60:19, NIV

My after-dinner walk takes me down the winding Palm Drive, past the open lot, the renovated home, the yapping Chihuahua, and to the mailbox. I retrieve my mail—my excuse for taking the afternoon stroll—and turn around to enjoy the walk home. The hillside views, verdant after recent rains and lying against a creative backdrop of patterned blue-sky clouds, send me home, refreshed and invigorated. In a few minutes, night descends. I no longer see the open lot or the houses. The clouds and the blue sky have disappeared. A black landscape is the only view from my now darkened deck. What a contrast to the lovely daytime views I had just experienced!

Day and night. Our Creator made them to be experienced as not only the sunny busyness of day but also the restful quiet of night. While we enjoy the vitamin D of the day, we also need the melatonin of the night. How marvelous of our Creator to plan ahead for our well-being!

Day and night. Do these words describe your life? Are your experiences sometimes wonderful and bright—like the day? At other times, do you experience a dark night in your life? Is it night for you right now? If so, it may seem unending. Maybe it would help to remember that "joy comes in the morning." (Psalm 30:5, NKJV). Morning will come.

We think of Jesus in the Garden of Gethsemane at night, praying. Maybe without the distractions of the day, we can spend our "night seasons" in prayer. How productive was Jesus' prayer session, alone, in that garden! Your "night season" will come as surely as the new moon reappears. Like me, maybe you have been trying to pretend that there is no night in your life. I now plan to embrace night with as much fervor as I embrace the day.

When I see the darkness approaching, I want it to meet me on my knees, in my Gethsemane, seeking the face of God. I want to reach out in faith, trusting when I cannot trace Him and praying my way through the dark.

Beloved, let us pray faithfully in our personal Gethsemane gardens until we assemble in the New Jerusalem where, we read in God's Word, there is no night. "The LORD will be your everlasting light" (Isaiah 60:19, NIV) when, finally, day and night will become one.

Annette Walwyn Michael

The Life Is in the Seed

"And I give them eternal life, and they shall never perish;
neither shall anyone snatch them out of My hand."
—*John 10:28, NKJV*

Springtime. My favorite season, when all nature seems to take on new life! This is the season when amateur gardeners shake off any winter doldrums and really get down to business.

Before his death, my husband found relief from a busy medical practice through his hobby of gardening. He worked hard at it and took satisfaction in harvesting good things to eat. Our five children were not all happy helpers, but our oldest son overcame his aversion. Now each spring finds him sowing and nurturing seeds and plants. One year he decided to plant not only on his own property but also where his dad had gardened some twenty-seven years before.

The additional garden plot had been plowed and prepared for planting, but no seeds had yet been sown. So what were those leaves peeping from the soil? Weeds? They didn't look like any kind of weeds my son was acquainted with, and he is now an experienced gardener. We puzzled over the mysterious new leaves until they were large enough to be identified. Almost unbelievably, they turned out to be okra from seeds planted almost three decades ago! These numerous plants bore prolifically. During all those years, the seeds had lain dormant, waiting for the right opportunity and conditions to spring to new life. The harvested okra was just as if it had been planted the same year it was gathered. We ate some fresh. We froze some and also saved some seeds to plant another year as a witness to the continuity of life.

As with the forgotten, apparently dead okra seeds, so will it be with those who are sleeping in Jesus. Though dormant, we who are asleep in Him will be "activated" by the triumphant call of the Life-Giver. "For the Lord Himself will descend from heaven with a shout, with the voice of an archangel, and with the trumpet of God. And the dead in Christ will rise first" (1 Thessalonians 4:16, NKJV). The promise is sure; the assurance, ours.

Someday "the heavens shall be rolled up like a scroll" (Isaiah 34:4, NKJV), and the earth will be harvested. Eternal life is offered as a free gift. Let's embrace it! Nothing in this world can compare with the joys that await those who look for His coming. Are we ready?

Lila Farrell Morgan

Lord, I Submit

Looking unto Jesus . . . ; who for the joy that was set before him
endured the cross, despising the shame,
and is set down at the right hand of the throne of God.
—*Hebrews 12:2*

You undoubtedly know the story of Naaman, the leprous captain of the Syrian guard. A captive Hebrew slave girl advised him, through his wife, to seek the prophet Elisha for the cure of his leprosy. Naaman went to seek the prophet, hoping for displays of magic and miracles. Instead, the prophet, through his servant, told Naaman to go to the river Jordan and wash seven times.

"What! The Jordan River?" questioned Naaman. "That's not even a nice river! It was bad enough that the prophet didn't even come out to see me. Now, he tells me—Naaman, captain of the king's guard—to go and wash in the *Jordan* River?" Ready to storm away in rage and, perhaps, convinced that the prophet was a quack, Naaman was detained by his servants, who convinced him to do what the man of God had instructed. So Naaman yielded to their entreaties, dipped seven times in the river, and was healed of his leprosy (2 Kings 5:14).

If Naaman hadn't bent his pride and submitted to the instruction of the prophet, he would have remained a leper all his life. He would not have had the testimony that there is no other god but the God of the Israelites (verse 15).

What a lesson to us! If we don't submit to the humbling process that God wants to work in our lives—through a particularly unfriendly neighbor, an illness that has us on our backs (or hobbling, as I am right now), a habit that seems impossible to break, a troubled marriage, or a difficult child—we too may miss out on some victory God wants to work in our lives. And we'll miss out on having a testimony that proclaims God is able to save, deliver, and heal.

Our supreme example is Jesus. Submission first, then new life. Jesus endured the humiliation of the cross so that we would be able to endure the chafing of everyday life with its many challenges, which help polish our rough edges. Submission is a crucial ingredient in that process. Submission may hurt now and rub and confuse and make us want to cry "Stop!" But I promise you that at the end of it all, you will testify that our God saves, delivers, and heals.

After submission comes resurrection—to a renewed life and a powerful testimony.

Greta Michelle Joachim-Fox-Dyett

The Fox, the Crow, and the Eagle

And now these three remain: faith, hope and love.
But the greatest of these is love.
—*1 Corinthians 13:13, NIV*

I t's not easy to drive at night in rural Australia due to numbers of kangaroos and other roaming creatures that come onto the roadways. Unfortunately, hitting them is quite unavoidable at times, and some are killed. This provides carrion for birds and other animals to feed on. I shall never forget the day I saw an amazing scene where a fox, a crow, and a large wedge-tailed eagle stood together over the remains of a carcass. It's very rare to see these three creatures together, for normally they are not at all sociable with one other. It appears, at this instance, they were drawn together by a common need.

This experience brought to mind a wonderful story in Luke 23 about three men. First, we see Simon of Cyrene caught up in the crowd making their way to Calvary. He was not a disciple of Jesus but was astonished at the treatment being given Him. As Simon expressed his compassion, he was seized, and the cross of Christ was put upon his shoulders. Bearing the cross was a blessing to him, and he was ever grateful for this providence, for he found the Savior.

Next, we see the thief on the cross whose mind grasped the truth. Recognizing Jesus as the Lamb of God, he cried out, "Lord, remember me when thou comest into thy kingdom" (Luke 23:42). To this penitent thief came the peace that comes only with acceptance by God. The third man, the Roman captain in charge of the crucifixion, touches us by his amazing praise to God. As he beheld Jesus hanging on the cruel cross, he also recognized the Son of God and could not refrain from confessing his faith: "Truly this was the Son of God" (Matthew 27:54). On the day of Christ's death, these three men declared their faith: the one who bore the cross of Jesus, the one who died on a cross at Jesus' side, and the one who commanded the Roman guard that put Jesus on the cross. These three men were drawn with a common need: to have a relationship with Jesus, whom they acknowledged as truly being the Savior.

As the hymn says, "Faith is the victory." Faith was their victory, and it can be ours too. For the common need to have a relationship with Jesus can draw us together to proclaim Christ as the risen Lord and Savior of all who accept Him.

Lyn Welk-Sandy

And a Paper Cross

Now therefore, our God, we thank thee,
and praise thy glorious name.
—*1 Chronicles 29:13*

An old man lived alone in a two-room shack. Nearby, the bricks were falling off a broken-down well, and a '48 Ford stood rusting in the grass. In a tiny alcove, under a stack of old newsprint, lay a few pairs of well-worn boots. He stoked his stove (which served for both heat and cooking) until the coals flamed before putting on some water for tea. Enjoying the increasing warmth from the fire and the newly made cup of tea, he relaxed and watched the resident squirrel outside running across the broken-down fence.

Before preparing his morning bowl of porridge, he made his way to a wooden dresser, made years ago from a tree of the forest. He pulled open a drawer and took out a box, woven together with reeds from the marsh just over the rill.

On his table he arranged the possessions from inside the box. A picture of two children cut out of a magazine—thoughts of the grandchildren he never had the privilege to enjoy. A dusty but pretty feather from a bird that had ended its life against his window. A tie, given to his son on his sixteenth birthday but left behind when he moved to the city, where he had passed away of a drug overdose.

The old man touched a small pile of tattered love letters from his wife of sixty years. Then, handmade get-well cards from a distant neighbor. And a stained dog collar worn by a faithful canine companion, long gone. The next item was a pressed, fallen leaf representing the arrival of his eightieth year of life, though he still was able to walk the two miles each Sabbath to the tiny country church.

One item remained. Slowly and tenderly, the old man's calloused hands lifted from the box what was possibly his most prized possession, a tiny worn Bible. From between its pages fell a paper cross cut out of an old Shredded Wheat cereal box. With shaking hands he pressed it gently to his breast and closed his eyes. His lips slowly moved as if in prayer. Then gently he returned the items to the quiet of the box and the dresser drawer.

What do you cherish in your life? What means a lot to you?

How thankful are you for the things that mean the most to you?

Vidella McClellan

The Explosion

Give thanks to the LORD, for he is good;
his love endures forever.
—*Psalm 106:1, NIV*

How are things going in your life? Is it busy? Full of joy? Full of grief? Personally, I am blessed. Overall, I am happy. However, I don't always appreciate how good my life is. Recently I was reminded quite dramatically of just how blessed I am and exactly how amazing God is. Let me tell you about it.

I went to bed as normal one Saturday night, but that night something completely unexpected occurred. About two-thirty in the morning, I suddenly woke up. A loud boom that shook the house had awakened me! We'd been having some stormy weather, so, at first, I thought that lightning had hit the house. I also noticed a strange smell. But the electricity hadn't gone out; the fan was still running. Various little lights on the various appliances in the bedroom and living room were also still on.

My husband checked the kitchen and discovered a fire! He quickly put it out. Then he went around the house checking for anything else amiss but found nothing wrong.

So what had happened? As near as we could tell, the chemicals from the cleaners that we store under the kitchen sink must have somehow gotten mixed together and caused an explosion. The explosion blew open the cupboard doors and set on fire the rug in front of the sink. What I do know for certain is that God was looking out for us and our home. Amazingly, the cupboard wasn't even singed! The rug had to be tossed, but the floor was fine. The smell of chemicals soon disappeared. Just the week before, we had been away from home. If the explosion had occurred then or any day when we were away from the house at work or at church, or even just out running errands, it could have all ended very badly. Since our home is an older one and constructed of wood, it wouldn't take long for a fire to consume it.

As Matthew 6:8 affirms, our Father knows what we need before we ask. He protected us, our home, our pets, and possibly even our neighbors' homes. He provided protection from something I never even expected to happen! This experience reminded me that God pours out blessings all the time! Sometimes we don't even know how He is showering us with blessings. Let's all praise God for His wonderful goodness!

Julie Bocock-Bliss

Jesus Goes to the Mall

Be ye holy; for I am holy.
—1 Peter 1:16

We sing the words of that old hymn, "Live out Thy life within me, O Jesus, King of kings!" But do we mean it? What would it look like when we're shopping, for instance, if we really allowed Jesus to live through us? If we allowed ourselves—through His Spirit—to look like Him? If I spotted a sales garment on the floor, would I bend over, retrieve it, and replace it back on the rack? Would I invite another shopper with just an item or two to step ahead of my loaded cart in the checkout line? Would I share a sympathetic smile with an embarrassed mother trying to keep her toddlers under control as she pays for her purchases? What would Jesus do?

And what would Jesus say to people in stores at the mall? He often impresses me to choose a checkout line where the cashier looks weary-eyed or long-faced, someone who might be able to use an encouraging word. And Jesus does set up conversation appointments. Sometimes it's as simple as changing my routine exit line—"Have a nice day!"—with an additional word back over my shoulder, "I just did!" and watch the cashier smile.

Once I whispered to a young cashier, "Are you working here to get through school?" Yes, she was, and the floodgate opened as she quickly shared how she was just one year away from a degree but not sure she'd make it with the pressures of employment and caring for her children. Jesus, living in me, offered a word of encouragement and cheer.

Another time a store employee asked whether she could help me carry out my groceries. I prayerfully observed her obvious weariness, touched her arm, and quietly asked, "Are you OK?" No, she wasn't. Her son-in-law in faraway Ohio had just abandoned his family, leaving her daughter's emotions in turmoil as she scrambled to reorganize her life, move, find a job, and change the children's schools. And all this with no income as of yet. The burdened mother sharing with me was herself working two jobs in an effort to forward one income to her daughter in Ohio. Again . . . a word of comfort from Jesus.

When Jesus lives in us, we're doing more than routine errands or weekly shopping.

Lord, where and to whom—with You living in my heart and walking on my feet—am I making my way just now? How do You want to be seen and heard through me today?

Janet Lankheet

Celebrity Watch

But as it is written, Eye hath not seen, nor ear heard,
neither have entered into the heart of man,
the things which God hath prepared for them that love him.
—*1 Corinthians 2:9*

I was raised in Los Angeles but retired to the state of Washington. I had experiences in Los Angeles that just don't happen here in the Northwest.

In Los Angeles I walked out of a building once and bumped into former American football player and actor Rosey Grier, and another time into the boxer, actor, and TV personality "Slapsy Maxie" Rosenblum. I stood in an elevator with actor Cornel Wilde, walked behind American character actor William Schallert on Hollywood Boulevard, and stood in line next to another actor Eddie Quillan. I was at a meeting with Mike Connors, best known for portraying a TV series detective, and I saw Bill Murray riding an elephant down Broadway.

But what encounters can we expect in heaven? The Bible explains heaven in detail.

It will last forever. We will build houses and live in them. Children will play safely with lions, and we will explore the universe with angels as guides. Yet we are told we really have no idea what God has already provided for those who love Him. I want to go to heaven and meet those who formed the basis of our faith and wrote the Bible. I especially want to meet our Father God and Savior Jesus and see and learn all they have for me there.

Encounters with biblical celebrities such as these don't happen, of course, on earth today. Yet in heaven I'll be walking on streets of gold a few steps behind Abraham or Daniel. I'll step out of a building and see Joshua or Matthew. Perhaps I will ride in the same vehicle as Paul or Jeremiah and live next door to Ellen White or Deborah. I will spend eternity in conversation with great Reformers such as Jerome, Wycliffe, and Martin Luther. I'll have the privilege of walking hand in nail-pierced hand with my Savior, Christ Jesus. I will sit at His feet and look into the holy, pure face of the wonderful God I love so dearly.

Thank You, Lord, for the promise of heaven. I want to go to heaven and meet those who formed the basis of my faith and wrote the Bible. I especially need to meet the Father God and Savior Jesus and see and learn all They have prepared for me there. I love You. Please, may I go to live with You there? Amen.

Darlenejoan McKibbin Rhine

April 6

To Inspire and Delight

Open my eyes that I may see wonderful things in your law.
—*Psalm 119:18, NIV*

The Library of Innerpeffray is a little "treasure box" on the tree-lined banks of the river Earn, close to our house. It's the home of the oldest free lending library in Scotland, founded by David Drummond in 1680. David was passionate about reading and learning and wanted to share his books with the community around his estate. More than three hundred years later, those precious books can still be borrowed for free. I hold them in my hands and turn the pages without protective gloves.

Two elderly gentlemen work as volunteers in the tiny library. When there aren't any visitors, they explore the different books, searching for literary treasures and interesting details. Their faces light up when my husband, Bernie, tells them he's a pastor. They pull out some huge Bibles and lay them gently on the sloping reading desks. Some have embossed leather covers and ornate brass clasps. There are massive Bibles with engraved prints and illuminated letters, and a miniature Bible with a tiny magnifying glass slipped inside the marbled endpapers. We pore over the pages, and they point out interesting details in the pictures and the beauty in the words.

It's after closing time, but our guides are still wandering along the shelves, gently easing out a book here and a volume there. They show Bernie a book of old sermons, and they bring me a book of Christian poetry. The autumn sunlight flickers through the leaves outside and dapples the pages. "We ought to go," I say. "We're holding you back."

One of the elderly men smiles and bows slightly. "No, dear, you stay there. Our job has no limits. Our role is merely to inspire you and delight you." And they do. They love this precious library. They know the inspiration and delights of every book. They take the time to listen, to discover each visitor's passion, and then introduce them to the books they'll enjoy the most.

I am inspired, and delighted. When it's time to go, we walk past the open Bibles. An engraving of the Creation story is bursting with life and joy. Some of the animals look a little odd because the artist is drawing animals he's never seen. The flowers are still vibrant, and there are tiny rabbits scampering in the grass.

How does God want to inspire and delight me with His Word today? How can I make the time to sit in His sunlight and read? And how can I share my inspiration and delight with others?

Karen Holford

Buying a Car

Oh, taste and see that the LORD is good;
blessed is the man who trusts in Him!
—*Psalm 34:8, NKJV*

I had been in an accident, followed by months of recovery; now I was able to walk. We had been praying and saving for a car because I would need one in order to go to work. My son, John, and brothers had been looking for a car for me. We had saved some money, but I thought I would need to receive my tax refund before I would have enough to buy a car.

Malachi 3:10 says, " 'Bring all the tithes into the storehouse, that there may be food in My house, and try Me now in this,' says the LORD of hosts, 'if I will not open for you the windows of heaven and pour out for you such blessing that there will not be room enough to receive it' " (NKJV). So God wants us to obey. He also wants us to tell Him what we are thinking because He can do things for us if we ask that He wouldn't do if we didn't ask. After reading about a vision Ellen White had about buying a horse, I realized God understands our need for transportation.* One Thursday I borrowed the church van in order to go to the dentist. While driving, I prayed, *I appreciate using Your van, but if I am to be driving, I need to have my own transportation.*

That night when John came home, the first words out of his mouth were, "I found your car." I talked to God again. *You are the One who knows whether this is a good car or not. You know how much money we have. If this is the car we are to have, let the seller either take what we can give him or be willing to wait for the rest of the payment while he holds the car for us.*

On Friday we went to look over the car and take a test-drive. We talked with the man and made an offer. He was not willing to take the offer but was willing to hold the car for us, so we knew this was the car we were to buy. We scraped together all the money we had and then paid for the car. We also had enough money to license it. By the time I needed to be at an appointment that day, I had my own transportation. John was able to be at his appointment also. The checks I had written for bills cleared, with a few dollars still left in the bank.

Praise God! He wants us to talk to Him, try Him, and watch for results. In the middle of the next week, my tax refund arrived to help me even more. God is good.

Ruth Middaugh Goodsite

---

* William C. White, "Sketches and Memories of James and Ellen White: VIII. The Home in Oswego, New York," *Review and Herald*, April 25, 1935, 11.

April 8

He Filled My Cup

You revive my drooping head;
my cup brims with blessing.
—*Psalm 23:5*, The Message

Have you ever felt empty? Like God was far away? Have you ever found yourself just "going through the motions" because you just couldn't or didn't take time to do anything more than have a quick prayer in the morning as you walked out the door? I've been there. Several years ago, our church voted to reopen a school, with me as teacher. The first school year flew by—until my stepsister died of breast cancer. Stunned, I managed to finish the year before spending the summer, for the first time in more than twenty years, in summer school. Another school year. More summer study. On November 27 of the third school year, my mom passed away. That year I "celebrated" Christmas with my family, but in a fog. A January 1 telephone inquiry to my husband put us on a three-month roller-coaster ride as we felt our way through a decision process—whether or not to move to a distant location where he had been invited to pastor. In the end, we didn't take the call. Just days later, we began a full-scale evangelistic series while my school went through a full-scale evaluation. After our daughter's graduation from a Michigan university, we headed—that same day—to Pennsylvania for a weeklong school field trip. My school year ended a couple weeks later amidst several other stressful events. Then it was off to camp meeting, after which my husband and I immediately headed to Texas for pastors' meetings and our the General Conference session, which occurs every five years. *That's* when I finally realized what kind of shape I was in—*empty*!

I knew I needed God and began praying in earnest and spending quality time with Him. Suddenly I was like a sponge, soaking up everything of Him that I could. I also began exercising again (half an hour each day) and spending an hour each day in worship and Bible study.

Slowly my world improved. Four months later, I felt more alive than I have in many years. I have been blessed with a closer walk with God than I have ever had. I am losing weight and feeling great. Most amazing of all, I recently was made aware that despite my busyness and emptiness, God still used me to bless others even as I was going through my dark valley. I praise the Lord for the valleys that help us to grow. I praise the Lord for using me, despite myself. And, most of all, I praise the Lord for filling my empty cup and making me whole once again.

Kathy Pepper

Up Early With Birds

Let the saints be joyful in glory:
let them sing aloud upon their beds.
—*Psalm 149:5*

Are you a lark or an owl? Larks twitter, sing, and flit around first thing in the morning, but by day's end, there isn't much of a twit or flit left. Owls usually don't do mornings! However, come early evening and through the night, owls are swooping around with their wings spread, ready for taking to the skies!

You may agree that the best time to talk with God is when we are fresh and alert, be it morning, noon, or night. I'm very much a lark, but I certainly did not plan to begin my "larking" at four o'clock in the morning!

A number of years ago I awoke and glanced at my bedside clock. The display read 4:05 A.M., but I felt refreshed and wide awake. I thought, *Well, now what am I going to do? It's too early to get up and start my day. I guess I'll just talk to God for a while.*

Thereafter, I awakened—totally refreshed—right around the same time each morning, so I took advantage of this early time to visit with God. Ten years have passed, and I'm still waking up every morning somewhere between four o'clock and four thirty, when I really enjoy my special prayer time.

One morning I decided to add a little song of praise to my prayer time, but it didn't turn out so well. I tried to hum a favorite hymn as softly as I could, so as not to wake my husband.

Bad decision!

My little hum came out sounding like a squeak, which caused my husband to rise up and say in alarm, "What's the matter?" Needless to say, I decided thereafter to sing just in my head.

First Corinthians 14:15 says, "I will sing with the spirit, and I will sing with the understanding also."

While singing silently in my mind, I find it easy to really listen to and understand the words of even the simplest melody, such as "Jesus Loves Me."

I believe the Lord started waking me up all those years ago because He knew it was the best time for us to communicate with each together.

I'm so glad that I started talking to Him at that early hour—and "singing" like the birds—instead of turning over and turning off.

Terry Wilson Robinson

What Are You Worth?

*"Do not fear therefore;
you are of more value than many sparrows."*
—Matthew 10:31, NKJV

Traffic hurtled past me as I ran along the wide shoulder of Highway 97, a main artery running north-south through central Oregon. It carries 18-wheelers, tour buses, vacationers, and local traffic throughout the summer months. Ahead of me was a long hill. The only way to tackle it was one step at a time while keeping firmly away from the trucks barreling past.

Looking to the ground, I noticed a small roll of something ahead. No more than two inches long, this little parcel of something lay directly under my descending foot. I adjusted my step in midair and noticed a tiny flash of yellow in a little roll of feathers. A lesser goldfinch probably. I took two more steps and saw another little parcel of feathers, this time brilliantly yellow, lying quietly on the shoulder. Had these two little lives been lost in one moment? Flying together and dying together, unnoticed by the people whizzing by but noticed by God? Matthew and Luke record Jesus saying that God notices every ordinary little sparrow that dies (Matthew 10:29, 31; Luke 12:6, 7). He surely saw these beautiful birds, each weighing no more than a few grams, die.

By the time I reached the brow of the hill, I had recalled many Bible stories that illustrate Jesus' compassion toward the unimportant people of His time while on earth. He noticed the virtually insignificant offering the widow brought to the temple that reflected her total commitment to God. He did not find children a nuisance, and He used a boy's lunch of a few loaves and fishes to feed the growling stomachs of the peasants and their families who listened to His words of hope. In the Sermon on the Mount, Jesus did not praise the Roman rulers, noblemen, Pharisees, and community leaders, but He apportioned blessings to the meek, persecuted, peacemakers, righteous, downtrodden, and bereaved. He spoke tenderly to the common people as He touched the untouchables; restored sight to the blind; and healed the crippled, demon possessed, and society's lowlife. Jesus recognized the true worth of a soul.

Two days later I ran past the same spot on the shoulder of the highway, searching. Searching for two little rolls of feathers. Nothing. The little finches had disappeared—but were still imprinted on God's heart. Just then a beautiful butterfly fluttered across my path and into the forest, a sure reminder of God's continuing love for us.

Tabitha Abel

Brother John

Be kindly affectioned one to another with brotherly love;
in honour preferring one another.
—Romans 12:10

I belong to a small church, the Lily of the Valley church, on the beautiful island of Dominica. Our membership consists of about forty members, but that's what I love most about the church I belong to. Though small, we care about each other. Love can be felt among the brethren.

It's almost impossible to feel left out there.

The first elder of our church is Brother Rennick John. I've always seen him as not just a leader but an encourager. I believe that when that time comes in the last days, when we are separated as believers and are being persecuted for our Lord's sake, I will remember Brother John.

If one needs help in any way, just ask Brother John.

You need a ride? Call Brother John.

You need someone to talk to? Brother John is there.

Even when you just feel like being alone, along comes Brother John, who has this way of making you feel better, whether you like it or not.

Brother John accepted the call as first elder to our church and has never been less than that. His prayer is to see each and every one of us saved. That's the kind of love you expect from a leader. But I also hope that those who read this devotional will be encouraged to treat others as our head elder treats us. Today's text tells us to "be kindly affectioned one to another with brotherly love; in honour preferring one another."

In today's world we need each other more than we did before. I know that our Father in heaven expects us to stick together as a family, as His coming is so much nearer than it was before. "So we, being many, are one body in Christ" (Romans 12:5). If, perchance, one part of the body is sick, the entire body is sick.

My prayer today is that we continue to love each other as Christ loves us, making it our duty to encourage each other as we journey to God's eternal kingdom.

Amanda Amy Isles

April 12

Wise, Saving Words

My son, if sinful men entice you,
do not give in to them.
—Proverbs 1:10, NIV

Words of wisdom are important lifesaving messages. In fact, they are in demand when we are in serious trouble (see Proverbs 4:6, 7). The devil is the great deceiver and can use even a friend to destroy us. One summer morning in Cornwall, Ontario, while I was having breakfast with Celia, my roommate, John, a taxi driver friend, called, inviting us to join him for a drive in the country. We gladly accepted the invitation.

We drove along beautiful country roads, laughing all the way. Then John stopped to share some refreshments he had made. But as he offered us drinks, I was reminded (by an angel, I'm sure) of my father's word of wisdom not to accept any drink from others unless it is sealed in a can or an unopened bottle because someone, having an assault in mind, might have spiked the drink. In our Filipino language, I warned Celia not to drink it. The effects of a spiked drink can affect one's mind and body within only twenty to thirty minutes and last up to eight hours.

Within twenty minutes John stopped at the only house in a small village. As he walked toward the house, Celia and I immediately discarded the drinks and locked all the car doors. I moved to the driver's seat without a clue how to drive, but I knew God would show me (see Isaiah 41:13). Then two men approached the car. I started to panic. They quickly knocked on the car window. John arrived on the scene with a spare car key. I took a deep breath and called upon the name of Jesus Christ to save us (see Psalm 91:15). While John was opening the door, the hand of God was upon me as I turned the ignition key. The taxicab took off! Both my hands and feet were shaking. God knew what He was doing though I did not know how to drive (the car even had a standard shift). The rough country road, paralleled by ditches, runs up a *steep hill*. At the speed I was driving, we could have ended up in the ditch. Approaching town, I removed my foot from the gas pedal, and the car slowed down. We got out and ran into a store. The man in the store quickly ran to stop the car and park it before calling the police for us. John was arrested.

Although my father was not present at the time, his words of wisdom saved us.

Likewise, though our Father in heaven is not visible, He has given us words of wisdom that are able to save us if we will remember and heed them (see Psalm 119:105).

Nena A. Wirth

O Love of God

But God demonstrates His own love toward us,
in that while we were still sinners, Christ died for us.
—*Romans 5:8, NKJV*

O love of God, how strong and true!
Eternal and yet ever new;
Uncomprehended and unbought,
Beyond all knowledge and all thought.*

I stood on the top of the cliff, looking out to the sea. It was early in the morning; the sun was rising and the waves were crashing on the rocks close to the shore. The clouds were low and gray, and I knew that soon it would rain. As I stood on that cliff looking out at those rocks that seemed immovable and the unending power of the sea that crested over and over and yet still kept coming, I thought of God's love for me.

The seeming stubbornness of the rocks that would not be moved and the sea that kept coming to the shore reminded me that God's love for me will never end. No matter what happens in my life, no matter what I've done, the love of God keeps washing over me in unending waves.

Paul wrote that even when we were sinners, even before we knew Him or gave our lives to Him, Jesus died for us. Christ's death on the cross is the greatest evidence of God's love for humankind. Amazing? Yes. Unbelievable? Yes. Stubborn love? Yes. And so the words of Horatius Bonar's beautiful hymn came to mind, "O love of God, how strong and true." The love of God for each of us goes beyond our behavior, our attitudes, our own stubborn will, and even our sins. And we see this love culminating in the death of Jesus on the cross for each of us.

We read thee best in Him who came
To bear for us the cross of shame;
Sent by the Father from on high,
Our life to live, our death to die.†

Sometimes we feel unloved or unlovable. When Satan brings those thoughts to mind, remind him—and yourself—that God loves you, and His love is more powerful than negative feelings or thoughts. So rejoice in that love today.

Heather-Dawn Small

---

* Horatius Bonar, "O Love of God, How Strong and True," 1861.
† Ibid.

SHE, the Definition of ME!

Older women . . .
may encourage the young women.
—Titus 2:3, 4, NASB

It was 1990, and I was in my thirties when Deborah Harris, commissioner of Women's Ministries for the church in our area, asked me to organize and plan a program of mentoring, motivating, and inspiring our young girls (ages five through seventeen). At that time, Deborah's daughter, Tonya, was eight and my daughter, Danyielle, was six.

I organized the girls and put them all under the umbrella of BUDS, which included BUDS (ages five through eight), Blossoms (ages nine through twelve) and Blooms (ages twelve through seventeen). I even reached into the cribs and organized Bulbs (birth through four). However, the group ages eighteen and older, at the other end, became a concern. We tried all kinds of programs. But it was not until we spent a weekend in Charlotte, North Carolina, that BUDS who had grown up in the program organized themselves and launched the phenomenal "SHE, the Definition of Me!"

Tonya and Danyielle, both now in their thirties, cochaired a ministry that has caught the attention of other millennial Christian women. Deborah and I smiled with humility as they both heralded, "This is not our mothers' retreat."

With simple guidelines, Tonya Fewell-Mobley and Danyielle Jackson sought other talented young women who had grown up as BUDS and captivated their audience. Together with Carla Clary, Enjoli NeSmith, Vershonda Waiters, and Carla Edwards, they motivated and managed SHE, a program for young women (ages twenty-five through forty-five) who want to do for the church. Young women who love God and who are willing and desirous to serve God but who are technically and creatively able to do it all differently than those of us who are older.

God simply wants us to love Him and to express that love though obedience and service of ministry. How we minister is the manifestation of the gifts or talents that God Himself gives to us. In fact, we have a responsibility to nurture the next generation (Titus 2:3–5).

SHE! Twenty-five years after the former director, Deborah Harris, asked me (the current director) to work with girls of our area, those very girls are now working with each other to help the church "hold on" to them. Today's mentoring results in tomorrow's leadership!

Sylvia Jackson Wilson

Brownie Blessings

And Samuel said, Hath the LORD as great delight in burnt offerings
and sacrifices, as in obeying the voice of the LORD?
Behold, to obey is better than sacrifice,
and to hearken than the fat of rams.
—*1 Samuel 15:22*

My husband loves brownies, so I decided to make him a batch this evening. This is not my first time to make them, but I still read through the instructions.

As I read, I asked myself, *Only* two *tablespoons of water will be enough for those brownies? But how?* Though that seemed impossible, I finally decided to follow the instructions. I figured that the manufacturer must know best. If they didn't, who would? So, two tablespoons of water it was.

As I stirred the batter, my unbelief turned to disbelief! The two tablespoons of water were indeed enough, for the formidable powder soon turned to a rich, creamy chocolate batter. After the brownies were baked, I was pleased to note they had turned out pretty well. I doubt this would have been the outcome had I just added water, willy-nilly, as I thought best.

Many times in life we set out on a particular course of action toward a goal. Or maybe we have received instructions from God that defy our own reckoning. At these times, we are tempted to do things our own way. *But how can I forgive? But I do not have money for . . . But I do not see the way. But this seems to be better.*

Those brownies this evening taught me that in these times it is essential to "trust in the LORD . . . ; and lean not unto [my] own understanding" (Proverbs 3:5). Trust and obedience require faith, and then our hope is never disappointed.

My brownies turned out just the way that they were supposed to.

And if, in simple faith, you adhere to His instructions, your destiny will unfold according to God's plan. Trust in His instructions, along with two tablespoons of obedience, can bring a batch of joy. Always trust and obey.

As I watched my husband devour his first brownie, I was thankful that they were brownie blessings and not "burnt offerings." I hummed to myself,

Trust and obey, for there's no other way
To be happy in Jesus, but to trust and obey.*

Judelia Medard-Santiesteban

---

* John H. Sammis, "Trust and Obey," 1887.

Lesson From a Pizza

Wait on the LORD: be of good courage,
and he shall strengthen thine heart:
wait, I say, on the LORD.
—*Psalm 27:14*

The Cedar Hall ladies' end-of-semester social activity for the summer semester had been planned weeks ahead. Everybody was bubbling with anticipation as they prepared to go off campus to dine.

However, deep inside, I felt like the weather outside—cold. The Sabbath had just ended, but the load of the previous week, in addition to the new week just ahead, was already on my shoulders. All I wanted to do was to go to bed and sleep—just escape life's reality for a little while. All I knew was that I was not satisfied with my present situation.

Since it was raining, we ladies changed our plan and decided to go to one of the closer pizzerias. Soon giggles, smiles, jokes, selfies, pictures, and recalling memories of the semester were part of the "lime," as Trinidadians call their social gatherings. Being the only vegetarian among my dormmates, I decided to order a veggie pizza pan. Surprisingly, my friends ate their pizza, while I continued to wait for the smallest item that any of us had ordered.

When I questioned the waitress about my order, she replied, "Oh, do not worry; your veggie pizza pan is in the oven." However, she returned five minutes later. "We are really sorry, but the veggie pizza pan burnt in the oven—instead, we are making a small veggie pizza for you." In other words, instead of four slices, I would receive eight.

While the others were murmuring, I finally understood the lesson.

Even though I had not been pleased with my predicament, God was preparing something better for me. All I had to do was wait. God's thoughts are not our thoughts, nor are our ways His ways (Isaiah 55:8).

Your life might not be as you would like it, but wait on God. When you wait on God's plan, you might not receive what you want immediately, and you might never receive your desire. Yet God is still planning something better while we are in the waiting room. This blessing might not be on this earth, but the present trial could certainly be a way to prepare us for heaven.

Wait on the Lord today . . . and forever.

Nahomie Daubé

Divine Appointment

"Then the Lord said to me,
'Go; I will send you far away to the Gentiles.' "
—Acts 22:21, NIV

Recently I attended a women's retreat in Mauritius with my friend, Rhoda Nthani. Our hotel rooms were next to each other. One evening after a hard day's work, we went back to our rooms to rest. The door to my room would not open. The reception desk was far away, and I was too tired to walk there. So I requested to use my friend's phone to call for assistance. My friend offered to let me wait in her room until help arrived. A few minutes later, hotel security personnel arrived and solved my problem. So I gathered up my belongings from Rhoda's room and went to open my door. Again, it failed to open. Again, I called for help. This time the supervising employee suggested a change of door handle. He had to go to the storeroom to fetch the item. In the meantime, one of his assistants seemed to be reluctant to leave our area. He remained near us, though his doing so made us feel very apprehensive.

The man introduced himself and asked what our mission was. When we told him our reason for being there, he opened up, saying he'd been hoping to meet Christians. Born into a poor Buddhist family, he had grown up worshiping idols. One day he met with a group of Christians who taught him about God and Jesus. They taught him how to pray and gave him a Bible. He read the Bible and prayed to God every day, but his mother did not want him to be a Christian. God answered his prayers about finding a job, so he was able to rise out of poverty, build a house for his family, and provide essentials for them. He was now looking for Christians so that he could have spiritual encouragement. On the day my door wouldn't open, he had asked God to help him meet some Christians who would pray with him and encourage him. Right away we knelt with him in prayer. As we finished encouraging him, security personnel returned and fixed my door handle for the third time. This time it was *fixed*! What a divine appointment! I was humbled to know that God used the problem of my door to minister to a lonely heart.

There are times when we do our duties as usual but forget that God has set up divine appointments for us. This fact calls for each of us to listen and look for Him in every situation.

Lord, help me listen to Your voice every minute. Help me to see the many appointments You have placed on my daily schedule.

Caroline Chola

April 18

The Call

I press toward the goal for the prize
of the upward call of God in Christ Jesus.
—Philippians 3:14, NKJV

The 2015 General Conference Session in San Antonio was one of our denomination's largest gatherings. The many thousands of members from all over the world, assembled in one place, was a heavenly sight. Yet, at times, the crowds were overwhelming. There was little personal space and little control over one's own movements, as though we were just parts of the whole of a moving mass swept along from place to place. The meetings started for many in Austin, where the North American Division of our church held its CALLED ministerial convention, which drew thousands.

One afternoon, in a riptide of moving people, I found myself searching for my husband, Nord. We were looking in the large convention center to find the age-specific meetings for our grandsons. Now, trying to find Nord was like looking for that proverbial needle in a haystack. The bustling crowds were thick and loud with boisterous greetings and sideline reunions. Echoes doubled the volume. Then, in the midst of that consuming multitude, I heard my name called out softly. Instantly I recognized that it was Nord's familiar deep voice that had called to me. For a split second I wondered whether I had imagined or actually heard Nord through the reveling crowd.

Nevertheless, I stopped and turned toward the direction from which he called. I could not see him but was certain it was he and certain of where to look. There he was, fifty yards back, moving toward me. His walking companion, Alvin, was astonished. He exclaimed repeatedly that my distinguishing Nord's voice was not possible. He declared that had he not witnessed this, he would never have believed it. How, he asked, could I hear this one voice, spoken at normal volume and pitch, amid this multitude? Without any thought, my quick response was, "I know that voice! I'm attuned to it and can hear it anywhere." Then we paused as each was suddenly and simultaneously struck with the spiritual significance of the event and my explanation. Are you attuned to God's voice? Jesus said, "My sheep hear My voice, and I know them, and they follow Me" (John 10:27, NKJV). God has a unique call for each of us. Have you heard His call through life's vexations? What is your calling? Will you move toward His voice today?

Ella Louise Smith Simmons

The Phone Rang

"For I know the plans I have for you," declares the LORD,
"plans to prosper you and not to harm you,
plans to give you hope and a future."
—*Jeremiah 29:11, NIV*

As I turned the doorknob to walk out my front door, the phone rang. I wondered whether I should go back to answer it or continue walking out the door. I remembered the rain and the gloomy sky outside. This encouraged me to go ahead and answer the phone.

On the other end of the phone was a very familiar voice. It was Mrs. Dean. I was so surprised to hear her voice. She was one of my favorite substitute teachers in grade school. I loved to hear her stories about Jesus and knew, by her demeanor, that she loved Him with her whole heart. I had not spoken to her in years, probably about ten years or more at that point in time. Why was she calling? How did she get my number?

After we greeted each other, she told me the reason for her call. After worship that morning, the Holy Spirit impressed upon her heart to call two of her former students: one was currently a pastor, and the other person was me. I remember her saying, "I don't know what you are going through but God asked me to tell you that He has a special plan for your life and that He loves you."

She went on to encourage me to remain forever within God's will for my life. When she said that, tears streamed down my face, for I knew that it was God speaking through her to me. Mrs. Dean then prayed a prayer that melted my heart and reminded me of why God called me to be a Christian educator. Little did she know that I had been headed to apply for a reading specialist position at a brand new public school across the street from my condominium.

I often shared this story with my students. This was one of the joys of being a Christian educator. It afforded me opportunities to share real stories of faith with my students. I often reflect on this experience—and several more like it. Within the will of God is where I want to be. What about you?

Dear God, thank You for speaking to us through others and through Your Word. May we forever be within Your will for our lives, and may we trust You more each day.

In Jesus' name I pray. Amen.

Kalisha A. Waldon

Accents

Let your light so shine before men, that they may see your good
works, and glorify your Father which is in heaven.
—Matthew 5:16

I was a transfer student at a college hundreds of miles from home. One day in the cafeteria, people asked many questions and then smiled when I answered. It was all so very puzzling to me. Similar scenarios continued. My fellow students asked that I repeat what I had just stated very clearly. I became uncomfortable around people and reticent to speak. A couple of weeks were all it took for me to develop a complex. I was tired of being the obvious brunt of sly grins and whispered comments. Exasperated, I exploded to a friend after dinner one evening.

"Oh, that's simple to explain," she calmly replied. "It's your accent."

"Accent!" I responded incredulously. "*What* accent?"

"Why, your Deep South 'southerness.' People enjoy hearing you talk."

"But I don't have an accent!" I objected. Ironically, my ears had been enjoying the crisp, staccato sounds from my classmates. They were the ones with the accent, not me. Always having lived among those who spoke as I did, my method of speaking had never been questioned.

Most of us have a built-in loyalty to the state or country in which we were born. Attached to our loyalty is an accent. If you don't think you have one, try going to Alabama or Australia. You'll find out quite quickly who the foreigner is! All people everywhere emanate at least three accents: physical, verbal, and spiritual. From deep within come impulses, actions, and words by which others read our lives. The most noticeable are the physical accents. Others can detect what type of person we are by our manners, conduct, and looks. "Our words, our acts, our dress, our deportment, even the expression of the countenance have an influence."* Our verbal expressions, with their color and class, lose all their sparkle if spoken in an unkind tone. Of course, the most important in this trio of accents is our spiritual accent. As people observe us, they are influenced to either think more—or less—of Christ. In Matthew 5:16 we are admonished to let our light "so shine before men, that they may see [our] good works, and glorify [our] father which is in heaven." What is light, if it's not our expression or our positive accents?

Marybeth Gessele

---

* Ellen G. White, *Christ's Object Lessons* (Hagerstown, MD: Review and Herald®, 2003), 339.

Facing Raging Rivers

Put on the whole armour of God,
that ye may be able to stand against the wiles of the devil.
—*Ephesians 6:11*

Have you wondered how a loving God can watch the tragedies in our world? Why is He so selective when intervening? This question leads me to compare today's fluffy white clouds with destructive black clouds experienced a few days ago. Within twenty-four hours, thirteen inches of rain fell on a village near my home. Beautiful houses were flooded; some were completely washed away. One vacation home was swept down the river with six adults and three children still inside. A forty-foot wall of water raged down the river, lapping up everything in sight and snapping one hundred-year-old cypress trees in two as one would snap a toothpick in two.

On the other hand, Texas has experienced an extensive drought for several years. Farmers were fighting to survive, trees were dying; the ground was cracked—looking like a jigsaw puzzle. Animals suffered. Where is God during these life-threatening situations? In asking this question, I had to reestablish my belief that God is merciful and filled with compassion. He proved His love and sovereignty by having Jesus come to earth to turn the disaster of sin into the blessing of salvation. God can take catastrophic events caused by Satan and use them as stepping-stones to draw us closer to Him.

Because of the flood, formerly parched ground is now soft and covered with green grass. The trees are full of leaves, providing a home for the birds of the air and shade for the animals of the fields. The lakes are full, adding beauty to the landscape and supplying water for thousands.

These events remind me that a celestial war rages between good and evil. Satan has accused God of ruling without giving created beings the power of choice. Yet sinful choices have resulted in a rebellious planet. As in any war, innocent people are hurt. If He overruled our power of choice to stop the battle, Satan would win. Our mighty God mercifully waits, letting sin run its course until all have made their final selection.

We still have time to handpick who will claim our allegiance: God or Satan. In spite of tragic situations around us, we may still seek God daily, acknowledge Him as our Commander-in-Chief and—throughout this war for souls—cling to our faith in His gentle love and mercy.

June Ayers

My Banner

Thou hast given a banner to them that fear thee,
that it may be displayed because of the truth.
—*Psalm 60:4*

My husband, during the second year of his ministerial internship, was called under the supervision of his senior pastor to prepare for a four-week public evangelistic effort. We had been married for only seven months, so this would be our first public evangelism meetings.

I was very fearful. The area in which these meetings were to be held had never had a public evangelistic effort. In addition, this community was known as the "forbidden territory" in the town. Many crimes took place in this community. I knew there was not anything we could do on our own to guarantee the success of the meetings. We had to depend on our Lord.

Our months of preparation included revivals, seminars, training programs, prayer sessions, and many other events. Then the day of the meetings arrived. This being my first meeting as the pastor's wife, I eagerly welcomed this day. Yet the strong fear about this area did not go away, for I knew we were a part of a great battle. I prayed, *Lord, please help us.*

When we got to the venue of the meetings, my eyes looked up at the banner that had been erected to notify the public about these meetings. It was beautifully done. It was tall with beautifully colored paintings. Then the words, "The Truth Be Told. Gospel Explosion 2013. Evangelist Pastor Mark McPherson. Features—Dynamic Preaching, Bible Seminars . . ." As I kept reading, I felt a peace come over me. I remembered one of the purposes of a banner. When used in conflict, military companies use it as a signal for the battle trumpet to be blown. I recalled a biblical account (Exodus 17:8–16) of a battle in Rephidim between Israel and Amalek, the first enemy nation to war against them after leaving Egypt. Moses held up the rod in his hand as a symbol of the presence of God to help His people win the victory. They won the victory, not so much because of the "banner," but because of the presence of God.

The message of Psalm 60:4 comforted me because God had also given me a banner. I smiled and thanked Hm. During the four weeks of meetings, the battle was great, but—praise be to God—we endured the battle. God was our banner. At the end of the fourth week, ninety souls accepted the Lord as their banner too. God wants to be your banner. Will you allow Him to be?

Jenel A. N. Campbell McPherson

Moons Can Do Anything

Jesus looked at them intently and said, "Humanly speaking,
it is impossible. But with God everything is possible."
—Matthew 19:26, NLT

In our family, we grew up with a saying, a mantra: "Moons can do anything!" The Moon family had five children, the last three of us being adopted. My younger sister, Jean, and I were seventeen months apart and both adopted from Korea as infants. On a summer vacation trip to the Badlands of South Dakota, my mother offered to have us sing for special music at a church program. Being only six and eight years in age, we were shy. Singing in public was like a nightmare for us, but we managed to make it through.

The next Sabbath we were in Arkansas visiting some cousins. The leader of a children's division at that church asked whether we could sing, and if so, would we sing for church. I shook my head but didn't realize that my mom was sitting behind me. She gently jabbed me with the pointed toe of her shoe (it was not really "gently"). So we acquiesced and nodded that we could sing. As we were singing in church later, our mom kept coaching us to sing louder. Again, we made it through, but with a lot of stress and anxiety.

Years later I took nursing. The first bed bath I had to give was for a young male patient who was about my age. I was so nervous while reading his chart that night that I asked God whether the patient could do most of the bath for himself. The next morning as I was preparing the bath water and putting it in the basin, I tried to be calm. Thankfully, the patient needed help with only his back, legs, and feet. I know that my face felt very warm and was flushed during this trial. I breathed a prayer of thanksgiving after my hospital clinical was done for that day.

Throughout life we all have been faced with difficult times, most of them more stressful than the ones I have shared from while I was growing up. As Matthew 19:26 says, though, "With God everything is possible" (NLT). God allows us to go through these experiences to prepare us for His kingdom. If we don't go through them, we won't be able to handle things that come our way. May I suggest that our theme be "With God all things are possible"? He wants us to be an example that other people will want to follow, an exemplary servant for Him. Nothing can hold us back if we are doing His will and following the example of Him who is blameless!

Gyl Moon Bateman

Planting Time

Whoever watches the wind will not plant.
—*Ecclesiastes 11:4, NIV*

Driving home from Grand Forks, North Dakota, we crossed the Red River of the North and continued on Highway 2 toward home. Looking out on the rich, fertile, black ground of the fields, we were reminded that this is the season to plant the crops. Farmers were busily working the ground and seeding in preparation for a harvest to come. It was a joy to observe.

However, there was an element that did not bode well for the coming weeks. We are in the midst of a drought. The winter snows had been minimal, so they did not add to the needed moisture. With no rain yet this spring, it takes a large amount of faith for farmers to invest thousands of dollars into planting seeds with the anticipation they will grow and produce a harvest. A strong wind was blowing, depleting the soil of what little moisture there was. Clouds of black dirt were flying through the air. In fact, the amount of dirt in the air made it difficult for the farmers to see, and we had trouble seeing where the tractors and machinery were. Every farmer dreads seeing his soil blown about by the wind. For a farmer, this is the time when faith becomes their strength and gives them the courage to go into the fields and sow. It is a time to recall this verse: "As long as the earth endures, seedtime and harvest, cold and heat, summer and winter, day and night will never cease" (Genesis 8:22, NIV). Trusting, praying, and believing, a farmer goes to the fields every spring and seeds his crop. Some years the harvest season does not bring a good harvest because of the lack of rain or because of hail, winds, or insects that come and eat the plants. Extreme heat and freezing temperatures late in the spring or too early in the fall all contribute to a loss of hoped-for yields. The loss of needed revenue from the small or nonexistent harvest brings hardships upon the families. In addition, there is less food to feed the people of the world. Yet year after the year, the farmer remains optimistic—planting and praying for rain and temperatures that will enable a bountiful harvest. Farmers look to their harvest for their yearly paycheck that will carry them through another year.

As with the farmers, we also endure the winds that batter us and beat upon our families. There are windstorms that threaten our health and cause pain and suffering. Through it all, if we trust in the Lord, He will lead us through to a place where we have peace and comfort.

Evelyn Glass

A Polished Cornerstone

That our sons *may be* as plants grown up in their youth;
that our daughters may be as corner stones,
polished after the similitude of a palace.
—*Psalm 144:12*

One question still niggled at the back of my mind. My husband and I had been in Egypt for five whole days and would be returning to England in less than twenty-four hours. Our tour guide, Waheed, had taken us to temples, where we had been dazzled by the intricacy of the carvings, the reds, yellows, and blues still vibrant after three thousand years. I had been mesmerized by the mirages glimpsed across the vast desert and captivated by the skill of the local craftsmen fashioning translucent vases and sculptures of polished alabaster stone and marble.

Now, on our last day, I stood beside our guide in the Valley of the Kings—the final resting place of the pharaohs—as Waheed described how each succeeding ruler spent the bulk of his reign overseeing the preparation of his tomb. Waheed showed us one tomb with hardly any carvings—the pharaoh had died before his tomb had been completed.

I listened attentively but eventually asked the question that was on my mind.

"Waheed, where are the palaces? Where did these kings actually live?"

"Ah," Waheed smiled, "I'm so glad you asked that. It is a very good question. You see, the ancient Egyptians believed that living here was only temporary. So they built their homes and palaces from mud bricks. However, they believed that after death they would inhabit the afterlife forever. That is why their tombs and temples are made from stone—a more enduring material—and finished with such lavish detail."

We too are on a temporary earthly journey, preparing for an eternity with Christ, our soon-coming King. Sometimes, though, we confuse our priorities and neglect the things that really matter. Being kind to one another, investing time in our children, making an effort to improve our characters—these are the things that count. Those ancient craftsmen attended to every detail to produce temples and tombs that stood the test of time. *Master Craftsman, I put myself in Your hands and invite You to define my contours and to smooth every coarse habit and inclination until I am "polished" like the cornerstone of a palace that will stand forever.*

Avery Davis

God Understands Loneliness

For I am convinced that neither death nor life, neither angels nor
demons, neither the present nor the future, nor any powers, neither
height nor depth, nor anything else in all creation, will be able to
separate us from the love of God that is in Christ Jesus our Lord.
—*Romans 8:38, 39, NIV*

Moving to a new country can be a little scary and also very lonely, even after many years. After being married and living in Sri Lanka for seven years, I still found parts of my life empty, vacant. I found myself trying to fill this vacancy with friends from church, coworkers at the office, classmates back in India, and my best friend in Australia—but to no avail. Something seemed lacking, and I couldn't put my finger on it.

Then one day, while preparing for a feature talk in Sabbath School, I came across a verse I had often overlooked—the verse that comes after the famous "a father to the fatherless, a defender of widows" (Psalm 68:5). Verse 6 told me that "God sets the lonely in families."

Although married to a wonderful man, I knew he was struggling to juggle studying and working at the same time, while keeping up with his exercise regime. Often he was hard-pressed to find time to spend with me, though he tried his utmost.

Having grown up in a very close-knit, fun-loving extended family, my now being in a family of two suddenly seemed quiet, although, being somewhat of an introvert, I enjoyed time on my own as well. And then suddenly, in the fifth, most difficult, and final year of my husband's pursuit of a degree, one of my cousins decided to work in my country. She moved in with us for one year. With her living with us, we had several visits from her family (and a bunch of her friends) as well as one from my mother.

It was a fabulous year. My cousin and I share many similar interests and quirks; even our careers are in a related field. We cooked together. We baked together. We watched movies together. We sang together. We made our own Christmas tree.

She's back at home now. But I am better for the year she spent with us. Whenever I feel alone, while praying, I know without a doubt that God is looking after me, because He loves me. Nothing can separate me from that love. And that's all I need.

Cheryl Howson

Key Holders

Casting all your care upon him; for he careth for you.
—*1 Peter 5:7*

"Have you seen my keys? They're not on the hook." My daughter and her husband, Dennis, didn't remember seeing the keys, so we began to search pockets and tables and to look under cushions and behind the couch but . . . no keys. We drove ten miles back to the park where we had eaten our picnic lunch and searched the area. Still no keys. My biggest worry was for the church keys that were among the missing keys. I would need them in the morning. We searched again at the house without success before saying good night.

Too uptight to sleep, I knelt down and prayed about the missing keys. Still kneeling with my eyes closed, I thought of us sitting in the living room, talking. While Becky checked on the baby, I remembered Dennis picking up keys from the coffee table and dropping them in her purse.

Although close to midnight, I knocked on their door and asked them to check Becky's purse. I hated to disturb them, but this couldn't wait until morning. Yes! The keys were there! Thinking they were Becky's, Dennis had put them in her purse but had forgotten the incident. Seeing the unintended humor, we had a good laugh and said good night again.

Thank You, Jesus! sprang from my heart. Happy praises kept me awake while I thought about how God had shown me what had happened. In that moment of epiphany, I also saw that God really does care for me. I still hold that thought. It still comforts me. Knowing He cares so personally inspires greater faith in His love and the promises written in His Word.

Whether it's lost keys, time, money, health, or opportunities, Jesus always takes interest in everything that concerns us. He invites: "Be careful for nothing; but in every thing by prayer and supplication with thanksgiving let your requests be made known unto God" (Philippians 4:6).

But most of all, Jesus cares about our soul. "For the Son of man is come to seek and to save that which was lost" (Luke 19:10). God knows us so well. He understands our every need, our haste and hesitations, our heartaches and joys, as well as our limitations and weaknesses—and our tendency to stray from His side. Jesus asks each of us: "For what shall it profit a man, if he shall gain the whole world, and lose his own soul?" (Mark 8:36).

So here is a key thought to hold in your heart: Jesus cares for you!

Jeanne B. Woolsey

April 28

No Matter What

Whenever I am afraid, I will trust in You.
—*Psalm 56:3, NKJV*

The emergency room doctor pointed to the words "lymphoma" and "enlarged spleen" on the final CT scan report. Her fingers trailed over to the abnormalities on the laboratory results. We exchanged glances, not words. The doctor knew I was a registered nurse and completely understood the implications. Tears welled up in my eyes as I began to process the impending diagnosis that wasn't mine; instead, it was for Reece, my sixteen-year-old son.

Only four days earlier, our long-awaited family vacation had begun. On the final day, Reece developed symptoms consistent with appendicitis. As the hours passed, the symptoms grew worse. My husband and I agreed that a hospital visit was in order before making the long trip home. An ultrasound, X-ray, and CT scan revealed a normal appendix. However, the technician discovered an unusually large spleen and lymph nodes that demanded attention. This was going to be simple—it had to be mono! Much to our disappointment, the mono test was negative. Then the medical team shared the final impression of the CT scan. With medical reports and a referral to a pediatric hematologist/oncologist in hand, we were on our way.

The return trip home was long and somber. We pressed on with prayer, having enlisted a host of faithful prayer warriors located all over the country. The appointment with the specialist was a long two weeks away, and I just couldn't seem to shake the fog. I needed quiet time with God, so I retreated to our spare bedroom, where I keep many of my favorite books. Immediately my focus was drawn to *Leaning on God's Heart* by Carolyn Sutton. Navigating through the pages, I felt peace and inspiration swell within my heart as I took the journey of trial and triumph the author described regarding her own bout with cancer. Finishing the book in just hours, I walked out of the bedroom with new courage and hope, determined that *no matter what* . . . I would trust the Lord with Reece. Appointment day came along with more tests. The spleen had reduced by two centimeters, and most of the lab work was normal. Three days later, it was absolutely conclusive that Reece had had mononucleosis all along! Yes—we were praising God for mono!

Three weeks later, God allowed me to meet Carolyn face-to-face. We praised God together and determined to keep leaning on God's heart—*no matter what.*

Cindy Mercer

Becoming a Princess

*Yet to all who did receive him, to those who believed in his name,
he gave the right to become children of God.*
—*John 1:12, NIV*

I n the late 1980s I decided to follow Jesus after I awoke one morning to peace in my heart and a voice in those early hours that simply said, "Good morning, child." I wish I could tell you that I walked the straight and narrow from that point on . . .

But my path was filled with backsliding, selfishness, a toe in the church, and a foot in the world. Yet God never gave up on me. I was His prodigal daughter, His problem child, more times than I care to admit, but He kept calling me back. He has worked in my life the principle in Romans 8:28 for His good and glory even though I did not give up alcohol for some time. Though a churchgoer, alcohol was like a god I served. It was the place I went for comfort and peace—instead of going to prayer and the Bible. Finally, when I was sick and tired of being a hypocrite, I gave myself *wholly* to God. One Friday night, April 26, 2008, I got on my knees and asked Him to take away my desire for alcohol. Nothing happened. When Sabbath ended, I went to the kitchen and looked at the two bottles of alcohol with which I could make a White Russian. Then I remembered my prayer. At that instant, God answered my prayer. I walked out of the kitchen and have been sober for seven years without suffering DTs (delirium tremens) or drinking again. James 4:2 states, "You do not have because you do not ask God" (NIV). This was a major milestone in my life and relationship with God. Like the healed demonic in Luke 8, I must now tell everyone what God has done for me.

Though I have weathered many trials since then—including that of becoming a widow in 2014—God has carried me through, and I treasure what His Son did for me. Even though our righteousness is like filthy rags (Isaiah 64:6), God still loved the world so much that He gave us His Son. Anyone who believes can be saved (John 3:16).

How about you? Have you been a prodigal daughter? You can become a princess. Jesus says, "I am the way, the truth, and the life: no man cometh unto the Father, but by me" (John 14:6). Why not pray this simple prayer: *Lord, I am tired of the poor decisions I've made and where my life is today. I don't know how to do this, so I humbly ask You into my heart as my God. Help me this day to turn my life and will over to You. In the name of Your Son, Jesus.*

Candy L. Bedford

Letter to a Son

I press toward the mark for the prize of the high calling
of God in Christ Jesus. Let us therefore, as many as be perfect,
be thus minded: and if in any thing ye be otherwise minded,
God shall reveal even this unto you.
—*Philippians 3:14, 15*

Dearest Aaron,

In the game of life, we know that the Saints will ultimately win over the Wicked. To be a winning Saint, you must listen to the coach, Jesus Christ. He guides and gives instructions on how best to make the winning plays. He provides cheerleaders, such as parents and teachers, who will support and cheer you on. We also know that good "D"—or discipline—is essential for overcoming the lust of the flesh, the lust of the eyes, and the pride of life. A winning Saint presses toward the goal and never gives in to fatigue. What's awesome about Coach Jesus is that He will give you many assists and set up a screen so that you can score!

Players on the opposing team, the Wicked, don't follow the playbook. They will commit flagrant and technical fouls under the direction of their coach, Satan. Their coach will try to *lure* you to his team. He puts his "cheerleaders"—so-called "friends"—in your way with many temptations. He wants you—and any of us—to switch sides and start playing on his team. But we know he is not only a liar but also a destroyer.

In the game of life, we must protect—with all diligence—the special interest of both coaches: our hearts. Often getting into a huddle with supportive and committed friends, parents, and teachers—under the leadership of Coach Jesus—will get us hyped about living the Christian life. We will become excited about playing our best for Jesus, keeping our eye on the real goal—spending eternity with Him. In the meantime, Jesus will help us develop skills and multiply them as we daily "practice" with Him through prayer and Bible study. It takes more than good ballhandling skills to win in this game. We each need to be committed to the divine game plan.

Right now, son, you are in double *overtime*. So transition, cut past your opponents, block their shots, and let your Coach show you how to play in such a way that the end result for you will be certain victory. You *will* win because you are a Saint and your Coach is Jesus Christ.

I'm rooting for you. You are a winner. Your forever supporter, Mom.

Raschelle Mclean-Jones

Kindness Repaid

Be kind and compassionate to one another.
—*Ephesians 4:32, NIV*

A song I know suggests that when we give kindness away, it will come back to us. Many people who share love and kindness know this to be true.

My husband, Roger, is in charge of infrastructure development at a university. He used to go to work early with his workers, helping them to do their job accurately and quickly. He offered incentives for those who performed their tasks well.

Very early one day, a visitor came to the university campus. When he saw men at work so early, he was very impressed and asked, "Why are you up working so early?"

One man answered, "Our supervisor does the same; thus, we follow his example." The visitor, in further discussion with the worker, learned the supervisor was actually a missionary who had come to help out at the school.

Why would a foreigner work so early and so hard at his job? the visitor wondered.

"Have you had breakfast yet?" the worker asked the man.

"No, I haven't," responded the visitor.

The worker kindly offered, "Then I will ask the university cafeteria to prepare a meal for you."

Later the visitor revealed his identity: He was a minister from the government's department of education. He had heard positive things about the work that missionaries were doing at this university, so he had come to see for himself whether what he had heard was true or not.

As he left the campus, the government official said, "If you people need my assistance at the department of education, please feel free to contact me at any time." Since his visit, the minister has made obtaining work permits for the missionaries much easier than before.

When we do our best, without reservation, to extend kindness on God's behalf, blessings come back to us unexpectedly. Abraham and Sarah experienced this principle in their lives. After they entertained a visitor in their tent, they were promised—and given—a son in their old age.

It is true that, in one way or another, the one who shows kindness will be repaid with kindness in unexpected ways. How will you extend kindness to others today?

Evelyn Gabutero Pelayo

Trouble at Work

Let the morning bring me word of your unfailing love,
for I have put my trust in you. Show me the way I should go,
for to you I entrust my life.
—Psalm 143:8, NIV

I had prayed the words of Psalm 143:8 that morning before going to work. About thirty minutes after I got to work, one of my managers asked me a series of questions that seemed innocent enough, but I was intuitively alarmed. "Am I in trouble?" I asked.

"It's bad," she replied. And thus began what could probably be termed the worst day at work in about seven years. I called my husband to let him know that things weren't looking good and that I might be coming home early (and possibly permanently). I cried and prayed. After meetings, conference calls, and e-mails, I understood that a quality improvement training I initiated had spiraled into something ugly because of an error on my part. A sense of finality darkened my spirit as I collected my personal items and cleaned my desk midst more tears, while simultaneously trying to take care of my most urgent responsibilities in the event I was terminated. One of my managers came to me and, in a show of support, hugged me and told me to "hang in there." Her compassion opened the floodgates again and sent me rushing outdoors for privacy.

Why God? I cried out. *I prayed and asked You to show me Your loving-kindness. This is how You show love?* The enemy wanted to deafen my ears to the still, small voice: *Yes, it is, My child. Open your eyes and look.*

Then, even while the tears streamed down my face, I felt praise bubbling up in my soul. I started singing, "Praise Him. He's worthy to be praised." I felt a calm steal over me. *You're right, Lord,* I replied. My entire management team had rallied around me, taking the brunt of the pressure, fighting the battle on my behalf. They instinctively came to offer support even though they didn't know what was happening. When I got back inside, my manager told me that I would be either suspended or terminated instead of simply receiving a letter of warning. Even that news couldn't steal my calm. I serve an Almighty God who loves me. He will never forsake me.

As I write this, I still don't know the outcome, but I am confident that God will take care of me. That assurance is yours as well. The loving-kindness God displayed toward King David is the same loving-kindness that He displays toward me and toward you.

Aminata Coote

Music for the Soul

Praise GOD, everybody! Applaud GOD, all people!
—*Psalm 117:1*, The Message

Praise from all who love GOD!
—*Psalm 148:14*, The Message

Traveling in our state from church to church with my preacher husband, we share in many different worship styles. Some are pretty traditional church services, while others are more contemporary. At some services we sing the old familiar hymns, while at others it's the newer praise songs. As I like singing both, I'm blessed.

I'm so thankful for the sacred artists who write praise music *to* God rather than *about* Him. For years we have sung about God but rarely directly to Him. I'm blessed by the words of Scripture put to music. I praise God for the men and women who write sacred songs and lift their voices to God in appreciation of who He is and all the wonderful things He has done for us—not to mention what He is doing in our lives each day. I'm thankful they have chosen to use their talents for the Lord! Isn't it amazing how many different songs can be written from just the number of keys on the piano?

Since *grace* is a word often found in contemporary worship songs, we sometimes think it is a new word and not found in older hymns. Yet I'm rediscovering that some of the old hymns do extol God's grace. The next time you sing, really concentrate on the words of the hymn and sing from your heart. Even if you can't sing, read the words and focus on their meaning.

I'm so grateful the Lord created us with ears to hear music and voices to sing it! I always have some song running through my mind. A concern I have lately is the fear that I'm losing my singing voice. I know how frustrated I feel when I have a cold and lose my voice so I can't sing. For years I have led out in the praise singing and still do on occasion, so I would miss doing that if I couldn't sing. Also, I have enjoyed singing duets with my husband and participating in cantatas. I want to use my voice each day to uplift Jesus and the Godhead. David wrote so many psalms about lifting our voices in song.

May I encourage you to read the praise scriptures in Psalms and even in Revelation? They are music for the soul.

Remember, God inhabits our praise, so let's keep using our voices for Him!

Louise Driver

Getting Rid of the Feeling of Guilt

They said to one another, "Surely we are being punished
because of our brother. We saw how distressed he was when
he pleaded with us for his life, but we would not listen;
that's why this distress has come on us."
—*Genesis 42:21, NIV*

Guilt can be a self-destructive feeling that imprisons us physically and mentally. When we feel guilty, we become victims of fear, anxiety, and pain.

There was a time when I felt guilty for something, and it was taking away my peace. I did not talk to anyone about it because I thought that, gradually, I would know how to get rid of that feeling. But that is not what happened. To my sorrow, the pain increased. But one day, though, everything started to change. My eyes opened after watching two movies. The first, *Love Happens*, tells the story of a man who felt guilty for his wife's death in a car accident. The other movie was *Love and Other Impossible Pursuits*. This movie portrays the drama of a mother who felt guilty for the death of her little baby. In each movie, the lead character could not handle the weight of the feelings of guilt. Therefore, they became bitter, not even smiling anymore. I identified myself with the two stories because I also felt guilty for the death of someone I loved. I felt guilty for the death of my mother.

When my mother died, I was with her in the hospital. While I was dozing, she passed away. Something made me think that if I had not dozed off, I would have had time to call a doctor. For two long years, I suffered silently as I thought about this.

Yet, in both movies, the characters managed to free themselves from guilt when they felt the need to talk to someone and to share the pain that they had kept silent. So I did the same. I talked with God and opened my heart to Him in tears. It made all the difference! I realized that I was not responsible for the death of my mother. She would have died regardless of the person who was with her. She would still have passed away in her sleep, quietly, without any fanfare. She died because God understood that it was the best for her.

I do not know what kind of guilt entraps you today, but I know that you need to get rid of this evil. Open your heart to the Lord. Shout. Cry out. Tell Him everything that ails your heart. Allow Him to set you free from this burden and to live free. Without guilt. And without fear.

Carmem Virgínia dos Santos Paulo

Praise God! Praise God!

Therefore, my beloved brethren, be steadfast,
immovable, always abounding in the work of the Lord,
knowing that your labor is not in vain in the Lord.
—*1 Corinthians 15:58, NKJV*

Women are sometimes nosy," Mom said. "I'll leave *The Great Controversy* book open right here on the dining room table. It is a great book about end-time events." Quite a number of years ago, Mom, a widow, had decided to rent some rooms to supplement her income, and a single older woman had just arrived to teach at the local country school and was renting from her. Sure enough, Ann picked up the book to see what it was all about. Soon she asked whether she could take it to her room for a closer look.

Ann was very interested in what she was reading, and it wasn't long until she started going to church with us. She was so impressed with the orderliness of the service, the neatness of the deacons attired in suits and ties, and the reverent atmosphere of the Communion service. Yes, she eventually took Bible studies and was baptized into our little church.

Ann lived with Mom for seven or eight school years, so she had a lot of time to read from Mom's extensive home library. She read books that helped her in her new walk with God. After retirement, Ann went back to her home. We didn't keep close contact over the years, but later we did hear that she had passed away.

For the exciting ending to this story, we will fast-forward several years. I was now working in customer service at a Christian publishing company. The caller on the line was a woman who lived in the same small town where Ann had lived. I asked whether she knew of Ann or her sister. "Why, yes," she exclaimed. "We gave Bible studies to Amanda after Ann had shared her faith, and she was baptized too." I sensed the excitement in her voice as she continued. "And that's not all. Ann used her retirement funds to purchase a church for our town!" My response was just, "Praise God! Praise God!"

I recall some of the old, familiar songs Mom used to play on the church piano or hum while working her flower beds: "Will There Be Any Stars in My Crown?" and "When He Cometh to Make Up His Jewels." Mom hasn't heard the rest of this story as yet. But I imagine *she* will be a little nosy when she tries to find out why her glittering crown is so bright.

Rosemary Byrd Hickman

The Lost Pocketbook

I called on the Lord in distress; the Lord answered me.
—*Psalm 118:5, NKJV*

The big day had arrived for my younger sister, who was finally graduating from medical school in Buffalo, New York. Our entire family was excited, so we planned out our trip to Buffalo. My family in Florida decided we would meet at my brother's place in Atlanta and drive together in caravan fashion up to Buffalo. It was a long and difficult trip with my two toddlers and a baby (less than a year old). With my husband driving, I was responsible for taking care of the kids and also for our traveling money.

One of our stops for lunch was at a restaurant in Cleveland, Ohio. We got the kids settled in the booth and ordered our food. Then, with everybody fed and cleaned up, we hit the road again. When we arrived in Buffalo, we stopped for gas and my husband asked me for the money. I reached for my pocketbook but couldn't find it! We frantically searched the van but . . . still no pocketbook. Then the awful realization struck me: the Ohio restaurant, now hundreds of miles away. I remember paying the bill, then placing the pocketbook on the floor of the booth while I got the kids ready to travel. With no cell phones at that time, I couldn't call the restaurant until we arrived at my sister's place. All I could do was pray that the pocketbook was still in the restaurant with our money in it.

When I was able to phone, the restaurant manager came on the line. "Yes," he said, "one of the waitresses found it on the floor of the booth." My heart jumped for joy and I said, "Thank You, Jesus! Thank You, Jesus!" But wait—were the money, credit card, and everything else still in the purse? The manager would not check the contents, but he said he would keep it there until someone with ID came to pick it up. *Now what?* But My God already had it worked out. One of my brothers said he had a friend who lived not far from that restaurant. The manager said he would allow the man to pick up the pocketbook. The friend picked it up and sent it by FedEx. I had it in my hands the next day. Nothing inside had been touched. God allowed the right persons to come in contact with that pocketbook. He had someone in the area at the right time.

What an awesome God who heard and answered my call of distress!

He hears *every* call of distress.

Dorett Alleyne

How Prayers Help in Daily Life

Do not be anxious about anything, but in every situation, by prayer
and petition, with thanksgiving, present your requests to God.
—Philippians 4:6, NIV

Years ago, my whole family decided to visit my parents during the holidays. We traveled by public vehicle with many other people. When we were almost at the midpoint of the road going through a forest, two armed men stepped out in front of our vehicle, blocking it, forcing it to stop. We were all scared because they looked very suspicious.

We were told to come out of the vehicle and leave everything we had. The men went inside and took our money and many other belongings. While this was going on, my heart was beating so fast because of the unexpected turn of events. I recognized one of the men and said loudly, "I think I know you from somewhere." He immediately ordered me into the bush so that they could kill me there. He knew that if I stayed alive, I would go to the police station and report what I had seen, and he would be caught. I refused to step where he had indicated, but they forced me to. Our daughter, only ten at the time, was very scared; she started praying in her heart. She told God that if He saved our lives, we would always testify about His grace and love. She promised she would always sing for Him wherever she went (that is what she does now). In that vehicle, we had a pastor and an elder from our local church. However, they were both so frightened that they forgot to pray.

None of us said anything else while the men were still there. Then God did a great miracle. As these dangerous men rushed through people's things in the vehicle, they forgot about me! After eight long minutes passed, they quickly left us, disappearing from sight. We were terrified but went back into the vehicle and continued our trip—praising God for what He had done. Everyone began saying they had seen our daughter praying. Truly God had answered her prayer. He did so by chasing away these evil men so that we wouldn't get hurt.

God is always there whenever we have problems. He does not want us to suffer. Surely in life we will have problems, but prayers help so much. We might feel as if we are too insignificant to do something that will have a positive change. But with God, we are not. Let's step forward in prayer and have faith. Doing so can save lives.

Debbie Maloba

God Knows Your Name

"For I know the plans I have for you," declares the LORD,
"plans to prosper you and not to harm you,
plans to give you hope and a future."
—*Jeremiah 29:11, NIV*

That little girls are killed in India is not a hidden secret. In the midst of social workers, NGOs (nongovernment organizations), women's organizations, and many government regulations, this social evil is not preventable. Most of the time, when these heart-wrenching incidents occur, the murder of the latest little girl floods the news. This defies reason and begs us to ask these questions: Where is God? Why should such evil prevail? Is there hope in the midst of despair? As these painful events roll into history, they still trouble my mind.

One day I became terribly sick and was rushed to the hospital. The doctor's report declared that I was suffering with fibroids and needed an immediate operation. Surgery was performed, and I knew that I would never be able to give birth to a baby of my own.

A few years passed. One day a pastor rushed into our house with a newborn baby in his arms. He explained that he happened to be present during its delivery and that the parents were planning to kill the baby if it was a girl. It was. Quickly he saved the baby by offering money to the parents. He thought of me and felt impressed that I would be the best mother for the child.

Words fail to express my joy! My husband and I embraced the baby girl. Each time I look at her, God's words ring in my mind: "For I know the plans I have for you, . . . plans to prosper you and not to harm you, plans to give you hope and a future" (Jeremiah 29:11, NIV).

Each passing day, when I look at our growing baby, she anchors the truth of David's words concerning God: "Your eyes saw my unformed body; all the days ordained for me were written in your book before one of them came to be" (Psalm 139:16, NIV). What hope filled my heart that God knew, beforehand, my medical plight and that of the baby girl—even before she was conceived! He had already planned to put us together as mother and child. This, my friends, tells us that no matter how discouraged and heartbroken we are by poverty or circumstance, the Maker knows us by name!

Never lose heart when facing the darkest moments of your life. Somewhere between the life pages in your personal story, you will hear God whisper your name. For He knows *your* name.

Anita Livingston Hayward

"Gleams of the Golden Morning"

The moon will shine like the sun, and the sunlight will be seven times brighter, like the light of seven full days, when the LORD binds up the bruises of his people and heals the wounds he inflicted.
—Isaiah 30:26, NIV

I watched in horror as the news report I saw reminded me of a similar tragedy in my personal life. I had wrestled with a power that could only have come from God when the perpetrator set me free just when I thought I had lost the battle. As other crimes of the day were reported, including an attempted baby abduction by two teenagers, I had great concern at the increase of what are called "adult crimes" among young offenders. That day, there was no good news. Mothers were weeping and fathers were threatening. Children were hiding in foxholes from the firepower of weapons being used to destroy their families. Periodically their heads would push above ground as they expressed words of bitterness against those who had disrupted their lives. I cried for their lost childhood, lack of joy, and absence of light.

A figurative night of gloom has overtaken the world. The darkness is becoming denser as the inhumanity of man spreads. As predicted by Paul, "People will be lovers of self, lovers of money, proud, arrogant, abusive, . . . ungrateful, . . . not loving good" (2 Timothy 3:2, 3, ESV). Paul refers to this time of spiritual darkness as "perilous times" (verse 1, NKJV).

In contrast, I looked at the dawning sun from my eighth-floor living room window—breathtaking. I stood spellbound, watching the golden rays spread over the eastern sky, dispelling the darkness of night. I was not the only enchanted observer. The birds were singing their beautiful melody of praise. It brought to mind that comforting song penned by S. J. Graham, "Gleams of the Golden Morning." In it he describes the coming of Jesus, who will soon return to take his "faithful and happy children" to their heavenly home. The chorus of this song proclaims, "O, we see the gleams of the golden morning."

That early morning I joined the birds in singing as I claimed the promise of Christ's soon return. In heaven any negative memories will not return. No more foxholes, no more abductions, no more death, and no more crying. Yes, this world's night of gloom will soon come to an end.

I can already see the glorious rays of that new dawning. Can you?

Sonia Kennedy-Brown

The Prayer Room

Delight yourself also in the LORD,
and He shall give you the desires of your heart.
—*Psalm 37:4, NKJV*

For some years we lived in a one-bedroom apartment. God had provided this fully furnished apartment, and all our utility needs were taken care of. It continued to serve us well even when our first daughter was born. At the time, we were living in a foreign land. Knowing that we would not be living away from our home country forever, we made serious plans for building our own house back home. My husband and I exchanged ideas as to what kind of house we wanted. In that process, we realized that one important thing we both desired was to have a dedicated prayer room where we all could meet for our morning, evening, and private worships. We sketched a diagram of the house, got someone to draw a plan for us, and started to pray about it.

We still have not built that house, but God, in His infinite love, has granted our hearts' desire in a very remarkable way. Just a few weeks before our second daughter, Kristen-Sara, was born, university officials where we work decided to give us a bigger house. Up until then, we were living in the studio apartment. When university authorities decided to give us another house, they upgraded us, not to a one-bedroom house or even to a two-bedroom house—but to a three-bedroom house!

When we entered this house, we saw an extra room intended to be a maid's room. We immediately knew that this was what we had been praying for: our prayer room. There we now meet with our heavenly Father almost every morning, afternoon, and evening, as well as for private prayers. This room has seen tears turned to joy and despair turned into bright hope.

God promised that He would provide " 'houses full of good things, which you did not fill, hewn-out wells which you did not dig, vineyards and olive trees which you did not plant' " (Deuteronomy 6:11, NKJV), as well as give us the desires of our hearts.

Do you have a pressing need whose fulfillment would glorify God's name? He is still in the business of granting our desires according to His will.

Today may He give you peace and assurance as you lay your heart's desires on His altar, as we did with our prayer room . . . which He delivered to us.

Lynn Mfuru Lukwaro

God's Dream

The LORD of hosts hast sworn, saying, Surely, as I have thought, so
shall it come to pass; and as I have purposed, so shall it stand.
—*Isaiah 14:24*

At the end of May in 2003, I was thirty-two and still single. I asked God whether I was wrong to trust Him with the choosing of a husband, considering that someone told me I should not place my responsibilities on God's shoulders. Given that God had already guided me through a decision between two jobs, I asked him about the choice of a husband.

That night I had a dream. When I awoke, I remembered a man from my dream. He had long, curly hair and smiled at me while we talked and played with two little boys.

As the years went by, I was impressed that God was giving me the freedom of choice regarding a husband. I sensed that He wanted me to know that I should not worry because, in His timing, He would have me at the exact place I needed to be in order to meet my future husband.

Many years have passed by since then. The decision to continue the wait is mine. Many dear people had advised me to forget about my long-ago impressions after the dream that followed my prayer. "Time is passing by," they remind me. Yet I want to continue to spend my time with God and to know His voice.

Today, while I am still waiting, I want to encourage you also to wait for the promises God has made to you. Even if decades pass by, do not try to help God or run ahead of Him

That's what Abraham did when his promised son didn't arrive as soon as he had hoped. Yet having a son with Sarah's servant girl, Hagar, or thinking about adopting his servant, Eliezer, could not fulfill the promise of the child God had promised to him. God had promised Sarah that she would give birth to a son, even if that was rationally and biologically impossible. In God's time, the son would be born. And he was. This story reminds me that, all too often, when we try to "help" God, it often brings catastrophe!

I promise to write the end of my story someday. However, today I encourage you to cling by faith to the promises God has made to you. Wait patiently for their fulfillment—even if it takes many years. In God's time and way, your "promised child" will come, as will mine. Not because we deserve it but because God is the One who has promised!

Kênia Kopitar

The Gift of Forgiveness

Bear with each other. . . . Forgive as the Lord forgave you.
—*Colossians 3:13, NIV*

Shellie Renee is my firstborn. She's quick-witted, fun loving, compassionate by nature, and straightforward by design. Shellie is a fighter—starting when in my womb due to my complicated pregnancy, which challenged us both. As a toddler, Shellie became my traveling companion. I delighted in watching her grow with each passing day.

After Shellie's father and I were divorced, our lives changed, as they do when loss occurs. Time, when given its proper respect, has a way of bringing about healing. Yet my low self-esteem and poor self-worth did not, and would not, allow the proper passing of time. So I found myself in another "committed on paper" relationship much too soon. Before that union ended, I gave birth to my son, Jonathan. I felt lonely and looked for my own ways to numb the pain. In a sense, I "abandoned" my little ones with hurtful looks, words that often pained more than cheered, and raised hands that inflicted bodily harm instead of the hugs they both deserved and needed. Over the years, and with more emotional loss, I started to withdraw deeply into a harder, complicated shell. Sadly, one consequence of my doing so was a growing distrust between Shellie and me. I missed opportunities to celebrate my daughter. With each failed attempt at reconciliation, I fell more deeply into shame, guilt, and loss.

David once cried out, "My sin is ever before me" (Psalm 51:3). Mine was too—but Shellie forgave me, again and again. She wrapped her forgiveness in encouragement, affirmation, and peace. We have, in recent years, visited with each other and loved ones on three different continents, including Africa, where I now live. She and I are purposeful about being there for each other. It's called healing, restoration, and reconciliation. Her gift of forgiveness, as she extends her hand and heart to me, flows over my being as a wellspring of promises made and kept to one another. I've seen her grow as an author of two books and public speaker. She advocates for the downtrodden, using skills and personal experiences to teach unwed mothers and those with dysfunctional pasts so they can turn their lives around and have a better tomorrow.

I am so grateful! What a beautiful world this would be if we gave to one another what Shellie—my daughter, sister, child-friend, and hero—has given to me: the gift of forgiveness!

Gail Masondo

Mother

Her children arise and call her blessed; her husband also,
and he praises her: "Many women do noble things,
but you surpass them all."
—*Proverbs 31:28, 29, NIV*

I enjoy writing and designing the cards I give to my loved ones. I keep interesting magazine pictures, paper with different textures and colors, paper scraps, anything to use for different occasions: Mother's Day, Father's Day, birthdays, births, baptisms, Valentine's Day, graduations, quinceañera celebrations (special celebration on a girl's fifteenth birthday), engagements, weddings, and anniversaries.

I remember a time when I had so many commitments that I could not stop to reflect and write calmly, as I like to do. After all, each message on each card is unique, special, and personalized. Also, I noticed that everybody at home was already up. I needed to finish my card. I read, reread, and finished the card just in time to share the special moments that day.

I also recall one Mother's Day when my mother was greatly moved by the words that I wrote on her card! For all the mothers reading this devotional today, I want to share the message I gave to my mother on that long-ago day. Here is what I wrote for her:

"The word *mother* has always been synonymous with love and giving. For nine months, a mother donates her body as a temporary nest with warmth, affection, and food for the growing child—and without charging rent. Then there is an intense and painful delivery of the baby from her womb into the world. She has to protect, feed, teach, and love that child. Her love cannot forget her child even for a minute. Her love does not miss opportunities to show affection, listen to, and advise her child. She has a love that impels her to pray and to nurture the object of her affection. Her love patiently waits to see what the future will bring for her children. And while she waits, she does everything she can to make good use of the time that she still has with them."

Whether you are a biological mother, a spiritual mother, or both, I pray that today will be a day full of God's love and special meaning for you, your children, and your family.

Ellen Diniz de Andrade

In His Time

Be still in the presence of the LORD,
and wait patiently for him to act.
—*Psalm 37:7, NLT*

My husband had just been called to serve in another country. I was supposed to follow him by February 2016. He left for the mission service in January. I was very anxious to go with him, but there were many loose ends to tie up. In fact, I was waiting on a major decision from the Office of Immigration and was not sure when that would come through. This is often the case with work permits, permanent residence, and citizenship documents. And you have to wait until the Office of Immigration gives you an appointment.

I remember the morning when my boss came in. She said she needed to talk to me and added, "I need to know a time frame concerning when you think your last day of work will be here in the office." She needed to know in order to have enough time to look for my replacement.

That morning, I prayed before going into her office. I decided to go by faith and told her I would be leaving at the end of February. I was not sure whether I was doing the right thing, but I knew my God somehow would come through for me. After coming out of her office, I just said, *This is it, Lord. Now everything is in Your hands. Please help me get the letter from the Office of Immigration before the end of next month.* I felt at peace, trusting Him to work out the details.

The day went by quickly as we got busy with work. I even forgot about that morning's appointment and my not knowing when the Office of Immigration would make their decision. When I got home that evening, I checked the mail. Lo and behold! At the bottom of the stack of envelopes was a letter, addressed to me, from the Office of Immigration. My heart leapt as I stood staring at the letter. I knew right away that God had answered my prayer!

There are times in our lives when we want to rush God because we want something now and not tomorrow, but God knows and provides at the right time—not necessarily what we expect but when we need it most. His timing is always perfect—just as with Rachel and Sarah. They received their firstborn sons at the time God deemed best for them. He will gladly do the same for you. Just wait patiently on Him, and He will act on your behalf in His time.

Judith M. Mwansa

The Yellow Carnation

"For with God nothing will be impossible."
—Luke 1:37, NKJV

One Sabbath each month, our church group visits a local nursing home, where we have an afternoon praise service with the residents there. Many of those who call this home are members of one of our area churches. This past Mother's Day weekend, our group decided we would take colorful carnations to give each resident at the end of our program. It was fun to see them smile, accept the flowers, and admire them. No one in our group wanted the one remaining purple-fringed, white-petal carnation. I picked it up along with my songbook. On the way out, I stopped to chat with a gentleman in his wheelchair. I sat down to listen to his family story and placed my book and the flower on a nearby table as I listened.

When I got up to leave I saw a beautiful, large yellow carnation by my book instead of the much smaller white and purple one. I looked around to see who might have exchanged flowers. No one was nearby. As I walked through the lobby, I offered this beautiful yellow carnation to a couple of different ladies but each declined, showing me they already had their carnations.

As I stepped outside into the sunshine, I noticed a couple sitting off to the side. I walked over and greeted them. He was bent and in a wheelchair as she held his hand. She said, "I just love flowers but when my husband moved in here we had to sell our house. I no longer have a garden. When I visit my husband here, I can enjoy all the beautiful hanging baskets." I held out my beautiful yellow carnation and said I'd like for her to have it in honor of Mother's Day. "Yellow carnations have always been my favorite," she said, her eyes growing misty.

Some of my friends suggested this was a "lucky coincidence." However, I am convinced that our loving heavenly Father, with whom nothing is impossible, worked one of His many wonders that day. I have no other explanation as to how a scrawny white-and-purple carnation "coincidentally" became a beautiful, large yellow carnation—other than the explanation that "coincidence is nothing other than God working anonymously." In Isaiah 65:24 God promises that "before they call, I will answer; and while they are yet speaking, I will hear."

I am sure that while I was talking with the retired pastor that day, our God transformed that little flower into something more beautiful so a burdened elderly woman could have her "favorite."

Beverly D. Hazzard

Mistaken Identity

*Speaking to yourselves in psalms and hymns and spiritual songs,
singing and making melody in your heart to the Lord.*
—*Ephesians 5:19*

A funny thing happened while I was studying in my college dormitory room during my freshman year. The loudspeaker blared, "Retha Butcher— telephone." I questioned, *Who could be calling me?* Nevertheless, I raced four floors down to the lobby phone and breathlessly answered, "Hello, this is Retha." When the person on the line asked whether I would sing special music for church, my mind ran the gamut of emotions: shock, perplexity, and disbelief. I regained my composure and replied, "You must have the wrong Retha."

Though Retha isn't a common name, another individual by that name, a junior at the college, was talented enough to fulfill that request. Not knowing the reason for the call, the front desk receptionist had assumed the call was for me, attached my last name, and summoned me. I could not stifle my chuckling on the way back to my room as I pondered that hilarious request for me to sing a solo. At the same time, the caller had no way of knowing about trauma from my childhood. It probably started when someone told my guardian aunt, who was within my earshot, "Retha will never amount to anything." Although those words were hurtful, they did not need to rule my life. Another traumatic event during adolescence was when the choir director of our small youth group stopped us in the middle of a hymn that we were practicing and yelled, "Someone is singing off-key." I knew it must be me because the others were more musical than I. Both those incidents played havoc with my wannabe-singer confidence level. I began lowering my volume almost to the point of lip-syncing to spare people from hearing me sing off-key.

Later I became passionate about providing piano and instrument lessons for my two daughters so that they could be of service in their respective churches. My confidence level has risen over the years, and I no longer lip-sync the hymns that I love. "My mouth shall praise thee with joyful lips" (Psalm 63:5).

Now, realizing that I am a child of many prayers, my motto is, "The task ahead of me is never as great as the Power behind me." I wake up each morning exclaiming, "This is the day which the LORD hath made; [I] will rejoice and be glad in it" (Psalm 118:24).

Retha McCarty

Mechanical Miracle

Before they call, I will answer;
and while they are yet speaking, I will hear.
—Isaiah 65:24

Like so many countries around the world, New Zealand attracts many tourists. Every Friday my husband and I travel into Blenheim (a town twenty-six miles from where we live) to do our weekly shopping. We often pick up hitchhikers—mostly young people on a working holiday. How we enjoy chatting with hitchhikers from England, Australia, the Czech Republic, Taiwan, the United States, Canada, China, France, and Germany! Most, without doubt, are from Germany. So it was no surprise that a lovely young lady named Sophie who visited our church one week was from Germany.

On Sunday afternoon we received a phone call from a church member and learned Sophie was having problems with her car, a rather old car she had bought in which to travel around New Zealand. Time was of the essence because Sophie still had plans to travel to more places, do more sightseeing, and take more photos. Then she would sell her car before her visa ran out in a few short weeks and return home to Germany on the flight she had already booked.

Because both my son and my husband are qualified motor mechanics, Sophie stayed in our home while the two men spent time with their heads under the car bonnet (hood). However, as they prayerfully identified the problem, another issue arose: How long would it be before they could find and purchase a needed replacement part? The model of Sophie's car is not common here in New Zealand. With prayer on his lips, my husband phoned a friend of his who ran a secondhand car part business in Blenheim. When my husband described the part and its number, his friend said, "Yes, I have one." It was the exact part and was located in nearby Blenheim! How we praised God! He had known which car part Sophie would need.

After a ninety-minute round trip and a ten-minute installation, the car was running again sweetly without black smoke pouring out the exhaust pipe.

Soon Sophie was happily on her way, pleased that she had listened to her mother's advice to attend church on Sabbath in whichever town she found herself and in whichever country she was touring. How blessed we are to be members of His big family and to know that He provides for our individual needs even before they arise!

Leonie Donald

Relationship Takes Time

Now when I passed by thee, and looked upon thee, behold,
thy time was the time of love; and I spread my skirt over thee,
and covered thy nakedness: yea, I sware unto thee, and entered into
a covenant with thee, saith the Lord God, and thou becamest mine.
—Ezekiel 16:8

An old hymn admonishes us to "take time to be holy."

In our fast-paced society, we hardly have time to unwind. Our minds are working and planning ahead while we sleep. But one thing that can't be rushed is the building of a lasting relationship. In fact, anything worth pursuing takes time. We learn a great deal when we take time to grow and understand. Often we tend to hurry into a love relationship without taking the time to seek God's will or get to know the other person. Sometimes, when we seal a business transaction with the stroke of the pen, we haven't taken the necessary time to read the fine print. Then when problems arise, we wonder, *What did I get myself into?*

When it comes to building a relationship with Jesus, it is vital that we spend time getting to know Him. The writer of an old hymn understood this when he wrote "In the Garden." The song talks about waiting and listening for the voice of God's Son. The song goes on to use words of relationship, such as *walks, talks,* and *tarry.*

When we are in love, time seems to stand still. Instead of taking the bus, the train, or driving with our special friend, we often choose to walk together because we have so much to talk about. Sometimes we tarry longer than we should. Jesus wants to walk with us; He is not rushed. He wants to tarry a little longer with us. He wants to listen to our concerns, joys, and sorrows. He wants to repeatedly express his love, saying, "My daughter, I want to cover you with my love again today. You are mine." What sweet communion we can have with the greatest of all lovers if we would just take the time to get to know Him. This Lover will not leave us stranded. He will never divorce us. A break in the relationship would be our choice.

My sisters, would you join me in recommitting to spend quality time for a better relationship with Jesus? Slow down, unwind, chill, relax, and do whatever it takes. Another hymn, "O Love That Wilt Not Let Me Go," describes the reward of a close friendship with Christ: We can rest our weary souls in Him, forever sure that we are in a forever relationship.

Joan M. Leslie

Watery Wall

If the LORD had not been on our side . . . , the flood would have
engulfed us, the torrent would have swept over us, the raging waters
would have swept us away. . . . Our help is in the name of the LORD,
the Maker of heaven and earth.
—Psalm 124:2–8, NIV

On Friday, November 8, 2013 (also my husband's birthday), the world had its eyes on the Philippines as Haiyan, the strongest typhoon ever recorded in history, hit. As winds increased momentum, the drumlike beat of raindrops on the roof became deafening. At seven o'clock in the morning, water began seeping in under the door. We moved to the next room, where the babysitter, my eldest daughter, and my two-year-old girl climbed onto the double-decker beds.

Suddenly, with a loud crack, the door was cut in half by a wall of black, rushing water. Knees quivering and hearts gripped with fear, we—including my husband—climbed to the upper deck and tried to break through the ceiling with the handle of a broom we had grabbed from the top of a cabinet. Since the only hole it made in the ceiling was the diameter of the broom handle, my husband inserted his fingers into it and pulled. Thank God, the whole ceiling square gave way!

We quickly climbed up as the water inside our house now churned up to ceiling level with a sucking sound resembling that of a washing machine. Outside, winds howled and huge waves repeatedly struck our building, threatening to collapse it. Aloud we repeated God's Bible promises of deliverance, prayed, and sang my baby's Sabbath School songs. Repeatedly we sang, "My God is great, so strong and so mighty. There's nothing my God cannot do."*

Around ten thirty that morning, the water subsided. The highest outside watermark was fifteen feet; inside the water had reached a height of eleven and a half feet. And what devastation: missing houses along the shore, vehicles—some upside down or piled one atop the other—scattered like litter, and only concrete posts where concrete houses had once stood. The scarcity of food, water, and clothing resulted in great suffering, not to mention the loss of lives.

That night we gathered for worship, thanking God for His wonderful deliverance.

Once again, He had proven Himself faithful and true to His promises. Truly, "my God is so great, so strong and so mighty. There's nothing my God cannot do." Praise His holy name!

Fe C. Magpusao

---

* Ruth Harms Calkin, "My God Is So Big" (Nuggets of Truth Publishing, 1959).

Forgiveness

*"Brothers, listen! We are here to proclaim
that through this man Jesus there is forgiveness for your sins."*
—Acts 13:38, NLT

Monday's page in my Bible study guide describes the incredible circumstance of Pentecost; the amazing phenomenon—fiery tongues of the Holy Spirit conferring special powers on the people who were to be the first emissaries of the gospel.

Honestly, I've always been intrigued by this story. As the nucleus for Christ's formative church, the little group of men and women was ready to receive the outpouring. They were of one accord and unified in purpose. And yet, just days before, they had gone into the upper room, dragging all their old emotional baggage with them. Notwithstanding recent events, their attitudes of intolerance, self-promotion, doubt, and legalism were still alive and well. These were, after all, the same disciples who wanted fire rained down on a Samaritan village, little kids kept away from Jesus, and Him not talking to certain women. They didn't like Gentiles or foreigners, and they weren't crazy about each other. And in that same room a few weeks before, they sat with folded arms, immersed in their own pride, while Jesus took the role of servant and washed their feet.

What could possibly have changed them so completely in so short a time? Jesus had told them to go there to pray and wait, but He had returned to heaven. They sat in that room facing each other. What happened, I wondered . . . what changed them?

In a word, I think the answer is *forgiveness*. Jesus had told them that the work of the Holy Spirit was to "convict the world of its sin" (John 16:8, NLT). And in that upper room, I believe the Holy Spirit brought their collective conscience to understand how importance forgiveness is. They needed to *get* forgiveness. They needed to *give* forgiveness. One thing prayer will do is help you understand how much you need forgiveness. And imagine the list of people they needed to forgive: the Roman soldiers who nailed Jesus to the cross, the Jewish leaders who orchestrated the destruction of their dreams. Not to mention . . . each other.

And they needed to accept forgiveness for *themselves*.

In truth, the good news is that forgiveness is still available. Any time, any place. And for anybody.

Linda Nottingham

A Painful Journey

I look up to the mountains; does my strength come from the
mountains? No, my strength comes from GOD,
who made heaven, and earth, and mountains.
—*Psalm 121:1, 2*, The Message

My sister, Joyce, phoned one Friday to ask that I pray for her grandson, Colton, a sturdy, strong, active twelve-year-old. A few days before, he had started complaining about having pain in his leg. Now he was running a temperature and couldn't put any weight on his leg because it was so painful. His dad, Mike, had to carry him to the car before stowing a wheelchair in the car so that Colton could be wheeled into the doctor's office. Colton's two younger brothers and a younger sister would be picked up by their grandmother, who would care for them in her home. After a brief examination, the pediatrician told my niece, Tami, and Mike that she was calling a pediatric orthopedic surgeon at the hospital in Asheville with a request that he see their son that day.

Several tests were done, which revealed that Colton had sepsis (a systemic infection) in his hip. Tami and Mike learned that if they had waited another day, the surgeon might not have been able to help their son. Even now, Colton would have a long, painful journey to be healthy again. So a week later, after two surgeries to insert drains, high doses of antibiotics, blood tests, an MRI, and a PICC line inserted (for intravenous administration of antibiotics), Colton was finally released from the hospital. Tami, who had been trained at the hospital, administered Colton's antibiotics for the next few weeks and kept sterile the area around the PICC line. Of course, he had to keep unnecessary weight off his leg and use a walker and wheelchair. This different, if not boring, lifestyle change for an active twelve-year-old kept him from running, jumping, and biking. Yet, thank the Lord, his life had been spared.

Many people, prayer groups, church members, friends, and relatives have covered Colton with prayer. Thankfully, no damage was done to Colton's bone structure in the hip area. We know Jesus, the Great Physician, will heal him completely. How thankful we are that we have such a precious, always available Friend!

How about you, my sisters? Is Jesus your dear Friend? Do you communicate with Him daily and trust Him with yourself and your family members? You can. He is always there.

Patricia Mulraney Kovalski

Waiting on the Lord

I waited patiently for the LORD;
and He inclined to me, and heard my cry.
—Psalm 40:1, NKJV

had recently moved to an apartment closer to the hospital where I was receiving oncology treatments. The small one-bedroom apartment reminded me of how simple my life had gotten. One night, boxes still unpacked, I called my parents 1,200 miles away. I told my father: "I think my prayers are making it only to the ceiling, Dad."

He said: "Wait on the Lord."

Wait on the Lord. Yet I wondered what would happen next. *Where will I go after treatment? What will God do with my life? How will I minister?* It was then I consistently began to pray: *I will wait on You.*

Seasons changed, and soon it was fall. I awoke one morning to the sounds of a moving truck. Someone was moving into an apartment across from mine. Movers were unloading a bench for the front porch. It made me smile. Weeks later, my new neighbor, Sarah, was sitting on the porch, blanket over her legs, reading the Bible and drinking hot water with a wedge of lemon on the cup. *She must be at least eighty.* We exchanged pleasantries. That evening, Sarah was sitting on the porch and invited me to join her. She told me of her childhood in this town, her husband's death, and time spent with her daughter after the funeral. We sat, enjoying the sunset and cool breeze. She patted my hand and said: "It's hard to wait, isn't it? It is hard to wait." *How does she know?*

The following day, I found that the treatment made me dizzy and nauseated. I called Sarah. I remember watching her walk toward me and then darkness. I woke up in the hospital with Sarah sitting next to me. She was reading a psalm from her Bible. She stopped and held my hand as the doctor walked in and explained the treatment complications that added up to spending a few days in the hospital. It suddenly became too heavy. My pain weighed me down.

I began to cry, but through my tears, I listened as Sarah hummed "How Great Thou Art." When she was done singing, Sarah opened her Bible to read to me until I fell asleep. This woman that I had known for a few weeks was looking out for me. God knew I needed Sarah in my life right then. Someone God placed in my path at the right time. Someone God knew would remind me of His promise. As I dozed off, I heard Sarah's voice: "I waited patiently for the LORD; and He inclined to me, and heard my cry" (Psalm 40:1, NKJV).

Dixil L. Rodríguez

God Is in Control

And my God shall supply all your need
according to His riches in glory by Christ Jesus.
—*Philippians 4:19, NKJV*

Moving time always brings up gushes of anxiety from my normally tranquil mind. I imagine and dread all the things that can possibly go wrong.

My hubby and I had decided, for health reasons, to move to a seniors' residence with access to resources we would need in the future. My husband's Internet search revealed a housing complex that appeared suitable, so we submitted our names. A few years on the waiting list should give us time to adjust to this massive venture. But within weeks, a call came saying our three-bedroom apartment would be ready in two months. We were unable to view it, but pictures and friends assured us it was great except for a rather tiny kitchen.

We sorted items, held a yard sale, arranged for movers, and said goodbye to our lovely home with a huge modern kitchen. Everything went so smoothly that even an observing neighbor commented this must be God's plan for us.

On moving day we loaded our cats into our little car and headed out from our rural abode to a very large city.

Our first view of the living center was positive. Though older, it was well cared for. The dining/living area was enormous. But, oh, the kitchen! My hubby named it the "intimate kitchen." We promptly added an extra cupboard and counter in the dining room. And surprisingly, it worked just fine. As for the rest of the complex—well! There is a swimming pool and hot tub, a dozen or so quality exercise machines, a library, myriads of lounges, activities including movies and concerts to games and bus services, pleasant grounds, and lovely people. Meals, laundry, housekeeping, and nursing care are available as needed. Some of the best medical facilities in the province are just a short drive from our place. Vegetarian food is abundant in restaurants and stores. Great friends from years gone by live five minutes away and have adopted us into their warm family.

Do we miss our old place and friends? Sure. Are we happy here? You bet! God not only met all our needs but also fulfilled our wants and added blessings in abundance!

Dawna Beausoleil

Zigzagging Along

And it shall come to pass, that before they call, I will answer;
and while they are yet speaking, I will hear.
—Isaiah 65:24

Mother, be ready. After school I'll come to take you to town for your hair appointment," I had said. Now I was ready to leave my classroom and drive home. Assignments for all classes were on the blackboard, my daybook was completed, and the room was tidy.

Carefully I drove, for only recently had I passed my driving test, and my car and I were just getting acquainted. Slowly I started out on the snowy road. At Farm Hill, where the red barn stood, I heaved a sigh of relief. So far, so good. Imagine my horror when I glanced down the next flat stretch of road, where I could see the glare of ice on the road! There was no alternative now, I must go forward. Mother was waiting for me.

I said a quick, silent prayer and began to inch forward. Of course, I turned the wheels too quickly and in the wrong direction. Oops! Zigzagging to the left, then to the right, my car traveled the length of about one half of a mile. Suddenly my vehicle slid to the right and flipped over into the ditch.

Now I was really stuck. Snow was piled around the car. The right door was jammed into the snow; the left door pointed skyward. What a situation to be in! All I could do was pray and wait. After some time, a very frightened face peered through the windshield. What a welcome sight! "Harvey, please get me out of here!" I shouted to an acquaintance, and he did. He drove me home. All I said to Mother was that, due to the icy road, Harvey would take us to town.

While Mother was in the drugstore, I quickly arranged for a tow truck to get my car out of the ditch. But the story soon came out. "Muriel, I saw your car in the ditch," boomed the loud voice of Abe, from Lamming Mills. Mother heard this comment, and an explanation had to be forthcoming. She never did make her hairdressing appointment.

My silent prayer had been answered. I had not been injured, the car was not damaged, and I had learned a driving lesson regarding icy roads. No matter where we are, no matter what time it is, no matter what circumstances, we can be certain our heavenly Father is aware of what is happening to His children. We are precious to Him, and He keeps His promises—always.

Muriel Heppel

The Bigger Picture

For my thoughts are not your thoughts,
neither are your ways my ways, saith the LORD.
—Isaiah 55:8

Did you look in your office?" my husband asked, trying to be helpful.

My eyes rolled in his direction. "That's the first place I looked!" I wanted to do some holiday shopping using a bank card received as a retirement gift from my former employer. I had been holding on to the card for months, with plans to spend it on a new computer tablet.

"It will surface," my husband said, trying to console me. "When you least expect it, the gift card will appear."

I nodded and then added, "I'm going to pray and keep looking." So for several days I prayed and continued to search. But despite my best efforts, I couldn't find the gift card.

Finally I decided to call my former employer, explain the loss, and ask for a replacement. Within a few days, the new card arrived. By now, sales had passed. Sadly, I knew my item would cost more. Upon entering the store, I asked the sales clerk whether the particular brand of tablet that I planned to purchase was still in stock and possibly on sale. She checked and then told me that my selection was sold out; the new inventory would be priced higher. Disappointed, I left. On a whim, I tried a different store in the same chain but over in the next county. Again, I asked the clerk whether the tablet was in stock and what its current price was. The clerk hesitated a moment, then said. "Miss, you walked in at the right time. We just adjusted the price on this tablet, and it is selling for considerably less today—much less than it sold for during the sales."

I asked him to repeat himself, in case I had misunderstood. Dutifully, the young man responded to my request, presenting me with the boxed tablet and keyboard. I handed over my gift card for payment.

The following day, as I was writing in my journal, it became clear to me how good God really is. Here I was, upset over the lost card and lamenting the missed holiday sale. But God had something better in mind—He saw the bigger picture, where I would secure the desired product at a much better price. I am so grateful that His ways are not our ways.

Thank You, Father, for always dealing with us according to Your bigger picture. Amen.

Yvonne Curry Smallwood

The Twelve-Month Move

We are not fighting against human beings but against the wicked
spiritual forces in the heavenly world, the rulers, authorities,
and cosmic powers of this dark age.
—*Ephesians 6:12, GNT*

There was a time—or two or three—in the past year that my husband, Jordan, and I felt like everything was off balance and couldn't get any worse. We had made the decision to sell our home on the east coast of Canada and move to the Nashville area in the United States to fully pursue Christian music ministry. Our prayerful decision had seemed to have the go-ahead from God. But the execution of our decision was unimaginably challenging. Our home buyer turned out to be a seasoned scam artist. My husband's temporary employer withheld funds and disputed his hours worked (we walked away). A self-proclaimed concert promoter took funds for never-before-mentioned expenses for several shows together. Everything was going wrong!

Our security was jeopardized by strife on all sides. Though grateful for our health and physical safety, we watched as our financial world crumbled. What was originally meant to be a two-month stay in Ontario, Canada, at my parents' home (while our house closed) turned into a twelve-month process. A time during which we had to put our house back on the market, still travel for concerts, and temporarily live wherever we were welcome. However, in the chaos of miserably failing plans, we never once felt as if God were telling us we'd made the wrong decision. After our house finally sold, we moved our furniture to a Nashville storage unit. Then, like the first glimmer of hope midst a long, grueling time of disappointment, Jordan's initial paperwork was approved by the government to proceed with his obtaining a green card!

No matter how much the devil tried to discourage us, God brought positive reinforcement at every turn. At times we felt we'd be living out of a suitcase forever. But now we are situated in our new home and looking back on what turned out to be one of our most successful years of ministry. Ephesians 6:12 reminds us that "we are not fighting against human beings but against the wicked spiritual forces in the heavenly world, the rulers, authorities, and cosmic powers of this dark age" (GNT). No one ever said life would be easy, especially in ministry. It's in our difficulty, though, that we are privileged to see God shine. In times of upheaval, we can watch Him bring amazing *possibilities* from the disorder of our *impossibilities*.

Naomi Striemer

Enditnow

"Come to me, all of you who are tired from carrying heavy loads,
and I will give you rest. . . . Learn from me, because I am gentle
and humble in spirit; and you will find rest. . . .
The load I will put on you is light."
—Matthew 11:28–30, GNT

God offers rest to everyone, especially to His daughters who have cause to wonder and perhaps doubt. The familiar words of Matthew 11:28–30 flew off the page of my newest Bible, not verbatim, but in metaphor to personal experience. The pivotal point continues to be that God is love!

Jesus' words call us to be faithful, joyous, and persevering. They call us to minister, pray, and praise even in circumstances that are negative, abusive, and chaotic. Church members are not immune to evil influence. Enditnow and other such outreach programs deserve our support. We have sisters in the faith who are just beginning their journey of finding a way out of their abusive surroundings, or protecting others younger and more innocent, or seeking the reality in their lives that God truly is love.

Let's seek out these sisters, share our journeys, and encourage promise-application to their lives as we've experienced God's faithfulness in ours. A godly woman pastor once explained to me, "Husbands living in community do not hit." When others are not, God is a gentleman. He always allows the evil one to have the first turn; then, in His perfect timing, He gets His dustpan and methodically cleans up the ensuing unpleasantness. I don't know how all the pieces to our life puzzles fit, but God does. Somewhere in the mix, there is a final testimony for good; remember, there are *two* in the yoke of Christ!

The Holy Spirit has special comfort for widows and the fatherless, singles and defenseless people, who put their trust in Him. Jesus is our best friend, benefactor, protector, husband confidant, and companion. He's constant and trustworthy! He cared for His own mother.

Kind sister, dwell in Psalm 37. Take on the honesty of Esther; the faith and courage of Rahab; the joy of Elizabeth; the tenacity of Abigail, Tamar, and Miriam; the loyalty and submission of Ruth to a noble husband; the prayer life of Hannah; the empathy of Naomi; the praise of a forgiven Eve; and the justice-seeking of Deborah. Kneel with Mary at the foot of the cross, and know you are a daughter of the King and a personal friend of Jesus! *Absolutely!*

Darlene Grunke Sanders

Cooking School

"Ask, and you will be given what you ask for."
—Matthew 7:7, TLB

t was exciting! The pastors' wives had been invited to come with their husbands to their own meetings during the regular church workers' gathering in Kisii, Kenya, East Africa. Special sessions had been planned that included the preparation of children's Bible study materials, the learning and singing of songs, and a discussion on birth control (with great laughter when contraceptives were passed around). Now it was time for the cooking session, and chairs were lined up on the school veranda. We discussed how to fix foods that were easily available in local gardens and in the marketplace.

An oven, in the form of a debi (a square tin for storing and transporting cashews), had been made by the fundi (workman) in town. I shared with the women how to use this oven for making Communion bread and baking potatoes and squash. I also said I would demonstrate how to make banana bread in it. We fired up charcoal in the jiko (small stove) before placing the oven on top of it to heat up. I demonstrated the making of banana bread. I mashed bananas, mixed oil and flour, and poured it all into a bread pan. But was the oven hot enough? With no thermostat, I could judge only by feeling the sides of the oven and hope that it had heated enough to bake bread. A helper fanned the coals in the jiko.

As the bread baked, we spoke with the women about other recipes. Eventually the coal fanning slowed down and stopped. A light shower began to fall outside the veranda and close to the oven. By now the once-hot oven began to cool. I touched the sides of the oven without burning my hands. Consternation! My sweet bread would be a flop.

Our discussion ended. It was time to take the banana bread out—cool oven or not. I said a quick prayer, telling the Lord that I really couldn't wait any longer and really needed this bread to be good to prove the oven's worth as an extra way to add to the menus of these women. Evidently He had already realized that, for when I pulled the bread from the oven, a miracle had taken place. The bread was nicely browned and had risen perfectly. God knew my needs. As we savored our samples, I knew that God had baked the bread for me. It was only a small request of Him, but His answer cheered my heart and provided a sweet ending to our cooking school.

Beverly Campbell Pottle

The Three-Point Landing

And then shall appear the sign of the Son of man in heaven:
and then shall all the tribes of the earth mourn, and they shall see
the Son of man coming in the clouds of heaven with power and great
glory. And he shall send his angels with a great sound of a trumpet,
and they shall gather together his elect from the four winds,
from one end of heaven to the other.
— *Matthew 24:30, 31*

Most of my life, as I grew up in the hilly country of Meghalaya, India, I walked wherever I went. Only later in my life did I travel by train or car. These modes of travel create a sense of security because we have the solid ground under our wheels. Traveling by air, however, is completely different because we see no road on which the plane travels. Though I can see the ground and airport from the plane window before the plane takes off, these scenes quickly disappear from view as we rise above the clouds. And I certainly cannot see the final destination.

Life in this world is like a journey with unknowns. In all my studies, plans, and work, I did experience some failure, disappointment, sorrow, and tears. Thank God, these were not fatal but rather lessons for me to learn about trusting God at all times. I thank Him that Jesus came down, even before I was born, to pay a ransom for me that I may have eternal life. Before He went back to heaven, Jesus promised to come back to take us home (see John 14:1–3). He has told us not to fear or be troubled because He will keep His word—even though our "sight" is by faith now.

I have enjoyed all my plane flights because I had faith in the pilot. The most exciting part of a flight for me is when the pilot tells us to fasten our seat belts for the landing. I gladly fasten mine because I know that as soon as the flight ends, I will be meeting my loved ones. Soon I would feel the jolt and hear the sound of the plane's tires touching the ground as the wheels of the landing gear made a perfect three-point landing.

Soon Jesus will return for us and take us on a wonderful flight to our heavenly home. He is the master Pilot of the most fantastic airliner ever seen. It will carry us home to a place whose beauty and perfection we cannot even imagine (1 Corinthians 2:9). Jesus will make a perfect three-point landing because our Pilot *is* "the way, the truth, and the life" (John 14:6). Even now He is our only way of salvation, the truth that protects us from deception, and the giver of eternal life. So let us fasten our seat belt (see Ephesians 6:10) and be of good courage. Bon voyage!

Birdie Poddar

Stinkin' Thinkin'

Commit thy works unto the LORD,
and thy thoughts shall be established.
—*Proverbs 16:3*

D o you love parties? How about birthday parties? My mother, while I was living at home, hosted some great birthday parties for me, complete with a special cake, sometimes topped with fluffy white frosting and decorated with colorful sprinkles. My friends were invited to enjoy the celebration. One time, my birthday cake was swan-shaped, covered with white frosting and coated with white flakes of coconut. Three times I've been given a surprise birthday party. One was the year I turned fifty. My husband and extended family gathered to celebrate; this party was totally unexpected and very meaningful to me. Some parties celebrate an upcoming birth or marriage. Others commemorate a holiday or a retirement. Some parties have no particular reason—it's just fun to get together and make special memories. Don't you agree?

There is another kind of party, though. While not my favorite, it is still one that I've attended—a pity party. You might be asking, "A pity party? What is that?"

A pity party can be created whenever one is feeling lonely, overwhelmed, or uncared for, or when one is nursing hurt feelings. "I have a right to feel this way," we may say. Have you ever attended a pity party for yourself?

That's a stinkin' thinkin' party, isn't it! Quite a lonesome party too, though we often try to throw that "poor me" attitude upon others, hoping to hear that we are correct feeling the way we are, that we have "earned" this pity party, fair and square.

One morning, I traveled down the pity party road and, before long, I was very messed up in my thinking. The "poor me" thoughts became overwhelming and kept me home from church that day. The very next Sabbath morning, negative thoughts again entered my mind. Praise the Lord, I realized those thoughts were a strategy the devil was using on my mind. So I chose instead to focus on Jesus and His love. In a short time my thoughts had left the beginnings of that new pity party and instead began dwelling on uplifting and positive thoughts.

When I choose to think about Jesus and His everlasting love toward me, I am changed into His thinking. I don't want stinkin' thinkin' to be a part of my life. I want His joy and happiness to fill my heart completely. Will you join me?

Valerie Hamel Morikone

Our Heavenly Father Cares

Casting all your care on him;
for he careth for you.
—*1 Peter 5:7*

During these past few weeks I have been reminded afresh of the need for us to exercise care for others in our daily life. In horror we've seen how the bushfires with indescribable devastation have destroyed homes and possessions, animals, and livelihood in South Australia.

Through it all, care shines through as we see firemen tirelessly fighting to save life and emergency centers providing shelter, food, and clothing for stricken families. Something stirs within the human heart as we seek to offer the precious gift of care in support of others.

Turning to a Bible story in 2 Kings 4, beginning at verse 8, we read of the Shunammite woman who invited the prophet Elisha to have meals at her home. She recognized Elisha as a holy man of God with a mission. In consultation with her husband, they built a room on their roof so that Elisha had somewhere to stay whenever he came to the town. As we read on, we learn how the Shunammite woman's son died from sunstroke. We see how Elisha was found by the mother at Mount Carmel, about fifteen miles from Shunem. In haste, they returned to the boy. Here we have not only a caring prophet but a caring heavenly Father who gave power through Elisha to restore life to the lad.

I am grateful I belong to a caring church that has responded to a special need my husband has with his hearing. Murray does specialty cooking and enjoys preparing dishes to share at our church lunches. One member was very appreciative when Murray prepared special food that catered to her dietary needs.

Often gestures of caring and sharing seem small, but they can bring so much joy to others. There are so many times we have been recipients of the care and kindness of others. True caring comes from a loving heart, and this example Jesus left for us to follow.

We can find much comfort as we reflect on today's text. The New Living Translation words 1 Peter 5:7 this way: "Give all your worries and cares to God, for he cares about you." This promise, along with many others, assures us that God cares about everything in our lives.

Until He returns, may we also show care for one another as we share life's journey.

Joan D. L. Jaensch

Wrestling With the People

For we do not wrestle against flesh and blood, but against
principalities, against powers, against the rulers of the darkness of
this age, against spiritual hosts of wickedness in the heavenly places.
—*Ephesians 6:12, NKJV*

There are times when I forget who the enemy is. I sometimes think it's the person who hurts me or creates an obstacle to where I want or think I should be. I get angry and want to fight. But when I remember that they are not the enemy, it gives me a different perspective. I can then recognize how the enemy is attempting to work in that person's life to keep them from living out what God has for them. Not just has for them in the way of work or ministry but has for them in terms of relationships, freedom, peace, and joy. And when I'm clear on who the real enemy is, I can better fight *for* them in prayer.

It's been easy for me to remember who the enemy is when fighting for my boys. I have always seen my role as a mom as fighting a spiritual battle for my sons. I think that's easier because they start out as babies, and we care for and protect them. But other people are harder because they're adults.

Our husbands are supposed to be the protectors and providers. In every story we've heard or read, the man is the warrior who fights for, and rescues, the woman. I think this applies to others too—whether they're friends, colleagues, or people we barely know. We don't see them as people for whose hearts we're supposed to be fighting. Yet I believe God calls us to fight. To be warriors. I love a scene in one of *The Lord of the Rings* movies (I can't tell you which because I haven't watched them—I just know this one scene). The enemy, Lord of the Nazgûl, says that no man can destroy him. He believes he is immortal. The warrior before him says, "I, sir, am no man," and then takes off her helmet to let her hair down, revealing she is a woman, Eowyn. Then she destroys him. When I saw this clip, something stirred inside my heart. I, too, want to be a warrior who fights the enemy.

I believe God calls us to fight for others. And maybe He chose us specifically for our particular husbands, friends, coworkers, and family members just because we're the ones who wouldn't give up or walk away. And because He knows we have the heart of a warrior inside of us. We just need to rise up and fight as only we can—through prayer and kindness.

Tamyra (Tami) Horst

Never Good Enough

Yet I will rejoice in the LORD,
I will be joyful in God my Savior.
—*Habakkuk 3:18, NIV*

My husband told me a story of a man who received a reprimand for not returning his tithe. Said a member to the offender, "Do you realize that you are a robber? That you have robbed the omnipotent God, your Savior?" Arrogantly and unapologetically, he retorted. "Yes! I know I have robbed God, but I gave a good reason." The response of the offender totally disarmed the member. As unbelievable as his response is, we sometimes fall into similar straits and, provided we can submit a rational explanation, consider ourselves justified.

Recently I visited a church for prayer meeting. I was disappointed to find the church in darkness with not a sound to indicate activity. I checked my watch to see whether I was too early or too late, but I was neither. As I was about to leave, another member arrived and pointed to a small opened door at the side; church was actually in session. When I inquired about the desolate appearance, he explained, "The attendance has been quite sparse and, with the rising cost of electricity, we no longer open the main doors, turn on the porch lights, or stream music." How was I to have known? To think that I almost missed the spiritual rejuvenation I craved because of the financial difficulties of the church.

This reminds me of Christ's indignation when the fig tree "expressed" prosperity but yielded barrenness. I am sure that there is a plausible explanation for full foliage and no fruit, but that would not suffice the hunger pangs of the expectant observer.

Can the same be said of us? Do others come to us expecting inspiration and a reason to hope, yet leave disappointed because "we had a good reason"? Is there ever a good enough reason *not* to be reflectors of God's love and faithfulness in our lives? Never! So what is your valid reason? You can't make ends meet? Parenting alone? Battling a chronic illness? Living in a strange land? Are you overworked? Easily misunderstood? Do you have a questionable past? There is never a good excuse for a failed testimony.

We are reminded to let our lives so shine before men that they may see God's good work and come to glorify our Father which is in heaven. Make the promise today to shine and, through Christ's strength, banish all excuses for not doing so, as they are never good enough.

Patrice E. Williams-Gordon

June 3

How the Mighty Have Fallen

Therefore let him who thinks he stands
take heed lest he fall.
—1 Corinthians 10:12, NKJV

Several years ago, I worked in a small community north of Ocala. The twenty-two-mile trip each way didn't seem long because I listened to good music and an audio Bible. On most mornings I watched a spectacular sunrise. The road took me through land heavy with large oak trees. I admired their giant trunks and the stunning canopies formed from their wide, spreading branches. At one place along the road, at least forty giant oaks sat on approximately three acres of land. I marveled at their age and noble bearing. No telling how long they had occupied that land; it seemed that nothing could ever move them or hurt them.

In late October one year, the threat of an oncoming hurricane closed schools for a couple days. After the storm passed, I drove slowly because of the debris littering the roads. I saw, in amazement, the devastation the storm had caused. Numerous trees and branches were scattered across roads and farm fences. The power of the destruction was visible everywhere.

I looked for my favorite trees to see how they had fared, but I didn't see them. Assuming I had passed them, I watched carefully when returning from work. And then I saw them—those once magnificent giants were lying on the ground. Shocked at seeing this unlikely scene, I wondered how these great giants could have been broken down so easily. Upon closer observation, I noticed that most of the trees were black on the inside, many being riddled with holes. From the outside they appeared strong and magnificent, but on the inside they were rotten. So when the storm came, it took them down with ease.

While mourning the fallen giants, I began thinking of people. Most of the time, we, just like the trees, look great on the outside—nicely clothed, working in the church, putting out our best for others to see. But what are we like on the inside? Do we have rotten spots in us that will grow even larger if they are not cut out soon? Are we spiritually strong enough to withstand any storm of life that might threaten us? Will we be resilient when Satan sends temptation? Only with God as our gardener can we be assured that we will be strong enough to survive the storms of life.

Zlata Sabo

Homeless or Going Home?

"In My Father's house are many mansions. . . . I go to prepare a place
for you. . . . I will come again and receive you to Myself."
—John 14:2, 3, NKJV

For many years we have lived across the river and through the woods in our peaceful mountain home. Because of our surroundings, we always try to keep the grass cleared away from our buildings in case a fire should start in the area, especially after several years of drought.

Then the day came when we heard of a forest fire not many miles away. As long as the winds blew in the right direction, we would not be in danger, so we didn't worry. We kept busy with our usual activities, which meant working in the garden for my husband, while I was also trying to preserve some fruit and vegetables for our winter use.

A phone call, followed by a visit from a sheriff, informed us we needed to evacuate. What were the most important things to take in case we had nothing to come back to? A phone call from our daughter helped us decide. Soon we were packed and traveling to the town a half hour away. We had made this trip many times before, but we always knew where we were going and when we would be coming back. What a strange feeling it was to know we were temporarily homeless! At church, we often helped the local homeless people who live in tents or camp in their cars. Now we were in the same situation.

Friends offered us a room to stay in, and each day we went to the Red Cross shelter for meals, updates about the fire, and visits with neighbors who were also evacuated. At times, the smoke-filled air made breathing difficult. While driving to the shelter for supper on the ninth day, we received a phone call letting us know that the road to our neighborhood area was open. We could go home! As we drove over the familiar road the next morning, it was raining. Showers of blessing because this was the first rain we'd had in four months. All was well at home, and our outdoor cats, which we hadn't been able to take with us, greeted us happily.

Soon we will be leaving this home again. It won't be so difficult to evacuate— this time we will be going to a much better place, to mansions that our heavenly Father has prepared for us. And He is coming to take us there! My prayer is that we will be ready for this great homecoming, along with our family, neighbors, and friends.

Betty J. Adams

June 5

Sowing Seeds

"God anointed Jesus of Nazareth . . . ,
who went about doing good."
—Acts 10:38, NKJV

My husband and I were just getting up to leave after a large memorial service at our local church. We had been impressed by many stories during the service telling how the recently deceased ninety-two-year-old man had shown his great love for people. We attempted to leave our pew so that we could view the many family pictures on display at the front of the church. We noted, however, that both ends of our row were blocked by groups of chatting folks. So we decided to sit and wait until the crowd diminished.

We suddenly became aware of a friendly lady smiling at us from the row of previously empty seats directly in front of us.

"Hello," she said, extending her hand as she introduced herself. Soon we were chatting away like old friends. She had noticed our "trapped" condition and made it a point to get acquainted. That was kind of her.

During our chat, I recalled an experience some thirty years earlier when we had first moved to Oregon. We had been impressed to invite this (now-deceased) man and his wife to lunch in our new home. Over lunch we shared with them the type of "home mission" work in which we were involved. Later during the visit, the man's wife came into the kitchen. She emptied the coins from her purse onto the kitchen table and said, "This is for your mission work." That really touched my heart. That was our first of many happy experiences with this couple.

Through the years, we found that mission work always has needs. When one asks a missionary what the greatest need is in a given field of work, the usual reply is, "We need everything!" Yet doing mission work doesn't have to cost a lot of money. Reaching out to others nearby is a form of mission work. For example, we love to welcome new people to our area. Recently I took a rose lei to a new neighbor lady. She was absolutely delighted and said, "I never had a lei before!" Immediately she put it around her neck. We can make others happy in very simple ways. Ellen White made this simple statement: "Every good deed is as a seed sown."*

After all, Jesus Himself "went about doing good" (Acts 10:38, NKJV).

Frieda Tanner

---

* Ellen G. White, *Testimonies for the Church*, Vol. 5 (Mountain View, CA: Pacific Press®, 1885), 18.

Hope From a Black-Eyed Susan

*Because Your lovingkindness is better than life,
my lips shall praise You. Thus I will bless You while I live.
—Psalm 63:3, 4, NKJV*

Countless black-eyed Susans grow in the gardens surrounding my home. This prolific plant blooms continuously from mid-July until after the first autumn frost. Even then the plant keeps on giving. Tiny offspring surround its roots. Dying blossoms leave seed-filled pods. Dozens of goldfinches perch on the stems and enjoy the tiny seeds.

Each spring, I have the fun of digging up and transplanting plants to new spots. In just two years, these perennials will brighten up my world. Even barren soil does not deter a black-eyed Susan from cheering the landscape.

This plant encourages me in my Christian walk.

There are times when the future seems bleak, but time spent in the Word strengthens and cheers me. As I read God's promises never to forsake me, I was reminded of what my salvation cost my Savior. As I appreciate the wisdom of Proverbs, collect embraces from Psalms, and gain life skills from authors like James and Peter, I am awed. God always has just the right words for me—almost like a smile of encouragement.

In times of loss and personal despair, I turn to Psalm 23:1 and read, "The LORD is my shepherd; I shall not want."

When I feel discouraged, I turn to Psalm 27:1, "The LORD is my light and my salvation; whom shall I fear?" When I need to be reminded of God's plans for me, I read Psalm 46:4, where the verse says, "There is a river, the streams whereof shall make glad the city of God." My heart thrills to this mental picture of heaven. Yes, God will be there in person.

It is good to remind ourselves of James's advice: "The wisdom that is from above is first pure, then peaceable, gentle, willing to yield, full of mercy and good fruits" (James 3:17, NKJV). When I look at the smiling face of a black-eyed Susan, I am reminded of how God "smiles" at me through His Word, reminding me to have humility and bear good fruit.

I look for the day when I will hear, "Come. Inherit the kingdom I have prepared for you" (See Matthew 25:34). In the meantime, I plan to spread cheer like a black-eyed Susan. Even like a sunflower.

Patricia Cove

What Do You See?

That person is like a tree planted by streams of water,
which yields its fruit in season and whose leaf does not wither—
whatever they do prospers.
—Psalm 1:3, NIV

A recent move to a lovely southern town found my husband and me searching for a park to sit in to enjoy a quiet and peaceful place. We found it. It's so small that it has only five parking spaces, but it's easily accessible along the street by footpaths.

We set up our folding camp chairs and enjoyed the view. Across the small lake we spied a large white manse complete with the Tara-type pillars depicted in the film *Gone With the Wind*. *Another era's construction*, I thought. "I must see this place," I cajoled my husband. "Let's drive around the lake to the other side to see it." As we sat resting for a while, I imagined a circular stairway, a beckoning music room, and all the touches of architecture such a home might possess.

After our resting time, we drove to the site. As we approached, I felt shaken as I saw knee-deep grass and "For Sale" signs all over the grounds. Why so many signs? The door of the large attached garage was caved in, as if a Humvee may have crashed into it. The once obviously gracious home now reeked of abandonment. The need for paint and repair of shutters almost shouted, "Please, fix me!" How could this have happened? My writer's mind went into imagination mode, and I visualized what unsavory scenes might have resulted in this fine home being left to rot with no loveliness left to be found.

As I thought about this old home, I kept lamenting its appearance . . . before I got to thinking, *It's just like me. That's what I'd be like if Jesus hadn't rescued me from myself.* Even so, I have no worthiness of my own. Scripture tells us, "As it is written: 'There is no one righteous, not even one' " (Romans 3:10, NIV).

Only the Lord Jesus is of worth. He is the One I want to keep my eyes upon, to emulate Him, to become like Him. Is it too much to hope? Of course not! Will you join me in being His in a new and better way as we drop off our old curled leaves and ask Him to water new shoots in our hearts? He wants us to reflect Him, to be like the blessed, whose hope is not in themselves. He wants us to bid others, "Come, see beautiful Jesus!"

Betty Kossick

Learned Lessons

It is of the LORD's mercies that we are not consumed,
because his compassions fail not.
—*Lamentations 3:22*

My older sister, a college student, and I were driving from Kingston to Westmoreland for the weekend when, while descending the steep Spur Tree Hill, the car brakes failed. We went into the lane of oncoming traffic, making a right turn onto a dirt road before crashing into a cubed concrete structure. We were all in shock. Though none of us was seriously injured, thank the Lord, we were taken and treated at a Kingston hospital, while a wrecker pulled the car to a mechanic. Yet I cannot underestimate the spiritual lessons I learned from this accident, which directed me to look inward, and then upward from whence my help comes. Here are four lessons.

First, I learned that even in this day and age, God's mercies and goodness fail not. To the extent of which the front end of my car was damaged due to the impact exerted from the crash, it was definitely because of God's mercies that my feet had not been pinned or that the steering wheel had not pierced my chest. All three of us exited the car without any major injuries.

Second, we saw the protection of the Holy Spirit at the location of the accident, for help was accessible and immediate, with a wrecking truck company only two blocks away. The owner of the property on which I crashed volunteered to take us back to Kingston and waited until we could be seen at the hospital. She explained that though she should have left her property earlier, she had lingered for no special reason. She now saw the leading of the Holy Spirit.

Third, we experienced a number of people willing to go the extra mile for us. I will be forever grateful to God for Dr. Carmelita Jones, Pastor K. C. and Mrs. Henry, Dr. Stephanie McFarlane, and my neighbor, Miss Juliet Patterson. They each extended themselves without reservation in my time of great need, which involved inconveniences for them.

Finally, it pays to serve the Lord. I experienced God's love, guidance, leadership, protection, and care in ways I could never have imagined. I know you have experienced His watchful care during lessons in your life as well.

God is good!

Theresa M. McDonald

God Showed Me the Truth

To the law and to the testimony: if they speak not according to this
word, it is because there is no light in them.
—*Isaiah 8:20*

Among the views presented by the evangelist was that Saturday is the Sabbath, the worship day that the Bible instructs us to keep holy. My sisters decided to continue attending the man's meetings in order to straighten him out, and I went with them. Instead, I found a new faith that filled me with joy. Though summer holidays were over and it was time for me to return to my own home, my newfound joy kept me with my sisters. Finally Mother sent for me. Arriving home, I told her I wanted to go to a similar church in Campbell's Castle. She said, "No!" The following Sabbath, I told her again that I wanted to go to church.

"No, child, I want you to go to the market with Mrs. Edmund." When I politely declined, Mother became infuriated. The next time I dressed for church, my mother tore off my dress. The following Sabbath, she took all my dresses and dipped them in a tub of water. After that, I decided to get dressed behind locked doors. Since Mother couldn't get to me, she told my brother, working in the garden, not to let me pass. When he saw me coming, he jumped into the street with his machete held high. Standing in front of me, he declared: "Either I die here or you, but you are not going to Campbell's Castle church today."

I turned back. To go home? No! I remembered a path through our neighbor's property that led to the main road that would lead to the church. My heart sang as I raced along the dewy path: "Today is the Sabbath, and I'm going to church." I kept singing until I reached the church. During this time I no longer attended my mother's church. Her minister asked to meet me at the rectory. I went. After talking with me, he said, "Let's pray." I thought he would read from the prayer book, but he just prayed. His last sentence was, "Lord, show Sylvia the truth."

My sister got a teaching job in another place, and she asked Mother to send me to be with her. From there I attended college in Jamaica, graduating from the teacher's education program.

While I was teaching at a Christian university in Alabama, my sister wrote to tell me that Mother had been baptized at the same church she'd worked so hard to prevent me from attending. To God be the glory! We must never give up on the workings of the Holy Spirit.

Sylvia Wright Barnes

Two Angels

For he will command his angels concerning you
to guard you in all your ways.
—*Psalm 91:11, NIV*

A few years ago, our family was invited to attend the birthday party of a five-year-old at a hot pools complex. At the time, my children were seven, five, and two years of age.

There were a lot of little children to watch, so I opted not to swim. Instead, I stood and supervised all the preschool children who were playing in the children's pool.

As a mother soon learns, little children can disappear fast. Very fast. I stood watching all the children who seemed to be happy as they played in the water.

Then something made me turn and look over toward the deep plunge pools. Those are the pools that adult swimmers drop into when exiting the huge tube waterslides.

That's when I saw my two-year-old son. He had somehow gotten out of the children's pool and was standing next to one of the adult plunge pools.

Then he jumped into the deep pool! I couldn't believe it!

I felt as if I could move only in slow motion. I started running and yelling, "Pull the baby out of the pool!" But the only people I could see were two ladies on the other side of the pool, standing and talking. Because they were in the pool, they couldn't see my little son. All they could see was a crazy lady running toward them and screaming! There was no one else around to help.

It felt as if it took me forever to reach the plunge pools. As I got closer, I could see my little boy's big eyes looking up through the deep water.

Just then, two men appeared out of nowhere. One of them reached into the pool and pulled out my child. I grabbed him, crying out, "He's mine!" I held him close. When I turned around to say Thank you to the two rescuers behind me, they were gone. All I can tell you about them was that they were two males with dark hair. They hadn't said a word to me. They had quickly appeared from nowhere to save my boy and then disappeared just as quickly.

To this day, I believe with all my heart that God sent two angels to answer my prayer.

Have you thanked God today for His protective angels around your family?

Donna Engu

My Meeting With God

"Please come and put your hands on her
so that she will be healed and live."
—Mark 5:23, NIV

At the age of thirty-five, I was suffering from depression and felt as if life had no meaning. Awakening one morning, I could see out of my right eye only. A month later, a specialist diagnosed me with retinal detachment and said I needed immediate surgery. My older brother, whose opinion I greatly respected, strongly advised me to go to a prestigious hospital in Sofia. While going through further medical examination, medical personnel criticized me for waiting too long to seek help. Discouraged, I intuitively started praying to God for His intercession. *Please bless the hands of the doctor who will perform my operation*, I prayed. During this period of waiting, I became increasingly convicted that God had something to show me that I could see only in darkness. *Lord, I believe You know exactly what You are doing and that You allowed this crisis in preparation for something important in my life.*

Surgery was scheduled for Monday, July 4. The previous Friday, I decided to undergo one more medical exam at another hospital. There, a doctor carefully examined me. Then she said, "You will choose whose hands will carry out the operation. I can guarantee you perfect vision. Here in this hospital, however, the conditions are not up to the same quality as at the other hospital. However, what really matters are the hands that will perform the operation." The care she had shown during the examination impressed me, but her words swayed my decision. She had repeated, almost word for word, the prayer I had prayed when alone with God about the hands of the surgeon. Immediately I transferred to the second hospital. The day after the surgery, when the blindfold was removed, I could see! Six months later, I was reading and working again.

Had my brother not been late to be with me—before I'd signed out of the first hospital and into the second—he would have prevented me from making that choice. Yet I was calm about my decision on surgery day and filled with assurance that God was taking care of me.

Soon after, wanting now to know much more about God, I accepted a friend's invitation to study the Bible. God had prepared me through crisis to desire more of His truth in my life. The following year, with much gratitude, I joined my church, and I now live with purpose and confidence instead of with depression and meaninglessness. I wish you this same peace and joy.

Anelia Panova

Cricket Counselor

And be not conformed to this world: but be ye transformed by the renewing of your mind, that ye may prove what is that good, and acceptable, and perfect, will of God. For I say, through the grace given unto me, to every man [and woman] that is among you, not to think of himself [or herself] more highly than he [or she] ought to think; but to think soberly, according as God hath dealt to every man [and woman] the measure of faith.
—Romans 12:2, 3

As I pulled my rake and let dirt fall into a rut, a cricket scurried out of the soil and then out of sight. *Does he think this is all about him?* I wondered.

In the past three hours, I'd tilled our garden spot, going north and south. Then, east and west. Then, I raked it in preparation for planting. This cricket's life had been turned upside down, stirred around, and covered up. He probably was just getting his wits about him from one onslaught when another hit. Whatever he did, trials kept coming at him. If a cricket brain could ponder the issues of life, he might feel like someone was out to get him.

From my perspective, the cricket had never entered my mind until I saw him. He just happened to be where I was accomplishing a good and worthwhile task. The soil stirring wasn't about the cricket. But I kept thinking about human life. On occasion, someone has made nasty remarks or done something obnoxious. Sometimes I've been tempted to focus on the disrespect shown me and the trials brought my way.

The cricket kept scurrying into my thoughts. If I saw the world as God sees it, perhaps when someone hurt me, that person may not have even thought about me. They may have just been busily doing the good and worthwhile task at hand. Perhaps their minds were somewhere else totally. *It's not about me*, I realized.

Even if a person did intend some slight or meanness, it's still likely not about me. If they're being unkind, it's really about them, about their heart. Good or bad, people demonstrate their own characters by the words they say and the actions they take.

The stirring is not about me. The world is bigger than me. "So," I told myself, "allow yourself to be transformed—renew your thoughts. Quit thinking about yourself. Look at your world through God's eyes."

Helen Heavirland

June 13

God Plans for Our Children

"For I know the plans I have for you," declares the LORD,
"plans to prosper you and not to harm you,
plans to give you hope and a future."
—*Jeremiah 29:11, NIV*

It was a warm summer day that my husband and I decided to spend at the lake with our two small boys, other family members, and friends. We had just bought a Jet Ski and wanted to try it out. Toward evening, I attached one end of the safety lanyard near the ski's starter and would soon attach the other to my wrist—as soon as I'd placed my three-year-old son on the front of the seat, before settling in behind him. But before I could settle in and attach the lanyard to my wrist, my son grasped the handlebars and, unknowingly, pulled back the throttle. The Jet Ski flew across the lake! Frantically I tried to swim after him, while my husband and a friend jumped on the remaining Jet Skis to pursue him. I watched helplessly as my little boy clung tightly to the handles, speeding away at full throttle. I watched my husband's and friend's Jet Skis fall further and further behind. My child, now barely visible, suddenly turned (at a speed nearing fifty miles per hour) toward the steeply angled, tree-, stump-, and boulder-lined shore.

As I saw the danger that lay ahead, I knew that my boy's only hope lay in the hands of our dear Savior. My sister, friend, and I pled for my son's life. My own prayer came from the heart of an inconsolable mother who knew it was her mistake that put her child's life in jeopardy. Soon a sense of calm came over me as I gradually began to let go and "let God."

Then, between a large boulder and tree stump that was jutting up out of the water (the distance between them being only a few inches wider than the Jet Ski itself), the vehicle carrying my son glided right between them and up the steep embankment. There it stopped, teetering from the vertical incline. My little boy somehow managed to stay on the ski until his father and our friend reached him and brought him down to safety, unscathed!

Throughout the following twenty-two years, my son's journey has taken different turns, sometimes along a good path and sometimes deviating down a wrong path. But God continues to hear my prayers for both of my children, and He continues to use the Jet Ski experience from so many years ago to comfort and reassure me that He has a plan for their lives. I encourage each of you to pray continually for your children. Never give up, and know that God never will either.

Terri Lutz

Be Grateful

Rejoice always, pray continually, give thanks in all circumstances;
for this is God's will for you in Christ Jesus.
—*1 Thessalonians 5:16–18, NIV*

I was tuned into a Christian television channel the other day, when I saw a minister who was speaking about "what women should know about men." I became very interested and listened closely. He asked, "Why do men ignore what their wives are saying and give other women second looks?" The preacher went on to say, "If their wives are always complaining, husbands 'switch off' and find other interests."

I'm afraid that some women do have the habit of complaining about everything. Maybe they don't realize how detrimental that is to their relationships. Sometimes we complain about the weather. It's too hot, too cold, too windy, or raining too much. We complain that we don't know what to wear, though our closets may be full. We forget about the person who has nothing to wear but rags or may not even own a pair of shoes.

If we are unemployed, we complain that we have no work. If we have a job, we complain about our salary being too low and that we wish we could stay home instead of having to go to work each day. We may complain that the price of groceries is too expensive. Again, we forget about the millions of people in this world who are starving, many scratching through dirty bins for a morsel of something to eat. Some women complain that they don't have all they would like in their homes—perhaps even the latest technological device. Yet many people have no home and must find shelter at night under a bridge someplace. What are we doing to help them? And Jesus did say that "you will always have the poor among you" (John 12:8, NIV). There will always be people who are worse off than we are.

Therefore, if we need anything, instead of complaining, let us pray about it. Let us go into our room, close the door, and pray to our heavenly Father who, though unseen, still sees us. He will hear us, for our Father knows what we need before we ask Him (see Matthew 6:6, 8).

May we be able to relate to Paul, who said, "I have learned to be content whatever the circumstances" (Philippians 4:11, NIV). Instead of complaining, let us count our blessings and thank our Creator for what we have. He knows what's best for us, so why should we complain?

Priscilla E. Adonis

Perceptions

Therefore, as God's chosen people, holy and dearly loved, clothe
yourselves with compassion, kindness, humility, gentleness and
patience. . . . And over all these virtues put on love.
—*Colossians 3:12–14, NIV*

My name is Hernando," he said softly as he leaned over my bed in the
semidarkness of the hospital room. "I will be your nursing assistant for
the night." *Well, let's see what the night will bring*, I thought. It didn't
take long for my roommate and me to find out.

Earlier, on the previous shift, our aide, Faye, had been in the bathroom
attempting to clean up my roomie after another incontinence "accident." A
strong, pungent odor permeated the whole room. Faye was unsuccessful at
keeping the disgust out of her voice.

"Stand still—don't move! Don't step there, I told you! And for heaven's sake,
leave that door open!" Mary remained silent. Since the enzymes in her digestive
system were not working properly, there was nothing she could do. "You can go
back to bed now," she was curtly told.

Now Hernando was cleaning her up once again. "I was having the nicest
dream," Mary said hesitantly. "I dreamed I was eating a huge bowl of ice cream,
and it tasted so good." She was obviously chatting to cover her embarrassment.
In his soft Hispanic lilt, Hernando replied that she'd had a "good dream."

"But I couldn't decide what to drink with it—Diet Coke or 7-Up." Hernando
gently asked what flavor of ice cream she'd been eating. "Chocolate chip," she
said, more relaxed now.

"Then I would choose 7-Up—not so sweet." A pause. "There, we're done. Is
there anything I can get for you?" He carefully guided her to her bed, smoothed
her sheets, and straightened her pillows. "Sleep well." His tread was soft as he
turned off the light.

The contrast between the two caregivers was obvious. Both had the same
opportunity, yet they were two minds with opposite sympathies. Two hearts with
differing degrees of compassion. Two opposite ways to touch—or wound—a
heart. The apostle John knew that difference when he pleaded, "Dear children,
let us not love with words or speech but with actions and in truth" (1 John 3:18,
NIV). *Lord, help me find someone today who needs to feel Your love through my
tender, gentle touch.*

Kathleen Freeman

Oh, Dear, What to Wear!

And he said, "These are they who have come out of the great
tribulation; they have washed their robes
and made them white in the blood of the Lamb."
—*Revelation 7:14, NIV*

Ever since Adam and Eve sinned, women have been accused of saying they have nothing to wear, but the fact is that Adam apparently also said he had nothing to wear. Whether or not women have more problems finding something to wear than do men, I know that I have a full closet but sometimes feel like I don't have the appropriate things for a particular occasion.

Clothes were an important topic even in Bible times. Clothing was very expensive and, of course, had to be handmade, a very labor-intensive project. Most clothing was made of wool, but some also of linen, animal skins, and possibly even some silk. And if you were rich enough, you might even have gold thread woven into the fabric.

Several years ago, I noticed how often clothing was mentioned in the Bible, so I decided that as I read through my Bible for the year, I would note any mention of clothing of any type. I found 359 references—and I am sure I missed some. There are literal passages, such as the detailed instructions as to how the priest's clothing was to be made and worn, symbolic references in which "God becomes like clothing to me" (Job 30:18, NIV), and spiritual clothing (2 Corinthians 5:1–5). Clothing was an important part of the spoils of war (Judges 5:30). It was as important as gold and silver for theft, and the sign of total despair was for one to tear his or her clothing (Josuha 7).

It is interesting that every time Joseph had a major change in his life story, he changed his clothes—or they were changed for him. Clothing also figures importantly in the Esther story.

Jesus began His life wrapped in swaddling clothes, people threw clothing on the ground in front of Him at the triumphal entry (Matthew 21:8), and He ended His life naked on the cross, while the soldiers gambled for his one-piece robe. He told stories such as the wedding guest who didn't have a garment (Matthew 22:11, 12) and rebuked the Pharisees for loving long fringes on their garments. He also cautioned us not to worry about what we are going to wear (Matthew 6:28–30). White cloth was difficult to get—the bleaching process was long and expensive—so when the Bible mentions Christ robed in white and Revelation tells us we will receive a white robe (Revelation 6:11), it is significant. Then, we will really be properly dressed for the occasion.

Ardis Dick Stenbakken

175

God Made Fathers

Our Father which art in heaven, Hallowed be thy name.
—*Matthew 6:9*

Advertisements in the shops remind us months in advance of holidays and events to come. Among these is Father's Day, which is celebrated in Australia on the first Sunday each September. Fathers have played a significant role through the ages since Creation. God designed the role of father to guide the welfare of the family unit.

In Genesis I read about the family life of Abraham. He was father of a number of children, Isaac being the promised child. Abraham was a mighty leader and protector of his large household. He made mistakes but allowed God to direct Him. He is an example for us today. "And he believed in the LORD; and he counted it to him for righteousness" (Genesis 15:6).

Another father was Job. Job 1:1–5 states he was blameless and upright and loved God. He nurtured the spiritual needs of his ten children. At set times, Job would ask his children to recommit themselves to God and then sacrifice a lamb for each of them, asking forgiveness of sin. Job had some trying times, but the Lord blessed him, and he lived a purposeful life.

Noah, the father of Shem, Ham, and Japheth, "was a just man and perfect in his generations, and Noah walked with God" (Genesis 6:9). His sons must have trusted in God to obey their father and work with him to build the ark, despite the ridicule thrown at them. When the great door of the ark shut, only Noah and his family were spared.

Joseph was a godly man and a father to Jesus while on this earth. It must have been a very special time working in the carpenter's shop together. I can't help but think how wonderful it will be when Joseph sees Jesus again.

I have been blessed to have a loving and godly father named Norm, who is still enjoying life at ninety-six. The time I've had opportunity to be with him will always be very precious. How thankful I am for all he has done for me, and I praise God!

Sadly, many find it hard to rejoice over the word *father*. Many undesirable situations affect relationships, but Jesus knows and cares. "He is like a father to us, tender and sympathetic to those who reverence him" (Psalm 103:13, TLB). That makes us all children of the heavenly Father and brothers and sisters to one another.

It will be such a happy "Father's Day" when we all see our heavenly Father.

Lyn Welk-Sandy

The God of Differences

A person's body is one thing, but it has many parts.
Though there are many parts to a body,
all those parts make only one body. Christ is like that also.
—1 Corinthians 12:12, NCV

Fifteen years ago, I was diagnosed with the autoimmune disease rheumatoid arthritis (RA). I continually experience mild to severe aches, pains, spasms, joint problems, and other distressing issues that make life a day-to-day roller coaster ride. There is no known cure for RA, but powerful medicines can help control or ease the resulting problems.

A few weeks ago, I joined a worldwide Facebook group for people with RA and other autoimmune diseases. Most members don't know each other, yet have found camaraderie with other members. I too have experienced a bond with these ladies (and a few men) who share about their diseases, complications, and challenges—something that isn't often experienced among family or friends who don't live with an autoimmune disease. But a member having a painful flare-up, new tests scheduled, or questions about symptoms experienced can connect with the online group. Then different members respond by asking for specifics or giving vital information; offering suggestions; posting funny tidbits to lift the somber moods; sharing encouragement, birthday, and get well greetings; or simply wishing members a great "pain-free" day (though not really possible with chronic diseases). Many request prayer for relief from suffering, and members readily respond. Reading these responses is heartwarming for me.

I've learned to appreciate each member who makes the medical issues we suffer more bearable by their thoughtful comments, helpful information, and professional medical experience. Member personalities shine through these posts, and I eagerly count on specific members for exactly what I, or other members, need to hear. I thank God for every one!

As I contemplate my closeness to others whom I don't know and will probably never meet, it affirms for me that we each have gifts and a special purpose tailor-made just for us. God will work through us in different ways and in any circumstance. God will use our unique gifts to reach persons who are sick, grieving, sad, depressed, confused, or ready to give up on life. Our actions matter greatly to others, but they matter most to God. Are you willing to allow God to work through you today?

Iris L. Kitching

God Intervened

If you say, "The LORD is my refuge,"
and you make the Most High your dwelling,
no harm will overtake you, no disaster will come near your tent.
For he will command his angels concerning you
to guard you in all your ways.
—*Psalm 91:9–11, NIV*

Lately I had had difficulty breathing. Though I tried to ignore it, I finally made an appointment with an ENT doctor. After examining me, he said, "Your nasal passage is very narrow and curves. I recommend surgery." So he set up an appointment for surgery. As the date approached, I got more scared, despite friends telling me this was only a minor surgery. I felt peace as family, friends, and my pastor were praying for me, putting everything into God's hands.

My husband drove me to the hospital to be admitted for final tests the day before the surgery, to be followed by five days of hospitalization. After six hours of tests and a procedure explanation by the anesthesiologist, I met with the four doctors who would perform the surgery the following morning. The head doctor, the ENT specialist who had recommended surgery, looked at me with a smile. He asked, "Why do you want to have this surgery?" I was puzzled by his question. Then he added, "It really isn't necessary." I was speechless!

"You mean I can still back out?" I asked. He nodded, as my true feelings came out in a loud "Hallelujah!" The doctors smiled. One explained that I might be able to manage my problem with some type of nasal spray depending on the outcome of one more test, an allergy test.

We went home praising God for His intervention in that surgery, though I called it a miracle. *Thank You, Jesus, for answering our prayers.* I needed to make some phone calls to inform several friends who had promised to visit me in the hospital after my surgery. One said, "Do not be afraid, Loida. God is with you, and we are praying for you. Everything will be OK." I finally had to interrupt her to tell her my good news. Now my friend was speechless!

In church the next weekend, the members were surprised to see me smiling. "You healed very quickly!" I told them that the God we serve had resolved the issue of surgery for me. This experience really strengthened my faith.

Friend, my God is your God too! We can lay all of our burdens on Him. For He has promised that He will carry them for us.

Loida Gulaja Lehmann

The Words of My Mouth

A word fitly spoken is like apples of gold in pictures of silver.
—Proverbs 25:11

My phone rang yesterday. It was a coworker asking me to rewrite a thank-you note for an interview. As soon as I hung up, I received an e-mail asking me to peruse a rough draft and make any appropriate changes before the e-mail was sent. This afternoon, I will attend a meeting with my administration to address concerns expressed by my coworkers. Although it is not in my job description, I am frequently asked to assist when the situation calls for a calming, well-spoken presence.

I wish I could say that I always apply these same skills in my private life, but that is not the case. When I get home, I am tired of being understanding and patient, and those closest to me often suffer from my rash words. I have spoken without thinking, hurting those I love with my words or with the harshness of my tone. Often, I wish I could take back what I have said, but the damage has already been done.

Not long ago, I hurt a dear friend, and to my shame, I was not aware of how my comments had been received. He had shared two very painful experiences: one, the loss of a parent, and the other, the betrayal of a close friend. My response, instead of comforting him, only caused additional pain.

This experience reminds me of Job. Job was suffering physically, mentally, and emotionally. His friends came to visit, surely with the intention of offering comfort and hope. They sat with him, saying nothing for seven days because they realized the depth of his pain and suffering. Yet when they finally spoke, their words did nothing to uplift him. Their words were condemning, only causing Job further pain.

I wonder, how often are my words like those of Job's "good friends"? Are my words healing like an ointment, or are they cutting like the thrust of a sword?

When I have to give an account of my words, as Matthew 12:36 states, will I tremble in fear, or will I stand confident that my words were gracious, like a honeycomb, bringing sweetness to the soul and health to the body? When that day comes, I pray that, as my friend did for me, God will forgive me for the words of my mouth.

Tamara Marquez de Smith

179

June 21

God's Intervention

"Before they call I will answer;
while they are still speaking I will hear."
—*Isaiah 65:24, NIV*

When I make jam, I purchase pectin in bulk from an online company called Nuts.com. For one order, I chose the shipping option that would deliver my order in three to five business days, rather than having next-day delivery. I wanted it to arrive on a day when I could be home to receive the package since we have had problems with packages being stolen.

The day after I placed the order, I was leaving the sanctuary after church, having just taken my mobile phone out of the "silent" mode. I received a message from my neighbor saying she had my order of nuts. The mail carrier had delivered it to the wrong house.

After some comments about the carrier's ability to read, I told my neighbor that it probably is just as well that the carrier had delivered the package to her. I explained that someone with bad intent might have seen "Nuts.com" on the box sitting at my door and stolen it, expecting to get a bounty of nuts. Instead, they would have gotten a package of white powder labeled "pectin" and thrown the whole thing out.

It occurred to me then that perhaps the mail carrier had not made a mistake after all. Maybe God had directed him to leave the package with my neighbor and friend. Yet our house numbers are vastly different, and we are several doors apart. How could the carrier mistake her house for mine? Could it be that God directed him to her house with my package? I believe that God intervened on my behalf that day to ensure that I would receive the item I had ordered.

This was not something I had prayed about, but I believe God had intervened nonetheless. Yes, it was a small, insignificant thing, and I probably would have been the only one who cared whether or not I received my order of pectin. Though the cost of a pound of pectin is small, I would have not been happy if I had had to replace it, but I could have afforded to reorder it, if necessary. Yet, without my asking, God jumped in to help me.

That day I learned that He really meant it when He said in Matthew 6 that though He feeds the birds that neither sow nor reap, we are much more valuable to Him than those birds.

So why would He not take care of us?

Jean Arthur

Why Didn't You Tell Us?

Come over into Macedonia, and help us.
—*Acts 16:9*

During our childhood years, my sister, Bonnie, and I dreamed of becoming missionaries. We wanted to get involved, share our talents, and do our part to make our little corner of the world a better place.

When student missionaries came from a Christian college in Collegedale, Tennessee, and introduced our little backwoods family to Jesus, we were thrilled and wanted to be just like them. Continuing our education, Bonnie became a church school teacher, and I trained to be a registered nurse.

More recently, a dedicated group of medical professionals traveled from their state to evaluate a low-income area of our state for the possible construction of a church and a school, and staffing the local hospital with Christian workers. It was their desire to "go tell it on the mountain." When Bonnie accepted the teaching position, she and I were asked to become a part of the welcoming committee for these missionaries.

To celebrate the arrival of our guests, we planned an outdoor event for vespers. Everyone was finally seated on the grassy slope, near a shaded wooded area, just above the hospital grounds, eagerly anticipating an old-fashioned "dinner on the ground." Everything was perfect, except it proved to also be a perfect habitat for chiggers, which *Webster's Dictionary* defines as "six-legged . . . mite larva" that suck blood from vertebrates and cause "intensely itchy reddish welts."

The next day, we heard many positive comments from our guests about our vespers program. But we also heard, "Why didn't you tell us we would be itching today? Those tiny red bugs were very sneaky!"

Our welcoming committee had not thought to put "avoid chiggers" on our agenda!

Dear friends, are we remembering to warn others that Satan, lurking in the shadows, is ready to devour them too? Let's tell them, with love, that Jesus is their refuge.

Won't you join me in recruiting others who will be able to say, "This is our God; we have waited for Him, and He will save us" (Isaiah 25:9, NKJV)? In the true spirit of missionaries, let's not wait until it's too late and they come to us asking, "Why didn't you tell us?"

Jane Wiggins Moore

God Talked to Isaac

*"He performs wonders that cannot be fathomed,
miracles that cannot be counted."*
—Job 5:9, NIV

It was a beautiful summer morning in Panama. Isaac, the taxi driver, and I picked up Brother Morris and Shirley to give them a tour of the city. The day before, Maria, a church-building ministry support coordinator, asked me whether I could show these church-building volunteers around the city of Panama. I had said Yes.

That afternoon, I met Isaac, and God put it in my heart to ask him whether he could take a couple in his taxi for a tour of the city. He consented. He and I had been baptized in 1983, but we had not seen nor spoken to each other in fifteen years. He told me that he had abandoned the church but now had the desire to return and take his daughter and wife with him. He also shared some difficulties he was experiencing: His daughter was sick in the hospital, his wife's brother had passed away two days earlier, and he himself had recently suffered a heart attack. Isaac was feeling a sense of urgency to return to God. I said, "I think God is telling you something, so take these visiting missionaries and me to the city." I could see some happiness in his eyes.

However, during the trip, something happened. After we returned to the car from visiting the museum, the missionaries saw hundreds of black ants coming from the seat where Brother Morris was sitting. They told us what was happening, so I asked Isaac to find a place to park the car. Hundreds of black ants were also coming, inexplicably, from the cover of Brother Morris's water bottle. I got out of the car. When I opened the water bottle, my hand and arms were covered with ants. Amazingly, they didn't bite us. Isaac, nervous and shocked, apologized. He believed the ants had gotten into the car when he had been parked under a tree. I prayed in the name of Jesus to rebuke the ants. It was unbelievable what was happening.

We got back in the car, and Shirley prayed. By now, Isaac had calmed down, so we decided to continue our city tour. We had a delightful day and eventually took Shirley and Brother Morris back to their hotel. Before leaving, Brother Morris prayed for Isaac that God would take care of him and give him courage to return to church. Isaac said he believed God used the ants to "talk" to him, further impressing him to return to church with his family.

God moves in mysterious ways!

Gloribeth T. Gancedo

A Day in Hope

Be joyful in hope.
—*Romans 12:12, NIV*

Let's go to Hope tomorrow," suggested our son. "It will be the perfect place for a day trip. It's relatively close to home, and there are lots of low-key adventures that we all can enjoy." Hope, Alaska, a gold mining camp established in 1896, is surrounded by mountains. It has a population of approximately 200; its roads are unpaved; and it has gift shops, fishing opportunities, swings and a slide, walking trails, and a library. All six of us—from ages one to sixty-nine— would be able to find several things to enjoy. We arrived near lunchtime. While my husband kept the young grandchildren happy running races, our son took pictures of the log buildings, and our daughter-in-law and I unpacked the lunch. We sliced tomatoes and cucumbers, popped lids off containers of guacamole and hummus, and pulled out tortillas.

After lunch, some of the adults looked for ice cream at "the world's greatest gift shop," while the grandchildren found a public sandbox. Four-year-old Derion filled a gold pan with black sand and dumped it repeatedly on his head; one-year-old Avril happily made roads for a collection of Tonka trucks. The adults took turns playing with the children and exploring the town. When my husband and I returned from a somewhat extended exploration, we found the sandbox deserted. Sure that the lure of water and fishing had attracted at least some of the family, we meandered down to Resurrection Creek. We watched from a distance as Avril played on the rocks and her mom basked in the sun nearby; Derion and his dad, Garrick, stood closer to the water. Garrick, always eager to learn a few more skills, had put on his hip waders, baited a hook, and cast his line into the river. The man upstream landed a fish, and almost immediately, the man downstream caught a good-sized salmon. But we could see that Garrick and Derion had caught nothing. Lack of fish, however, did not discourage our grandson. He waved when he saw us and announced excitedly, "We're fishing!" His eyes flashed happily.

Although I already knew the answer, I asked, "Have you caught any?" His eager reply startled me.

"Not yet!"

"How about Dad?" I pressed. "Has he caught any?"

He said, "Almost."

Not yet . . . almost. Derion wasn't discouraged. He was anticipating the future and sharing his joy with those around him. Clearly, in many ways, we were in Hope.

Denise Dick Herr

Jesus Christ Is the Same

Jesus Christ the same yesterday,
and to day, and for ever.
—*Hebrews 13:8*

During an evangelistic effort to large cities in our area, about five hundred people (one-fifth of them nonbelievers) came regularly to the big meeting hall. The meetings were also being broadcast on the Internet to other parts of the country. Thanks to the strong impact of the Holy Spirit, people's hearts were touched by the gospel. Then incomprehensible things began to happen that demonstrated that soul-winning efforts involve a big battle between Jesus and Satan.

For example, a forty-year-old church member, a successful businessman in excellent health, suffered a stroke; doctors said he had no chance of survival. Then a young family had to put their baptisms on hold when the mother was admitted to a hospital. During the premature—but necessary—C-section surgery, she became unconscious. "There's nothing we can do for her," declared the doctors. Then a twenty-five-year-old woman from a devoted pastoral family was hospitalized, along with her grandparents, for severe food poisoning. Emergency room doctors said, "They have only a few hours left to live!"

How our church needed to be united in prayer! My husband, a pastor and prayer request coordinator for our area in Bulgaria, began sending e-mails to his colleagues and sister churches, calling for prayer for all these people in such desperate need. Some of the sick were anointed, and churches with strong prayer ministries gathered daily to pray for God's answers to their requests. With enormous hope, we repeated the words of James: "Therefore confess your sins to each other and pray for each other so that you may be healed. The prayer of a righteous person is powerful and effective" (James 5:16, NIV). "God, I am not righteous," I prayed, kneeling beside my husband, "but, Lord, in the name of Your sacrifice, forgive our sins and hear our prayers on behalf of Your suffering children!"

And He did. God performed miracles in response to everyone's intercessory prayers! All of those needing healing were made better! Our great, almighty, and merciful Father in heaven revealed His power to re-create life in answer to our prayers. We succeeded in touching His miraculous power, declared in the Bible and displayed throughout the history of the Christian church. Indeed, Jesus Christ *is* the same yesterday, today, and forever!

Emiliya Stoykova

A Mother in Israel

Study to shew thyself approved unto God, a workman that needeth
not to be ashamed, rightly dividing the word of truth.
—*2 Timothy 2:15*

It was decided. The Lamb Wins team would attend a large youth conference to share our new musical project. "We'll sell thousands of CDs!" Delon proclaimed. Justin concurred with an "At least!" I tried to deflate them a little with, "Let's be realistic—" but they countered with, "No, let's not!" When I said I didn't want them to be disappointed, they said they wouldn't be.

We went, and we weren't disappointed. At one point, a friend said to me, "I love your little posse!" referring to our team—Delon Lawrence, Justin McLaughlin, Lee Givhan, John Millea, Matthew Redendez, David Kim, Hillary Blair, and my daughter, Kimmy Schwirzer. I thought, *I love my little posse too.*

I often ask myself how I ended up here, leading out in the production of a musical cantata based on the book of Revelation—with two rap artists from urban Philadelphia, an Asian cellist who played for the Hong Kong Philharmonic, and a gaggle of other musicians, most of them less than half my age and way, way outside my demographic. Truth is stranger than fiction.

On The Lamb Wins Web site, I'm listed as "Jennifer Jill Schwirzer—executive producer, composer, songwriter, singer, guitarist, pianist." I would like to add "Mother in Israel." Of all my roles, this is the most meaningful. In his process of pitching The Lamb Wins to the people sauntering by our booth, I overheard Delon say multiple times, "Jennifer Jill Schwirzer is the mastermind behind this project." I'm not sure I'm the mastermind, but through the grace of God I may be the master heart, the way a mother is the master heart of a family. University of Chicago professor John Cacioppo says that loneliness doubled from 20 percent in the 1980s to 40 percent today. Ironic that social isolation should increase with social networking, but it has. Studies show that Facebook use predicts declines in subjective well-being in young adults, some of which involves feelings of loneliness.* Facebook probably won't cure your loneliness—unless you use it to search for a vital, Christ-centered, active, Bible-honoring church near you and start attending. Get involved in service, outreach, and searching the Scriptures. In the process, you'll most likely form bonds that just may become your very own posse.

Jennifer Jill Schwirzer

---

* Ethan Kross et al., "Facebook Use Predicts Declines in Subjective Well-Being in Young Adults," *PLOS ONE* 8, no. 8 (August 2013): e69841, doi:10.1371/journal.pone.0069841.

The Voice

But now is the time. Never forget the warning,
"Today if you hear God's voice speaking to you,
do not harden your hearts against him."
—Hebrews 3:15, TLB

It was a Wednesday in June 2011. I had just ridden my bicycle three miles from work to home in Stockport, England. I planned to drive the car to prayer meeting. Though time grew close to the start of the meeting, my husband had not returned with the car, and I could not contact him by mobile phone. *Well, I can't go to prayer meeting*, I said to myself.

Then I heard a voice: *Go to prayer meeting*. I reasoned that I could not go: I had no car; I was tired; it would be dark when prayer meeting finished; I'd just changed clothes. I just could not go. *Go to prayer meeting!* The voice, like a drum, was becoming insistent, persistent, and louder.

Finally, I shouted, "All right, I'm going!" Resolved, I changed back into my cycling gear and rode several miles to church. When I arrived, I asked, "What now?" Silence. I quietly waited for the voice to instruct me, and it came through a young mother. Unbeknown to me, Sheila, a registered nurse from the Philippines, needed a twelve-week adaptation placement in order to practice as a nurse in the United Kingdom. She had secured her theoretical place at the local university but was unable to establish a placement near her family. She had only a few days left to find one before her work visa expired. Sheila and her family had been fasting and praying for a solution. Through my position at the time, as associate director in a community health-care organization, Sheila was able to gain the practical experience required for nurse registration and, eventually, a position as an oncology nurse in England.

Five years later, Sheila and I shared our respective experiences. She informed me that out of all the nurses on her same program, she was the only one who had obtained a position close to home. She only had to attend four to five hours a day, whereas her colleagues were working seven-to-twelve-hour shifts in their locations. Today she still praises God for miraculously answering her prayer. And I praise God that I listened to His voice and did not harden my heart so that He could use me to answer a prayer.

Today do not harden your heart.

Lucille Fifield

"Bloom Where You Are Planted"

"I delight to do thy will, O my God;
thy law is within my heart."
—*Psalm 40:8, RSV*

When we think of the story of Esther, the queen, we tend to look only at the last part of her story as a queen. But I want us to look at her beginning. She was a Hebrew girl whose family chose to remain in Persia, a foreign land, when they could have returned to their own. Life was simple compared to our lives today. Yet as an orphan now, she had been adopted by her cousin, Mordecai, and taken into his home to be raised as his child.

At some time during those years of growing up, Esther had to make a choice: complain about her misfortune, or look on the bright side and thank God for her blessings. She chose to be thankful, and she developed a relationship of trust in God.

In fact, she chose to bloom where she was planted and to become a blessing.

When it seemed there was no hope of deliverance for God's people, Esther realized that the crisis facing them would take courage and quick action, and she knew that only God could work to save them. She and the women associated with her fasted and prayed for three days. She told Mordecai to have all the Jews in Shushan fast and pray for three days also. She then risked her life to save her people, and God was able to use her to save thousands of Jewish people living in the land of Persia.

The Bible contains many stories of women who had a relationship with God and were willing to be used by Him.

God is still looking for women who are willing to work for Him.

When I was a young adult, I read an article by June Strong entitled "Bloom Where You Are Planted." In it she suggested we write our own epitaph. What do we want people to say about us after we die? I had never considered that before and, at first, thought the suggestion was morbid. But it did make me think! I took the challenge and wrote down what I would like to have said about me. That article changed my life.

What did I write? I wrote that I wanted to be remembered as a happy person who loved life and loved to help others. I wanted to be used by God wherever He planted me.

God can use you too, if you are willing to be used.

Celia Mejia Cruz

What Would Jesus Do?

Whether therefore ye eat, or drink,
or whatsoever you do, do all to the glory of God.
—*1 Corinthians 10:31*

The student was in tears and the teacher was visibly upset. At the beginning of class, the teacher had made it very clear that students who were tardy should be no more than ten minutes late for class. If they arrived any later, they would not be admitted into the classroom. The student had been ordered to leave the room and was angry at the treatment she thought had been unfair. The teacher immediately submitted a letter of resignation, along with her school keys.

Only four weeks into the semester, it would be difficult to find a replacement. As chair of the department, I knew I had to take this situation to God in prayer. After meeting separately with teacher and student, it was decided that all three of us should meet in an effort to resolve the situation. Thank God! His Holy Spirit was present at the meeting, and a positive and pleasant resolution resulted. After we prayed and hugged, we knew that God had allowed His Holy Spirit to reign in our deliberations. Indeed, His Spirit directed our thoughts, utterances, and actions.

This potentially explosive situation, which could have resulted in the disruption of the school's program, had a happy ending. But life is not always like that. We live in a world fraught with misunderstandings and problems. How often we complain that people do not treat us well or do not like us. And how do we respond? It is natural for us to try to get even or treat others as we think they deserve, but I would suggest that we be guided by the answer to this question, "What would Jesus do?" Over the years, I have tried to use my response to this question as a guide for my interactions with my fellow men. I have asked myself that question countless times when faced with interpersonal challenges. And interestingly, whenever I am honest in my response, the outcome is always positive and Christlike.

The words of a song I enjoy singing invite me to pray, "Give me, Lord, the mind of Jesus." The lyrics go on to request His holiness and righteousness in my life as proof that I've been with Him. We need the mind of Jesus to enable us to meet the challenges of life. We need the mind of Jesus to deal with difficult people. We need the mind of Jesus to prepare us for heaven. *Lord, please give me the mind of Jesus!*

Carol Joy Fider

Valley of the Shadow

He will wipe all tears from their eyes,
and there will be no more death, suffering, crying, or pain.
These things of the past are gone forever.
—*Revelation 21:4, CEV*

There are dog people and there are cat people, and then there are rabbit people. Anyone who has known me for five seconds can tell you that I am definitely a rabbit person. My love affair with rabbits started when I was a child, and today I love my Angora bunnies almost as if they were my children.

Cute bunny pictures and videos abound on the Internet, and one day I somehow stumbled from a sweet video of a white bunny eating a raspberry to a PETA video about how Angora rabbits are treated in some country whose name I am too traumatized to remember. I saw only a moment of the rabbit screaming while its fur was being ripped off. I stabbed at my keyboard, trying to make it stop! Make it stop! Make it stop! I promptly went into hysterics the likes of which I hope never to see again. Unfortunately, I needed to pick up my daughter from school. I was so upset when I arrived that I had to ask her to drive us home because I was in no condition. An hour later, I was still so distressed that I felt raw, as though all my skin had been peeled off and simply existing was painful.

It occurred to me, in the midst of my agony, as I was begging God to erase the horrible memory of that poor rabbit's suffering, that this must be a mere echo of the pain Adam and Eve felt immediately after the Fall. How they must have wished they could erase what they'd done and return to life before the Fall! How they must have wept, their grief so massive and overwhelming that they even hid from God. Imagine how they must have felt when, later, He handed them the pelts of the beautiful creatures they had petted and enjoyed only hours before.

It's all too easy to become complacent about sin, to allow it to creep into our lives. But we should never forget the cost of that sin; we should never forget the face of evil or try to dress it up. As dearly as I wish I had never witnessed that video, I am thankful for one thing. It reminded me that no matter how evil this world becomes, it is only a passing shadow. One day very soon, there will be no more suffering, no more sorrow. It is this hope that we must cling to when the flood of evil threatens to wash us away.

Céleste Perrino-Walker

Running With My Angel

For he shall give his angels charge over thee,
to keep thee in all thy ways.
—Psalm 91:11.

The sun shone brightly as I quietly shut the door. I set off running—after I successfully made an escape from my dogs that were "puttering" around outside. Then I realized I had forgotten my pepper spray. Almost everyone in our rural community had dogs on the loose, but I didn't want to go back home after outwitting my own dogs. With a prayer for God to protect me, I ran on. Having been a runner for almost forty years, I understand how hazardous running can be. So being visible and keeping pepper spray handy helps make running a safe sport.

At the house at the top of the second hill lived two dogs—a small mutt and a large German shepherd mix with big teeth. Would they come bounding out today? My usual habit was to look a dog in the eyes (or teeth), fling an arm up in the air, and yell loudly, "Home, boy!" That usually worked, but if it kept coming, I would fire the pepper spray. Today, though, everything was quiet. No activity whatsoever. *Thank You, Lord.*

I started down the winding hill. A white house on the right had a large, friendly Labrador mix that had a snippy, dark-brown friend. As I ran toward the house, a noisy tractor engine started up, camouflaging the crunch of my feet on the gravel. *Thank You, Lord.*

Gathering momentum, I ran down the hill, only to hear a car approaching slowly from behind. I ran on but it still lingered behind me. What was happening? Set back from the road was a house with a mixed bunch of noisy dogs that usually rushed to the roadside and barked loudly. None had ever bitten me—yet. The car tailed me by only a few feet as I avoided potholes and padded through a carpet of thick dust past the house, unnoticed by the dogs. The sound of the purring car engine had covered my footsteps and anxious breathing. Within seconds, the smiling driver passed me and sped away, throwing gravel and dust into the air. Another miracle.

Finally home, I realized that not once had I encountered a fierce dog on my run today. Coincidence? Perhaps. But if the Lord shut the lions' mouths so that they did not hurt Daniel (Daniel 6:22), He can surely use other means to distract dogs.

Yes, running has risks, but I can trust the Lord. He is in control of protecting us all.

Tabitha Abel

Thank You!

And as he entered into a certain village, there met him ten men that were lepers, which stood afar off: and they lifted up their voices, and said, Jesus, Master, have mercy on us. And when he saw them, he said unto them, Go shew yourselves unto the priests. And it came to pass, that, as they went, they were cleansed. And one of them, when he saw that he was healed, turned back, and with a loud voice glorified God, and fell down on his face at his feet, giving him thanks: and he was a Samaritan. And Jesus answering said, Were there not ten cleansed? but where are the nine?
—*Luke 17:12–17*

How could anyone healed of leprosy, the most dreadful of diseases, not say Thank You for miraculous healing? What makes the story even more disappointing is that *90 percent* of the lepers didn't say Thank You. I'm sure they had their reasons. They strictly obeyed Jesus' command to show themselves to the priests. Perhaps when they went back to say Thank You, Jesus was gone. We can all rationalize why we do what we do or neglect to do what we should have been done.

My heart aches for Jesus, who did a miracle in the lives of ten men, yet only one returned to give thanks. I know the feeling. Or do I?

There have been times in my life when I have been annoyed for lack of thanks from someone to whom I have given a gift or done a favor. Yet when I turn my thoughts to this story, I feel rebuked for feeling slighted.

Jesus has done great things in my life every day, and the ultimate gift was His sacrifice so that I might have eternal life. He has healed me of "leprosy" many times; have I expressed gratefulness? How about the minute miracles that come my way? They are deserving of thanks also.

I recall the time I needed six bananas. I grabbed a bunch off the fruit rack and counted six but when I got home there were seven. *Oh, well, no problem.* But it so happened that an unexpected guest arrived, and the extra banana came in handy. *Thank You, Lord!*

Let us begin each day by giving thanks to our Maker and Provider for the great and small miracles, and take notice of *each* one as they occur and give thanks—again and again.

Edith Fitch

July 3

Praise Him! Praise Him!

Let the peoples praise You,
O God; let all the peoples praise You.
—Psalm 67:3, NKJV

My dad, as many Germans did in those early days, played the violin. My mom, good Italian that she is, had me listening to early Italian opera singers, plus a good number of classical repertoires on our record player. All that musical influence rubbed off on me. Instead of playing with my little girlfriends, I usually preferred to make a quick getaway and practice on the nearest available piano. I studied piano from the first grade until I graduated from the conservatory some sixteen years later. By then it was clear, piano and music were the loves of my life.

Our lives are meant to give God praise. I wanted to be a concert pianist, but God wanted me to be a piano teacher and missionary. He provided me a pianist husband with an adventurous spirit, and, together with our two young boys, He sent us overseas to a mission field in faraway Asia! God needed a medical doctor and a musician to represent Him there. He guided and enabled us to follow Him and use our talents in that faraway place for His glory and honor.

I began giving piano lessons, starting with our sons. Younger members in our mission church joined the older ones in praising the Lord. Special musical, religious services, and social services were organized, known as Talent Nights, where the whole neighborhood came together in Christian fellowship. I believe that only in heaven will we know the full impact of our service for God. Our family's music ministry has been a lifelong experience. Whether at the piano, harmonium, pipe organ, or electric keyboard, and with my boys joining in on the baritone, the trombone, or the trumpet, we played and testified to the glory of the Master Musician. We were always ready to praise the Lord. And He accepted our praise and blessed us richly beyond compare (see Mark 10:29, 30).

"Praise the LORD! For it is good to sing praises to our God; for it is pleasant, and praise is beautiful" (Psalm 147:1, NKJV).

Will you join me in praising Him?

Marli Elizete Ritter-Hein

Memory of Millerton Lake

For he shall give his angels charge over thee,
to keep thee in all thy ways.
—Psalm 91:11

Excitement filled the air this Fourth of July weekend, as dozens of youth groups from surrounding churches headed out to a long-planned boating trip on Millerton Lake in central California. At the end of this two-hour drive through the beautiful San Joaquin Valley, the "food basket of the world," they would meet new friends and have lots of fun!

All sorts of boats on the clear blue water made Millerton Lake unusually crowded this hot summer day. Yet the teens enjoyed lots of water play and food. The hours passed quickly.

About four o'clock in the afternoon, a group of four kids—including our youngest daughter, Myrna, and her best friend, Bonnie—decided to go with the owner of a speedboat for one last swing across the lake. For some unknown reason, Myrna and Bonnie did not put on life jackets. The riders enjoyed the exhilarating travel speed across the lake. Then, without warning, the glare of the afternoon sun momentarily distracted the driver. In that second, another speeding boat hit them broadside. In an instant, the four kids flew out of the boat in different directions. The adult occupant of the other boat was unharmed, but the twelve-year-old girl with him was thrown out of the boat. Tragically, the propeller of the other boat struck her head and killed her.

Having heard and seen the collision, dozens of boaters swarmed to the accident scene to help with the rescue. Three of our four kids were fished out of the water and immediately brought ashore. Bonnie was shouting at the top of her lungs, "Myrna is missing! Myrna is missing!" I cannot tell you how hard we all prayed! The next forty-five minutes seemed like an eternity to us as both authorities and volunteers desperately searched for our daughter, Myrna. Finally they found her, caught in a bunch of seaweed-like water vegetation that had kept her afloat under the hull of the capsized boat! Our precious daughter was only semiconscious and suffering from hypothermia when she was handed to us. That incident made an indelible mark in our memories that will last a lifetime. We were unspeakably grateful for God's protection of Myrna but questioned why the twelve-year-old child in the other boat died. Only in eternity will we know why bad things happen to good people.

All we can do for now is trust in God's love, wisdom, and comfort.

Zeny Marcelo

Free Membership—Really?

God saved you by his grace when you believed.
And you can't take credit for this; it is a gift from God.
—*Ephesians 2:8, NLT*

t was that time of year again, when health insurance agencies advertise multiple times on TV and bombard mailboxes with flyers and booklets with claims of why their companies are the best. The deadline to make my own decision was fast approaching. I needed insurance and needed to decide quickly. *Why am I procrastinating when I know it has to be done?* As I looked over several of the health plans, I finally decided on one that I thought would best fit my needs. A company representative scheduled a meeting to explain various details to me.

"Oh, I like this one," I informed her. She asked me why.

I responded that even though the daily hospital rates were high, the plan had a low monthly premium, reasonable co-payments to my primary physician and specialists, and a free monthly membership to a gym called Silver Sneakers. What a bargain! Free membership to the gym! Since I was striving to be healthy, I didn't have any excuses not to visit the gym as many times as I wanted to—especially since it was only five miles away. I signed up for the plan.

I was excited when my health card arrived. All I needed to do was scan it every time I visited the gym. But something happened. Every day, I found myself making excuses to not go: *It's raining. It's too cold. I'm tired. I don't want to go alone. I'll go tomorrow.* The weeks and months gradually increased, and because I didn't take advantage of it, the free membership was useless. Another thought suddenly overwhelmed me: *God has offered me a free gift of His amazing grace. Am I putting it off each day with excuses by not fully accepting and using it?*

Although I know God will not force me to avail myself of His free gift, I also know He is so willing and generous that, if I accept it, He will guarantee me free membership in His family and a place in His kingdom. So I accept His marvelous plan that is always available to me. Even in my weakness, when I want to make excuses, He has promised, " 'My grace is all you need. My power works best in weakness.' So now I am glad to boast about my weaknesses, so that the power of Christ can work through me" (2 Corinthians 12:9, NLT).

Lord, help us daily to accept and use Your free gift of grace.

Vivian Brown

Two-Minute Warning

"When you see all these things taking place,
you can know that the Kingdom of God is near. . . .
Don't let that day catch you unaware, like a trap."
—Luke 21:31–35, NLT

Two-minute warnings come up at the end of every half of a National Football League (NFL) game (United States). Two minutes before the end of a half, a referee used to stop the clock and alert both teams that their game time was nearly over. With better technological innovations now, the NFL still uses the two-minute warning as an important strategy to build excitement.

At the end of Super Bowl XLIX (49), when the New England Patriots were playing the Seattle Seahawks for the coveted Vince Lombardi Trophy, the two quarterbacks, Brady and Wilson, battled it out. The two-minute warning came and went. Then, with only twenty seconds remaining in playtime, a Patriot's sideliner made an interception, and the Patriots prevailed.

A lot of things can be decided in the final seconds of a game!

The book of Revelation talks about the greatest competition of all time: the great conflict between Christ's team and Satan's team, the controversy between good and evil (Revelation 12:7). God has given His followers a two-minute warning in these final moments of this great controversy. This warning comes in the form of signs of the times just before Christ—who has already won the competition on the cross—returns for His team members to take them home to heaven. Matthew 24:7 tells us we can read of the signs of the times in famines, wars, and earthquakes. Daniel 12:4 talks about people running to and fro and knowledge being increased. Today travel takes less time than ever, and technology allows instant connectivity to information sources. God's two-minute warning also comes in the form of growing violence (Genesis 6:11), sexual immorality (Jude 7), the extinction of animal life (Hosea 4:3), and many great efforts behind attempts to achieve world peace—which will be short-lived (1 Thessalonians 5:3). Despite all this, Jesus promised that the gospel would be preached to the whole world, and many would come back to Him in earth's final moments (Matthew 24:14).

When you see these things, Jesus said we should "know his return is very near, right at the door" (Matthew 24:33, NLT).

Team Jesus, stay strong! Your two-minute warning is almost up, and He is almost here!

Suhana Chikatla

Is Your Sabbath a Delight?

Then he said to them,
"The Sabbath was made for man,
not man for the Sabbath."
—Mark 2:27, NIV

How wonderful to spend a Sabbath in Jerusalem! We felt at home worshiping with fellow believers—Jewish and Arab converts alike. Sabbath afternoon, we jumped into our rental car with trusty maps in hand, winding our way through unknown neighborhoods. Then we noticed small blockades in front of some streets. No signs. Just blockades. "Why the blockades?" we ventured. Then my husband spotted the street we were looking for and turned left.

Instantly we noticed that no one else was driving on this road. We were just beginning to wonder whether Sabbath driving was not permitted here when we heard something that sounded like hail "pinging" our car. "Dad," my son shouted, "people are throwing rocks at us! Go fast, Dad!" We had become a moving target for residents in this conservative neighborhood. Men and boys at street side were now picking up larger stones. The ping sounds turned to plunk sounds.

"How do I get out of this maze?" My husband drove faster and faster, as we seemed to be going in circles with every street outlet blocked by a barricade. There was no place to flee!

"Lord, help us!" we cried. Then a woman stepped out of nowhere! Pulling her long, dark, billowing skirt to one side, her other hand signaled wildly. What was she trying to tell us? We followed her hand signals, driving right across the sidewalk between two buildings. Amazingly . . . to freedom! We drove for several blocks before stopping to see whether there was any damage to the car. Thankfully, there was no damage! How we wanted to thank our unknown, darkly clad benefactor!

I've often thought of that Sabbath day's journey. We all enjoy the Sabbath, a day of rest like an oasis in a desert. But how do we keep this day special? Do we get hung up on the "rules" we've assigned to this special day? Do we, like our friends in that neighborhood, require others to live by a certain set of rules?

The Sabbath was created to be a delight. It is a time for worship, relaxation, sharing, caring, and—most of all—a time to reflect on the Creator, the One who established this magnificent day of rest and recreation. Let's enjoy it! *Shabbat shalom* (peaceful Sabbath)!

Harryette Aitken

Bread on the Waters

Cast your bread upon the waters,
for you will find it after many days.
—*Ecclesiastes 11:1, NKJV*

I walked into my hotel room at the anesthesiology conference I was attending. The telephone was ringing, so I picked up the receiver. "Hello," I said.

A voice on the other end of the line asked, "Is this Dr. Blaylock from Birmingham?"

"Yes, this is she," I responded.

"My name is Jeff. You may not remember me, but as a medical student, I did a one-month anesthesiology rotation with you twenty-five years ago. I was unsure how to proceed in medicine, and during that one month with you, I decided to become an anesthesiologist."

I listened in amazement as he continued talking. "I have been practicing the past twenty years here in Colorado and have never regretted that decision even once." Jeff, who was at the same conference I was attending, asked whether we could touch base in person. We met long enough to reminisce before parting ways. Yet those few minutes buoyed me up for days.

As I think on what Jeff shared, I am still astounded. We had interacted for only thirty busy days—twenty-five years earlier. I had been sleep-deprived and stressed with the demands of residency, as I tried to show students the basics of anesthesia. I also shared why I had decided to pursue that profession. I'm sure I had no thought of influencing the course of that young man's life. Then my thoughts moved to the spiritual. I had not been trying to convince young Jeff to become an anesthesiologist. I was just showing him what *I* liked about this branch of medicine. In the course of our time together, I had shared my reasons for making the professional decision that I had. That had been easy.

So . . . how many times have I felt that it was too hard for me to share *Christ* with others? In my busy stressed-filled days, it is not my "job" to convince someone else they need to become a Christian. I simply need to show people why *I* have chosen Jesus. I can simply explain why being a follower of His gives me lifetime satisfaction that will extend into eternity. That's all you need to do, as well, for the Holy Spirit will do the rest.

After we part ways, we might not think we've done anything special. Yet in the future—or in heaven—we will be surprised by the results of our influence in the lives of others.

Suzanne Blaylock

Storms

A furious squall came up,
and the waves broke over the boat,
so that it was nearly swamped.
—Mark 4:37, NIV

Storms sometimes arise suddenly in our lives. Storm clouds of perplexity fill our personal skies, eclipsing happiness and hope. Our calm has suddenly become a conflict. When chaos ensues, we feel as if we will perish, for there seems to be no solution to our problems. We are at the mercy of the elements that make the "boats" of our lives swing to the rhythm of the waves that threaten to submerge us. Storms come in the form of economic woes, personal ordeals, and spiritual crises. Or perhaps we live with chronic pain, unemployment, disrupted relationships, or the disapproval of others. We feel as if we have no strength to get up after a failure. We wonder, *Will I never experience a crisis-free day again?*

One time, Christ's disciples feared they would be swallowed up by a storm on the Sea of Galilee. Jesus, tired from His day of labor for, and service to, mankind, had fallen asleep. Peacefully He slept in the bow of their small boat. All day, He had used His power to heal the sick, multiply the loaves, being Himself the bread that came down from heaven to satisfy the spiritual hunger of the human heart. He had fed spiritual hunger with His words of hope and encouragement, while heaven's peace and inner calm flooded the hearts of His listeners.

Now Jesus slept like the man He was. Yet, as God, He was attentive to human need. So when His disciples awakened Him, calling for help, He used His divine authority to settle down the sea and calm the winds. Though the disciples asked, "Who is this man, that the wind and sea obey Him?" they already knew the answer (see Mark 4:41).

In our conflicts, in our storms that devastate our calm, we need the peace of knowing that Jesus is in our boat too. He is our Friend. He alone can resolve that which pains, saddens, and perplexes us. Only He understands that which throws our lives into crisis.

This same Jesus stretches out His mighty hand over our lives and says, "Peace, be still" (Mark 4:39). In His time, and in His way, He rides out the storm with us. We may not know when the sunny days of rest and reassurance will return, but we can know that they will come at a time of His own choosing. In the meantime, we are not left alone to face life's storms. Jesus is with us.

Maria Raimunda Lopes Costa

The Pine Trees

"Like an evergreen tree I will shelter them;
I am the source of all their blessings."
—*Hosea 14:8, GNT*

From my bedroom window I can see a group of very tall pine trees. Evergreens. When all the other trees are resting and no longer have color, there they stand. The dark, rich green on their boughs remains when other trees have lost their leaves.

Sometimes, on occasion, when I have been praying or meditating, a shaft of light shines through their treetops, and I experience something quite phenomenal. It is as though, for a brief while, my eyes and thoughts are transported up to where the warmth of that light is and where there appears to be complete peace. I am reminded that, detached from the world where I live, I can still know God's presence.

Where do you go, away from the secular, to experience God in special prayer? Perhaps into the early morning sunshine or out in a gentle breeze? Isn't this time with God enriching?

When I am alone with God, He brings a whole new concept of Himself to my world. Things that seemed so important fade into the background. I can focus more clearly on Him. There is a real sense of contentment in those precious moments with just God and me.

Isn't it wonderful to know that God can and does reach into our world? He can lift our thoughts to Him and touch us. It is completely different from anything else we can relate to—a time and place where we can enjoy a real sense of His beauty.

I often look up into the treetops, to that place where the sun shines down in a shaft, and I am reminded that there is a place *above* that is different from our busy world too.

Sometimes these days, it isn't always easy to slip away to my pine tree escape. On the other hand, there have been times when I rushed away too quickly from those moments with God. Yet I am grateful for the pine trees, which are a reminder to me that there is a place where I can sense His presence.

Although it is phenomenal and beyond our comprehension to grasp, we *do* have a Father who reaches down, longing to touch us.

Let us connect with Him today.

Laura A. Canning

Seeking the Lost

Even so it is not the will of your Father which is in heaven,
that one of these little ones should perish.
—*Matthew 18:14*

When my son, Richard, was just one month short of his third birthday, I went through a very traumatic experience. While he was playing around the kitchen with his toys, I went upstairs to make up our beds. Suddenly the house became very quiet; there was no sound of my child playing. I went downstairs to see why the house had suddenly become silent. Richard was nowhere to be seen. His rubber boots and cap were gone, so I knew he must be outside somewhere. I hurried outside and called his name, but there was no answer.

Now I became alarmed. The river, running very close to our house, was flooded. Furthermore, there had been bears seen in our area; we had no close neighbors. So many unsettling thoughts went through my mind! I ran partway out of our lane, calling his name. Since my daughter, Lois, only one year old, was inside the house, I could not go far and leave her alone. So I called our nearest neighbor and told her the situation. In the meantime, I went in all directions from the house, calling for Richard. I was frantic! And then, our neighbor's car drove in, followed by other neighbors whom she had called to help in the search. I could see a little head peeking over the dashboard of the car, and I knew then that Richard was safe. Tears of relief came to my eyes, and I held him close for a long time.

This experience reminded me how God feels when His children are lost in this sinful world and how He yearns over them. We are told that greater than the love of a mother for her children is Christ's love for His redeemed.

Are we doing what we can to help in finding those who are lost in sin? The Lord is asking us who have been privileged to know Him and have been recipients of His great love to share that love with others. We can't all go to far-off lands to share the love with those who haven't yet heard of it, yet there is something we all *can* do. We can pray for those who don't know Jesus. We can give of our means to help others go and be witnesses. We can witness in our own homes and communities.

Let us each do our part in searching out the lost and sharing the love of Jesus.

Miriam L. Thompson

Lights Out

"He that is unjust, let him be unjust still; he who is filthy,
let him be filthy still; he who is righteous, let him be righteous still;
he who is holy, let him be holy still."
—Revelation 22:11, NKJV

One Wednesday evening, while I was administering medication to my one-hundred-year-old mother, the lights went out. For that moment, all was quiet and very dark. I stopped, stood still, looked around. I thought of Jesus and Revelation 22:11. Though in the dark, I did not panic, for I know that when He comes, it will not be a quiet event (1 Thessalonians 4:16). I looked out the window and saw that the entire neighborhood was dark.

Reflecting some time later on the lights going out made me ask myself, *What will be the state of my spiritual life when it's "lights out" for this world? Will I be ready when Jesus calls for me?* Events oftentimes allow us to procrastinate until a more suitable moment. But not for the last "lights out," which will be final. When Jesus returns, He will declare, "He that is unjust, filthy, righteous, and holy, let him remain as such." So, in effect, choices I make today determine my final destination. With each choice, I want to choose eternal life. This brings to mind Mr. O, who is a devoted relative, friend, and neighbor. He has a warm personality and is greatly respected. He greets everyone with a smile and is greeted with much love and admiration. On several occasions, I have asked Mr. O to worship with us. Each time he has an excuse not to. Once he said he would. Yet, when I called to confirm with him, he said he was too busy. I was very disappointed at his decision since I had witnessed how God blessed him by giving him a new life by delivering him from alcoholism, illness, and unemployment. I found myself judging Mr. O.

Then God, my awesome Savior, convicted me not to judge Mr. O but rather to pray that he would hear the voice of God calling. Now I pray that Mr. O will not procrastinate in accepting God's invitation while he still has opportunity. I think of the text that reads, "If you seek Him, He will be found by you; but if you forsake Him, He will forsake you" (2 Chronicles 15:2, NKJV). Therefore, I also pray to be able to live *my* life in a way that reflects God's character.

May we each walk in the strength of God's amazing grace so that we will be found worthy of His blessing when it's the final "lights out" for this sinful world.

Sylvia Giles Bennett

Blessing at the Fair

Trust in the LORD with all your heart,
and lean not on your own understanding;
in all your ways acknowledge Him,
and He shall direct your paths.
—*Proverbs 3:5, 6, NKJV*

This year, I was helping with a booth sponsored by our church at the Western North Carolina State Fair. My schedule was from 3:00 P.M. to 7:00 P.M. on Tuesday and Thursday. The tables at our booth were covered with inspirational literature: Bibles and religious books, magazines, tracts, and children's materials. All this material had been donated by our area churches to offer encouragement and spiritual information to literally thousands of people who come each year to the state fair.

On Tuesday, my first day to help, Linda, one of the organizers of this booth, gave me a tour around the tables and showed me where to find extra copies of supplies when I needed to restock the items that had been taken. She shared tips on how to interact with the passersby but reminded me to let the Lord lead out in the conversations. It was a good experience for me.

When I got home that evening, I remembered I had some women's devotional books that I received from my mom. She had finished reading them and returned them to me to pass on to someone else. They were virtually brand-new. The thought kept returning to me that I should take them to the state fair. When the thought came again, I retrieved the devotional books from the bookshelf on our back porch. Four of the books were wrapped in a plastic bag. I wasn't sure whether I would need them or not. However, I took them with me to the fair the next Thursday and showed them to Linda. She said we could use them for the gift basket. So these four women's devotional books went into the basket, which already contained sermon DVDs and religious posters. In order to get an item from the gift basket, attendees needed to complete a short survey. That afternoon, two precious ladies requested a woman's devotional book as a gift. As I watched one lady choose from among the books, my heart overflowed with joy. My heartfelt prayer was that these books would be a means to draw them closer to Christ. I have to say I was so glad I listened to that still, small voice.

What is God telling you to do? Whether small or great, be assured there is a blessing in store for you too.

Rosemarie Clardy

Lightning Damage

Casting all your care upon him;
for he careth for you.
—1 Peter 5:7

Lightning accompanied loud thunder on that late summer Thursday night in 2014. I am usually afraid of these occurrences. Before being widowed, I would always snuggle beside my husband during these storms. One of these episodes was so dramatic that even the dog went for cover! I was certain there had been an incident nearby. On Friday morning, I realized I had no water in the bathroom, kitchen, or entire house. Although I am hesitant in dealing with any electrical problem, I checked the breakers and discovered that the breaker switch for the well pump was malfunctioning. It was then that my prayers began.

My son, who lives seventy-five miles away, had planned to visit that day. I was hopeful that during this visit he could help to determine the problem, but he could not resolve the situation. Eventually the well company made an appointment for the following Monday, since I had previously planned to go away over the weekend. So many times we take things for granted. During these hours, I realized how many times I turn on the faucet to get water, rinse a cup, or wash my hands or fruit for breakfast. Now I had to resort to bottled water.

On Monday, the well utility worker came and concluded my water issue stemmed from an electrical issue. Someone would have to burrow under the concrete walkway and garage entrance to access the well system in order to make repairs! Fighting panic, I asked God for help. An electrician I knew was unavailable to help, having had recent back surgery. Only God could solve this situation—and help with the anticipated high expenses. Two weeks prior, I had had to replace my riding lawn mower *and* repair the push mower.

The worker suggested placing a temporary external water line from the well to the house until final repairs could be made. In the process of attaching an external line, he smelled smoke in the pump house. When he removed the covering for the pump system, he discovered that the switch for the system had been hit by lightning and was completely shattered. With one simple switch replacement, the problem was resolved! I immediately shouted, "Glory to God! Praise Him!" And the bill was minimal—instead of costing thousands.

God cares for His children and is interested in our affairs. May He increase our faith!

Missilene B. Edwards

A Great Idea!

"Let your light so shine before men, that they may see
your good works and glorify your Father in heaven."
—Matthew 5:16, NKJV

For years I have gotten up early each morning to read the Bible and pray. This day, I was away at a worldwide ministry conference where our Women's Ministries department would be hosting a booth. I awoke with the joy of the Lord, for His mercies are new every morning. Prior to ending my devotional time, I committed my life once again to God, repeating this prayer: "Take me, O Lord, as wholly Thine. I lay all my plans at Thy feet. Use me today in Thy service. Abide with me, and let all my work be wrought in Thee."* Once finished, I left my hotel room and went to the exhibit hall where I would be serving.

At the booth, I met many of God's children. One lady stopped by our booth and asked for copies of the Women's Ministries instructional booklet "Great Ideas" in Spanish. She also needed instructions in Spanish to help direct Spanish-speaking ladies to our booth. I was the appointed vessel the Lord used to light up her day. This incident made me think about some "great ideas" for us to practice every day.

First, we can practice an attitude of gratitude, giving thanks to God for all things (1 Thessalonians 5:18). Second, we can consecrate ourselves early each morning to God. In so doing, we are seeking "first the kingdom of God" (Matthew 6:33). Third, we can remember that we are new creatures in Christ. Therefore, we must allow Him to shine forth from within—and not self. For "the life which I now live in the flesh I live by faith in the Son of God, who loved me and gave Himself for me" (Galatians 2:20, NKJV). Finally, we can treat everyone around us as part of our human family, doing "good to all" (Galatians 6:10, NKJV).

There are many more "great ideas" that we can find in our daily study of the Word of God. With prayer, the Holy Ghost who lives in us will guide us in the way He wants to use us each day. Then others will see Jesus Christ in us and glorify our heavenly Father.

My dear sisters, let us start this day with the "great idea" of praying: *Dear heavenly Father, my life belongs to You. Let Your light shine. Use this vessel to draw others unto Thee today so that Your love may transform and they will know Your salvation in Christ Jesus. Amen.*

Bezaida (Betzy) Castro

---

* Ellen G. White, *Steps to Christ* (Washington, DC: Review and Herald®, 1956), 70.

Wormy Apples

Great is the glory of the LORD.
For though the LORD is high,
he regards the lowly.
—*Psalm 138:5, 6, RSV*

We hadn't sprayed our apple tree with pesticide, so the apples were wormy. But the tree still abundantly scattered the apples onto the lawn. My husband kept bringing them in. "Can't you do something with these?" he asked. Well, yes. I could cut out the wormy areas and make all kinds of things: applesauce, pies, cookies, apple crisp—not to mention drying, freezing, or canning them. Ordinarily, when my garden or fruit trees produce more than I can handle, I share the bounty with friends—even strangers! But I was embarrassed to offer anyone wormy apples!

I tried to think of someone who would regard wormy apples as I did—more work to deal with but still of value. But I couldn't bring myself to offer them to even my closest friends. Yet, frugal as I am, I hated the thought of just discarding them. Then an idea came. It wouldn't relieve me of all the remaining apples, but at least some more could be enjoyed. At the time, I was a mentor at an agency that helps newly released prisoners find housing and jobs in order to get a good start on a new life outside of penitentiary walls. I cooked up a large batch of applesauce and took it there. Fresh applesauce would be a rare treat for them.

Ex-prisoners aren't accustomed to kindness. The public, and often even their families, don't believe they can change. They are painfully aware they have messed up, big time. I know that many of them feel like "wormy apples." They think God wants nothing to do with them. I have heard people speak admiringly of people who "go to church," as if we were a species apart, not regular human beings with faults and failings. What a pity! We can lovingly assure them that every person is important to God. For don't we all start out as wormy apples, "since all have sinned and fall short of the glory of God" (Romans 3:23, RSV)?

God sees beyond our "wormy" parts, our weaknesses and wrong choices, and knows our struggles to be the person we were created to be. We Christians carry the wonderful message that God loves everyone, including "wormy apples."

We can tell others that God has the patience and power to remove the "worms" and bruises and transform any "wormy apple" into a new creation.

Dolores Klinsky Walker

The Inspection

*While we look not at the things which are seen, but at the things
which are not seen: for the things which are seen are temporal;
but the things which are not seen are eternal.*
—2 Corinthians 4:18

Though my school had been due an annual inspection the previous year,
no such activity had been carried out. The principal and teachers all
knew that the inspection was inevitable, but we somehow failed to make
the necessary preparation in a timely manner. It might have appeared that we
had ignored the advice to be prepared at all times. Then the inspection notice
came—but only two days prior to the arrival of the inspector. We began rigorous
preparation.

We made sure that all potentially hazardous objects were secured, so as not
to be harmful to anyone, and that all solid waste was properly disposed of. A
general clearing of the outside grounds was done, leaving the campus a beauty
to behold. Walls were painted, floors were scrubbed, lawns were manicured, and
flower gardens were weeded. While the school grounds and buildings were being
attended to, the administration had to make sure that all requisite documents
were updated should they be requested. In order to be graded suitable for
operation, all of the standards set by the governing entity had to be met. When
the inspector arrived on the school grounds, I observed that nothing had been
left unfixed or undone.

My thoughts were raised heavenward, and I immediately reflected on my
personal relationship with God. I then started an inward inspection of my own
life and wondered: *If God were the Inspector this morning, what would His inspection
report reveal about me?* I reflected on the story of Noah and the warnings he gave.
In spite of his constant calls of repentance and heart preparation, the majority of
the people failed the "inspection" anyhow. Some were perhaps waiting to make
last-minute preparations, but the Flood caught them off guard. Quietly I moved
to a corner of my classroom and prayed that this experience would help me
change my perceptive on being prepared.

*Dear God, help me today, Your daughter, to fix all the negatives and clear all the
garbage from my life. Help me prepare my heart for the great inspection. And please,
may the grades I receive place me on the right side of Your throne, where I will see
Jesus face-to-face.*

Rose Coleman

I Will Be With You in Trouble!

He shall call upon me, and I will answer him:
I will be with him in trouble; I will deliver him, and honour him.
With long life will I satisfy him, and shew him my salvation.
—*Psalm 91:15, 16*

Mom," said my daughter Haley, "I don't think I want to go back to community college this semester, because I already have more than enough credits when I transfer to a Christian college for my last two years. This semester's credits at community college would just be wasted." I told her it was not a bad idea, as she could work more hours at her job and save money for college tuition. Haley worked extra time at her job.

In February, I had an accident and suffered a compression fracture in my vertebrae. The doctor said, "Essentially, you have a broken back." My pain, which hospitals rate from one to ten, was at least a twelve! I was immediately stuck at home and could do nothing but be waited on by my kids and husband. I had never even had a broken bone, and now I start with my back? Doing normal household chores was out of the question, as was sitting comfortably. For more than a month, all I could do was sleep or sit. Now I would not be able to work at my two jobs. I had been working mornings cleaning three post offices. I also worked second shift, forty hours a week, at a local factory. I have never been one to miss work, so the thought of my not being able to go to work made me miserable. However, my daughters and son came through for me. They said they would help me with cleaning the post offices, so I would not lose that job. This did not lessen my pain, but it made my situation more bearable.

Not being in school, Haley was free to work in the morning, cleaning offices and driving more than fifty miles, three days a week, to cover my work. That certainly has helped me out, as I have been off more than nine months to heal. God knew this was going to happen, and perhaps that was why Haley did not attend school. God knows the end from the beginning, and His way is the best way. When Haley had to leave for college, my older daughter, Jessica, quit one of her jobs to take on the three post offices for me. Though none of us had planned for all this inconvenience, God has made it work. I praise Him that my children have been so willing to help their injured mother.

Let's praise God today for His loving care over all of us! Truly He is with us in trouble!

Charlotte Robinson

Sometimes, Yes; Sometimes, Wait

Wait for the LORD; be strong and take heart and wait for the LORD.
—*Psalm 27:14, NIV*

I was only a child in kindergarten when I first heard the saying, "God always answers prayers—sometimes, 'Yes'; sometimes, 'No'; and sometimes, 'Wait.' " It sounded so simple back then. Yet many years later, I know this is really a complex spiritual concept because sometimes, when answers to prayer don't seem to come, we wonder, *Jesus, are You listening?*

When God obviously answers "Yes," this becomes the source of many testimonies at midweek prayer services. We love the many "Yes" stories in the Bible:

- Eliezer, the praying servant, searching for a wife for Abraham's son, Isaac
- Jacob being delivered from Esau's vengeance after wrestling all night with the angel
- Moses crossing the Red Sea on dry land
- The three Hebrew boys in the fiery furnace not getting burned
- Daniel being kept safe in the lions' den
- Peter walking on water

These stories encourage us. These stories speak of the majesty and power of God. These stories provide us with hope as we proceed along life's journey.

However, sometimes God says, "Wait." Now, I have to be honest—waiting is really hard. We live in an age of instant mashed potatoes and grits. We microwave our meals, which can be prepared in just minutes. Our entire culture is built on speed. But God reminds us, at times, to wait. Waiting often frustrates us and causes us to be confused and to question. Unfortunately, we sometimes expect God to move as quickly as we see our computer programs move.

Yet the concept of waiting has meaning to God. Sometimes our prayer requests are frivolous and not well thought out. Perhaps God delays an obvious answer because He wants us to think seriously about what we asked of Him. Do we really need what we asked for? The delay may be about increasing our heart searching and the enhancement of our spiritual growth.

Both God's "Yes" and "Wait" answers are easier to accept when we remember who is in control. Reflect on your prayer life today. Is God asking you to wait?

Edith C. Fraser

Sunshine

Let the one who walks in the dark, who has no light,
trust in the name of the LORD and rely on their God.
—*Isaiah 50:10, NIV*

"I will turn the darkness into light before them."
—*Isaiah 42:16, NIV*

Summer was late in the Northwest, where I live. Usually the longer days bring lots of sunshine, from early morning until evening, but not this year. The clouds had gathered and continued to hang on. It seemed everyone was anxiously awaiting summer's return. As the Fourth of July weekend approached and the days were still cloudy and cooler than usual outside, attitudes changed. Many people seemed depressed and complained about the weather. When would the sunshine come to stay? Clouds were also gathering in our minds. On one of these cloudy days, I took a short walk outside. While on this walk, I saw the clouds in the sky suddenly roll back and the sun begin to shine brightly. Instantly my heart sang. I told God how much I appreciated the sun and its brightness. My endorphins were bubbling up, and joy filled my heart!

At that moment, a thought occurred to me. God never intended for it to be cloudy. It is no wonder we become depressed when the sun hides behind the clouds. Dark clouds are the result of sin. Until Jesus returns for us, we will have some dark days. We have an enemy of our souls, and he delights in causing spiritual darkness.

When our lives seem dark and we can't see through the gloom, we need to remember not only is God walking with us, but He is also on the other side of the darkness. He knows the outcome of what may be troubling us and wants us to trust Him. He will see us through. Satan wants to rob us of the peace and joy that God has for us. He wants us to look at the circumstances surrounding our lives and feel hopeless. He wants us to lose sight of God.

Our enemy, however, is a defeated foe. One day soon, we will look up and see a small cloud, as it nears the earth. The entire sky will light up. Thousands upon thousands of angels will fill the sky. In their midst, riding on a white horse, clothed in a linen robe dipped in blood, and wearing many crowns, the King of kings and Lord of lords descends. We will be gathered together with those who are risen from their graves and join Him in the air. No more tears, no more death, and no more dark clouds. We will live with Him eternally and bask in His light!

Sue Anderson

A Slice of Bread

*For all the promises of God in Him are Yes, and in Him Amen,
to the glory of God through us.*
—2 Corinthians 1:20, NKJV

Several years ago, I was given a Daily Bread promise box containing cards bearing verses from the Bible. Each verse contained a promise from God. I set the "bread box" on my desk at work. However, I paid so little attention to it that it eventually got misplaced.

Recently I thought of a practical use for the contents of my misplaced Daily Bread promise box. Why couldn't I take out a promise card each day and apply it to my life by memorizing it and meditating on it throughout the day? But when I looked for my Daily Bread promise box, I could not find it.

So I set out to find another bread-shaped box that contained Bible promises. I did find one, identical to the first one!

I have placed the new Daily Bread promise box in a unique location that is accessible to everyone in my family. Now I include them when I pull out a "slice" of bread each day and invite them to apply the promise to their lives as well. What a blessing I have received using a slice of God's promises every day with my family. In fact, doing this has proven to be such a blessing that I have purchased several more Daily Bread promise boxes to share with others. When I have given a box to someone, I first explain what I am doing with my own promise bread box. I tell them I would like to know about their amazing experiences after applying these promises to their lives.

I share that each verse has been meaningful to me. For example, one of my "slices" reads, "As I was with Moses, so I will be with thee" (Joshua 3:7). As I meditated on this promise and trusted that God was with me in my challenges too, I am reminded that through my struggles, God is also with me. Rejoicing in God's blessings has become my daily theme. Also, I am inspired to read beyond each day's Bible verse of promise for more blessing.

As I have given out Bible promise bread boxes, I have challenged others to be surprised with each wonderful promise, memorize it, and bask in God's presence all day long.

You can do the same with your "bread box," the Bible.

Margo Peterson

Protected

My help comes from the LORD, who made heaven and earth.
He will not let your foot be moved; he who keeps you will not
slumber. Behold, he who keeps Israel will neither slumber nor sleep.
—*Psalm 121:2–4, ESV*

One day after Georgia, my almost eighty-four-year-old stepmother, passed away, one of her friends shared an amazing insight into God's care of her. About ten years ago, when conditions in the family home became unsafe for her, several individuals cooperated to get Georgia moved into low-income housing because she was intensely desirous of remaining independent. Each day, however, Georgia insisted on walking back "home" to feed the cats and shop in town. The distance each way was more than a mile on a narrow road running up a steep hill.

As the years took their toll, Georgia became stooped until she was almost bent double. Yet she walked, day and night, with a purse on one arm and a plastic bag from a department store on the other. I had been unaware that each time Georgia slowly walked "home" or to stores, she passed through the part of town that had the highest crime rate. Her daily walks, during which she must have appeared increasingly vulnerable, took her past a couple of crack houses, often with more than twenty people hanging around. In 2014, while walking home one day, Georgia fell. One of the young men hanging around the front yard of a crack house noticed and went over to help her up, offering to take her for medical treatment. Georgia refused, but he insisted on seeing her home. The next day, the same young man, a friend of drug dealers, requested that Georgia's friend double-check whether she needed medical care. He followed through. Indeed, Georgia's arm was broken, and she spent time in the hospital and nursing home until she recovered. Georgia's friend was convinced that God had been protecting Georgia. Though everyone in town thought she was very poor, she obviously carried some money to shop but was never robbed or assaulted.

We traveled to her funeral and helped clean her apartment. As we sadly drove home, I opened Georgia's purse. Yes, money. Eleven months' worth of Social Security income! In her old age, Georgia had come to fear banks. But God had protected her—and her income!

If God could use someone viewed as a social outcast to come to the aid of a vulnerable elderly woman, what can He do for you today?

Dora Hallock

God's Autograph

"This is the covenant I will make with the people of Israel after that time," declares the LORD. "I will put my law in their minds and write it on their hearts. I will be their God, and they will be my people."
—*Jeremiah 31:33, NIV*

Jeremiah 31:33 portrays God talking to the Israelites, but the message applies to all of God's people today.

I spent a lot of my free time in January 2016 watching movies on the Hallmark Channel. One of my favorite movies was *Love on the Sidelines*. It is a love story about a romance between a struggling fashion designer (Laurel) and a quarterback (Danny) who is sidelined with an injury. One scene in the movie is what inspired this devotional.

The scene zeroes in on a young fan approaching Danny while the injured quarterback is dining in a fancy restaurant. The child goes bonkers over being able to meet his hero and asks Danny for his autograph. Danny smiles, takes the pen that the boy offers, and writes his name on the blank sheet of the boy's notepad. The boy leaves with a bliss-filled look on his face.

The autograph scene of this movie made me think of something greater because I realized how we, as humans in real life, get stars in our eyes when we see our favorite famous people and seize the opportunity to get autographs. Sometimes we go to drastic and dramatic lengths to get the signature of a famous person. In some cases, fans not having a pen and paper have asked celebrities to autograph their bare arms, hands, chest, or back!

We may think it's a bit crazy to go to such lengths to get the signature of a favorite person. But while we may be chasing celebrities, God is chasing us! He went to great lengths to save our souls (John 3:16), and He wants to give us more than His autograph—He wants to write *His* name on *our* hearts!

That's beautiful, isn't it? So while chasing celebrities and seeking autographs is a part of some people's human experience, I challenge you to remember who sought *you* first—God, the Creator of the universe.

Go ahead and ask for His autograph. He's more than willing to give it to you, and you won't have to go above and beyond to get it.

Alexis A. Goring

"Tomorrow"

Moses said to Pharaoh, "I leave to you the honor of setting the time
for me to pray for you and your officials and your people that you and
your house may be rid of the frogs. . . ."
"Tomorrow," Pharaoh said.
—*Exodus 8:9, 10, NIV*

When we understand what God wants to teach us, we will have a completely different picture of His Word. For example, when His children were captive in Egypt, God wanted to help them. How? God sent a series of plagues to soften Pharaoh's heart. One of these plagues was an infestation of frogs. God did not leave one inch of Egypt untouched: frogs were in the kitchen, beds, ovens—everywhere.

I can imagine Pharaoh's wife saying, "I am done! I am sick of all these frogs." Quite possibly Pharaoh listened his wife. Then he came to Moses and asked him to get rid of the frogs. "Pray to your God," said Pharaoh. Moses replied, "I leave you the honor of setting the time for me to pray." In other words, "I will give you the honor to set the time for God to remove the frogs from your life." He was saying, "Just tell me when. God is ready, God is able, and God is powerful. Just tell me when you want this to happen, Pharaoh."

I consider Pharaoh's answer odd. He says, "Tomorrow." Think about that. God was ready to take the frogs, but Pharaoh's answer was, "Not today, tomorrow." Amazing! Yet how easily we perhaps do the same. "Lord, I can deal with this situation. Tomorrow I'll ask for your help."

Tomorrow.

Are we allowing God to deal with the "frogs" that are plaguing us? I am thinking of things such as harmful emotions we are willing to live with rather than turning them over to God today: worry, fear, an unforgiving spirit, envy, sadness, shame, guilt, jealousy, bitterness, or resentment. Perhaps we try to solve those problems by procrastinating or avoiding the issue. Avoiding turning them over to God.

Today Christ wants to take away the "frogs" that plague us. "For we do not have a high priest who is unable to empathize with our weaknesses. . . . Let us then approach God's throne of grace with confidence, so that we may receive mercy and find grace to help us in our time of need" (Hebrews 4:15, 16, NIV).

Raquel Queiroz da Costa Arrais

All Things Are Possible

"Fear not, for I am with you; be not dismayed,
for I am your God. I will strengthen you, yes, I will help you,
I will uphold you with My righteous right hand."
—Isaiah 41:10, NKJV

Mowing the lawn is something I enjoy doing. Last year, we purchased a self-propelled walking lawn mower. It is so much easier to use than the push mower I was used to.

After several days of rain, then two beautiful sunny days, I needed to finish mowing the large expanse of lawn at my son's home where we were spending the summer.

The grass appeared to be dry on top but, once mowed, much moisture was exposed. The back wheels of the lawn mower were caked with wet grass when I finished mowing, so I cleaned them off. Upon checking the underside of the mowing deck to see how much grass had been trapped there, I couldn't believe the amount packed in above the blades. I was truly amazed at how those blades kept operating with so much grass stuffed in all around them. The mower had continued to persevere despite the obstacles.

As we strive to serve and win others to Christ, we also encounter frequent obstacles. How do we deal with them? Do we believe the promise in Philippians 4:13 that says, "I can do all things through Christ who strengthens me"? (NKJV). Then, do we persevere as did the clogged up lawn mower, or do we become fainthearted and decide persevering is too hard, so we give up?

Jesus is our great example. Tremendous barriers confronted Him—from His own people and family. In spite of being bombarded from every side with unbelief, hatred, abuse, and scorn, He continued to preach, teach, and heal until His own people, the religious leaders of His day, crucified Him. Compared to His suffering, what we deal with in striving to serve others or win them to Him is trivial. When we believe His promises and claim them, all things are possible, despite any lack of support or unexpected obstacles with which we are confronted.

Many times, when working for Christ, we plunge ahead with very good intentions but in our own strength. Giving our issues, problems, and challenges over to Him frees us up so that we can proceed with His work in spite of our circumstances—without fear or stress. Let's unclog the "blades" of our human efforts by turning all our concerns over to our heavenly Father, as He invites us to do. Then we have can have the assurance of great blessings and positive outcomes.

Marian Hart-Gay

God's Angel With Me

For he shall give his angels charge over thee,
to keep thee in all thy ways.
—*Psalm 91:11*

One lovely sunny morning. I was getting ready for my doctor's appointment, knowing I would have to take a long, familiar route from where I live along the Baltimore-Washington Parkway. Upon entering my car, I paused, asking God to take charge of my trip by sending His angels to be with me.

My examination ended with a good diagnosis. I thanked God and got back on the parkway to head home. When approximately one half mile away from the doctor's office, my car began slowing down. I decided to pull over on the side of the road. The engine stopped. Within a few minutes, I remembered how I had prayed, asking God to protect me as I traveled. So I pressed the accelerator. Surprisingly the car started but moved only slowly. Again, I moved to the side of the road before my car stopped again. I called my son and the insurance company to inform them of the problem I was having.

During my wait time, a blue car pulled up behind me. The driver, a woman, approached, saying she had followed me because she suspected I was having a problem. She waited with me until the automobile technician arrived. With heartfelt thanks, I told the woman, "God sent you as my angel just at the right time!" My son had also arrived.

Upon walking to the front of my car, the automobile technician said, "I smell gas." Checking further, he then looked at my son and me. "You have a gas leak," he said. "You are lucky that your car stopped running. If it hadn't, it would have caught on fire!"

Being previously unaware of my immediate danger, I now shed tears of joy and thanksgiving on the journey home. It had not been a coincidence that my car's engine had kept cutting off and then dying completely. Rather, it was the same God who sent His angels to free Daniel from the lions' den and now had sent an angel to free me from being caught in a burning vehicle.

God knows why things happen in our lives along life's pathway. Let's join together, trusting in faith as I share words from a favorite song little children enjoy singing in their Sabbath School class: "Angels are watching over me. . . . Thank God for angels bright."

Annie B. Best

July 27

"Peace, Be Still"

But the LORD watches over those who fear him,
those who rely on his unfailing love.
—*Psalm 33:18, NLT*

What started out as a peaceful day ended in chaos. I decided to make a quick stop at a mall in Johannesburg after a long, tiring day. I needed something to eat before proceeding to the hotel. As I entered the mall, rain began to fall. I thought I'd just window-shop until it stopped, but after two hours passed, I ventured out into the storm.

After driving a few kilometers, I noticed a heavy traffic jam ahead. I did not worry because the off-ramp to the hotel was just a few meters away. As I made the turn, I lost control of my car and drove into a ditch! It was flooded, so I panicked. I stayed in the car because I can't swim. I rolled down the window and beckoned for help but to no avail. The entire road was flooded, and everyone was fighting for survival. I cried out to God to save me. Then I made a quick call to my sister, Betty. Her last words were, "May the angels of the Lord encamp around you and deliver you from the storm." I started singing, "Master, the tempest is raging." When I got to the words, "Peace, be still," I was engulfed by His peace that surpasses all understanding. I only remember letting go of the steering wheel and watching my car float on its own until it reached dry ground. How I praised God for His protection and unseen angels!

I quickly drove on for several more kilometers to the next off-ramp. It too was flooded. I parked by the roadside. Again, I prayed for help. Suddenly a brand-new car stopped right beside me. A young man beckoned me to follow him. I protested, but in a firm voice he said, "This storm is only going to get worse!" I followed him through the water until we reached dry ground. He stopped in the middle of the road and motioned for me to drive past him. I saw him in my rearview mirror, but when I looked a second time, his car had vanished.

I drove on, wondering about the mysterious young man. I walked into the hotel lobby, where I collapsed from exhaustion. I was carried to my room. Four hours later, I was awakened by the telephone ringing. My family was phoning to say they had prayed for God to send an angel to protect me and steer the car through the storm. I praised God!

Today who do you need to pray for?

Edith Kiggundu

"What Are You Doing With What You Have Left?"

Each of you should use whatever gift you have received to serve
others, as faithful stewards of God's grace in its various forms.
—1 Peter 4:10, NIV

In one of my reflective moments as a retiree, I found myself musing about my life and was forcibly struck by this question: "Shirley, what are you doing with what you have left?" Pondering the ideas that surfaced, I began to think about these women's ministries devotional books and how articles written by God's messengers have blessed, inspired, and encouraged me on my Christian journey. For many years, I have shared devotional books as gifts to family members, neighbors, friends, and doctors' and dentists' offices. Now I was impressed to expand this ministry to include women I meet during my travels.

Several months ago, I received an e-mail from a lady I met on a cruise. She was requesting prayer for her upcoming surgical procedure. I prayed but also sent her the devotional book *Breathe*. She responded: "My *Breathe* book arrived the day after I completed my therapy! The short stories allowed me to look outside myself and appreciate the love and caring sent through God's messengers to remind me of the care we are given daily . . . sick or well, in pain or joy. Your story about the birds let me see the caregivers as the birds outside your window. Thank you." I thanked God for the opportunity to minister to someone so far away.

Another ministry God placed on my heart is encouraging women to write. Currently, twelve articles from these women have been published. Maple, upon receiving her complimentary book, was so excited to see her name in it that she called to express her gratitude: "I didn't know I could write, but you kept insisting that I should just write. And I did. Now I hold a book in my hands with my name in it. I can't hold back the tears." I'm enjoying this newfound ministry in my senior years.

Dear Christian traveler, what are you doing with what you have left? You haven't any idea? Well, why not ask God to reveal something to you. He has entrusted all of us with talents. Maybe yours is helping an abused neighbor, praying with the bereaved, visiting someone in a nursing home or who is incarcerated, or sharing a "Thinking of You" card. If you're willing, God will provide the opportunity. Don't delay. Start today! Touch a life; make a difference for Jesus!

Shirley C. Iheanacho

Encouraging Others

In all your ways acknowledge Him,
and He will make your paths straight.
—Proverbs 3:6, NASB

I enjoy my Tuesday morning volunteer time in the hospital Pastoral Care Department. The morning after newly admitted patients arrive, I visit with them and advise them regarding our chaplain's services. I offer to call their pastor if he or she is not aware that the patient is in the hospital.

My visits are brief unless the patient indicates a desire to talk. If so, I remain as long as someone needs a listening ear. It amazes me that, as ill as many are, in the five years I have been involved there, none have ever been rude or unpleasant. Occasionally someone will indicate they are not interested in anything of a religious nature, and I quickly assure them the choice is theirs.

When training other volunteers, I make a point to tell them that if we leave and the patient does not feel as though someone pleasant has been in to visit them, then we should not have been in their room. It is always a blessing to encourage a patient with a word of prayer.

Before I began this work, I was not sure I would be comfortable offering to pray with strangers. Now I find that those are the moments I look forward to the most, and I am grateful for the opportunities.

I find other Christians are happy to hear and/or talk about Christ's love and care for them. Non-Christians or former Christians often react with emotion and gratitude.

What a privilege to respond when the Holy Spirit reminds me to offer a prayer for a person who appears gruff or uninterested in prayer. Yet I see how genuinely touched and appreciative they are.

The few hours of my volunteer time each week are outweighed, by far, by the manifold blessings and joy I receive in return for this ministry.

Having volunteered in other areas of the hospital and community, I find the satisfaction of this endeavor the most rewarding.

My purpose in sharing this part of my life with you is to encourage you to venture out for the Lord in ways you have not yet tried.

Dorothy Wainwright Carey

The Power Source

"I am the vine, you are the branches. He who abides in Me,
and I in him, bears much fruit; for without Me you can do nothing."
—*John 15:5, NKJV*

One of the most frustrating things for me is to wake up in the morning and find that my phone is dead. *What? I made all the preparations for it to be charged overnight. I connected the charger to the phone and plugged the other end into the electrical outlet.* That was last night, though. Somehow, the charger became disconnected from its source of power. Perhaps I forgot to plug it in—it doesn't matter *how* it happened—my phone is dead.

So it is with my spiritual life. If I am disconnected from my Source of power, Jesus, I'm essentially useless and, for all spiritual purposes, dead.

At times I'm close to Jesus. I speak to Him, pray, and study His Word. His Holy Spirit gives me grace to trust Him with all that is important to me: my life, children, marriage, work, and relationships. During those times, the Spirit enables me to regard others more highly than myself and to love God above all else. Life becomes bearable because I trust the One who stands behind, who leads the way, and who goes before me.

At other times, though, I feel completely disconnected from Jesus. Stress, sadness, or struggles so overwhelm me that I lose sight of Him. In the course of my disquieting times, I "obsess" over my obstacles. I focus on those who have hurt me or when I might have hurt my loved ones. I begrudge the ungrateful and detest the malicious. All my energy is wasted on those who have slighted me, and my unsettled spirit blames myself, others, and the world.

During those times, the Spirit of God is relentless in His goal to reconnect me to the Vine, the Rock, the Light of the world, who is Christ Jesus. The Spirit may touch me through a sermon, a Bible verse, or one of God's friends. But He never fails to speak to me even in my darkest moments. When the Spirit reconnects me to Jesus, I'm able to live my life according to God's plan. Just as my newly charged phone is able to live out its purpose again.

My sisters, how is it with you today? Are you connected to the Source of power? My prayer today is that the Spirit of God will keep you connected to the power Source—Jesus Christ, our Lord.

Rose Joseph Thomas

My God-Dependence Coach: Turning a Limitation Into a Blessing

*"My grace is sufficient for you,
for my power is made perfect in weakness."*
—2 Corinthians 12:9, NIV

I woke up at 4:30 A.M. on Thursday, January 21, 2016, to realize that the vision in my right eye had undergone a drastic change. Three days later, I was completely blind in that eye. That was my abrupt introduction to the world of multiple sclerosis, or MS.

A week later, I discovered my legs could hardly move, though I'd walked a mile the day before. In the hospital, I underwent intense treatment to bring the symptoms under control and to learn how to live with my new "normal." I've improved a lot, but still there's a great deal of uncertainty. One day I'm almost normal. The next, I need a walker because it's hard to move my legs or keep my balance. Sometimes I have to let others do things for me, and it's frustrating. I want to do everything myself. I feel unsure of what each day will bring.

I have chosen to let MS be my coach for living a life of complete dependence on God. I'm taking my cue from the apostle Paul, who struggled with his own "thorn in the flesh." He wrote: "I was given the gift of a handicap to keep me in constant touch with my limitations. . . . At first I didn't think of it as a gift, and begged God to remove it. Three times I did that, and then he told me, My grace is enough; it's all you need. My strength comes into its own in your weakness. Once I heard that, I was glad to let it happen. I quit focusing on the handicap and began appreciating the gift. It was a case of Christ's strength moving in on my weakness. Now I take limitations in stride, and with good cheer, these limitations that cut me down to size—abuse, accidents, opposition, bad breaks. I just let Christ take over! And so the weaker I get, the stronger I become" (2 Corinthians 12:7–10, *The Message*).

Do you have a limitation? God's grace *is* sufficient for us. He will help us choose to relate to our disabilities as gifts and learn how to let them be a blessing both to us and to others.

Rachel Williams-Smith

Getting to Know the Author

"My sheep hear my voice, and I know them, and they follow me.
I give them eternal life, and they will never perish,
and no one will snatch them out of my hand."
—*John 10:27, 28, ESV*

Since I was a little girl, I have loved to read books. But it wasn't until the era of Facebook and Twitter that I discovered a major opportunity and blessing—I could use social media to connect with my favorite authors! Most authors with books on the market today love connecting with their readers through social media. They invite their readers to follow them on Twitter and to "like" their author page on Facebook. Sometimes, they will even respond to friend requests and add new friends on their personal Facebook page.

I absolutely adore it when the author of one of my favorite books and I become Facebook friends! As a writer, there's something special about connecting with one's favorite author. It's like a bond that no one else really understands except you and your writer friends—because writers are unique. They don't see the world the same way that most people see it. It's always wonderful to be friends with people who truly "get" you and understand your viewpoint.

One Sabbath morning during worship service, the praise team was singing songs about how great our God is, and I felt God impress me with the idea for this devotional. I entitled it "Getting to Know the Author" because I realize that there's one Author whom we all should know, the One who is eager to call us His friend. The Author that I am referring to is the Creator of the universe. He's truly in love with you! God is passionate about reconciling you to Himself, which is why He sent His Son, Jesus Christ, into this world to save our souls.

I think it's pretty awesome how the Author of our faith, the Creator of the entire universe, wants to be our friend.

But how do you get to be friends with God?

The answer is simple: You spend time getting to know Him through prayer and studying His Word, the Holy Bible.

As you grow close to Him, you will know His voice. Then your relationship with Him will inspire others to know Him personally too.

Alexis A. Goring

August 2

Oh, Yes, He Cares

I will lift up mine eyes unto the hills, from whence cometh my help.
My help cometh from the LORD, which made heaven and earth.
—Psalm 121:1, 2

On the Friday before Father's Day in 2010, my late husband was admitted to the Brookdale University Hospital and Medical Center. He was released the evening before my family was scheduled to drive from New York to Atlanta, Georgia, for a big church conference. My seventy-five-year-old mother rented a fifteen-seat van to carry family members, which included six of my nieces and nephews. My husband, who had a United States provisional driving permit, agreed to drive if my mother would ride in the front passenger seat. It seemed that my dear husband specialized in missing exits and getting us lost for hours even though we were using a GPS. We eventually got onto the right highway and arrived in Georgia around ten o'clock the following morning. We were happy to see many of my siblings and families that congregated at the home of one of our brothers who resides there.

Using my brother's car on Friday morning, my husband and I set out for the Georgia Dome to attend meetings. Since we got lost, however, we didn't arrive at our destination until the afternoon. Yet it was a wonderful experience to meet old friends and be blessed in the meetings by hearing what God is doing in the lives of people around the world.

One of my sisters, who had flown in from New York, had originally planned to fly back home Monday. However, she changed her plans so that she could do the return road trip with us. After the weekend, as our rented van backed out of my brother's garage, he suggested that my sister do the driving, with my husband giving her a break, now and then, when she got tired.

During the trip, I observed that my husband's breathing was not normal. With prayer on my heart and keeping an eye out for hospital signs, should we need them, I heard my husband complain about frequent bouts of shortness of breath. He was unable to do any more driving. Thankfully, we made it back to New York with no emergencies.

Truly God impressed my sister not to fly home and my brother to suggest that my sister do the driving back to New York. God always has a plan for us, even though many times we do not acknowledge it. Our God always makes a way because He sees, He knows, and He cares.

Ruby H. Ennis-Alleyne

Hope, Joy, and Love

"But those who drink the water I give will never be thirsty again.
It becomes a fresh, bubbling spring within them,
giving them eternal life."
—John 4:14, NLT

As I sit here in my living room, I enjoy looking at a Webcam on my Kindle Fire. I can go around the world seeing beautiful landscapes and scenery. Sometimes I catch a glimpse of people snow skiing in Norway or swimming in the clear waters of Hawaii. I wonder about the lives of those I see in those moments of time and sometimes stop to pray for them. I don't know their situations, but God does.

Our planet is full of all kinds of people in different cultures, different countries, and different ways of living. But in reality, we all want the same things—to love, be loved, take care of our families, and contribute to society in some fashion or another. We are all God's children and important to Him.

Our importance is never clearer to me than when I think of the plan of salvation through God's Son, Jesus Christ. The sacrifice He made on the cross is the most important event in human history. He gave Himself so that anyone who chooses may have eternal life. That makes God the ultimate equal opportunity provider! When life feels like a challenging climb up a ladder, remember that He has your back. When we feel as if we are slipping down that ladder, we can know that He is waiting for us with His arms wide open to embrace us with His love. And when we come to know Him, we experience joy like no other. He gives us strength when we're weary, peace when we're anxious, hope when we're discouraged, and affirmation that all is going well.

God alone can save us, as we cannot save ourselves. When we come to the One who was willing to have nails pierce His hands and feet and to suffer the pain of our sins, we can become whole. Jesus said, "I am the way, the truth, and the life" (John 14:6); and "I am Alpha and Omega, the beginning and the end, the first and the last" (Revelation 22:13).

I believe God's promises. He has shown Himself to me in so many ways. I know He is who He says He is. He was resurrected from the dead. I know that He loves me and that He loves you more than life itself because He gave His life for each one of us.

Opening our hearts to Him today will bring hope for all our tomorrows.

Jean Dozier Davey

The Flood—Part 1

"There will be . . . anguish on the earth among nations bewildered by
the roaring sea and waves. People will faint from fear. . . . Then they
will see the Son of Man coming. . . . But when these things begin to
take place, . . . lift up your heads, because your redemption is near!"
—*Luke 21:25–28, HCSB*

Rain fell that July 26 afternoon in 2008 as I worked in my small house in the village of Makotsevo. Then walnut-size hail turned my yard white and pelted off pieces of my tile roof. Soon water leaked through the ceiling and accumulated everywhere. Two hours later, the rain stopped and the sun appeared. Nine days later, however, on August 4, the heavy afternoon rains came again. Gradually, they intensified into such a heavy downpour that I could not see objects as close to me as sixteen feet (five meters) away. Again, my roof began to leak. In no time at all, it was actually raining in my house! I put buckets and large bowls on the floor in an attempt to catch the incoming water. I covered the beds with big plastic bags to keep them dry.

Alone at home, I felt a mighty shudder as something powerful hit the back of the house. It was a big wave of flood water rushing down from the nearby mountain. My house parted the wave so that two turbulent rivers now flowed— one on each side of my home. As thunder rumbled and lightning flashed, the terrifying sounds reminded me of bombings during a war. Pine trees sixty-five to ninety-eight feet (twenty to thirty meters) tall bent in agony beneath the windy gusts and downpour, causing me to fear that they would fall within seconds and crush me. This severe storm lasted for thirty-six hours! For another two weeks, however, floodwaters continued to flow and to rise. They dug trenches twenty-seven to thirty-one inches (seventy to eighty centimeters) deep in the streets around my house, washing away some of the foundation soil.

Surrounded by water on all sides, and with three nearby railroad bridges destroyed, we were cut off from the village and nearest city, leaving us without electricity, bread, or drinking water. My three neighbors and I shared our food stores until we ran out. Then we prayed.

I read from the Bible and explained to my neighbors that catastrophes such as these would occur more and more frequently, serving as signs pointing to the return of Jesus, who is coming to save us. These signs warn us to prepare our hearts to meet Him. Are you getting ready?

Slavka Simeonova

The Flood—Part 2

"You will call to Me and come and pray to Me,
and I will listen to you. You will seek Me and find Me
when you search for Me with all your heart."
—Jeremiah 29:12, 13, HCSB

On Sabbath, August 6, after reading from the Bible and discussing what we had read, my three neighbors and I finished the last piece of food we had left. We said Goodbye to one another, determined to pray earnestly that God would somehow help us reach the city of Sofia, despite the high floodwaters. Later that evening, I heard someone calling my name from the street. I saw another neighbor, Margarita, and her daughter, whom I did not know very well. However, my late husband had talked to them about God shortly before his death. Margarita shouted, "Come, I've got something for you, and I must tell you something." Excited and shaking, she said, "My husband had just put wood inside the fireplace when I heard a whisper. It said to me, 'Get up and take some food to Slavka because she is alone.' Then, as I was preparing the evening meal, I heard the same words whispered to me again. So my daughter came with me to bring this to you." They held out some delicious zucchini and bread. I thanked them.

I was deeply moved by this encounter. I felt such inner joy and peace. God was taking care of me, meeting my needs, and using people who had not been much interested in Him! The next day, August 7, our electricity came back on. By August 12, the three ruined railroad bridges had been restored enough so that I could travel to Sofia to shop for my needs. I still wonder how I was able to live in my very humid house between July 26 and August 12 without becoming seriously ill. What would have happened to me if God had not intervened, if He had not provided food and medicine, since I have a heart disease and diabetes that necessitates my taking insulin? And why did God use that particular family of unbelievers to provide for my needs?

Yet God's ways are unique. After this experience, that particular family and I became very close. I was able to start telling them more about God. Now they too know that Jesus loves us just as we are: imperfect. And they know that "all things work together for good to them that love God" (Romans 8:28), for God has promised to hear our pleas.

When we seek Him with all our hearts, He promises to let us "find" Him. For He is always close by—to each one of us. We do not have to fear the "floods" of this life. Amen!

Slavka Simeonova

Control and Freedom

*"So if the Son sets you free,
you will be free indeed."*
—John 8:36, NIV

In my counseling practice, I often need to remind people that true control comes from giving freedom. God designed us to resist efforts by others to control us. This resistance was also built in to give us the ability to resist temptation. The curious thing is that we use this feature to resist and break free from those who would like us to do things their way and to think like they think. Strong messages of nonacceptance or disapproval are sometimes communicated to us by others when we do not think or behave the way they want us to. Fear of anger, threats of physical or emotional pain, or withdrawal of love pollutes the joy God has in store for us.

So, then, when we comply in that context and do what another person urges us to do, we are no longer motivated by love but by *fear*. We fear losing a relationship or connection with the other person. When we feel trapped or stuck, resentment begins to deteriorate that relationship. This may be equally true if we are the party attempting to control.

God's design is that true control comes only when freedom of choice is available. Only then can joy replace fear. Intimacy cannot be forced or coerced. Yet intimacy is what all humans most desire.

How different would life be if, instead of trying to control others, we gave others the freedom we ourselves value so deeply? Stress and frustration would evaporate if we implemented the principles of God in our intimate relationships with family members and friends. All the wasted energy of trying to control—or resisting control—would be free to generate enthusiasm, attachment, and love. Imagine a world full of the wonderful creations we were designed to be! What a privilege!

And how different would our world be if we simply expressed how we felt, declaring our opinions in calm, kind, and loving tones? What if we could all have the privilege of being ourselves?

Control only begets control. Only when a human being is given the freedom of choice to give love and respect, can loving and respectful behaviors really be reciprocated.

What a paradox—to have control we must be willing to give freedom!

Arlene West McFarland

He Will Command His Angels

For he will command his angels concerning you to guard you
in all your ways; they will lift you up in their hands,
so that you will not strike your foot against a stone.
—*Psalm 91:11, 12, NIV*

My husband, Rick, had major back surgery before sustaining significant damage to the muscles in his right leg. That leg is not fully reliable yet, as he discovered recently. While taking a load of garbage to the dump in his pickup, he was on a major, heavily traveled two-lane highway across the state of Washington. A piece of cardboard lifted off the load, taking with it several chunks of wood of various sizes as it flew onto the highway.

Rick pulled off when he could and ran back to retrieve the debris before it could cause an accident. Cars, freight trucks, and vacation vehicles barreled by him. He carefully timed his first pass, picking up several pieces of material on his way. He got safely to the other side of the highway, caught his breath, and prepared to cross again in the other direction to gather up the rest of the debris. The nearest vehicle coming toward him was a semi, and it was about one hundred yards away, moving fast. Rick ran onto the roadway, got near the debris—very close to the center line—and his weak leg gave way.

He started to fall, then heard an urgent voice say, "Roll!" The word meant something to Rick. He'd rolled plenty of times as a gymnast in academy and college. He'd not performed the maneuver in at least forty years, however, and that long-ago concept was not on his radar at all. The idea didn't come from within. Without any hesitation, however, Rick tucked his head down into his chest, hit the asphalt with his left shoulder, and rolled. He remembers nothing of the actual rollover movement, since he became "aware" again as he came up onto his feet on the side of the highway. He turned around immediately, and the truck roared by.

One glove had been torn from Rick's hand; the other had been shredded but was still attached in places. Otherwise, there was no damage anywhere. The rest of his clothing was intact, and more importantly, so was he! He sustained no breaks, cuts, scrapes, bruises, or even soreness in the days to follow.

We don't doubt that Rick heard the Holy Spirit's voice and was rolled out of the way of traffic by an angel. Praise the Lord! And how important that we all listen for that voice today!

Carolyn K. Karlstrom

Acts of Kindness

Let love be without hypocrisy. Abhor what is evil. Cling to what is good. Be kindly affectionate to one another with brotherly love.
—*Romans 12:9, 10, NKJV*

After many years of hard work, I was at the end of completing my doctoral dissertation. I needed to return to my research lab during the lunch hour to drop off a final draft of my dissertation. It was a normal afternoon in busy California. The freeway was full with traffic. I entered the on-ramp to Interstate 10, which had rows of cars and trucks in each lane. I proceeded to the left lane of the freeway. As soon as I reached sixty miles per hour (ninety-six kilometers per hour), a car in the middle lane drove into my lane. The driver was on the phone and didn't see my car in the left lane. I had no time to brake before his rear bumper hit my front bumper, sending my car into an uncontrollable spin. He drove away as my car spun across four lanes of traffic. All I could think was, *Oh, God!* My car spun off the freeway and came to a stop on its side in an embankment. My car had miraculously avoided a cement barrier and four lanes of traffic.

As I lay in my car, I heard the voices of the many people who stopped to help me. Then I saw the individuals. I will never forget the faces of the men and women who stopped to help me. Each person was as different as could be. They were from diverse walks of life and of different ethnicities. Yet despite their differences in ethnicity, age, and gender, they all manifested great kindness toward me when they stopped to help. Whether it was the men who pulled me from my car, the nurse who held my head steady, or the elderly gentleman who placed his loving hand on my shoulder as he checked my injuries, each person reached out to me in love.

I will also never forget the same comment made by each of them. "God was with you!"

God was truly with me. The injuries I sustained healed over time and were not life-threatening, nor did they cause me chronic pain.

Racism, ageism, and sexism are all too common in today's world. These forms of discrimination fuel acts of hatred rather than acts of kindness. More acts of kindness are needed. Not just acts of kindness to those who are like us, but especially to those who are not like us.

As we go about our day, let us "not be overcome by evil, but overcome evil with good" (Romans 12:21, NKJV).

Beatrice Tauber Prior

Courage to Stand Up for Our Faith

"Whoever acknowledges me before others,
I will also acknowledge before my Father in heaven."
—*Matthew 10:32, NIV*

When I went to school, we still had a six-day week, with classes on Saturdays. On my first day in my new school, some teachers spoke to me about subjects that were offered only on Saturdays, and they wanted to see how we could solve the problem, since that was my day of worship. The girls questioned me continually, "Why don't you come to school on Saturdays?" During each break, some of my new classmates wanted to walk with me in the adjoining park so that they could hear the reasons for my strange lifestyle. I had never ever had to answer so many questions about my faith. Yet standing up for our faith strengthens our spiritual backbone.

When I started at the university, all freshmen had to take a placement test for French. Among other things, we had to write an essay in French. Having spent a summer in France, I had no problem and enthusiastically wrote page after page—unaware I was being watched. Later one of the other students came and sat down beside me in an English lecture. He had also taken the French test and considered the essay writing difficult. He said, "You wrote so much during the French test. How come it was so easy for you?" We started talking. He often came to sit beside me. I had told him early on that I kept the seventh-day Sabbath. He had never met anyone else who did. One day he said, "Listen, one day I will be a teacher. You are the only seventh-day Sabbath keeper I have ever met. You have positively influenced my impression of those who believe this. It will influence my attitude toward any future pupils I have of your denomination."

I can't remember what I said, but his words just bowled me over. I can't even remember his name, but I will never forget his words. He had been watching me and formed his impression of me as a representative of my church. I was just a young girl, and I was not even aware of being watched. But, yes, people do watch us and what we do or don't do. And they categorize and pigeonhole us.

It is a privilege to be a Christian and follower of Jesus. It is nothing to be ashamed of. That is why Jesus told us: Don't be afraid to acknowledge me! (Matthew 10:32). He will be with us to the very end of the age (Matthew 28:20).

Hannele Ottschofski

Would You Like to Have Joy at Home?

"And when she finds it, she calls her friends and neighbors together
and says, 'Rejoice with me; I have found my lost coin.' "
—Luke 15:9, NIV

Has your house had great moments of joy? Luke 15:9 tells of a house party that included neighbors and friends for the purpose of rejoicing. This get-together's joy was the opposite of sharing pain or an uproar created by some tragedy. Joy drives away despair. And in this particular text, we find the context. It is a celebration of joy that is overflowing . . . at home.

We need a lot of joy at home because when it exists there, we leave in peace to go to work, to school, to church, or even for a holiday trip. When coming from a joy-filled home, we work better and produce more. We are anxious to get back home and are happy to linger there. Many students do not succeed in their studies because the family environment is not joyful. How important is a healthy home for better academic performance!

Sometimes, people who come to church have just left a home that is disturbed. They are in search of hope, of receiving a blessing to rebuild the family at home. Imagine what it would be like if each family that attended church was coming from a joyful, spiritually healthy home! How fantastic would be their worship and praise experience! I like to think that the parable from which I chose today's text has to do with the family. The woman in the story had lost a valuable coin—inside her own house! So I wonder, what of value might have been lost in your house or mine? Respect comes to mind. Respect of one family member for another. Just listen to conversations between many parents with their children or exchanges between husbands and wives. In some cases, no respect is shown. One who respects another listens with attention. Sadly, we see much disrespect—and even selfishness—in homes today. I do not think it would be difficult to identify other "coins" that are disappearing from homes today as well.

So let us do what we can to maintain what God deems as valuable. Then we will experience real joy and happiness at home. However, if we realize that the "coins" of respect, dignity, or love are missing from our home, let us diligently search for them, as did the woman in the parable, through prayer and making sure our own words and behaviors show the kindness of Christ. Then what has been lost at home will be found, and Jesus will be our permanent Guest.

Meibel Mello Guedes

Let the Children Come to Me

"Let the little children come to Me . . . ;
for of such is the kingdom of heaven."
—Matthew 19:14, NKJV.

Early one the morning, around one thirty, I had a respite from making rounds at the hospital. This is the quiet half hour before more patients arrive. I went to my locker, took out my lunch box, and headed to the third floor pavilion, where it is quiet. Waiting for the elevator, I saw her sitting alone in the lobby. I asked the receptionist about the little girl, Namina. Her mother was brought in an ambulance that morning. *I started my shift six hours ago. Why did I not notice her?* I sat next to her and introduced myself. She was quiet but looked at my lunch box. *She is hungry.* I opened the lunch box and extended it to her. She grabbed the sandwich and the apple and took turns biting into each. *She's a forgotten little girl, hungry, wondering where her mother is.* I left the lunch box with Namina and returned to the desk to ask for information.

I returned to Namina, who had eaten everything in the lunch box. I asked whether she was still hungry. She nodded, and I explained my plan. In the cafeteria, she carefully selected food and then pointed at a bagel and spoke for the first time: "Mom likes that. I wait for her after school. A truck hit the car." *Silence.*

The sweet lady behind the counter smiled at Namina, and said, "Why don't I toast it for her?" *There it is. The generous gestures placed in our heart, words that mean so much and are so precious because the Holy Spirit inspires us to utter them.* In the private room, the nurse told me the mother would wake up in a while. We opened the sofa bed for Namina, where she could sleep.

I knelt next to her bed, told her that she was safe, and placed a pillow next to her. I told her that her mother is resting, and nurses would be visiting the room. She held my hand and said, "Like you visited the room with the lady crying or the place with babies to pray with family, or stopped at rooms to pray for the one inside?" *She followed me?* I asked why, and she pointed at my small Bible and told me she has one too. She yawned, and in no time she was asleep. I exited quietly, glancing at Namina. *Truly the kingdom of heaven is yours.*

Lord, grant me wisdom and strength to be an example of Your love, especially when I don't know who is watching.

Dixil L. Rodríguez

Be Encouraged

But God, who encourages those
who are discouraged, encouraged us.
—*2 Corinthians 7:6, NLT*

The God of peace will soon crush Satan under your feet.
—*Romans 16:20, NIV*

You may be wounded emotionally, even hurting on the inside when challenges seem to have taken over your life. When I feel like this, I remember that I am a child of the living God. I feel encouraged and strengthened. This is because I know God is the restorer of my soul. God Almighty will bring healing and give me beauty for the ashes; He will turn my battlefield into fields of blessings. The Lord, who has a plan for both my present and my future, is on the throne and always in complete control. He is all-powerful.

Let me suggest that when challenges and adversity come your way and barriers block your path, you call upon the name of Jesus. He wants to save us. He is our Encourager, Provider, Healer, Strength, and Protection. Jesus encouraged His own disciples with these words: "Don't let your hearts be troubled. Trust in God, and trust also in me" (John 14:1, NLT).

The Israelites, when about to enter Canaan, sent twelve spies into the land that they were to conquer. Among the spies were Joshua and Caleb. Ten of the spies brought back a discouraging report: "We saw giants and fortified cities. We can't conquer that land!" But Joshua and Caleb silenced the discouraged people, and Caleb said, "Let's go at once to take the land. . . . We can certainly conquer it!" (Numbers 13:30, NLT). They, speaking on behalf of God, were encouragers. The God of the Israelites is the same Lord today who will still encourage us when we are discouraged.

Don't settle in the valley of darkness. God will turn our valleys of weeping into pools of blessing. "When they walk through the Valley of Weeping, it will become a place of refreshing springs" (Psalm 84:6, NLT). What encouraging words those are to us who are presently walking through this world of sin. A place full of suffering and pain is not our permanent home. God has better plans for us. In the meantime, He has a purpose for everything He allows into our lives. If we fix our eyes on Him, we *will* be encouraged!

Thank You, God, for being greater than whatever Satan brings into my life. Kindly give me Your strength and Your calm, encouraging hand during times of pain and difficulty.

Pauline Gesare Okemwa

Local or Loco?

The Lord GOD hath given me the tongue of the learned,
that I should know how to speak a word in season to him
that is weary: he wakeneth morning by morning,
he wakeneth mine ear to hear as the learned.
—Isaiah 50:4

I had not yet purchased a women's devotional book for the coming year. Time and life had just gotten in the way of my taking care of this important part of my life. So I quickly called my local Christian bookstore to see whether they'd be open the last few days of the year.

After talking for a few minutes with a man named Skip about the availability of the women's devotional books, he asked me whether I was local. Because I had just returned from a road trip to California and was still rather tired, I misunderstood what he had asked. I thought he had asked if I was "loco." I was quite taken aback and really had to think for a few seconds before it dawned on me what he had really said to me.

After gathering my thoughts, I told him, "I am local. And I am also *loco*!" I could tell that my response stunned him somewhat. After a few seconds, we began to laugh as I explained why I had responded as I did. There was more snickering between the two of us as we finished our conversation and arranged a time when I could go to the store and purchase my devotional book. Poor Skip. I wonder whether he thought, *Maybe I'm going to meet a nut.* However, when we met, he was gracious and kind, and we found some more things to laugh at.

Often we tell others what we mean to say. Yet other times we are not really listening to what has been said to us. Why? Perhaps we're tired or just plain not paying attention. Depending on the understanding of what is said, an interaction can either be lighthearted or can degenerate into discord. Not only should we try our best to speak in a clear manner, but we should also try our best to listen well.

Jesus was very clear and loving when He spoke in any situation. I do not want to misunderstand a single thing He has for me to know. I want my ears to be open, my eyes to see, and my heart to be loving and open to His calling.

Won't you join with me in being one of the sheep that knows the Shepherd's voice and desires to be part of the flock dwelling within the safety of His fold?

Mary E. Dunkin

God Comforts Us

Yea, though I walk through the valley of the shadow of death,
I will fear no evil: for thou art with me;
thy rod and thy staff they comfort me.
—*Psalm 23:4*

Sometimes things happen so suddenly that we aren't prepared for them at all. My sister-in-law, Marge, and I do almost everything together. We live next door to each other. We call each other to go on errands or shop. One spring day, after shopping for groceries, she dropped me off at my house. After unloading her groceries at home, she phoned to let me know she was safely home. We kept track of each other's well-being that way. Unbeknownst to me, Marge remembered she had left a bag of cards in the car. She went back but didn't take her cane. Due to trees that had fallen some time before, the ground there was uneven. In addition to her sack of cards, Marge decided to carry in a pack of bottled water. Usually she asks my daughter or granddaughter to carry in water that she buys. Losing her balance, Marge fell and wasn't able to get up. Having her cell phone, she called my son, Garry, at the garage next door. He arrived quickly and helped her into her house. Then Kathy, my daughter, came home. When she heard what had happened—and that Aunt Marge had hit her head and her right wrist was in pain—she decided we should take my sister-in-law to the hospital to have her injuries evaluated.

In the emergency room, X-rays and tests revealed Marge had fractured her right wrist and also several places in her neck and back. She was fitted with a large, long brace, which proved to be very uncomfortable. Though moved to a hospital room, she could hardly move because of the brace and needed help taking medicine, eating, and getting to the bathroom.

After three days, Marge's caregivers allowed her to go upstairs to begin physical therapy. She began working with four therapists from 8:00 A.M. to 4:00 P.M. each day, taking short breaks between workouts and no long naps. She was tired because she had been in the hospital four days now. The next morning, Wednesday, the individual making rounds at 4:00 A.M. found her to be doing well. However, when Marge was checked at 5:30, a caregiver discovered that her heart had stopped beating! Medical personnel rushed her to the intensive care unit. Marge never regained consciousness and died.

We were shocked! The good thing was that she had lived her life for God and was ready to go.

What about you and me? Life is uncertain. Are we ready to meet Jesus?

Anne Elaine Nelson

God Never Overlooks

If either of them falls down, one can help the other up.
But pity anyone who falls and has no one to help them up.
—*Ecclesiastes 4:10, NIV*

My daughter's car was having problems. So Monday morning she and her dad, a pastor, went to the nearest bus stop to catch a bus to work. After an hour, Adjei, my husband, called and told me that they were still waiting for a bus! I was surprised because three buses regularly pass that bus stop every day. In desperation, I just whispered a prayer: "Father, sometimes life gets so difficult for us, but I know You never overlook anything. Please help Abby and her dad get to work if it is Your will."

Just then, Adjei called and joyfully told me that Ernest, a member from our church, would be giving them a ride to work. He said Ernest told them that there had been an accident on that particular bus route, so no buses would have passed that bus stop for the rest of the morning. All traffic was being detoured. Of course, Abby and Adjei had no way of knowing that.

Though Ernest lives around that area, he never takes that particular route to work. Yet that day, about the time I prayed, he chose to take that route and found his pastor and the pastor's daughter stranded!

"I suspect God had an assignment for me today—to take you two to work," said Ernest. "That is probably why I was impressed to take this particular route this morning. I'm glad to be used by God to help my pastor, and I believe God will bring me extra blessings for doing that," he added.

I know God is always near and ready to help. In a sense, I had sent him a "text message" in the form of a prayer. He had chosen to reply instantly!

Yes! Our heavenly Father never delays, ignores, disappoints, nor overlooks any detail in the lives of His beloved children. His promises are sure. One of them assures us that if we will only ask, God will give us what we need (see Matthew 7:7).

This experience also reminded me about the importance of taking every life situation to God in prayer. No wonder one songwriter tells us to whisper our prayers all day. We can whisper a prayer at any moment, and God will answer it right on time! He never overlooks a thing!

Mabel Kwei

August 16

Jesus and You: Essential Self-Care

And He said to them,
"Come away by yourselves to a secluded place and rest a while."
—*Mark 6:31, NASB*

For several years, I have taken an annual personal retreat—to catch up on sleep, spend quality time with God, and plan for the following year's ministry projects for my work. At times, I am able to combine a work trip with a one-day retreat by myself in a nearby area, but at least once a year I take several days off work to be alone with God. I choose a different location each year—within a half-day's drive from my home—to sample various natural settings: mountains, forest, botanical gardens, or the ocean. In each place, God speaks His love to me through His second book and shares His plan for me. In only a day or two I feel like a new person and am ready to tackle projects that, before my retreat, seemed like too much work to even think about.

I know several super-busy women who take regular spiritual alone time. One takes one day a month to visit an especially beautiful garden, where she is revived by communing with God and nature. Another friend takes a day or two each quarter, walking woodland trails and talking with God. Other women stay home and each day, while their children are napping, retreat to closets they have repurposed with relaxing pillows, soft light, and music.

Often women feel guilty taking time for themselves. Satan whispers that there's work to do. It would be sinful to rest before it's done, right? Consider this: None of us has a busier schedule than Jesus did. He had just three and a half years to accomplish the most important mission ever undertaken. Satan bombarded Him with every possible roadblock and temptation to prevent Him from completing His task. Though He didn't waste a minute, He repeatedly took time, the Bible records, to rest and pray. He also encouraged His disciples to rest and rejuvenate.

Our Creator knew that taking time to regenerate isn't wasting time; it's essential to our physical and spiritual well-being. The One who loves each of us with an everlasting love knows that a change of pace is therapeutic, especially when coupled with communion with Him. The busier you are, the more you need "me time." Jesus invites you to rest a while with Him.

If you ask Him, He will show you how to find regular time to be revived by Him. Why not accept His invitation?

Carla Baker

The Finish Line

I have fought the good fight, I have finished the race, I have kept the
faith. Now there is in store for me the crown of righteousness, which
the Lord, the righteous Judge, will award to me on that day.
—*2 Timothy 4:7, 8, NIV*

It was a perfect day for the 2007 Rock 'n' Roll Marathon in San Diego,
California.

Henry, my husband, was running the marathon, again! The night before, he
was nursing an injured foot. I was tempted to discourage him from participating
in the race. But, knowing his determination, I kept the thought to myself. As I
stood in the bleachers with the cheering crowd, I had visions of Henry limping
toward the finish line, his injury compounded. To ease my fears, I focused on the
race, cheering as runners ran past me.

The mood was festive, with the announcers congratulating those who made it
to the finish line. Tunes such as "Celebrate Good Times, C'mon!" and "We Are
Family" played as cheers filled the air and runners came streaming past the stands
in an effort to reach their goal. Many runners were dressed in costumes. Some
were dressed like Elvis or Disney characters. Purple shirts identified members
of the Leukemia and Lymphoma Society Team in Training. As I watched this
group, I noticed one runner with the word "Coach" printed on his shirt. He
ran next to a team member having a difficult time, encouraging him as they ran
together the last mile of the race. Several times the coach ran back to the crowd of
runners to encourage some other member needing a morale boost. This gesture
of teamwork went on throughout the race.

Then I saw Henry cross the finish line with a smile on his face. What was I
worried about all this time?

I am running the marathon of my life. I imagine the cheering crowd of fellow
Christians encouraging me as I race toward the finish line. I hear my Father's
voice saying, "Evelyn of California is approaching." But I falter on the way as I
struggle toward my goal.

Then Jesus, my Coach, reaches for my hand and gently encourages me: "A
few more steps, and you're there! We'll run the race together."

As I cross the finish line, I hear heaven's version of "Celebrate Good Times,
C'mon!" The rest of the crowd joins in with, "We Are Family," as one of their
own finishes the race.

Evelyn Porteza-Tabingo

Help!

God is our refuge and strength,
a very present help in trouble.
—*Psalm 46:1, NKJV*

Three thirty. The end of another school day. Before I leave school, there is one thing I need to do—use the bathroom. I enter the first part of the teacher's bathroom and close the door. Then I enter the toilet stall and close the door. I turn the small knob and lock the door. I proceed to use the restroom. Once finished, I turn the knob to unlock the cubicle door, and to my surprise, I am unable to turn the knob. Locked? This can't be! I try again. Definitely locked. Now what?

Three forty-five. Most teachers on my side (I'm in the upper school building) have left for the day. What now? I imagine spending the night at school. *Since I will get home late, surely my husband will notice and come looking for me . . . but at school?* This is so embarrassing. How could I have done such a dumb thing? I call out again. Maybe the school secretary will hear me, as her office is nearby and she finishes work at four thirty. "Mrs. Place! Mrs. Place! Are you there?" Silence. Finally I remember to pray. *Why didn't I think of that before?*

"Hello? Hello?"

"Bean? Is that you?"

"Yes, I've locked myself in the bathroom stall."

"I thought I heard someone calling out." Mrs. Pachai opens the door. "I just happened to be coming back over this way."

"I thought you had left." As I told her what happened, we decided to write a note and place it in the bathroom so that this does not happen to anyone else.

"Thanks." I tell her. "I'm glad that you were still here."

Have you ever found yourself "locked in"? You're locked inside a relationship. You're locked inside a job. You're locked inside family. You're locked inside a noncommitted relationship with God. You think that you can't get out. You've tried every possible solution, and nothing works.

Then you remember there is God, who can work things out for you. He will turn the knob, unlocking the door on your situation, and set you free.

Then you can say, "Thank You, Jesus! I'm glad that You were still here."

Dana Bassett M. Bean

The Amazing Race

But they that wait upon the Lord shall renew their strength;
they shall mount up with wings as eagles; they shall run,
and not be weary; and they shall walk, and not faint.
—Isaiah 40:31

A s I flicked through the different television channels, my attention was drawn to a program: *The Amazing Race*. Normally I would turn to a Christian TV station and be inspired by the wonderful messages from the Word of God. However, on this particular night I paused to watch *The Amazing Race* show. It was about a race that would give the winner—whoever endured to the end—the grand prize of one million dollars.

And what does it take to get the grand prize? A contestant could get that prize only if he or she followed all the steps correctly and completed the race.

After watching the program for a few minutes, I began to draw spiritual insights from this race. I was extremely impressed to see how each contestant tried to follow all the steps carefully, steps that would eventually help them win the race.

The following week, I thought, *I want to follow this race to see who will be the next person to be eliminated.* To my dismay, the two people who had run the race the previous week were eliminated. Why? They were eliminated because they made one simple mistake: They did not read the directions properly. They took a taxi when they had been instructed to walk!

Lord, although what I was watching was not spiritual in substance, I gained a spiritual blessing from it. It taught me a valuable lesson. If we are not careful as Christians, we too will lose the grand prize—a place in Your kingdom. This is a race that we must personally run so that the victory will be ours.

Sometimes, Lord, simple mistakes can cause us to lose focus and eventually lose out on heaven. Yes, along the way we will meet many obstacles and challenges. Yet if we persevere and press on, You will give us the strength and power to endure.

In the end we will hear Your words, "Well done, good and faithful servant. You have been faithful over a few things; I'll make you ruler over many things. Enter now into my joy."

Please, Lord, help me to stay in that race to the very end.

Patricia Hines

He Restores My Joy

Restore unto me the joy of thy salvation;
and uphold me with thy free spirit.
—*Psalm 51:12*

What trials has God brought you through recently? There is an abundance of pain, sadness, and sorrow in our world that are the result of evil, sickness, violence, starvation, and infidelity. These social ills plague our society. The smile has been wiped from many faces and the joy ripped out of many hearts because of the blows life has dealt. It is the enemy's desire that God's people be unhappy. Sadness literally saps our life energy, whereas laughter and joy tend to health and longevity. Satan, though, wants to keep us in a state of depression. Many in our world are losing their sanity because they have lost their joy. Consequently, they are also devoid of peace and hope. Such people often turn to drugs, alcohol, or a promiscuous lifestyle in order to fill that vacuum in their lives. Sadly, some even commit suicide.

Unlike the enemy, our heavenly Father wants us to be happy. The apostle Paul wrote this blessing to the Christians in Rome: "Now the God of hope fill you with all joy and peace in believing, that ye may abound in hope, through the power of the Holy Ghost" (Romans 15:13). The Holy Spirit is anxious to give us joy, with which come hope and peace.

We may have lost our joy due to the death of a loved one, the loss of a job, abandonment by a spouse, betrayal by friends, the ungratefulness of children, or our own unfaithfulness to God. In spite of life's misfortunes, however, God is willing and anxious to forgive us of our sins and restore our joy, if we only call on Him, asking Him to do so.

Jesus found comfort and joy in communion with His Father, and that should be the secret and source of our joy as well: communion with our heavenly Father. We should devote quality time each day to communing with Him through prayer and the study of His Word. We can claim the precious promises in His Word. Truly He has provided a promise for every situation we might find ourselves in. That should continually cheer our hearts.

Let's pray today and every day for joy, a gift of the Holy Spirit. Furthermore, as did the psalmist David, let's ask our heavenly Father to restore unto us the joy of His salvation. This will enable us to smile again and enjoy abundant life regardless of the challenges that confront us. Indeed, the joy of the Lord is our strength (see Nehemiah 8:10).

Gerene I. Joseph

My Boss Has Been Watching You

"Before they call I will answer."
—Isaiah 65:24, ESV

It was a cold snowy day, but my mother-in-law wanted her paycheck. When Dad refused to take her to get it, she decided to walk and get it herself. As she told me, it was *only* a mile. Yes—a mile on icy, snowy streets. Check in hand, she began the walk back through worsening snow conditions and wind. Nearing her street, she decided to take a shortcut through a large cemetery. From a certain gate, she lived just a few houses away.

When Mom reached the gate, much of it was buried in snow. For a long time, she worked to free it from the snow so that she could swing it open, but it would not budge. Disheartened, she began the long, cold walk back to the cemetery entrance. Just then, a cemetery grounds truck pulled up beside her. A man leaned across the cab and told her, "Get in."

Mom protested that she was all right. She was on her way home. The man said, "My boss has been watching you for a long time. He sent me to get you. Just look at your bare legs. They're blue. You're freezing. Get on in." Reluctantly Mom climbed into the truck. She never wanted to be any trouble. The driver repeated what he'd said earlier. "My boss has been watching you. You need to get home."

Later Mom realized it was impossible to see that troublesome gate from the cemetery office. Also, the driver never asked where Mom lived. Leaving the cemetery, he simply turned toward her street. As they stopped at an intersection, Mom gasped. In a car right in from of them, staring right at them, she saw Dad. "That's my husband!" she moaned. "He's going to be so mad I've been gone this long."

At that (she told me later), the driver looked at her with great love and sorrow in his eyes. Then he made the turn and soon pulled up in front of her house. Before she got out, he cautioned her, "Be more careful in the future. You could have died." Quietly Mom went inside, afraid of the explosion she'd meet from Dad. He simply said he'd gone out to find her. She told him that they'd seen him at the end of their street. "We were in a truck. You looked directly at us."

"I didn't see a truck," he said. "There was no truck." And Mom pondered the driver's words: *My boss has been watching you for a long time. He sent me to get you.*

Penny Estes Wheeler

A Common Ground

But you are a chosen people, a royal priesthood, a holy nation,
God's special possession, that you may declare the praises of him
who called you out of darkness into his wonderful light.
—*1 Peter 2:9, NIV*

Since June 2013, I have frequented an open-air market (known in my country as a hawker center). God has led me to look for "common ground" I might have with those I encounter. Discussing a commonality helps build friendship and win trust before the Holy Spirit eventually leads discussion into spiritual matters. Since a number of people I meet in my Asian country come from one of the ancient traditional religions, one of the commonalities I have with many is vegetarianism. I am often able to have a casual chat with other food customers when they are enjoying their vegetarian meals, as I am enjoying mine.

"Are you on a long-term or short-term vegetarian diet?" I might be asked. (A short-term diet means a person eats vegetarian on the first and fifteenth day of each lunar month.) I share that I have chosen a vegetarian diet since December 2009.

A few years back, in 2014, an acquaintance, Kelly, and I were chatting. It came out that I was a vegetarian as well as a Christian. She seemed surprised when I said that. She remarked, "I hadn't heard about some Christians being vegetarians." She shared with me that some of her friends, after leaving their traditional Eastern religion, had shared their newfound Christian faith but in a way that was putting undue pressure on her to make a decision.

"No worries. I understand what you are saying!" I assured her. "Many years ago—while still practicing my traditional beliefs—some new Christians tried to 'pull' me into Christianity. But I wasn't ready. Besides, being a Christian means you choose to believe in Jesus Christ and accept what He did for us personally. It's a personal choice when the Holy Spirit convicts and draws us into relationship with Him." She thanked me for sharing my beliefs in a way that didn't put pressure on her but gave her food for thought. We cordially parted ways.

Let's be alert for people whose pathway God crosses with ours. Let's be aware if the Holy Spirit points out "common ground" we might have with them. Then we can stand confidently on that common ground and share the love of Jesus in word or in deed.

Yan Siew Ghiang

A Tool

"But the king of Assyria will not understand that he is my tool."
—Isaiah 10:7, NLT

God, in His divine wisdom, made each of us to be unique. While we are unique as individuals, there are also other differences that exist between the genders. These differences can be seen in our choice of foods, hobbies, and entertainment. For example, I enjoy spending time in our local hardware store, not for the tools but for viewing the household items. My husband also enjoys spending time in hardware stores, but in a different section of the store. He enjoys the tools and home repair areas.

After spending some time with him in his favorite sections, I have come to develop a deeper appreciation for the importance of having the right tool to complete a job. I sometimes find myself with household problems that need quick solutions. At these times, I turn to my husband and his tool kits for remedies. Any given task can be made much easier with the aid of the right tool in the right hands.

In Isaiah 10:7, we hear God speaking to the prophet. In previous verses, God describes the fact that He is planning to bring down His wrath on His people because they have become a godless nation. In order to do this, He is going to allow the armies of Assyria to plunder them. Yet in this verse God tells His prophet that the King of Assyria will only be a tool in His hands to accomplish His will.

God seems to be in the tool industry. He can use us as His tools, or He can use others as tools in our lives. Could the persons and circumstances we encounter be striking tools, like hammers and sledges, to beat out traces of sin in our hearts? Or how about a holding tool, like a clamp, to help hold the lives of our brothers and sisters together when things seem to be falling apart for them? Or could we serve as safety tools, like goggles and vests, to protect each other?

I also believe God has some greater good to accomplish in our lives through the tools of painful circumstances such as sickness, death, disappointments, or financial hardships. Tools, in general, are used to resolve an issue, so I would like to challenge you today to look at the difficulties that come your way as tools that God is using to fix problems for His glory.

Perhaps, more important, will you consider allowing yourself to be a tool in God's hands?

Taniesha Robertson-Brown

August 24

The Price of a Soul

"Is anything worth more than your soul?"
—Mark 8:37, NLT

Two dollars and eighty-nine cents: the price of a jar of spaghetti sauce.

As I drove to my favorite farmer's market, I planned my dinner—baked potato, corn on the cob, green salad, and veggie meatballs in spaghetti sauce. The jar of sauce I selected was labeled "chunky with olive oil and garlic." Perfect. At the checkout counter, the cashier seemed unusually friendly. She smiled and commented on the weather as she added up the total charges of my vegetables and fruit. Then she came to the spaghetti sauce. When she picked up the jar, she stared me straight in the face, looked into my eyes, and quietly placed the jar into my grocery bag, unchecked. Had I seen correctly? The cashier and I stared at each other again. Then I found my voice. "You did not charge me for the spaghetti sauce," I quietly pointed out.

She stared hard at me, suddenly silent. Then, looking toward the cash register, she pushed a button, ringing up the total. "Twelve forty-nine," she announced.

"No," I reminded her. "That should be about fifteen dollars. The spaghetti sauce . . . remember?" The cashier abruptly took the jar from the grocery bag and scanned it. I paid for my total purchases, thanked her, and left, though not sure of the motives behind her actions.

I can just imagine her thoughts after my departure: *How could that customer have been so foolish and ungrateful? Why was she so unwilling to accept my "kindness"?*

I was unwilling because, plainly and simply put, I didn't want to steal from the grocery store. I would not exchange my soul for two dollars and eighty-nine cents—or any other amount. How bitter that sauce would have tasted had I been an accomplice in its theft!

Although the cashier had not scanned the spaghetti sauce originally, I know that God's eyes were scanning this entire scene. Like Job, I too may have been an unwitting protagonist in a drama watched by the universe. Would I pass the test? How delicious my entire meal tasted that evening, especially the veggie meatballs in that chunky, *paid-for* spaghetti sauce! But I tremble, knowing that amount could easily have been the price of my soul.

Lord, keep us alert to the wiles of the evil one and show us how to witness for You in matters great and small.

Annette Walwyn Michael

Third Time's the Charm

Everything you ask for in prayer will be yours,
if you only have faith.
—Mark 11:24, CEV

Blood in the toilet bowl: something that sends a pregnant woman into immediate panic. I was six weeks pregnant with my first child. I had already suffered two miscarriages prior to this and thought for sure my fate was yet again determined. After falling to my knees to beg God that this time would be different, I called my doctor, who sent me for an emergency ultrasound.

My husband was away at the time, so I had to drive myself to the appointment. With previous ultrasounds, I could barely walk, let alone drive, after drinking a liter of water in preparation for the exam. Somehow, this morning was different, and I was able to drive with ease to the appointment. I silently sent a prayer of thanks above.

As I waited in the office for the technician to call my name, I opened my daily devotional that I had brought along with me. I was directed to a story whose message was that only God can do the impossible. I knew that stumbling across this particular story was no coincidence but, rather, the Holy Spirit speaking to me. Then my name was called.

Moments later, my thoughts were racing as I lay waiting on the ultrasound table. According to my research, I knew at this early stage in my pregnancy, it would be very difficult to see a heartbeat with an abdominal ultrasound. My doctor told me that it was very unlikely. But by the grace of God, within seconds of the technician's placing the ultrasound probe on my abdomen, a heartbeat was found.

Tears of joy streamed down my face. Maybe this third pregnancy would go full-term.

As weeks went by and my first trimester continued successfully, I prayed daily that God would keep my growing baby safe. I had a few more scares in the months to come, but in the end, God always looked after me and my baby. You see, God doesn't promise to remove the obstacles or pain from our lives, but He does promise to see us through them. As Moses tells us in Exodus 14:14, "The LORD will fight for you, and you won't have to do a thing" (CEV).

Prayer and unwavering faith in God and in His plan for our lives is all we need. Faith is a sixth "sense" that transcends all others, but it is up to us to choose to put it to use.

Have you put your prayer and unwavering faith to good use lately?

Renee Farmer

Successful Outcomes

God blesses those who patiently endure testing and temptation.
Afterward they will receive the crown of life
that God has promised to those who love him.
—*James 1:12, NLT*

As Sonny would say, we "zoomed" past the billboard on Highway 395 on the outskirts of Hermiston, Oregon. My sister Jan, Sonny (my twenty-eight-year-old autistic son), and I were out joyriding and having fun going shopping. I had only a split-second to read the message written on the billboard. *That "Love Thy Neighbor Thing." I Meant It! —God.*

Since Sonny's birth, I've felt that my family has been fortunate to live in Alberta, Canada. I'm sincerely thankful for our health-care system. However, I'm ever mindful of the many concerns and challenges that the government faces regarding adequate care and funding for persons living with lifelong developmental disabilities. It takes dedicated people and teamwork to keep the system going in a compassionate and positive direction. With his day programs, which are coordinated through "excellent" service providers, Sonny lives a happy, meaningful life. Our Family Managed Supports (FMS) agreement provides funding for educational purposes—this was "why" we were going shopping!

It's a pure joy to shop with Sonny in search of inexpensive inspirational items for him to decorate and to give away as guided by the Holy Spirit. Through sharing, Sonny continues to develop his social skills. He's become an ambassador of good will and an advocate for others living with developmental disabilities. Sonny has very limited speech, but his gentle spirit speaks volumes. Along with his heartwarming artwork goes a small, homemade booklet filled with amazing stories about our family's ministry and spiritual journey. With the passing of time, these stories just keep getting better and better. Around the time we began using FMS, Jesus gave our ministry a mission statement: *We Are In It—To Win It . . . The Crown of Life.* It is our job as Christians to help others be winners too!

In his 2014 televised Christmas message, Prime Minister Stephen Harper said, "Canada is a compassionate nation!" I wholeheartedly agree. Stories about "successful outcomes" for the money and time invested in the lives of persons with developmental disabilities and their families are empowering. *We* are God's living billboards!

Deborah Sanders

The Missing Devotional Book

Judge not, that ye be not judged. For with what judgment ye judge,
ye shall be judged: and with what measure ye mete,
it shall be measured to you again.
—Matthew 7:1, 2

My husband and I were going to Toronto, Ontario, to surprise his mother for her seventy-fifth birthday. I always buy extra copies of the annual Women's Ministries devotional book to give away as gifts. I knew that Jen, my niece, was going through a rough time in her life, so I took for her the last copy of the devotional book *Grace Notes*. I wrote her name in it, signed, and then dated the book. Jen was so excited when she received her gift. I knew that Jen believed in God and that she would draw strength from the inspirational experiences shared in the book by her sisters in Christ.

Jen took the devotional to work with her so that she could read it on her break. She enjoyed the daily readings and rejoiced that God was speaking to her through those pages. After reading each day's devotional, Jen would place the book on the corner of her desk. One day, when Jen reached for the book, it was not there. Surprised, she searched her entire workstation but did not find it. The day before, Jen had worked a late shift, along with a few other employees. So she approached these colleagues to ask if anyone had accidentally "borrowed" her devotional book. No one had seen it. Despondent, Jen related the incident to her supervisor, who sent an e-mail to the staff asking whether anyone had seen the book or taken it by mistake. If so, would they please return it. Days turned into weeks, and the book did not turn up. Jen eventually called me to tell me what had happened. I was ready to pass judgment on the unknown culprit, for I knew the book could not have grown legs and walked off on its own!

Almost immediately I "heard" a still, small voice telling me all was well. In fact, the book's disappearance might have turned out to be good thing. I quickly changed my judgmental perspective.

"I'll get you another book," I assured Jen. "And who knows? Perhaps someone else needed God in her life and that book is blessing her right now!" We both laughed and began to praise God, hoping it had ended up in the hands of someone who needed it more than Jen did.

To God be the glory for what I believe was a double blessing!

Sharon Long (Brown)

The Keys

"Before they call I will answer."
—*Isaiah 65:24, NIV*

My husband and I were so excited. Our family had given us an early sixtieth wedding anniversary gift, a cruise to Alaska; we were ever so busy getting packed and ready to go. As I went through my purse, I removed things I would not need, including my keys. I dropped them into the drawer of my nightstand, along with the other things I was leaving at home. Then I shut the drawer.

Almost immediately I was impressed to reach in and take the keys out again—which I did—even though it seemed against my better judgment.

We drove to Seattle the next morning, left our car in a special parking area, and shuttled over to the pier where our cruise ship awaited us. After getting through all the lines of people and forms to fill out, we were finally on the ship.

All through that week we were so blessed by the breathtaking beauty of Alaska. We met many wonderful people and had a fantastic time. All too soon, our cruise was over.

The morning we were to leave the ship, my husband awoke in a panic. It had occurred to him that he had no idea where his car keys were, and he wondered how we were going to get home. He mentioned several places where he might have put them.

We searched but to no avail. Our larger pieces of luggage had been picked up by the staff during the night and were already on their way to the terminal, where we would pick them up later.

How thankful I was to be able to tell my husband that I knew exactly where *my* keys were. As soon as we retrieved our luggage, we were able to open the suitcase where I had placed them, and we moved on from there.

God knew we would need those keys and impressed me not to leave them at home.

And my husband's keys were not lost either. When we unpacked our suitcases at home, there they were in the pocket of his shorts, right where he had left them.

I thank and praise Him that we can always safely trust in His leading. What if I had not listened? Let's each resolve to listen and follow God's voice today.

Anna May Radke Waters

Guardian Angels

This poor man cried, and the LORD heard him,
and saved him out of all his troubles.
—*Psalm 34:6*

We have a neighbor, "Bob," who lives across the paddock from us. A retired police officer, he is a very kind and loving friend. He is always helping people, the young as well as the elderly. For example, an elderly single man lived alone across the street from Bob and Myra's house.

Bob visited this neighbor one day to see how he was doing. He found the man on his kitchen floor, partly unconscious. Quickly Bob rang for an ambulance. The man was taken to the local hospital, but sadly, he passed away.

One day after finishing our dinner, I went to get myself a hot drink. As I was returning to the dining table, I said to Murray, my husband, "I don't feel so good." He helped me to my chair. As I started to sit down, I completely blacked out. Murray had to hold on to me in order to keep me from falling off of the chair. Though he wanted to ring for help, Murray has a cochlear implant and is unable to hear on the telephone.

"God, help us!" he cried out in his distress. In just a few minutes, the Lord answered his prayer. First of all, I recovered a little. Murray was then able to help me to the bedroom, where I would be safer. That freed him up for a moment to run out and get help from our neighbors, Bob and Myra. Myra was soon attending to me as we waited for the ambulance to arrive.

I was taken to the nearby hospital and kept under observation for a few days.

Due to help from my husband, neighbors, and my guardian angel (whom I suspect helped Murray hold on to me when I blacked out), this experience had a happy ending, and I am now doing well. Praise God for His wonderful ways of protecting us! He is so good.

In His matchless love, our heavenly Father cares for each one of us. One of the most personal ways He does this is through the protection of our guardian angels. We receive even more blessings when we commune with God each day through prayer and the study of His Word. To be able to praise Him for all these gifts brings even more blessings into our lives.

How wonderful it is to know that we are never alone in our day-to-day activities, no matter what is occurring in our lives, for the "angel of the LORD encampeth . . . and delivereth" (Psalm 34:7).

Joan D. L. Jaensch

Don't Give Up

Trust in him at all times; ye people,
pour out your heart before him: God is a refuge for us.
—*Psalm 62:8*

Before we moved to Florida, I contacted the board of education in the city where we were going to reside.

After my arrival in town, I made it my business to go to the office of a woman who might help me become licensed in my new state. But she had to leave earlier to be with her ailing husband. Her assistant took my information and submitted it to the proper authorities, who could help me get a state license from the Department of Education.

The wait began. More and more time passed. When I thought it appropriate, I decided to contact the license division of the Department of Education.

What a shock to be told that no one in the department could locate the information that had been sent to them!

My information was lost? Really? I could not believe this!

I would have to resubmit school transcripts, fill out the proper forms, and initiate the whole process again. I looked at my husband and said, "Road trip." I would hand-deliver this information to the appropriate individuals next time. I *would* obtain my license.

When I had gotten all the necessary information together and the forms filled out, my husband and I set off to our destination. After providing the necessary personal information to obtain clearance to enter the education building, I finally located the appropriate office. A gentleman was assisting people. However, when it was my turn to speak with him, he abruptly said, "You need to get on the phone and call for assistance because I am going to lunch." I picked up the phone, made the call, and was helped by a very kind lady.

A few days and one office visit later, I had my license.

My husband and I went to seventeen schools with my resumé, but no one offered me a job. Though greatly dejected after my second interview, I went to my heavenly Father in prayer and told Him how I was feeling. He understood and answered my prayer. Soon I had a job.

What situations and feelings do you need to take to your heavenly Father today?

Bertha Hall

A Prayer Answer Delayed

Trust in the LORD with all your heart,
and lean not on your own understanding; in all your ways
acknowledge Him, and He shall direct your paths.
—*Proverbs 3:5, 6, NKJV*

I treasure the promise in the following quote: "To every sincere prayer an answer will come. It may not come just as you desire, or at the time you look for it; but it will come in the way and at the time that will best meet your need."*

How true this promise proved to be in the experience of my mother! She was a single parent with three girls to raise and support. My father left us and moved to another state so that he wouldn't have to provide child support. It was a struggle for my mother, who had to work in a factory as an unskilled worker because she hadn't even completed her high school education.

We lived in a small apartment and made do with hand-me-down clothes from other people. Our food was simple but nourishing, with dessert only on Sabbaths, our birthdays, and some holidays. My mother's goal was to see that each of us had a Christian education and a profession. She took extra jobs cleaning offices at night. Each of us was blessed with summer jobs and, sometimes, jobs during the Christmas holidays. Whoever in our family didn't have a job during the holidays did the cooking, the laundry, and the cleaning of our apartment.

Years passed with no child support relief for my mother. After we girls finished school and married, we learned our father had died. My mother was now remarried to a fine Christian man. Not only was he a great husband, but he was also a wonderful stepfather and grandfather. And he had a car! Mother's life, for the next sixteen years, was easier. Then he passed away.

Through a phone call, my mother learned she could collect more Social Security income from my late father than from my stepfather. I drove my mother to the Social Security office, where they had no idea who had phoned her! However, they totaled the figures. To her amazement, Mother learned that the amount she would receive each month from my father equaled the child support amount she *should* have received from him decades earlier!

Her response was, "The Lord knew I would need extra income more in my old age when I couldn't work than when I was younger." God knew what was best for my mother.

And God knows what is best for each of us as well.

Patricia Mulraney Kovalski

* Ellen G. White, *Gospel Workers* (Hagerstown, MD: Review and Herald®, 2005), 258.

Cultivate the Heart!—Part 1

Seek good and not evil, that you may live; so the LORD God of hosts will be with you, as you have spoken. Hate evil, love good; establish justice in the gate. It may be that the LORD God of hosts will be gracious to the remnant of Joseph.
—Amos 5:14, 15, NKJV

My vegetable garden is a special place for me. It is where I interact with Creator God in deep reflection. Last year, I planted a new vegetable that taught me a profound character lesson.

The garden was created to satisfy a number of culinary desires. There was a salsa garden with the requisite Mexican cilantro, tomatillo, jalapeño, and tomato. In another section grew Japanese eggplant, okra, Jamaican Scotch bonnet pepper, and Georgia peanuts; and there was a medicinal section to my garden where basil, parsley, peppermint, lemon balm, lavender, English thyme, rosemary, sage, and echinacea provided healing and a fragrant breeze to my backyard oasis. All were planted within my small twelve-foot by twelve-foot kitchen garden.

Yet this story is not about any of those plants, it is about the sweet potato. I studied the space and fertilizer requirements for every plant, but the sweet potato required more thought because of the kind of sweet potatoes I wanted to enjoy. They were to be sweet visions of perfection. I wanted perfectly shaped sweet potatoes. But my garden was not cultivated to grow perfectly shaped sweet potatoes.

After the builder had constructed the house, I had simply asked for a section under my kitchen window to be defined with brick pavers and provided with a water irrigation system. The garden, from all appearances, looked perfectly ready for planting. But to grow sweet potatoes, I had to remove the unseen rocks and even the small pebbles and the construction debris that were buried six inches under the beautifully smoothed soil. Cultivating beautiful sweet potatoes was more than adding fertilizer and water—the soil has to be loose and free of impediments to grow potato tubers.

Have you ever considered impediments that might compromise spiritual growth?

Prudence LaBeach Pollard

Cultivate the Heart!—Part 2

And may the Lord make you increase and abound in love to one
another and to all, just as we do to you, so that He may establish
your hearts blameless in holiness before our God and Father
at the coming of our Lord Jesus Christ with all His saints.
—*1 Thessalonians 3:12, 13, NKJV*

wanted to grow perfectly shaped sweet potatoes. This required that I carefully cultivate the soil in preparation.

It was early fall when I harvested the sweet potatoes. They were visions of perfection, plump and free of irregularities. My hard work preparing the soil and removing the foreign objects paid off!

At harvest time, I stood in my garden in deep appreciation for the character lesson.

Is my character free of stones, pebbles, the construction debris of life, and all the impediments to growth of a character acceptable to God?

Jesus reminds us in Matthew 5 and in Luke 6 that the character He desires in us begins with the internal attitude of love.

A heart of love shines forth in actions that demonstrate my love for God and my love toward others.

Such a heart cannot grow accidentally; it requires cultivation of the heart of love, much like the cultivation of my sweet potato garden.

My prayer today: *God, please cultivate my heart as I meditate on the attitudes that You desire to demonstrate through my character. I want to discern Your way, to surrender my own will to do what is right in Your sight and, with Your promised help, to resist the wrong even when under pressure and temptation.*

Prudence LaBeach Pollard

September 3

Pure, Living Water

But whosoever drinketh of the water
that I shall give him shall never thirst.
—*John 4:14*

As you read the story of the woman at the well, have you ever considered how thirsty she must have been? The weather was hot; the road was dusty. Jesus was thirsty and asked for water. When was the last time you were desperate for a drink of water?

I once attended a large conference in August. The Texas summer heat surpassed one hundred degrees. Since I use a walker (following a double knee replacement and other complications), it was difficult for me, at the end of one meeting, to make my way through the crowded hallways, along with thousands of others.

My husband and I slowly made our way around the large coliseum, only to find the front plaza totally congested. As we worked our way through the crowd, he noticed an open place on a wall that I could lean against. He needed to meet someone with whom he had previously made arrangements to take us to our car. The only parking place he could find was in a hotel garage five stories underground and about one half mile away. Approximately thirty minutes later, my husband returned, disappointed that the person had not met him. So we both slowly walked quite a distance to a rest area under an interstate freeway that offered shade and a few crowded benches.

By now I had to stop every few feet. My husband realized I could not make it the rest of the way. He spotted one open seat on a bench where I could rest as he went for help. Close to an hour passed; I had had nothing to drink in more than seven hours. The thought of a heatstroke loomed in my mind, for I was very dehydrated by now. As my thirst increased, I thought, *God, some water would surely be nice.* To pass the time, I continued intently watching hundreds of people walk by.

Then a man approached my bench, bent over, and looked me directly in the face. In broken English, he asked, "Would you like some water?" With that he handed me a bottle of pure, cool water. Whenever I tell this story, I still feel chills down my back. How the sudden kindness of that stranger reassured my faith in Jesus! Christ still taps us on the shoulder, offering not only cool water in a time of need but also His pure water of life to all who will accept Him.

June Ayers

Seeing the Bigger Picture

And my God will meet all your needs
according to the riches of his glory in Christ Jesus.
—*Philippians 4:19, NIV*

There are many times in my life when I am struck with awe at how God's elegant works are manifested even in difficult times. My parents, wanting their four children to have a Christian education, chose to live in the small Filipino village of Tacras because of its Christian school. Unfortunately, Tacras had no nursing jobs for my mom. Nevertheless, she worked as a volunteer nurse for nearly a decade, and my dad served as the head elder of the church. Living a lifestyle that relied entirely on faith, we noticed that God always provided for us, though our home was like a local hospital. I vividly remember hopping over patients and assisting my mom with delivering babies and patient visits. Though my mom was unpaid, we never went hungry—which still puzzles my family. How did we manage all those years?

One particular night, we had run out of food, and we were almost out of faith. We prayerfully prepared to go to bed before hearing a knock on the door. A former patient of my mother's had brought food. Another time, a stranger dropped off a sack of rice at our house. Food and money would show up just when we needed them the most, though my parents had no permanent jobs.

Finally, my aunt Lourdes was able to arrange for Mother to take nursing tests and find work in Canada as an immigrant nurse. Through her employment, God provided means for the rest of us to come to Canada in June 2006. Life was still difficult, yet God never left us, even when we were cheated in business, were hurt by people we trusted, or underwent relocation hardships. God was always there, guiding our family. Perhaps we sometimes fear that life will be difficult when we choose to surrender everything to God. Yet even in my short life, I've already learned that without God, life is even more difficult to face. When we walk in the path He has prepared for us, though, we need not worry. He promised He would carry our burdens. I learned to trust that God saw the bigger picture, even when I was at a point of near starvation or life didn't make sense. Looking back, I see how God has led my family in difficult times so that we would become reliant upon Him.

Take comfort—and have faith—that whatever you face, God still sees the bigger picture.

Ellen Jane Tejano-Galupo

God's Intervention

In all your ways acknowledge Him,
and He shall direct your paths.
—Proverbs 3:6, NKJV

Wanting to attend a large church conference in 2015 to be held in San Antonio, Texas, I began planning a year ahead. I thought it would be exciting to visit another state, see the sights, and hear the sounds. So, after asking God to be in my planning, I began making financial commitments for the travel and hotel accommodations. There would be bus transportation, and I would share a hotel room with someone else. During the ensuing months, I continued to pray frequently for God's leading and for safety on the upcoming trip, a twenty-four-hour bus trip from Georgia to Texas.

By April 2015 all my financial obligations for the conference were met. Friends who knew the San Antonio area encouraged me to visit certain attractions and experience the river boat ride before I returned home. The last week of June was exciting as I finished packing my suitcase. Though we were scheduled to leave on Wednesday, I was ready to go by Monday.

Then it all happened! On Tuesday morning, about six o'clock, a dull pain in my upper right abdominal area awakened me. The pain intensity increased and was soon accompanied by nausea. I thought the symptoms were temporary because I'd had a gallbladder removal in 1986. Yet the symptoms became so severe that I called 911 and was transported to the emergency room of the nearest hospital, eighteen miles from home. I was immediately given medication for the painful symptoms, which quickly subsided. Blood work, a CT scan, and other tests were done. I was now feeling better and asked the attending doctor whether I could travel to Texas the following day. He replied emphatically, "Under no condition! Your liver enzymes are twenty times what they should be, and your bile duct is grossly distended. I am arranging to transfer you to another hospital to have the duct cleaned out." The transfer occurred within minutes. An MRI revealed a cyst surrounded by stones in the common bile duct. A medical procedure cleared the blockage, and three days later I was discharged, symptom free, but not able to travel to the conference.

Each of us has to trust our plans to God and thank Him for His all-wise leading.

Missilene B. Edwards

The Harvest

And another angel came out of the temple, crying with a loud voice
to Him who sat on the cloud, "Thrust in Your sickle and reap, for the
time has come for You to reap, for the harvest of the earth is ripe."
—*Revelation 14:15, NKJV*

As I drove through the central Florida countryside, I noticed several new citrus groves adjacent to mature ones. It was evident that the grove owners were thinking ahead to when the mature trees would no longer produce at a profitable level. It takes several years of watering, pruning, and fertilizing for a young citrus tree to produce fruit. As with any business, maximizing production for a favorable bottom line is important.

Harvest time is always anticipated with the expectancy of gathering in quality fruit to be sold at a good price. The harvest either makes or breaks an enterprise.

There is an extra special harvest coming soon. It's a harvest of souls. Christ's second coming will be the grandest harvest of all, the culmination of the sanctification process for all those who love God and want to live with Him forever. All that God can do He will have done to make this final harvest as inclusive as possible. He is not willing that any should perish.

Everyone can be included in this harvest. The invitation is generously given to join our hearts to the heart of God by abiding in Him daily and making Him our very best Friend. We can do that by reading His Word each day and internalizing it. He also invites us to talk to Him in prayer, cultivating a relationship and level of comfort with Him that will make us want to live with Him forever. When this happens, we can't help but share our love for Him with others. Then perhaps they too will fall in love with Him and want to be a part of this great harvest.

God never forces us to make Him our Lord and Savior. He values nothing more than our freedom. He will leave no stone unturned to win our hearts to Him. The bottom line of this harvest is of utmost importance to Him.

What a thrill it will be to see our heavenly Father and Jesus face-to-face! I want to be a part of this great harvest, don't you? Let us daily allow the Holy Spirit's pruning, watering, and fertilizing of our hearts, which will fit us to live in heaven forever.

Marian Hart-Gay

Let's Go Fishing

And Jesus said unto them, Come ye after me,
and I will make you to become fishers of men.
—*Mark 1:17*

I'm a novice fisherwoman who likes to toss a line into the river or sea when my husband and I go camping.

One really looks the part with rod over the shoulder and bucket, tackle box, and bait in hand, not forgetting the floppy sun hat. With hook baited comes the great expectation that my brilliant cast will land in the midst of big fish. Then it's time to wait impatiently for that first nibble, but too many minutes pass. I sit down a while, and although the scenery is pleasant and the sun is warm, nothing is happening. So I reason that maybe if I reel in the line and cast out again in a different place, I might get results. It's usually at this stage my husband appears with the inevitable question, "How many have you caught?" My deflated answer most times is, "Nothing."

It was fishermen that Jesus first called to leave their nets and follow Him to become fishers of men. Things weren't always easy for them. However, they accepted the commission Jesus gave them, leaving great examples for all to follow through the ages.

Matthew 24:14 tells us, "And this gospel of the kingdom shall be preached in all the world for a witness unto all nations; and then shall the end come." We can all play a role in bringing this text to fruition. Many of us aren't missionaries, teachers, or preachers. No matter how inadequate we may rate ourselves, we can still work alongside others, using the gifts and talents God has given each of us (Matthew 25:14–29).

We need not be disheartened if there are no responses to Bible study invitations we put in mailboxes or visits with others. Keep doing what you can, and let your light shine, for God sees our every effort to share His Word and His love. Matthew 25:35, 36 instructs us to care for others and provide for their needs. Keep praying for others and be kind, living as an example to all. We don't know what seeds we are sowing. It matters not if my fishing ventures fail. What is most important is the answer I give should Jesus ask me what I have done for Him.

Be encouraged, accept His commission, and let's go fishing. We can all be fisherwomen for Jesus.

Lyn Welk-Sandy

I'll Be There!

"It is the LORD who goes before you. He will be with you;
he will not leave you or forsake you. Do not fear or be dismayed."
—*Deuteronomy 31:8, ESV*

My aunt had enrolled me in a private school a few miles away from home. Each morning, she dropped me off at school, and one of my relatives met me after school. As we traveled to school, my aunt would reassure me that someone would be there waiting for me when my classes ended and that I shouldn't worry. All I had to do was sit near the front of the school so that the person coming to pick me up would see me.

One morning as we traveled to school, my aunt told me that she would be the one coming to get me after school. She said she would be there as soon as she could. I would have to wait only a few minutes.

Once classes let out, I went to the school entrance. I sat watching and waiting for my aunt to come. At first, it wasn't too bad; other children were waiting for their parents as well. As I saw each child going home, I got worried that my aunt would not come for me. Then I was there all alone. I didn't want to cry, so I paced up and down the school yard. The janitor sat with me for a little while—until she went home. There was no sign of my aunt.

In our morning devotion time, my aunt had reminded me that she would be there to get me. She also said that if I got a little scared, I could talk to God. So I said a short prayer. However, at the age of seven (even with prayer), waiting is the hardest thing to do. Thirty minutes later (what seemed like hours), I saw my aunt coming toward me. She had gotten held up doing an errand and had been unable to make it to my school on time. However, because she promised to come and get me, she wanted to make sure that she came through on her promise. Was I ever glad to see her! My aunt had kept her promise despite the challenges she faced.

Likewise, God always keeps His promises. Sometimes we feel scared about events in our lives, and we doubt that God is going to be there when we need Him to be. We feel like we don't have a way out. Today's Bible verse serves as a reminder, though, that God promises to be there with each of us no matter the situation.

Remember, God will not leave you or forsake you. His promises are sure and true.

Diantha Hall-Smith

September 9

Cloud Cars

The Lord Himself will descend from heaven with a shout. . . .
And the dead in Christ will rise first. Then we who are alive
and remain shall be caught up in together with them
in the clouds to meet the Lord in the air.
—*1 Thessalonians 4:16, 17, NKJV*

A study in contrasts, our six-year-old grandson quietly waits for me to join him in the living room. Gentle in spirit, with golden blond hair and great blue eyes, he is seated in his small wheelchair. A black patch covers his left eye, for he is dealing with the ravages of brain stem cancer. In spite of his limitations, his little face radiates with joy in anticipation of our visit and my reading him a new book about heaven that someone had sent him.

Clutching a Matchbox car in his little hand that day, he settled back with me to mentally explore the possibilities and surprises that await God's people who anticipate eternal life in and through the sacrifice of Jesus Christ on the cross of Calvary. This wonderful book encourages one to expand the expectation of heaven beyond the stereotype of sitting on a cloud all day while playing one's harp throughout eternity. Truly we can't begin to imagine the wonders our Father in heaven has prepared for us.

Knowing my grandson's love for Matchbox cars and "driving" them, I asked, "Jeffery, how do you think we are going to get around in heaven?" With little hesitation, I suggested that we might have "cloud cars." Raising my hands to grip my imaginary steering wheel, which I quickly "turned" to my left, I quipped, "We could just jump on a cloud and take off!"

His lopsided grin, caused by facial paralysis, and the sparkle in his one visible eye spoke volumes as he paid this treehouse-sleeping grandma the greatest compliment ever by asking, "Grandma Dottie, will you go on a 'cloud car' with me?"

My response was super quick! "Yes, Jeffery, we will just jump on and take off!"

His attitude changed abruptly! With great seriousness, Jeffery said, "Grandma Dottie, this is our old home. Jesus has gone to make a new home for us. Nobody there will ever be afraid or die. And . . . we have to make preparation to go." So reads the final testimony of a little boy who possessed faith beyond his years. He did not celebrate his seventh birthday but went to sleep in death a few weeks later, awaiting the second coming of his best Friend, Jesus.

Dottie Barnett

Finding Healing
Through Forgiveness—Part 1

"Whenever you stand praying, if you have anything against anyone,
forgive him [drop the issue, let it go], so that your Father
who is in heaven will also forgive you your transgressions
and wrongdoings [against Him and others]."
—Mark 11:25, AMP

I still remember the first time I saw the movie, *The Hiding Place*. I was fourteen and attending a Brazilian boarding high school. I was deeply moved by the story of Cornelia (Corrie) ten Boom, a Dutch Christian who, along with her family, helped many Jews escape the Nazi Holocaust during the Second World War, before her family was imprisoned in 1944.

While incarcerated, Corrie experienced mistreatment and the loss of her beloved sister, Betsie, who died after whispering the inspiring words, "There is no pit so deep that He [God] is not deeper still." As a teenager viewing this movie for the first time, I was impressed by Corrie's faith and how God miraculously freed her ten months later. What I did *not* quite grasp then, however, was how forgiveness played a key role in her life at the camp and afterwards.

Sixteen years later, as a thirty-year-old in the United States, I was experiencing the pain of injustice and rejection. It was then that God reminded me of the story of Corrie ten Boom. I listened to her own testimonial, as she told of her struggle to forgive. It was when she realized that she also had wronged God and needed *His* forgiveness that she was able to "let go" of the bitterness in her heart.

In her book *Tramp for the Lord* (1974), she wrote of an encounter she had with one of the cruelest guards at the Nazi camp where she'd been imprisoned. She was teaching at a church in Germany three years after she was released. The guard did not recognize her as he stood in line to greet her at the end of the service. She had not forgotten his face and prayed that God would help her forgive him. She wrote, "For a long moment we grasped each other's hands, the former guard and the former prisoner. I had never known God's love as intensely as I did then."

Corrie opened a rehabilitation center for concentration camp survivors while in the Netherlands, before sharing, around the world, about the healing power of forgiveness and God's love. What an inspiration for us to practice forgiveness!

Katia Garcia Reinert

Finding Healing Through Forgiveness—Part 2

So, as God's own chosen people, who are holy [set apart, sanctified
for His purpose] and well-beloved [by God Himself], put on a heart of
compassion . . . ; bearing graciously with one another, and willingly
forgiving each other if one has a cause for complaint against another;
just as the Lord has forgiven you, so should you forgive.
—*Colossians 3:12, 13, AMP*

At the time I recalled Corrie ten Boom's story, I was living with hurt. Having moved from Brazil to the United States, I was experiencing the pain of injustice and rejection by people I trusted and loved. In order to encourage me, I am sure God brought Corrie's story to my memory (as preserved in her own writings as well as in the movie *The Hiding Place*, which I'd seen as a fourteen-year-old).

As a young adult now, I pondered my own hurt as compared to what Corrie had been through. My hurt suddenly seemed smaller.

I asked myself, *How can I hold off forgiving others when God continues to offer me forgiveness again and again?*

Later on, I began to study the personal implications of forgiveness. I also went on to study forgiveness among our own church members, ones who had had a history of child abuse.

Among other things, I learned that those who more easily forgive others have better mental health than those who do not. Corrie ten Boom had also noted, in her experience with other victims of Nazi brutality, that those who were able to forgive others were better able to rebuild their lives.

Over the years, I have learned that forgiveness is a process. It may take time to forgive someone who has caused us deep pain and trauma. I also learned that forgiveness does not always mean reconciliation, and it does not always require the other person to feel sorry for what they did. In addition, I learned—especially from personal experience—that forgiveness *does* take work and that we cannot do this work alone. God, and God alone, can enable us to truly forgive others.

I chose to allow God to heal my pain through forgiveness. What will you choose?

Katia Garcia Reinert

What's in a Name

But now thus saith the Lord that created thee, O Jacob,
and he that formed thee, O Israel, Fear not: for I have redeemed
thee, I have called thee by thy name; thou art mine.
—Isaiah 43:1

I was born Rita Faye. *Rita* means "open and communicative. Extrovert. Thrilled to be alive. An individualist." *Faye* means "confident and trusting. Strong belief system." I lived out the meaning of my name for four years, until I was adopted and my name was changed to Dorcas, which means "determined, motivated and energetic." My birth mother gave me up, and my adopted family introduced me to God. All of my names were positive and powerful; I've always been proud of them. Then life happened, and I began allowing situations to change my open and communicative personality into one that was closed and introverted.

Then, questioning who God created me to be, I started losing confidence. By the time I was twenty-five years old, I had contracted "doubting Thomas syndrome." As a result, my name—self-given this time—I changed to Rejection. The devil made sure he reminded me of my name as much as possible. I answered to the name Rejection in relationships, marriage, and friendship. I experienced rejection in my failed marriage and in not having friends or people that I could trust. I actually found comfort in my new name. I liked it so much I wanted to name others Rejection before they even rejected me. I could relate to Naomi in the Bible, whose name meant "pleasant, delightful, lovely." But when the women of Bethlehem called her name after she'd experienced bitter blows that crushed her spirit, she was quick to say, "Call me not Naomi, call me Mara [bitter]: for the Almighty hath dealt very bitterly with me" (Ruth 1:20). Who could blame her? Looking at the circumstances, she took it upon herself to change her name and blame God for the reason she had changed it.

I wonder whether you, in times of discouragement, have felt you had the authority to change your name. Yet in Isaiah 43:1, the Lord who created you says, "Fear not . . . ; I have called you by your name; you are Mine" (NKJV). I suspect that if Naomi had continued living with the name Mara, she would not have become the great-grandmother of King David. And if I had not allowed God to call me by my true name, I would not be Reneé (my middle name), which means "reborn."

If you need a name change, tell Jesus. It will be all right if *He* changes your name.

D. Reneé Mobley

September 13

Let Us Run the Race

Wherefore seeing we also are compassed about with so great
a cloud of witnesses, let us lay aside every weight,
and the sin which doth so easily beset us,
and let us run with patience the race that is set before us.
—*Hebrews 12:1*

In early 2012, I set myself the goal of running a half marathon (21 kilometers) in order to raise money to build a classroom at the small village school that my late father had attended. Having never run such a distance before, I followed a training program that would take me from running ten kilometers to running the twenty-one. This involved running three days a week, slowly building up my endurance, strength, and speed. On rainy days, my running was restricted to the treadmill. Always I aimed to finish the goal for the day. I trained diligently for several months, keeping in mind my targeted date of September. All my running was on relatively flat surfaces, and I became quite familiar with the routes I used. Sometimes I met the same individuals as I ran. In order to better prepare myself, I ran at different times, early morning or evening.

During my months of preparation, I had to attend a work-related meeting out of town. The small town had beautiful sloping hills and fantastic sunrises and sunsets. The hills tested both my strength and my endurance. On the first day that I went running, the uphill route was quite a challenge, requiring great discipline and determination. The downhill was different: faster, exciting, and almost exhilarating. By the end of the week, I looked forward to my training, though with a bit of trepidation regarding the uphill stretch.

One day as I sat to have my devotional time with God, it dawned on me how very much like physical training our spiritual life is. God is ever calling us to a higher place, deeper relationship, and greater commitment. We desire these too, but sometimes the discipline of the upward trail seems too much for us. On the other hand, the slide down into sin is so much easier—even exciting, almost exhilarating, and before we know it, we have happily run into the mire of sin. Satan makes our descent into sin attractive and blinds us to the fact that we are heading downward. He blinds us to the destruction ahead.

I thank God that He doesn't give up on us. He reminds us that even though we walk (or run) through the valley of the shadow of death, His rod and staff still comfort and keep us.

Mukatimui Kalima-Munalula

Trust and Obey

But let all those rejoice who put their trust in You;
let them ever shout for joy, because You defend them;
let those also who love Your name be joyful in You.
—Psalm 5:11, NKJV

One of the biggest challenges in a Christian's life is the challenge of trusting God consistently. I can think of times in my life when I doubted God—not in His ability to help me, but I did not trust that He would help as I wanted. I think of Gideon in the Bible, who had a difficult time trusting God's call on his life, so he tested God (Judges 6). Do we trust God as we should, or do we try to test His promises, always unsure whether He will do as He says or answer as we desire? A hymn I love is entitled "Trust and Obey." Those two words, *trust* and *obey*, are so important to our spiritual growth. Not only should we trust God, but we must also obey His Word. God said to Gideon, "Go . . . , you shall save Israel from the hand of the Midianites" (Judges 6:14, NKJV). If Gideon had obeyed God without doubting, how much stronger he would have been as a leader. God did not get angry with Gideon. He gave Gideon proof of His power (verses 36–40). That action of God increased Gideon's faith and strengthened his trust in God.

As I look back on my life and see God's hand at work, I also see that each time He answered prayer or worked miraculously on my behalf resulted in increased trust and greater faith. However, when a new trial comes across my path, do I remember God's leading in my life and feel confident to face the trial? Do I move forward in obedience, knowing that God is in control and He will and can do all things for my good, or do I find myself doubting Him once again and stumbling in my Christian walk?

The Bible is replete with stories of those who obeyed God's Word and trusted in His wisdom, goodness, and guidance. As a result, the relationship that these people had with God grew from strength to strength. People such as Daniel, Deborah, Ruth and Naomi, Abraham, Hannah, Abigail, Elijah, and Elisha, and the list goes on. Being a Christian is not easy, and faith in God develops through seeing Him work in our lives—especially when things seem at their worst. But in order to see God at work in our lives, we must also obey His Word, follow His leading, and surrender to His plan for us. Through it all, let's give Him the praise and thanks.

Take heart, my sisters, put your trust in God, and you will shout for joy.

Heather-Dawn Small

Animal Protest

The LORD appeared to us in the past, saying:
"I have loved you with an everlasting love;
I have drawn you with unfailing kindness."
—*Jeremiah 31:3, NIV*

I learned to live with two indoor animals—a dog named Rufus and an unnamed cat. I soon learned their "languages." Rufus let me know he was ready to eat when I entered the kitchen to prepare breakfast. He did this by jumping up to the cupboard where he knew the bag of food was. Sometimes he followed me around the apartment; when thirsty and his water bowl was empty, I would hear him banging the toilet seat, somehow lifting it up and letting it fall as he protested his predicament. I'd say, "Oh, Rufus wants water."

The cat, on the other hand, was more on the quiet side. Yet after a few months, he too learned to protest when he was hungry, crying and pacing the kitchen until food was placed in his bowl. Sometimes he would follow me around the apartment. Occasionally I would not put out his food immediately because I wanted to learn more about how he communicated. Sometimes he climbed onto a chair or jumped up on the counter or washing machine. Other times he'd simply cry and rub against my leg or against Rufus. When the cat learned to protest his hunger, Rufus began to lie silently in the kitchen, while the cat did all the work. I would finally feed both Rufus and the cat.

Observing these two animals over time was a joy for someone who was formerly opposed to indoor pets. I'd see the cat rub against Rufus, lick the dog's fur, and try to play with him. They even slept on the same sofa. Yet I never observed any demonstration of love from Rufus toward the cat, though the cat would "protest" on his behalf for food and make friendship advances. This made me think about Jesus' love toward us and our occasional unresponsiveness. He demonstrated the greatest love by dying for us. He continues to work on our behalf. On a daily basis, He manifests His love toward us, just as that cat does toward Rufus.

Jesus continues to "protest" our needs before His Father. Though our actions hurt Him at times, He—like that cat—never tires of showing His love for us. The love of Christ continues to pursue us so much more than the cat pursued a relationship with Rufus.

How long must He "protest" on our behalf before we reciprocate such perfect love?

Nadine A. Joseph

Not My Will but Yours

"For I know the plans I have for you," declares the LORD,
"plans to prosper you and not to harm you,
plans to give you hope and a future."
—*Jeremiah 29:11, NIV*

After I completed my college degree in business management in December 2011, finding employment was difficult. So much so that I became very discouraged. Not only is it often more challenging for a woman to get a job than a man, but I also needed a job that allowed me to have Sabbaths off because of my religious beliefs.

Though I found temporary work at a nonprofit organization, my three-month tenure there was soon over, and again I was unemployed. I resented being idle. Thus I began to consider all my options. In next to no time, I had traveled from Dominica to Saint Lucia, where I have family. My plan was to continue my job search there. At this point, I was more than certain I would find a job there because the economy seemed to be better than it was at home. I spent two months searching tirelessly but to no avail. I began to get discouraged again.

One afternoon, I received a phone call from my mom (a prayer warrior in church) back in Dominica. She told me that Sister Christine (another prayer warrior) had seen an ad in the newspaper for an opening as an accounts clerk. I must admit that I was a bit hesitant because I felt that if I applied and was called for an interview, my making it back to Dominica in time for the interview would be almost impossible. Though I don't always remember it, God *does* have plans for my life (see Jeremiah 29:11). I applied for the position—and *was* called in for an interview. Since I was in Saint Lucia, I asked to have the interview via Skype. I knew, of course, it was best to leave everything in God's hands.

I believe that I serve the most wonderful, loving, and awesome God! The company with the accounts clerk opening agreed to the online interview, and I got the job!

Throughout the trial of unemployment, I also forgot the lovely promise in Psalm 27:14, "Wait for the LORD; be strong and take heart" (NIV). As Christians, we ask God to come through for us, and we pray that His will—not ours—be done in our lives. Yet, at the very same time, we attempt to help Him do His work. If only we would *wait* on the Lord and allow Him to reveal the plans He has for us! Today let us "stand still, and see the salvation of the LORD" (Exodus 14:13).

Amanda Amy Isles

Under His Wings

He shall cover thee with his feathers,
and under his wings shalt thou trust:
his truth shall be thy shield and buckler.
—*Psalm 91:4*

I was suffering with severe abdominal pain and spotting. My concerned husband had me visit the doctor for an ultrasound. Because my husband was conducting evangelistic meetings, he was unable to go with me; so my aunt did.

After a thirty-minute ultrasound test, the doctor said he was seeing a little bulge in my uterus. He was not sure what it was, so he recommended I have a pregnancy test done. I accepted the recommendation and prayerfully had the test done. "You are six weeks pregnant," the doctor told me when he came out. I was surprised and happy. Then he shared the rest of the news: "The spotting might be the threat of a miscarriage." Though saddened by this last bit of news, my husband and I still thanked God and prayed for our baby's safekeeping. The doctor had also prescribed tablets and told me go on complete bed rest. At this point, my husband was in the third week of his evangelistic meetings. *How can we survive this?* I asked God. Then, because severe lower back pain and spotting continued, we decided to visit a specialist two days later. "It appears you have an ectopic [outside the lining of the uterus] pregnancy," he told me. My husband and I prayed and fasted for three days. At this point, I was comforted with the words in Psalm 91:4, which assured me I could trust my situation to God.

On my return to the gynecologist, she confirmed that there was a gestation sac in my left fallopian tube and I needed immediate surgery, during which I would risk the loss of the tube. Frightened, I prayed and cried. A family friend accompanying me phoned my husband and told him the news. He too prayed and cried. He was still in evangelistic meetings. "Why don't you get a second opinion from another gynecologist?" suggested a very close friend. So we did.

That new doctor put me through a quantitative blood test, the results of which were negative. He told me I had had a miscarriage and no longer needed surgery. I was happy to give my husband the "no surgery" news, though the miscarriage saddened both of us.

I believe God heard our prayers and delivered me from surgery. He is ready and waiting to deliver you from your fears as well. Will you allow Him to do so?

Jenel A. N. Campbell McPherson

A Day in the Garden

A cheerful heart is good medicine.
—*Proverbs 17:22, NIV*

With winter approaching, it was time to harvest the garden. My son and daughter-in-law dug potatoes and pulled carrots. They cut chard and plucked Brussels sprouts. Besides harvesting, they had to keep their children occupied and happy. This was not difficult with their daughter, who was only a few months old, but it proved more of a challenge with three-year-old Derion. He wanted them to play hockey or to throw stones in the lake with him. Eventually he decided that he'd like to pick the snow peas from the vines. He picked and ate happily, renaming the peas "beans." Garrick and Stephanie were delighted; the three of them could talk together about the interests of three-year-olds: fire engines, airplanes landing on the lake, the dog playing in the yard. Derion pointed out where a moose had lain beside the garden last winter; they chatted about how they could bake the potatoes and crunch on the carrots.

It was a long day, spent in the sunshine and breeze. By five o'clock, Garrick and Stephanie were tired but happy and hungry, eagerly anticipating a meal from the garden. But not Derion. Like many three-year-olds who miss their naps, he was grouchy. While Garrick cleaned pails of potatoes before storing them in the cold room, Stephanie nursed their daughter, and Derion started throwing stuffed animals around the living room. As Stephanie cooked, he crashed metal cars in his parking garage and tossed plastic cows and pigs from his farm set. Although supper was ready, Stephanie hoped to calm him down by suggesting, "Let's find a book to read."

"No!" shouted Derion, his eyes flashing as he hurled another stuffed animal.

At that moment, Garrick walked up the basement steps. "Derion," he said sternly, "you have a choice. You can be a nice boy, pick up your toys, and come eat supper with us, or you can go to your room by yourself. Supper or your room," he repeated. "What do you pick?"

Sniffing loudly, Derion announced, "I pick *beans!*"

Suddenly the tension in the room vanished. Stephanie laughed. Garrick swung his son into an embrace. "Yes—you did pick beans! Now, let's all eat supper." With plates piled high with produce from their garden, they bowed their heads and thanked God for their blessings—good food and cheerful hearts that healed discord.

Denise Dick Herr

God of the Second Chance

*And we know that in all things God works for the good of those
who love him, who have been called according to his purpose.*
—Romans 8:28, NIV

While lying in the hospital bed, I could not believe what I had just heard: "You had a heart attack." There had been no recognizable warnings. I did not have hypertension. Cholesterol was a bit high, but I was on no medication. I had thought all was well. Then it happened. As I was preparing to do something for my mother, the chest pains had hit. Pressure. Tightness. Neck and shoulder discomfort. I took my blood pressure. The display read 200/103. I said, "That can't be right. I don't have high blood pressure." I waited a few minutes before I took a second reading on the other arm. This time it read 200/95. "Something's wrong," I said. I notified my husband, who was working under his truck: "I think I'm having a heart attack."

He dropped everything, and we went to the hospital. Of course, this was all new to us. Thanks be to God, I remembered to pray. I told Him, *I do not want to die. But if that is Your will, then it would be mine too.* All along the way to the hospital, I was not afraid nor did I ever panic. I just prayed, thanking God for His rich blessings and asking forgiveness for sin.

After much testing and consultation, I was diagnosed with having had a myocardial infarction, a heart attack. Emergency room personnel transported me to the nearest heart hospital, where I was scheduled for cardiac catheterization. That procedure revealed no blocked arteries or damage to the heart. "Praise be to God!" I said. The doctor said, "Whatever you had going on is gone now. Maybe it was just a spasm. You are good to go and in great health."

So what purpose did my heart attack serve? Romans 8:28 states, "And we know that in all things God works for the good of those who love him, who have been called according to his purpose." Perhaps the heart attack was to serve as a wake-up call for me to prioritize my responsibilities and slow down. This I do know: God allowed it to happen for a reason.

I remember lying in the hospital Friday evening when all was quiet. I reflected on how God had set me aside in this quiet place to talk with me about prayer and how important it is in my daily journey. Maybe that was the purpose behind my heart attack.

Our loving Savior quiets us sometimes so that we can reflect on His love for us.

Sylvia Giles Bennett

Control of Emotions

Better a patient person than a warrior,
one with self-control than one who takes a city.
—*Proverbs 16:32, NIV*

The skater exults that he or she has control over legs and feet in order to perform intricate maneuvers. The basketball player is happy for the ability to control arms and hands in order to direct the basketball up and into the basketball hoop. The pianist has mastery over hands and fingers across the piano keys. The gymnast delights in the discipline she has over her body, and the singer is happy because he can control his voice. Yet we all need self-control.

When somebody hurts you with words and you can control yourself without giving an answer that will also hurt the other person, you feel victorious, don't you?

From childhood, we should be learning self-control, especially over our emotions. As the gymnast feels good about controlling the movements of her body during a gymnastic routine, controlling one's emotions is also very gratifying.

Learning to control our emotions adds to the quality of happiness in our lives. Controlled emotions are basic to healthy and happy relationships.

One of the greatest virtues we can teach our children is the virtue of learning to control one's own emotions. Emotions often influence behaviors that, again, affect the quality of relationships. Dealing with children, in particular, we can affirm each choice they make to control their emotions in a way that results in acceptable behavior. These positive choices of theirs we must praise, showing we are interested in everything they do.

They will learn, as we have, that self-control not only brings happiness but also contributes to the success we can experience in various areas of our lives. Few undisciplined people attain enduring success. The writer of Proverbs 16:32 stated, "Better a patient person than a warrior, one with self control than one who takes a city."

God will help us learn patience. He wants our families to be representative of the heavenly family. He wants to see us, along with our children, control our emotions, have good relationships, and succeed in life. The more we seek God's presence in our families, the happier they will be. Friend, may you invite Jesus to be in your home.

Meibel Mello Guedes

No Fear in Love

Perfect love casteth out fear.
—*1 John 4:18*

I love 1 John 4:18 (today's verse). It's concise. Succinct. John didn't waste words. He knew what he was talking about; he lived with perfect love for three years.

For many years, I tried to have that perfect love, a love that would help me get past my overeating, my impatience, my lack of faith, and all the other things that bombarded me. I tried, I really tried. I worked so hard at finding perfect love that I worked myself right into a black abyss.

If I can't be perfect, I'll be bad, I finally decided.

I found out that bad is not very good when it comes down to it. So I'm back in the fold again, thanks to God's unconditional love. Yet I was still trying to understand perfect love.

So what's the secret of perfect love? I wondered. *And whose perfect love is John talking about?* I thought that it needed to be mine. Even after striving for perfect perfection years ago . . . even after God's revelation to me on my Damascus road when I was reconverted . . . even since then, I'd been asking, *When will my love be so perfect that I won't have any fear? It won't happen. Not in a million years. So where does that leave me now?*

I eventually realized that it left me right where I belong: praying for *God* to make me the totally submissive clay for the Master Potter. The clay that doesn't jump off the table and run away like the gingerbread boy. I submit to a total dependence on the Master to break me, make me, mold me, and use me.

When I'm submissive, filled, and empowered, perfect love will take up all the space in my life and heart, and there will be no room for fear. "Perfect love casteth out fear" (1 John 4:18). My Jesus is the "perfect love" John is talking about. Now, that makes sense.

After watching a powerful movie on the life of John Hus, I asked myself, *What will it take to get me to the place where I would be faithful all the way to the flames as John Hus was?*

I decided that all I can do is continue to love my Savior so that I may "know Him." I hold on to this prayer: *Oh, God, continue to grow in my heart and mind so intimately that Your perfect love will cast out all my fear no matter what comes.*

Jodi Eulene Owens Patterson (Dodson)

Sing Praises to the Lord

When my heart is overwhelmed:
lead me to the rock that is higher than I.
—*Psalm 61:2*

It is a good thing to give thanks unto the LORD, and to sing praises
unto thy name, O Most High: to shew forth thy lovingkindness in the
morning, and thy faithfulness every night.
—*Psalm 92:1, 2*

For those of us with debilitating diseases, it is easy to become overwhelmed when our doctor declares, "There is nothing more I can do for you." We fervently pray for a miracle of healing, but we know that is not a desire granted to all of us. So what do we do?

As I thumb through the book of Psalms, I notice that David constantly reminds us to "praise the Lord" and "sing praises to the Lord." I have been able to do this when He sends special mercies when I need them the most.

One weekend as I struggled to breathe comfortably, I debated whether or not I should go to the emergency room at the hospital. I have been there several times, so I know the routine. I wouldn't see my doctor, and the doctor on call would likely admit me to a bed and order oxygen. I wanted oxygen at home, but it would likely be a long process to have this available. If I were on oxygen at home, however, I could still get my own meals and continue to do projects for the university archives in my town.

God was listening to my quandary and sent a visitor from my doctor's clinic who books all outside appointments for clients. Lois Hymanyk offered to talk to my doctor the next morning, Monday, and ask him to approve oxygen for me. That very Monday afternoon, someone from the medical equipment company came to my door with an oxygen tank.

What a boost that was! I sang praises to the Lord.

Another day, a former teacher and friend, Ellen Bell, visited. While she was here, I had a call from the medical equipment company. Someone wanted to ask me twenty-five questions to determine whether I could qualify for free oxygen. Since I'm hard of hearing and depend on lipreading, I turned over the phone to Ellen, who relayed the questions for me to answer. That shortened and simplified the phone call. Again, I sang praises to the Lord.

Please join me in my resolution. Even in difficult situations, I have resolved to "sing unto the LORD as long as I live: I will sing praise to my God while I have my being" (Psalm 104:33).

Edith Fitch

Tick

Hear my prayer, O Lord; answer my plea
because you are faithful to your promises.
—*Psalm 143:1, TLB*

My family and I moved and now live in a tropical island paradise! I didn't look for work straight away. I had the home to arrange and children to settle in school and church. Yet I was planning to look for some part-time work when I felt the time was right.

Then one day, my husband came home and said a friend had asked whether I was working or whether I wanted work. So my husband told him to phone me, which he did. I agreed to go in for an interview and find out what the prospective job would be about.

Two managers threw lots of information at me and said I would have to work from 8:00 A.M. to 4:00 P.M. five days a week. So straight away I thought, *No, this is not the job for me. My children are still too young for me to be gone so much.* I told my husband so when I got home. A couple of weeks later, I received another phone call from our friend asking me to please come in again for an interview with the "big boss." The "big boss" was very nice and flexible. I don't know what that entity had heard about my work history, but it must have been good. They offered to create a position for me! Best of all, I was told I could work whatever hours best suited me. Even my hourly rate was negotiable! I asked for time to discuss the job offer with my husband—which I did. It all sounded too good to be true!

After the second interview, I went down to a nearby lagoon. I love to sit midst its beauty and tranquility and talk to God. Now, I am a person who asks for specific signs; otherwise, I am scared I will miss knowing God's will. I guess I am funny like that! On this sunny day, I noticed white clouds in the sky. So I told God that if He would show me the shape of a tick in the clouds, I would take that as a sign that I was supposed to accept this job offer. I looked up to the sky, turned around in a full circle, and there it was: a cloud in the perfect shape of a tick! I was so excited—I had my answer. I accepted the job and was blessed!

I encourage you, when appropriate, to prayerfully ask God for His signs but especially for His leading when you are faced with decisions. It is exciting to see the ways that He answers.

Donna Engu

Rocks of Hope

"My word . . . shall not return to Me void."
—Isaiah 55:11, NKJV

What a fascinating ministry, I thought, listening to the singer explain the outreach project during a break in his concert. He knows an elderly lady who lives on a small island in one of the Michigan lakes, an island accessible only by boat. At times, the island is iced in and cannot be reached by the ferry. The woman has not minded the isolation of being the only person living on the island after her husband died. Well organized, she carefully stockpiles her supplies before ice storms develop.

One day, thinking she needed another outlet for her time and energy, she hit on the idea of collecting small, flat rocks along the lakeshore. She paints one side of the rock with a Bible verse and, on the other side, a colorful picture—such as a butterfly, flower, or bird.

By the time she has several rocks completed, the weather warms enough for the ferry to reach her and take her to the mainland, along with her painted rocks. She wanders through various stores and unobtrusively leaves a rock on the counter or on a shelf and then moves on her way, praying the Holy Spirit will lead the right person to that specific rock.

As the singer passed attractive samples of her rocks throughout the audience, he told us why he considers this to be an excellent project.

"Many people pass out pamphlets or lay them places where others will find them," he said. "However, some people will throw away a piece of paper. But when they find a painted rock, they are less likely to discard it. It becomes a conversation piece and will probably be retained by the finder or given to someone else."

The uniqueness of this ministry appealed to me. Though not an artist, I found, to my surprise, that I can produce acceptable illustrations.

So began a new ministry for me. It is simple to end up with presentable rocks by just spending a few relaxing moments at a time being creative. Since there's no place to gather the rocks near my home, I find suitable rocks in lumber or hardware stores.

Now, each time I leave my home I try to take along a rock or two as a fun way to remind others of God's love. You may want to consider trying it too.

Dorothy Wainwright Carey

God's Grace for Any Situation

For we are God's handiwork, created in Christ Jesus to do good
works, which God prepared in advance for us to do.
—*Ephesians 2:10, NIV*

My first job after college was a disaster. I had to enter machine part numbers into a computer, and my boss came in drunk most mornings. A month went by, and I was let go. Sometimes it takes a while to figure out your "calling." I finally figured out that what meant the most to me is sharing Jesus and His grace.

In 2008 I was on an Alaskan cruise ship with my friend, Corleen, and many other women and men for a Women's Ministries trip that we had named "Making Waves." At each port, we did some community outreach as well as sightseeing.

On board, for extra exercise, Corleen and I strode around the deck many times. When we would reach the back of the ship, I always felt a little strange looking over the edge, which was an abrupt, straight down drop-off. I'd feel myself wanting to stand back or hold on to something. I knew that at times people have fallen off of ships. I thought, *What if, when getting close to the enticing view, I stepped up on a ladder's rung and then accidentally slipped and fell off? However, I have a deep faith that the ship's captain would see me and turn the ship around for a rescue. Yet how long would I last—even with faith in the captain—if he didn't turn the ship around and save me? Maybe ten minutes in the cold Alaskan water?*

I realized that if, by God's grace, the captain did see me, turned the boat around instantly, threw out a life jacket, and pulled me aboard in record time, then it wouldn't be anything *I* did that saved me. Grace would have reached in and given me back my life. "For it is by grace you have been saved, through faith—and this not from yourselves, it is the gift of God—not by works, so that no one can boast" (Ephesians 2:8, 9, NIV).

Grace comes first. And grace can pull us out of our "icy water" situations. The next verse (10) says, "For we are God's handiwork, created in Christ Jesus to do good works, which God prepared in advance for us to do" (NIV). What is God calling you to do?

Diane Pestes

The Case of the Stinging Nettles

Where there is no vision, the people perish.
—Proverbs 29:18

My cell phone vibrated, breaking my concentration. Somewhat absently, I answered. "Melissa went on a school field trip this morning and now she's in the emergency department," the voice said. "Come, quick!"

Once at the emergency department, I could hardly recognize Melissa. Every square inch of skin that had not been covered by clothing now sprouted ugly scratches and puffy, angry, red welts. She had tangled with *Urtica dioica*, or stinging nettles. As the nurse spread anti-itch cream on Melissa's skin, the story came pouring out. "There was this big, beautiful butterfly," Melissa began, "with wings like stained glass." She paused to swallow a tablet of antihistamine. "I ran after it into the field. I had no idea those towering plants had hollow stinging hairs on leaves and stems, like tiny *hypodermic needles* that sting people."

When I expressed surprise that no one had thought to caution the students ahead of time, Melissa looked up, her excited recital skidding to a halt. "Ah-h-h," she began and paused. "They did, actually. Well, they tried to." She dug into her backpack and extracted a paper on which was a picture of stinging nettles, along with instructions for avoiding them on the hike. "I didn't take time to read it," said Melissa, honestly. "I was too busy talking with my friends. So I didn't learn about stinging nettles. I could have. And now look at me! I am stung everywhere!" She promptly burst into tears, creating rivulets that trickled over anti-itch cream and puffy, red welts.

"Reminds me of an old saying," I said, shaking my head sadly and sympathetically. "What you don't know you don't know can oft' become a lethal foe."

"How do you know what you don't know?" asked Melissa, puzzled.

"By studying and learning and turning what you learn into knowledge," I replied, "and then practically applying the knowledge. Fortunately, you won't be ruined this time for lack of knowledge! (Hosea 4:6, NABRE). At least not permanently. But many people have been."

Melissa looked down at her arms and hands, slathered in calamine lotion. "Next time, I will take time to study and learn, turn it into knowledge, and then practically apply it!"

Are you perishing in some aspect of your life due to lack of knowledge? You can do something about that if you want to. It's your choice.

Arlene R. Taylor

Lessons From the Pigpen

"But the father said to his servants, 'Quick! Bring the best robe
and put it on him. Put a ring on his finger and sandals on his feet.
Bring the fattened calf and kill it. Let's have a feast and celebrate.
For this son of mine was dead and is alive again;
he was lost and is found.' So they began to celebrate."
—Luke 15:22–24, NIV

What a familiar story, which has implications for family relationships—especially as parents relate to wayward children. What lessons do we learn about the father from this parable? We already know God, represented by the father in this parable, is caring. The first lesson is that *the father allowed the son to make bad decisions when the prodigal son came to the father and asked for his share of the inheritance.* The father did not stop the son from leaving. He did not have to give the son his portion because, frankly, the son did not have a portion. He was living in the father's house, eating the father's food, and sleeping in a bed his father had provided.

The second lesson we learn from this parable is *sometimes God has to allow us to go into the pigpen.* In the story, the young son wasted all of his father's money, and when that happened, he ended up in a pigpen. However, there are lessons in the pigpen! In the pigpen, the prodigal recognized his helpless state. He had thought he did not need the father or his rules. He thought he wanted to be autonomous, but in the pigpen he decided to give up his autonomy and go home.

A third lesson from this parable of Christ's is that w*hile the father did not rescue the son, he was always looking for him.* He eagerly wanted him home. Why? He loved him. He did not care that the son had selfishly demanded his share. He did not care that he had left without leaving a forwarding address. He did not care that there was no communication. He looked for his son because he loved his son and wanted the best for him, which leads to the final lesson.

When the son came home, the father celebrated! The father did not reprimand him or say, "I told you so." He ran out to meet his son, not caring that he was dirty and smelly. Why? Because he loved his son. So when the boy came home (after coming to his senses), the father celebrated his return with a party. He restored him to his original position, and he trusted him.

We serve a mighty God, represented by the father in this parable. No reminders of "you should have" when wayward children return. Just celebrations. Oh, to be parents like that!

Edith C. Fraser

Aprons

*But one thing I do: forgetting what lies behind
and straining forward to what lies ahead, I press on toward the goal
for the prize of the upward call of God in Christ Jesus.*
—*Philippians 3:13, 14, ESV*

My Grandma Altie was big on aprons! In fact, other than the times she went to town, or, of course, to church, I don't remember her without an apron. Nor do I remember her wearing one that didn't have a bib! My cousin, Norma, who lived on the same farm, has observed that Grandma's were usually pinned on with big safety pins at the shoulders; I'm guessing that because she had back trouble, she didn't want them weighing on her neck. Norma adds, "We were lucky growing up on the farm and enjoyed all the Grandma love those aprons put out!"

When you look at pictures of pioneer women, they almost always had on aprons. They didn't usually have many dresses, and aprons were so much easier to wash and iron.

I'm not a big apron wearer, but my daughter, Rikki, is, and she keeps urging me to wear one when I am cooking. Rose Otis gifted me with a lovely plasticized apron from Harrods of London that I do like to wear, and I have tried to find nice aprons for Rikki and my granddaughters. My husband even has a macho apron—it is patterned so that it looks like Roman armor. I have a couple aprons that were my mother's. One I had made for her has the outline of our son's hand embroidered on the pocket from about the time he was two. Obviously she treasured and kept it.

It is fun to look back on the past with nostalgia, but seldom was the past as good as we fantasize. It is so much better to look forward, for the future will be even better—at least it can be spiritually. We need to keep moving forward and not dwelling on the past, whether it is our personal spiritual journey or that of the church.

I looked up the word *forward* in the New Testament in a Bible search engine and was amazed at how many wonderful texts I found. One is Romans 8:24, "We are saved by trusting. And trusting means looking forward to getting something we don't yet have" (TLB). Another I love: "And you are looking forward to the joys of heaven, and have been ever since the Gospel first was preached to you" (Colossians 1:5, TLB). I like to personalize that one and suggest you do too: "Ardis has been looking forward to the joys of heaven ever since she knew Jesus."

Ardis Dick Stenbakken

A Prayer of Rejoicing

The LORD directs the steps of the godly.
He delights in every detail of their lives.
—*Psalm 37:23, NLT*

I was out of state to take care of family needs. I had had a very busy day figuring out details of assistance for Mom, as Dad had passed away the prior summer. The court had appointed a conservator to help with Mom's major decisions. That day I met with Jill, who had agreed to be the conservator. She was a lovely lady of similar religious beliefs who showed such compassion. She shared with me how she planned to bring my mom a dozen roses on their first meeting. I couldn't praise God enough for this miracle.

I returned to my motel realizing that I hadn't washed clothes all week. Finding a laundromat was my goal for the evening. I quickly drove to a local one, only to find it had already closed because of a snowstorm prediction. So I went to the next one, which closed as I drove up. Not to be discouraged, I drove north in the darkness until neon lights from a large, modern laundromat loomed ahead. It was perfect, with modern machines, a friendly attendant to help with the money cards, and a café next door. Soon I found myself peacefully sitting at a small table enjoying my dinner while my clothes were washing.

Back in the laundromat, I noticed a tall, young, and attractive woman watching a flat-screen TV off to one side. Before long, she came over to my table and introduced herself. She said that she was a new Christian and asked whether she could pray for me. I was unprepared for the question. My first thought was, *I don't need prayer at this moment.* Then I realized that, yes, I would be delighted to have her pray a "prayer of rejoicing" with me. I had experienced such a wonderful answer to prayer for my mom that day.

We stood, and she lifted her head upward to heaven and prayed the most beautiful prayer. As she prayed, she kept her eyes open and didn't say Amen as many people do. At first, I wasn't sure when she was done, but, in time, she finished. She left quickly after that. Then I realized that she had not been washing clothes at all. I was in awe as I realized how God had sent the young lady to rejoice with me though I was all alone in a strange city. I felt that heaven had been opened and was sharing my joy. I hadn't been alone after all.

Judy M. Helm

My Visitor

Thou art my hiding place; thou shalt preserve me from trouble; thou shalt compass me about with songs of deliverance.
—Psalm 32:7

I was home and lunch was nearly ready. Suddenly I heard a most unusual sound. It was definitely a sound from the direction of the kitchen.

Looking around, I saw a black bear just outside my window. It was standing to its full height and looking right at me! Why was it there? It looked upward and tried to grasp something. What was it after? The bear was after a cake of suet and birdseed in a wire cage. The birds had visited this spot all winter, but this food was not for the bear.

When deer had come onto my porch to have a good feed of birdseed in my bird feeder, I had chased them away by blowing a whistle while clashing two cooking pot lids together. As I opened the door and whistled and clanged the lids, the deer had jumped from the porch and leaped away. I would use the same warning sounds for the bear.

But the bear was too close to the door for me to go safely outside, so I prayerfully whistled and clanged the lids inside the house. All that did was cause the bear to drop onto its four feet and look around to see what all the noise was about. It still didn't give up the quest for food.

In the meantime, I phoned Mitch, my neighbor. Shortly he drove into the driveway and roared toward the house. This time the bear dashed behind the woodshed and fled into the woods between my neighbor's property and mine. It obviously was not afraid of people.

Now, whenever I go outside, it is my custom to look straight ahead to the meadow, left to the other neighbor's property, and behind to the front lawn. Then, since I cannot see past the shed, I take a chance and hurry prayerfully to the carport and quickly get into the car. My window carries reminders of my visitor, for his claw and body marks are still visible there. To keep this type of visit from happening again, Mitch took down the tempting bird food. I think I would recognize "my" bear if it came around again. The bear has a thatch of white fur, in the shape of a V, on its chest. That's an easy identification mark. The next time the bear comes around, though, I want it to keep its distance.

God truly will help us in any situation. We just need to remember to ask for help.

Muriel Heppel

281

October 1

Arms of Love

The LORD of hosts is with us;
the God of Jacob is our refuge.
—Psalm 46:7

*ord, should I change jobs, or should I stay? Yet my health is getting worse . . . but
then, we have expenses and bills to pay! I just don't know what to do!* This prayer
and these concerns had been in my thoughts for the past six months. We
concluded I should stay at this job until a better option came around. But that
never happened, so I continued working, despite my serious thyroid condition—
at a pace I could not maintain. God showed me that His will was for me to quit
that job, but I convinced myself that there had to be another way—something
less drastic. I finally admitted in prayer that I was wrong and knew the Lord
wanted me to take that first step of faith. After discussing the decision with my
husband, we both decided I should quit the job. Let's just say that God truly
works in mysterious ways!

We hear a lot about living by faith, but when the time comes for us to exercise
that faith, we often get scared. We constantly say "amen!" in church when we
listen to sermons and preachers who say, "The just will live by faith." But in times
of crisis, we sometimes realize just how little faith we actually have! But God is
there and reminds us in His Word that He will guide us and help us. He will take
care of us and even mend our brokenness.

Do you know what God's will is for your life decisions? Does it matter whether
or not you have people's approval? Do your loved ones understand why you are
making a certain decision? Do you have everything sorted out? These questions
point to the same principle: trust God. He takes care of the big picture as well as
the small picture—all the details in the creases and folds—and He will put the
finishing touches on our stories.

I have to say, God is surely good. He has solutions to our problems that we
never knew were options. Just *trust God.* Is our budget now covered? Yes. Is
health in order? Yes. Am I rested, happy, and grateful? Absolutely, yes!

Let God take care of the options. Let God take care of you. He made us, so
He knows very well what we need and how to provide it. His love and his mercy
will guide us. His Holy Spirit will comfort us.

Let us trust and praise God, for the best place to be today is in His arms of
love!

Yvita Antonette Villalona Bacchus

I Know He Loves Me Too

If the Son therefore shall make you free,
ye shall be free indeed.
—*John 8:36*

Feeling a lump in my breast, I visited my doctor. He confirmed my fears, and we planned for surgery. Leaving the doctor's office, I went to a nearby church, where I wept and handed myself afresh to God.

Before the surgery, I prayed without ceasing, asking God for healing. I reflected on my life in ministry with my husband. I recalled how we labored for the Lord at Owerri when I was the head deaconess. We had no church building, so we worshiped in a public school classroom without doors. Alone, I would brave torrential thunderstorms to get the church ready for services. Also, on Fridays I would go to the nearby secondary school to pick up students. After church the next day, we fed them before taking them back to their school.

During one of my prayer sessions, as I wondered whether I'd skipped over any blessing for which I wanted to thank God, a voice said to my heart: "How can you forget what happened to you at Aba?" I was reminded of how God had snatched me out of the devil's den during a college project there, I and thanked Him again.

My pastor came to the hospital the morning I had surgery, along with my husband and other family members. A series of chemotherapy treatments followed my surgery. Then the doctor ordered extra treatments. By now my husband had gone to the United States on a sabbatical before he could return to Nigeria. I was broke. My children, although studying on student loans, were helping to put gas in my car. My food consisted of spinach, mushrooms, and potatoes. I could not work. I was encouraged to find employment at a night shift job to bring in a little money to help pay my bills.

When I completed my cancer treatment, a voice said to me, "Everything is fine now." I was convicted then that the Lord had healed me. During worship one Sabbath day, our pastor's wife and my sister sang on my behalf. A week or so later, I gave my testimony and sang the hymn "I Sing the Mighty Power of God." The church members were deeply moved and sang along with me. Afterward, we hugged each other, and I had to ask, "Is any thing too hard for the LORD?" (Genesis 18:14.)

Margaret Obiocha

October 3

Trusting the Promise

And we know that all things work together for good to them that
love God, to them who are the called according to his purpose.
—Romans 8:28

On my way to the hairdresser one Thursday morning, I heard an inspiring story on the radio. It was about a Vietnamese Christian who, because of his faith, was imprisoned for many years. Miraculously, just when he faltered and decided to abandon his faith, God sent him an encouragement from Romans 8: "And we know that all things work together for good to them that love God. . . . Neither death, nor life, nor angels, nor principalities, nor powers . . . , shall be able to separate us from the love of God" (verses 28–39).

Impressed, I shared the story with my hairstylist and suggested she read Romans 8:28–39 when she got home from work, since I couldn't quote it in its entirety. The next day she texted me, asking for the Bible reference, which she'd forgotten. Thrilled, I sat down on my living room sofa and reached for the Bible on the coffee table and found the text for her.

On Sabbath morning, while getting ready for church, I noticed that my wallet was missing. Stressed when I couldn't find it, I decided to go to church without it but to drive very carefully. As soon as I returned home, I searched for the wallet again but to no avail.

Sunday came with new fruitless searches, leading me to believe that I had left the wallet at a meeting I'd attended the previous Thursday evening. That building, however, was closed for the weekend. After many phone calls, someone was finally able to open it for me, but my wallet wasn't there. I decided to search my house again. I prayed, *Lord, you know where my wallet is. I've looked everywhere and can't find it. Please show me where it is.*

Getting up from my knees, I decided to search my bedroom again. As I walked by the living room sofa, I thought, *I already checked behind the pillows on the sofa, but I didn't look underneath the cushions.* As I pulled the first cushion forward, my black wallet appeared. The Lord had led me directly to the place where it was hidden.

My wallet must have slipped underneath a cushion when I'd sat down to find the Bible verses for my hairdresser. One of the verses I'd shared with her now had new meaning for me: "We know that all things work together for good to them that love God" (Romans 8:28).

Zlata Sabo

When the Cats Spoke English!

The eyes of the LORD are upon the righteous,
and his ears are open unto their cry.
—*Psalm 34:15*

I once read somewhere that cats can make about sixty different sounds. I'm familiar with about ten of those. My husband and I flew from Virginia to Phoenix, Arizona, to help our daughter, Julie, transport her two pets to Texas. She had just finished five years of medical studies at a California medical school and was joining her husband, Craig, in San Antonio.

Otto was Siamese and Jeff was a black-and-white tuxedo cat. We spent the night at an inn, then resumed our journey the next day. Each kitty weighed sixteen pounds and hated being crated. They became very restless. Jeff protested constantly. "Oh, ohh, hhh!" he cried, sounding just like a person. Otto sympathized with an intermittent, "Ow! Oww! Owww!" The poor cats probably thought they were on the longest trip to the vet ever!

Carl and Julie took turns driving. I was the "cat whisperer." *Music soothes the savage beast*, I said to myself. *Let's see whether it will help* tame *ones*. I started singing children's songs and nursery rhymes about cats and other animals to them. I also reached into their crates to pet them and rub their backs and necks. They settled down and went to sleep for an hour or so. When they awoke, still in the same situation, the cat chorus began again. This routine lasted our whole trip.

"Oh, ohh, ohh!" Probable translation: "Will this trip *never* end?" "Ow, oww, oww!" The likely meaning: "Being so closely confined is really hurtful!" Even with their one-word "English" vocabularies, they vividly conveyed how distressed they were.

We, too, at times, have troubles that seem too hard to bear. Some of us may be quite vocal. Others of us may grapple with finding words to express the feelings that surge through our souls. But God understands every human language. And if we can't speak, we can send Him thought prayers.

The kitties were much relieved—and so were we—when we reached San Antonio. Their cries for help had been heeded.

And help is at hand for us as well. We just need to tap into it. Jeff and Otto weren't too proud to cry for help. Nor should we be either.

"God is our refuge and strength, a very present help in trouble" (Psalm 46:1).

Bonnie Moyers

Lydia

One of those listening was a woman from the city of Thyatira named
Lydia, a dealer in purple cloth. She was a worshiper of God.
The Lord opened her heart to respond to Paul's message.
—*Acts 16:14, NIV*

More than forty years ago, we visited the ruins of the old city of Philippi. I will never forget walking on stones where Paul and Silas might have walked and seeing a building that could have been their prison. But for me, Philippi is especially interesting because of Lydia, who lived and worked there. A prosperous businesswoman, she sold purple fabrics. She was originally from Asia Minor, where woven wool and linen fabrics were dyed purple.

I would have loved to visit Lydia's fashion shop, although I would probably not have been able to afford anything in her classy boutique. Her luxurious fabrics were very expensive, but it would have been wonderful just to touch and feel them between my fingers.

Lydia was not a Jew, but she was a believer and met with other women on the banks of the river to pray on the Sabbath. Paul and his comrades joined them and told them about Jesus. Lydia's heart was touched, and she was baptized. Paul met Lydia in a women's prayer group, and he shared the gospel with them. Is it significant that Paul was happy to meet with women? He was convinced that Lydia had a strong and genuine faith in Christ and was ready to be baptized. She was the first person baptized on the European continent. The first church in Europe was founded in her home! After Paul and Silas were released from imprisonment days later, they again met with believers at Lydia's house before leaving town. In a subsequent letter to the Philippian church, Paul mentions the special financial help they provided—Lydia was likely one of the contributors. A founding member of the congregation, she might even have been its first elder.

Lydia was a successful businesswoman, but she had a tender heart and a hospitable home. She probably had a large family, and she wanted all of them to accept Jesus as their Savior. We are told that her whole family was baptized with her. This rich and respected woman became a faithful disciple of Jesus. The truth she discovered in Jesus determined the course of her future life. This is something we can all learn from her.

Hannele Ottschofski

Gerbera Daisy

As Christ was raised up from the dead by the glory of the Father,
even so we also should walk in newness of life.
—*Romans 6:4*

Last fall, I left my gerbera daisy plant out on the deck, not knowing that it couldn't withstand the cold. As the cold weather came on, my plant appeared to have died. I wondered what would happen if I took that poor plant into the house. Nothing happened for about two weeks. I made sure the plant had sunshine, water, and warmth, which is just what people also need to be healthy. Then the stalk grew taller and taller, and new green leaves began unfurling.

One day, I spotted a drab flower bud, not pretty at all. Yet, day by day, it began changing from its drabness to a bloom with orange-tipped petals. Before long, it was a brilliant orange daisy. Beautiful! I was thrilled with this process. At the base of the plant, I even saw more tiny leaves being "born"!

That plant, miraculously coming back to life, taught me a lesson. God had created it and renewed it. It had made my life happier just doing what it could. I thought, *That plant is working for its Creator. What are* you *doing for God?*

I was ashamed of my answer: *Very little.* Shame on me—and after all God has done for me! Even if I am ninety-one years old and can't walk any distance without my walker, surely I could do something. *God, what can I do for You?* I prayed.

A few days later, I received a flyer in the mail. It came from a Christian bookstore. It was advertising, among other things, a packet of tracts entitled "Talking With God." This was an answer to my prayer! I ordered a packet of one hundred. *I may not be able to get around too well at my age,* I thought, *but I can certainly hand out encouraging tracts in the shopping strip near my house.* I was surprised to see how fast one hundred tracts disappeared into the hands of others! The warm, grateful smiles I received in exchange for them warmed my heart too.

The next time I will order four packs! It's money well spent!

To us, some people may appear to be as spiritually dead as did my gerbera daisy before I brought it into the warm indoors. Yet perhaps some people reading that tract on prayer will be spiritually revived. I pray they will bloom into newness of life and be ready to meet their Savior.

Dorothy Butler

Do It for Steven

"For I know the plans I have for you," declares the Lord,
"plans to prosper you and not to harm you,
plans to give you hope and a future."
—*Jeremiah 29:11, NIV*

I was able to retire at a fairly young age. I had worked for thirty years and considered working several more. My husband, Steven, and I started thinking of relocating to a state where we frequently vacationed. It was a family decision, and my mom, sister, and her husband were also considering the move. We are all so close that we couldn't imagine living apart.

As much as I felt I would enjoy the new location for its beauty and peaceful surroundings, my heart was not a hundred percent on board yet. It was a leap of faith to leave our familiar area and basically start over in a new state.

I was driving down the interstate one day, talking to God. I remember asking Him to give me guidance on this big decision. All of a sudden, I heard God's quiet voice saying, "Do it for Steven." I immediately felt at peace about the decision and knew we were moving. I came home and told my husband about what had happened. Then we called the rest of the family. We all decided to take that leap of faith! Little did we know what was going to transpire!

Eight months after moving to our new home, my husband was diagnosed with a rare autoimmune disease called granulomatosis with polyangiitis, or GPA (formerly known as Wegener's granulomatosis). It is imperative to get treatment quickly, and it is sometimes extremely hard to diagnose. In 2005 many physicians had never even heard of it. Our new internist, though, listened to Steven's symptoms and sent him immediately to a rheumatologist. She was able to quickly diagnose him due to her knowledge of Wegener's. She already had other patients who had this disease. The internist, years earlier, had treated a Wegener's patient. This was not a coincidence, and we know it was God working to help Steven get the best care and get it quickly.

Even though Steven has experienced many challenges over the years with this disease, we have felt God's love and care. The blessings have been abundant. We thank God daily for all He does in taking care of us and for providing for Steven's ongoing treatment.

Years prior to our thinking of moving, the Lord knew our future. He was putting a plan together to provide for my husband's needs. How awesome that He attends to each of our needs!

Jean Dozier Davey

God Does Not Give Up on Us

"All those the Father gives me will come to me,
and whoever comes to me I will never drive away."
—*John 6:37, NIV*

One day, I saw three friends talking. One of them said that he was having problems with his parents. The others asked, "And what does that have to do with us? It's *your* problem, not ours!" The boy was devastated and ended the conversation.

After overhearing that situation, I asked myself, What would have happened if Christ had done to us what those friends did to that boy? *Those young people closed the door on a friend in need of help,* I reflected. How would we feel if we were to tell God our problems and He ignored us, turning away from us? Thanks to God's great mercy, He does not do that. He says that if we know how to give the best to our children, He knows how to do so much more for us. Even if a mother forgets her children, He will never forget us.

During His time on earth, Christ sought to reach all people. He did not make distinctions among people. He wanted everyone to have the opportunity to go to heaven: tax collectors, sick people, thieves, and prostitutes. People who do not have a place on earth will be welcome in heaven, and His mission is to make this possible through offering salvation.

Christ showed that He was different when He chose His disciples. He could have chosen true scholars, doctors of the law, but He did not. He chose humble fishermen, sometimes even rude and ignorant men, to show that in His kingdom, everybody is welcome and equal.

Christ's mission here on earth was to reconnect the fallen human race with its Creator, reestablishing the bonds of love that had been broken. That is why He always listened attentively to each request and each cry. He supplied the needs of each person that approached Him.

Christ never closes the door on anyone. He is available to us twenty-four hours a day. We do not need to pay to speak with Him. It does not matter where in the world we live or when we need Him. All we have to do is speak and, in that same instant, He will hear us. Christ will listen, and in the right moment, He will answer our prayer. He never gives up on us!

May we follow the example of Christ and always be willing to have an open heart and mind so that we may be able to help our fellow man as Jesus helps us.

Carmem Virgínia dos Santos Paulo

First Things First

And God saw every thing that he had made,
and, behold, it was very good.
—Genesis 1:31

Misplaced priorities can cause a lot of problems in life, whereas a well-ordered life is a blessing. Doing the first thing first is always the best way to happiness. As a Women's Ministries leader, I have met with many mothers who suffer misplaced priorities. Some have sought for a marriage when they should have first sought a career in life. Some sought for pleasure when they should have sought after God, who alone can direct the course of their lives aright. Alas, the consequences have ranged from heartache to even suicide, in extreme cases.

Reading through the Creation week account, we see a God of order in action, a God filled with love and blessings for all His creatures that He created in the order of His priorities. He made first things first. In both Genesis 1 and 2, we see that God used the first three days of creation to transform our watery, formless planet into a comfortable and habitable place to live.

He created light to give us the day-and-night cycle. He created a firmament so we would have an atmosphere in which to breathe. The dry land He created provided for the needs of vegetation, which, in turn, provide for our need to be fed and nourished.

On the fourth day, God brought the sun, moon, and stars into existence.

The fifth day of Creation saw creatures spring into life both in the water and in the air.

On the sixth day, in God's perfectly ordered plan, He created land animals and human beings that could thrive in this perfect environment. All things were ready for them. Yes, God's orderliness made all He did during Creation week "very good."

This same Creator God longs to order the steps and lives of His children. The Bible says, "The steps of a good man are ordered by the LORD: and he delighteth in his way" (Psalm 37:23).

In your marriage, in your career, and in all your endeavors, God is more than willing to order your steps. He longs to keep you from making mistakes and to grant you blessings. His desire is to give you beauty instead of ashes. Even if you have previously misplaced your priorities in life, God is still able to replace your ashes with beauty. Choose Him as your Guide.

Lord, please order my steps in all my endeavors. Give me beauty in place of ashes. May I delight in doing things Your way. In Jesus' name. Amen.

Omobonike Adeola Sessou

What Teenagers Want Adults to Pray For

If we ask anything according to his will, he hears us.
And if we know that he hears us—whatever we ask—
we know that we have what we asked of him.
—*1 John 5:14, 15, NIV*

I am a thirteen-year-old young lady who lives in North Carolina. My grandma asked me to speak for her Praying for Our Children prayer conference call. My topic was "What teenagers really want adults to pray for—when we ask them to pray for us." I spoke from my heart. As I share these thoughts with you, I hope you will be inspired to think beyond what people typically assume teenagers need.

First, we need you to pray for our education but beyond just our grades and peer pressure. We need you to pray for our teachers. As teenagers, we really hope we get a good teacher so that we can get the best education. It really concerns me when I think I could go a whole year missing out on a great teacher. I believe if you pray for us, the Lord will make sure we get the right teacher.

Teenagers also want prayers for our families. Please pray for us to get along with our siblings, as well as with our parents or guardians. Teenagers live in many different situations, and we need you to pray that whatever is going on between our parents or guardians will not take a toll on us. We don't know how to deal with adult issues, so we just try to make it, and sometimes that's hard. It would be good if we knew someone was praying for us in that area.

Finally, we need prayer for what may seem strange to adults but is important to us. Teens seem to worry about little things, but it is not the little things that are getting to us. It is usually something much bigger, but we don't know how to express the real problem. We might seem to "freak out" because we have "nothing to wear." Instead of brushing us off or saying something that makes us feel bad, you could talk to us; try to figure out whether there is something else going on. If you don't know what to ask, then ask the question that stumps scientists: Why? Even if you don't get an answer . . . if you have been praying for your teenager, *God* will tell you how to help us with the real problem, which is usually much more than "nothing to wear."

On behalf of all teenagers, don't stop praying for us. Pray for what we say. This will allow you to hear what we *think*. More importantly, pray for what we don't say because that is what we really need. Thank you for praying for us today.

Briana Fewell-Johnson

From Rags to Riches

The LORD their God will save his people on that day as a shepherd
saves his flock. They will sparkle in his land like jewels in a crown.
—*Zechariah 9:16, NIV*

"They shall be Mine," says the LORD of hosts,
"On the day that I make them My jewels."
—*Malachi 3:17, NKJV*

From a small, dark shadow against a bleak gray wall emerged a shy little girl closely observing prospective mothers and fathers. She watched them talk with the other children on visitation day at the orphanage.

I wish someone would notice me, thought Darlene. *I wish someone would talk to me and then take me home to be part of their family.* Loneliness weighed heavily in her heart.

Years passed before Darlene was to have a family of her own. One day, a Christian family, already bursting at the seams with foster children, invited Darlene to come live with them. At last, she had been chosen! She had some rocky moments at first, including her breakage of a toaster. Yet her foster parents were able to repair it, and it worked for the next forty years!

Not only did the members of that family accept and love Darlene, but they also introduced her to Someone who would become her very best Friend, Jesus. Darlene knew how to make herself useful. Before long, her foster parents officially adopted this industrious teenager into their large family. They helped her obtain an education in Christian schools. Eventually she graduated from college with a degree in secretarial science.

We first met Darlene as church secretary at a church where my husband was called to pastor. In addition to being a faithful member, Women's Ministries leader, and church custodian, she excelled in electronics, the operation of public address systems, and the use of cameras.

Years later, one hour before our departure to visit our lonely son who was in the military, Darlene appeared at our door with a gift for him. We had prayer with her and hugged her with tears, as I had a sense of foreboding in my heart. A few days later, on a snowy Christmas Eve, Darlene was killed instantly in a head-on car collision. Yet from the emotional "rags" of her orphaned childhood, God had produced the "riches" of a jewel reflecting *His* love to so many.

May we allow Him do that in our lives as He did in Darlene's!

Patty L. Hyland

Beyond Imagination

*"No eye has seen, no ear has heard, and no mind has imagined what
God has prepared for those who love him."*
—*1 Corinthians 2:9, NLT*

The pathway through the familiar forest looked so different in the darkness. Flaming torches lit our meandering way between the autumnal trees. Gentle lights illuminated the different patterns in the branches and the shapes of the rocks.

A fountain danced on the tiny lake. A rainbow of lights played across the swirling water as it rose and fell, pirouetting to a symphony of sound. Spotlights swept the woods, accenting different trees, bringing them out of the darkness. Sudden starbursts highlighted the gnarled silhouette of an ancient oak, and fairy lights twinkled along the branches. Flames billowed and faded over the water of the lake, dancing in formation to the music that bathed the forest. We watched slender birches caught in a "lightning storm," their silvery bark flickering in the night.

We wandered in wonder. The air was perfectly still, and the October evening was surprisingly mild for Scotland. We tried taking photographs and movies, but nothing could really capture the magnificence of the experience. Tiny children in their buggies, disabled people in their wheelchairs, old and young, entire families—everyone was touched by the wonder, the peace, and the exuberant joyfulness that filled the forest.

The Enchanted Forest is a light, music, fire, and fountain display designed by lighting artists and composers. Each year, the Forest has a different theme, and the creative team experiments with music, lighting, special effects, and fountain choreography to shape their dreams into an award-winning experience. And even though the music and lighting are incredible, the God-created trees, water, and woodlands are the stars of the show.

At the end of the evening, my husband and I held hands, silenced, in awe. Something inside us wanted to stay forever. Both of us had the same thought: This is a taste of heaven. Every day will be filled with indescribable wonder; around every corner, a new delight. Every moment will fill our hearts with praise for God, the ultimate creative designer.

What fills your heart with wonder? Where will you taste heaven today? And how will you share this experience with those you meet?

Karen Holford

October 13

Angels

For he will command his angels concerning you
to guard you in all your ways.
—*Psalm 91:11, NIV*

Hours passed as bad weather delayed my flight from Bacolod City in the Philippines. I was sure I would not make my connection from Manila to Washington. My heart sank because the next day I was to meet my grandson, Benjamin, to spend a long and special weekend with him. Finally the last person in line boarded our delayed flight. *Good,* I thought. *I may still have a chance to make the connection. Oh, no! One more passenger.* A crippled man boarded the plane and took a seat beside me. He looked tired, and I was upset. As the plane took off, I shared with him my frustration and fear of not making my connection in Manila's busy airport, a transition that would involve a thirty-minute bus ride from the domestic to the international terminal.

When we landed in Manila and I was about to say goodbye, my gentle and attentive seatmate said, "Do not worry. You will make your connection. My personal driver is waiting for me, and I will drop you at the gate." Sure enough, the driver was there waiting. In five minutes, I was at the gate for my flight home. I was the last one to check in and ran to the plane. My last words to him were, "You are an angel. Thank you for making my way home possible."

The Bible teaches us that there is another world that surrounds our earthly realm. It's invisible to us, yet very real indeed. Traveling between these two worlds, the invisible spiritual world and the temporal world that we know, are good angels. What do they do? "The angel of the LORD encamps around those who fear him, and he delivers them" (Psalm 34:7, NIV). "For he will command his angels concerning you to guard you in all your ways; they will lift you up in their hands, so that you will not strike your foot against a stone" (Psalm 91:11, 12, NIV).

If you are a believer, expect powerful angels to accompany you in your life experiences. And let those events dramatically illustrate the friendly presence of "the holy ones," as Daniel calls them. Certainly, the eye of faith sees many evidences of the supernatural display of God's power and glory. God is still in business, and His angels are still at work on our behalf.

Flying home that night, I thanked God for the angels in my life. One thing I do know: "He will command his angels concerning you to guard you in all your ways" (Psalm 91:11, NIV).

Raquel Queiroz da Costa Arrais

Precious Words

Let no corrupt word proceed out of your mouth, but what is good for necessary edification, that it may impart grace to the hearers.
—Ephesians 4:29, NKJV

Today was one of those rare days when I was home all alone. Well, not totally alone because our two dogs and cat sat lovingly by my chair while I worked on a talk to present later this year. Searching God's Word makes time fly because the next thing I knew it was four hours later and my tummy was rumbling. I had been focusing on the connection between the heart and words. Years ago, Florence Littauer wrote a book, *Silver Boxes*, based on a sermon she presented at women's retreats. The point of her book is that we need to speak kindly to one another, sharing words as if they were gifts wrapped up in silver paper and tied in sparkling silver bows.

It seems to me that the angrier the world gets, the nicer we need be to each other. The world is a hard place in which to live because of so much stress. Yet if I could be nicer to others and speak kinder words, maybe it would help defuse some of the tension and anger around me. I realized I have to pray about this every day, because it's so easy for me to express frustration and negativity. My heart needs to practice what the Word tells me to do: "Speaking to one another in psalms and hymns and spiritual songs, singing and making melody in your heart to the Lord" (Ephesians 5:19, NKJV).

Too often I find myself sour faced and grumpy about things.

Oh, Lord, I long to have such intense joy from You that I am the voice of song to all those I come in contact with. It might not change the world, but I have no doubt that my home, work, and church would be happier places with my mouth speaking edifying and uplifting words.

Maybe you, like me, need more of the Lord's love in your heart. Maybe you, like I sometimes do, think you are justified in entertaining negative thoughts and words. I am going to try to remember to apply the ten-second rule and "silver boxes" when feeling negative. I will wait ten seconds before speaking. I will pray that words coming from my mouth will be precious words—wrapped in "silver bows" that help others and edify them. The astounding and capable love of the Lord will help us do this. "Let the words of my mouth and the meditation of my heart be acceptable in Your sight, O LORD, my strength and my Redeemer" (Psalm 19:14, NKJV).

Mona Fellers

The Miracle Jacket

"Don't be like them, for your Father knows exactly what you need
even before you ask him!"
—Matthew 6:8, NLT

The church moving van, surrounded by towering snowdrifts, picked up our belongings to move from northern Iowa to our new pastoral assignment in western Oklahoma. We arrived at our new home to find green lawns, birds happily singing, and summerlike temperatures.

There were many adjustments for us to make, not the least of which was a need for new wardrobes for all of us. Not only did we need lightweight clothing, our son grew six inches during his freshman year of secondary school! I made most of the clothes worn by our daughters and myself. My husband's one black suit took care of his Sabbath attire. It was soon apparent, however, that the heavy winter coats we wore "up north" would have to be replaced.

Being short of money was not an unusual dilemma. My husband's ministerial salary at that time barely covered our basic needs. My newspaper salary was applied toward the cost of Christian education for four children. We managed to get lightweight sweaters and jackets for the children, but I still needed a suitable church outer garment for myself. *Lord, you know that the heavy winter coat I wore in northern Iowa isn't appropriate for Oklahoma, not to mention its age. I desperately need something new to wear to church.*

During the twenty-five-mile drive to work one day, I had a strong impression that there was a special tan sweater-jacket waiting for me at a national chain department store in the town where I worked. I could visualize it on the rack—and even see the price tag, which was so low that even I could afford it. When my lunch break came, I rushed to the back of the store and found the very sweater-jacket I had been shown. It was my size, the only one of its kind in the store, and the price was exactly what I had visualized during my prayer.

When I took the garment to the clerk, she said, "Where did you get this? We don't stock jackets like this here." I pointed out their company's price tag on the garment. She took my money, mumbling under her breath, "This is just *too* weird!"

I wore that jacket for years and never put it on without remembering how my God had supplied my need in such a dramatic way!

Teresa A. Sales

Quiet Messages

God has put the body together, giving greater honor to the parts
that lacked it, so that there should be no division in the body, but
that its parts should have equal concern for each other.
—*1 Corinthians 12:24, 25, NIV*

Years ago, I attended the funeral of one of our church members. She was a quiet, soft-spoken woman whose presence was marked only by her smile. Never did she express her thoughts during a Bible discussion, nor did she voice her opinion in church meetings. So when I entered the sanctuary to take my place at her funeral, I was totally taken by surprise to find that the church was packed with more than two hundred and fifty people. During the service, I learned she had touched many people's lives by sending sensitive, handwritten notes to neighbors, friends, and coworkers. What an impression her ministry made on me that day!

Now, writing—be it just a short note or a Christmas letter—has always been a painful process for me. Yet I have discovered that notes can address assorted situations in very personal ways, whether they are notes of gratitude, encouragement, or congratulations. A personal note has a unique way of opening the door of friendship. With friendship often comes opportunities to share God's love. My notes aren't filled with wisdom or fancy words, but they do contain heartfelt feelings that I put down on paper for another.

Recently I noticed that a coworker of mine had become somewhat withdrawn and apparently sad. Though I was not sure of the reason for her change in demeanor, I couldn't help but wonder whether it had to do with her thirty-something son, who had committed suicide a little more than a year before. Hesitant to say anything, I turned to writing a note. I prayed as I drafted my note. I always write a draft first. I guess it's because I want to make sure of what I say and also allow God to correct my feeble thoughts. I sent her the finished note. In due time, she and I did have a heartfelt conversation about what was concerning her.

Certainly, many women have talents and ministries that God has given them. Some women are high profile, while others are quieter. Yet we are all valued in God's sight, and when our talents are used for His honor, we can provide untold blessings to those in our spheres of influence. Maybe the quiet, handwritten note can expand your scope of ministry too.

Lynn Nicolay

Infected!—Part 1

And I will bring the blind by a way that they knew not;
I will lead them in paths that they have not known:
I will make darkness light before them, and crooked things straight.
These things will I do unto them, and not forsake them.
—*Isaiah 42:16*

While traveling in Romania for our ministry, I suddenly felt a terrible pain along my left jawline. Knowing that I have TMJ/TMD (tempromandibular joint disorders), I thought at first that this condition was causing the pain. It would go away after a short time. After all, it had been a very busy trip, and now we were headed back to Bucharest, and the crazy drivers on the road were stressing me out!

It didn't take long to realize the pain was much more than my TMD flaring up!

I awoke the next morning with a large lump under my left jaw, and the pain was getting more intense by the moment. We had a full day of travel still and obligations the following day, since we were speaking at church that Sabbath.

I tried toughing it out. We got through the church service and all-day potluck and fellowship with the help of some pain relievers one of the parishioners shared with me.

Unfortunately, the pain and the swelling continued to worsen.

I ended up going to multiple hospitals on Easter Sunday (Romania's Easter is on a different date than the United States' holiday)—first trying to find one that was open and then trying to find one that could help me. By the end of the day, I had an antibiotic, a pain reliever, and a spasm relief medication. I was told to come back in five days if I wasn't better.

Well, a few days later, I was no better, and things had gotten worse. My husband even prayed for and anointed me in the middle of the night because I was crying due to the intensity of the pain. At this point, God intervened.

By this time, my tongue was swelling, and I was having great difficulty swallowing and could barely open my mouth. I ended up seeing two more specialists in Romania and obtaining an emergency letter so that we could return home a few days early and not have to pay a fortune to change our flights. How kind God was to provide this timely financial relief!

It reminded me of the promise, "God is our refuge and strength, a very present help in trouble" (Psalm 46:1). Truly God is faithful to help us in times of trouble and need!

Samantha Nelson

Infected!—Part 2

Be sure your sin will find you out.
—*Numbers 32:23*

After being awake for two full days of travel, we arrived home around midnight, slept for a few hours, and then went to the urgent care facility on Friday morning. That is where I met the doctor who told me how serious my infection already was, in the first place—and how much more serious it had become. I learned that two of my symptoms, the swelling tongue and difficulty in swallowing, along with barely being able to open my mouth, were critical symptoms of this dangerous and potentially lethal infection.

The doctor prescribed a new antibiotic, and I began taking it. Sabbath morning, I woke up in pain—everywhere! I called the doctor, and he told me to discontinue the medication. I was having an adverse reaction to it. In fact, it had caused me to develop polyarthritis—a type of rheumatoid arthritis.

The following Monday, I went to a dentist and was told I needed to see a specialist because my situation was complicated.

So what was the cause of all this pain, swelling, and suffering? Three of the doctors agreed that it was due to a very small infection that had started from a previous dental procedure! The small infection had gone undetected for years, possibly decades, and had finally erupted into a full-blown, serious infection that could cause death!

That led me to think about sin. Is there something that is seemingly small in our lives that we allow to persist for decades, thinking it's no big deal? Yet what will that small sin lead to eventually? Will it erupt into something major? Possibly even something deadly? Maybe even something that could cause us to lose eternal life?

We have a warning in Galatians 5:9: "A little leaven leaveneth the whole lump." A little sin is still too much sin!

My desire is for God to cleanse me, not only of this biological infection but also of the sin infection. I want the Lord to search me "and know my heart: try me, and know my thoughts: and see if there is any wicked way in me, and lead me in the way everlasting" (Psalm 139:23, 24). What about you? Will you choose to be cleansed from the infection of sin? I pray so!

Samantha Nelson

October 19

It's Not All About You

God works for the good of those who love him.
—*Romans 8:28, NIV*

I was coming to terms with being left out, yet again, by family. Things were not happening the way I wanted, but God had surely blessed me beyond my wildest dreams. So why was I so disillusioned that night? And I was. In my mind, I was feeling "woe is me." Yet hadn't God been good to me and performed miracles before my eyes?

God is patient with us and goes on loving and loving, which He did for me that night. In His infinite grace, He gave me the words I have used to entitle today's inspirational thought. He didn't give me this thought in a harsh way but rather in a soft, loving way. *It's not all about you.* And it isn't.

God helped me begin to see my situation from a different perspective. So in the early hours of the morning, I penned these words, which I felt came from Him: "When an artist paints a picture or someone creates a tapestry, it is not with one single brushstroke. It is a combination of many different strokes and many strands of thread. So it is [that] this is part of something bigger and more beautiful."

God was doing something amazing to bring about resolution, incorporating my loved ones and friends in the process. Things hadn't happened as I felt they should, but I just wasn't seeing—until then—that this situation wasn't all about me. It never had been, nor would it be. God wants to have my loved ones in the picture too. How silly I had been! These feelings of abandonment would pass. Yes, I had felt harshly treated by being left out, but I really wasn't being left out at all. As I was able to "stand back" and look at the broader picture, I realized that I really was included. I had a vital part to play in this situation, as each brushstroke does in a painting and each thread does in a tapestry. *All things are working together for good.*

It is true that God could use anyone, but He was choosing to use me. And He chooses to use you to complete His work of art. So let's not be disheartened, hurt, and upset if we are not where we want to be and doing what we want to be doing. When we better see the whole picture, we will shine, give God glory, and be so pleased that He has allowed us to be part of something bigger than ourselves. Be blessed knowing you are part of His amazing work.

Laura A. Canning

Answering the Call

Commit thy way unto the LORD; trust also in him;
and he shall bring it to pass.
—*Psalm 37:5*

Shortly after moving into a new community and connecting with a new church family, my husband and I became acquainted with some individuals who became friends.

Two of these individuals expressed their desire to learn more about God and His commandments. Bible studies were arranged with them, and their response to the presentation of its doctrines convinced us that their request for baptism was genuine.

Our new friends had a grandchild. He would be present at every Bible study, but he was hardly seen once the session started. He would go under the table where we were studying. We would be reminded of his presence only by an unplanned step on someone's toes or by a touch of someone's legs. Attendance at church was commonplace for this child, as his grandparents were always present.

One Sabbath, when the child was about three years old, he was sitting with his grandparents during the worship service. Apparently he was listening attentively to what the preacher had to say. The sermon was about Adam's disobedience to God and his hiding from God in the Garden of Eden after he'd sinned. As the sermon arrived at God's reaction, the preacher loudly proclaimed God's words: "Adam, where art thou?" (Genesis 3:9).

Suddenly, from a pew in the house of worship, and as distinctly as the question had been spoken by the preacher, the little three-year-old bravely responded, "I am here!"

Though a teenager today, that young man is still listening for God's voice in his life, and he is training to be a deacon.

Children are greatly influenced by parents and role models—but more by what they *see* their role models doing than by what the adults *tell* them they should be doing.

We parents and other role models are responsible for teaching the children in our families to do everything as if carrying out each responsibility for the Lord. We need to remind them frequently that God loves them unconditionally and that they have been committed to Him.

By our words and example, especially, we can instruct them to make choices that will help them listen for God's voice calling them. Then may they answer, "I am here!"

Quilvie G. Mills

Winter Is Coming

"See! The winter is past; the rains are over and gone."
—Song of Songs 2:11, NIV

My apartment windows look out on a small forest of trees, mostly evergreens, but also a few deciduous trees. Winter is coming, and the deciduous trees are shedding their leaves. A non-evergreen cypress tree is already bare, its spindly arms reaching skyward, seemingly in silent supplication to the God of nature.

Yet one deciduous tree is stubbornly protesting against the unrelenting onslaught of the cold wind. I see it close by my window. This deciduous tree, a Bradford pear, is bereft of leaves except for one lonely branch. The leaves of that branch are still green but precariously hanging on, fighting the wind, and seeming to defy the inevitability of their demise as winter closes in.

I am wondering why.

Maybe it is a lesson for us, one synonymous with human thinking of wanting to always be young. As we age, are we not often trying to hang on to aspects of our earlier life, denying the eventuality of what is to come?

Yet often we do not accept and appreciate the *wisdom* we have accumulated with age. It accompanies the appearance of "weathering" from the many storms we've endured throughout life.

I am waiting to see whether the tenacious tree branch of the Bradford pear survives until spring. Practicality tells me it will succumb to nature's natural cycle, just as we will do when the time comes. Still, we need to consider the advice of the famous poet Dylan Thomas: "Do not go gentle into that good night . . . ; Rage, rage against the dying of the light."*

Perhaps that is what those yet-green tree leaves are doing.

What did Thomas mean by the word *rage*? Though the word can mean extreme anger, according to a dictionary, it can also mean "an intense feeling." For a Christian, this could be an internal resolve to persevere and remain faithful so that as long as we live, we are able to witness for Christ.

As Christians, we rejoice and praise God as we trust Him to be our ever present help in times of trouble. Trusting Him, we can know that eternal spring will follow winter.

Peggy Miles Snow

---

* Dylan Thomas, "Do Not Go Gentle Into That Good Night," 1947.

Such a Good Hiding Place

The name of the LORD is a fortified tower;
the righteous run to it and are safe.
—*Proverbs 18:10, NIV*

As a young couple, my husband and I occasionally helped out our friends by babysitting their three young girls. We didn't have any kids yet, and these girls were a fun pack to spend a day with. They were curious and imaginative and could entertain themselves for hours. Nevertheless, once in a while they would ask us for an idea of what to play next. "Why don't you play hide-and-seek," my husband once suggested. Three sets of bright eyes became brighter.

"That's a good idea!" the girls shouted. "Can we play inside?"

"Sure," my husband said without much hesitation. After all, our home was scarcely furnished, so the little we had, we didn't worry about. Off the girls went to play. At first, they found many places to hide: behind the sofa, under the bed, and in the closet. However, after several turns, it seemed that they were running out of new hiding places.

"It's my turn to hide!" said Erin, the middle sister. She hid, and then the other two began looking for her. First, they searched in all the usual places, but they couldn't find their sister. *Where could she be? Where did she hide?* Finally, after a long search and a bit of a hint, Erin was discovered in the bathroom lying in the bathtub.

"Erin, that was *such* a good hiding place!" exclaimed Kimby, the youngest one. "You found a really good hiding place," she said again.

Now it was Kimby's turn to hide. She had no trouble figuring out where to hide. She dashed into the bathroom and lay down in the bathtub, the exact place Erin had hidden only moments before. In fact, every time it was her turn to hide, Kimby hid in the same place. Each time she was discovered, she'd say with a radiant smile, "Wasn't that just the *best* hiding place?"

I still smile at such childish logic. Yet I can't help but see a beautiful lesson in this experience for my life. No matter what I am going through, I can always come to Jesus. Sometimes I first run to other places or people, but none turn out to be that strong tower of safety that only trust in Jesus provides. And each time I come to Him, I am never disappointed.

He is my *best* hiding place!

Ida T. Ronaszegi

The Intruder

"An enemy did this," he replied.
—Matthew 13:28, NIV??

When I worked in the public school system, we regularly practiced drills—fire, tornado, and earthquake drills. But after the school shooting at the Columbine High School in Colorado, another drill was added—the campus intruder drill.

With this drill, it was assumed there was someone suspicious on campus. The principal would speak over the school intercom and announce, "We have an intruder on campus. Take necessary precautions." With that announcement, we teachers knew exactly what to do.

We first looked quickly in the hall outside our classroom and pulled into the classroom any student passing by. Then we securely locked the classroom door and placed cardboard in the window of the door. We turned out the lights, closed the window blinds, and made sure all our children were gathered in a corner of the room away from the windows. We instructed them, "Be very quiet. Don't make a sound." At that point, the principal would be in touch with the teachers by computer, relaying any information she had for us. Finally, after what seemed a long time, the principal would announce, "All clear," and school activities would return to normal.

Jesus created our world (Genesis 1:1) and placed a perfect man and woman in His Garden. All was complete happiness until an intruder entered. He is still prowling around "like a roaring lion looking for someone to devour" (1 Peter 5:8, NIV). We have all encountered that intruder and know how devastating his attacks can be. We have been warned to take the necessary precautions. Peter says, "Resist him, standing firm in the faith" (verse 9). *Resisting* means we spend time with Jesus every day in Bible study and prayer. Staying in touch with Jesus throughout the day is the only way to overcome and have a successful outcome from an encounter with the intruder.

Soon Jesus will come, and the intruder will be no more. No more guns. No more pain, sickness, tears, or death. No more school children huddled in the corners of classrooms.

Though campus intruder drills don't always work perfectly now, Jesus has a plan to come again and put an end to this intruder. And God's plan will work perfectly.

What a day that will be! "Amen. Come, Lord Jesus" (Revelation 22:20, NIV).

Sharon Oster

God's Work in Our Lives

"He who is faithful in what is least is faithful also in much."
—Luke 16:10, NKJV

I went shopping for myself and my daughter because her birthday was in a week. I purchased what I wanted and went home. One of the items I purchased was a pair of high-heeled sandals. Although I felt a bit uncomfortable that the heels were so high, I purchased the shoes anyway.

For the rest of the evening, I felt uneasy about this particular purchase. I woke up the next morning convicted that I must return the shoes.

Back at the store, the two sales associates carefully read over the receipt I provided, examining and matching the price of each item to the code of the item that I had purchased. The sandals were not listed on the receipt! Then a lady whom I assumed to be the senior sales associate or manager asked whether I had another receipt.

I quickly answered, "Yes, I think so—but not here. It's at home."

"Without the original receipt," she explained "we can refund only seventy-five percent of what you paid for the sandals. However, if you can bring us the original receipt, we can refund one hundred percent of what you paid for them. Why don't you bring us the original receipt?"

I thanked them and went home. What I had thought were receipts, however, were all coupons I could use toward future purchases. This suggested I had not shopped for a while. I took the time to add up all my purchases. The total came to the same amount as had been charged to my credit card. Going through this process, I made an amazing discovery. The shoes I thought I'd purchased for my daughter had been put into a bag but not charged to my account! I had not paid for them, so they didn't belong to me.

The next day, I went back to the store to return the pair of shoes for the second time. When the sales associate realized I had not taken advantage of their mistake, she was very thankful. "Never," she said looking at her coworkers, "have we had any customer do something like this. Thank you so much for your honesty!"

Driving home, I thanked God Almighty for the ways He works in our lives. I no longer had sandals I didn't want, but I had an opportunity to witness for Him.

Charity I. Ekeke

October 25

Angels in Charge

For He shall give His angels charge over you,
to keep you in all your ways. In their hands they shall bear you up,
lest you dash your foot against a stone.
—*Psalm 91:11, 12, NKJV*

It wasn't the horrendous scraping sound of metal against concrete that filled the vehicle and made the book I was reading fall from my hands. It wasn't the sudden lurch to the left that threw my children and me against our seat belts with a gasp. It wasn't the tire I watched with shock as it bounced between my door and a little red car beside us.

It wasn't the slide across the road into the graveled grass, making me slump with relief as momentum released me. It wasn't even my stunned gaze as I watched the tire roll through the ditch, and on and on, until it finally bumped into a fence post and fell over about a quarter of a mile ahead of us.

No, it wasn't any of the above.

What brought goose bumps to my arms and breathlessness to my lungs was the realization that we had just been held and guided by a Power greater than our own. A Power that held our van upright when it should have rolled—as the right front tire came off, shearing the bolts that had held it in place. A Power that allowed the bouncing tire to continue hurtling through the interstate traffic around us, not hitting the car we were passing, nor traffic behind us, but continuing rolling on and then into a ditch.

This Power helped my husband guide our van though it was sliding on the right front end and shearing off the brake mechanism almost to the axle. My husband maneuvered our van between other vehicles. We crossed the lanes of the interstate before skidding to a stop on the shoulder of the road. This Power guided us to find two different tow trucks, both drivers shaking their heads and saying they couldn't believe we hadn't rolled over. "Someone was watching out for you," they told us.

We continue to thank God for saving our family, for guiding us, and for never leaving us. What could have been a tragedy was turned into a stunning witness for God's strength and protection.

As we go about our busy lives, let us never forget that His angels are holding us.

Barb Engquist

Downsizing Blues!

We all come to the end of our lives as naked
and empty-handed as on the day we were born.
—*Ecclesiastes 5:15, NLT*

As the years are steadily creeping by, my husband, Will, and I have contemplated where we will spend the last years of our lives. Somber, I know, but important. I have often said I would never live in senior housing, but the prospects started appealing to me. I looked at places online, checked floor plans, amenities, and prices. Then recently, Will and I visited the first potential apartment, a place that would be convenient to family, church, and work. We were impressed with the front office and lobby, friendliness and professionalism of the staff, social room, library, game room, and exercise room, each on different floors. Disappointment came, however, when we saw the small but cozy apartment. It surely could not hold our furniture, personal items, and cherished treasures acquired over our adult lives. This was disheartening. *I need my things*, I told myself. *I can't sell or give them away or, worse yet, throw them out!* I recalled friends saying they had downsized, but this much?

On the way home, I felt myself becoming saddened at the thought of parting with belongings and of our existence relegated to basics, nothing decorative or creative. Depression set in as I envisioned life without what I was accustomed to and attached to. A question popped into my head: *Does this stuff really matter that much? You started with nothing and probably don't need all this anyway! You'll have much more to look forward to one day!* Much more? Where? How? And then I got it, *Ah, yes, heaven!*

It's only been five days, and if we finish the application and it all checks out, we're second in line for that apartment. As I contemplate a move soon, this one or another, I've spent time sorting and putting treasured things aside to give away. It's only a start, because the big stuff— furniture will need to be dealt with, but everywhere I turn, I want everything I see! Yet my mind is beginning to focus on even more—that beautiful, heavenly mansion.

Heavenly Father, empty me of self and fill me with Your Spirit. I was born with nothing and know that coveting my earthly possessions is pointless when You have given everything I need. Help me adore You completely and envision the heavenly mansion, my best home ever!

Iris L. Kitching

Dealing With the 80 Percent

Don't worry about anything. . . .
Then you will experience God's peace.
—Philippians 4:6, 7, NLT

Once, at a church conference attended by more than fifty thousand people, a little packet of cash disappeared from my purse—probably during a lunch break transaction—without my noticing it. I hoped no one had actually stolen this three hundred dollars I'd set aside for an unexpected emergency. In any case, the money was gone. Feelings of guilt and shame overwhelmed me. *How did I lose the money?* A sense of failure weighed heavily on my heart as I trudged back to the hotel room, where I would soon meet my husband. As I sat on the bed sharing my loss, Jim's eyes widened in shock. I expected at least a mild reprimand if not a stern lecture on carelessness.

Instead, Jim cleared his throat and said, "It's a significant loss, but we still have enough money to finish this trip. Besides, if this is the worst thing that ever happens to us, we'll be getting off pretty easy." His matter-of-fact response stunned me. The next day, I understood it better while in a seminar presented by Dr. Arlene Taylor, a brain function specialist.

Not only did she share how differently male and female brains react to stressors, but also information on how we can more effectively handle life's stressful losses. "Only *twenty* percent of any negative impact to brain and body is due to the event itself," she said. "The remaining *eighty* percent has to do with what *you* think about the event, the weight and importance *you* give to it. You may not be able to do anything about the twenty percent, but you can do almost *everything* about the eighty percent because *you* create your perceptions."

Wow! Whipping out a pen and notebook, I did the math. If I chose to "let it go," then—psychologically and emotionally—I'd lost about only seventy-five dollars. Whoa! That loss didn't "feel" nearly as bad as the larger amount over which I'd been grieving. Next, I prayed that whoever might now possess my missing money would find relief from financial need. In fact, I asked God to accept the lost money as an after-the-fact love offering to pass on as He saw fit.

Don't worry . . . experience God's peace. My burden of guilt and shame dissipated. I'd learned the secret of dealing with the 80 percent—find the silver lining and move on! What life loss can you better manage because of how *you* handle the 80 percent?

Carolyn Rathbun Sutton

A New Beginning

Create in me a clean heart, O God;
and renew a right spirit within me.
—*Psalm 51:10*

Come now, and let us reason together, saith the LORD:
though your sins be as scarlet, they shall be as white as snow;
though they be red like crimson, they shall be as wool.
—*Isaiah 1:18*

What can wash away my sin?" asks a verse in a beloved old hymn.* The next phrase answers the question: "Nothing but the blood of Jesus." The following line asks, "What can make me pure within?" Once again the answer comes: "Nothing but the blood of Jesus."

Each of us at some point—if not at many points in our lives—have desired a fresh start, a new beginning. Because of our choices, we have felt so messed up, even unclean! We wish we could revisit our past and make some changes. We sometimes even wish we could erase whole portions of our past, for we are filled with regret and embarrassment.

In the same way that the contents of a glass with milk, when overturned, cannot be gathered up again and put back in the glass, so are many of life's experiences. We simply cannot go back and change them. Time and consequences are not retrievable. How King David wished he could have changed his choices from the past! That's why he penned the prayerful words, "Create in me a clean heart, O God" (Psalm 51:10). He knew that only God could permanently deal with the fallen king's remorse and guilt.

Through these words, David also demonstrates that no one need be held captive by their past choices. David's decision to take his remorse and guilt to God shows us that no one needs to be held captive by the past. Provision has been made to keep us connected to God, for Jesus came to set us free. He assures us, "Neither do I condemn thee: go, and sin no more" (John 8:11). What a relief, what comfort and assurance we have in Jesus! Doesn't that make you joyful? Yes, we *can* start over again. A new beginning is possible for all of us. God, through Paul, tells us that "if any man be in Christ, he is a new creature: old things are passed away; behold, all things are become new" (2 Corinthians 5:17).

Jesus is a forgiving Savior who casts our sins into the deepest part of the ocean. Though David had badly messed up, he found a new beginning by taking his failures to the Lord.

May this be our experience too.

Jacqueline Hope HoShing-Clarke

* Robert Lowry, "Nothing but the Blood," 1876.

The Golden Rule

"And the King will answer and say unto them,
'Assuredly, I say to you, inasmuch as you did it to one of the least of
these My brethren, you did it to Me.' "
—*Matthew 25:40, NKJV*

"So in everything, do to others
what you would have them do to you."
—*Matthew 7:12, NIV*

I had just finished buying commodities at the store of a large discount chain when I remembered I needed to purchase some whole wheat flour at a nearby grocery store. I was halfway between stores when I saw an elderly man struggling to cross the street. He was moving in the direction of the grocery store entrance.

Quickly and carefully, I made my way through traffic and joined him inside the entrance. "May I help you out?" I asked him, extending my hand. Then I guided him to where the grocery carts were. I remembered that even a small deed done for others is done for Christ.

"Oh, thank you for your kindness!" he responded. His gratitude warmed my heart.

The following day, after fixing my husband's breakfast and lunch for work, I bade him goodbye and headed outside for my usual one-hour walk.

Before turning right at the next intersection, I spotted something on the ground I thought might be important. Stooping over, I looked at it more closely. My suspicions were confirmed. It was somebody's credit card! I picked it up. A few steps away, I saw a lady's handbag that had obviously been ransacked and then abandoned. A few steps further, I came upon a driver's license and another bank card on the ground. All revealed they belonged to the same person.

I hurried home to give these things to our neighbor who is a policeman, but no one responded to my knocking at his door. So I quickly called 9-1-1 to report what I had discovered. Not long after, a police officer knocked at our door to pick up the important personal documents that I had recovered on my walk. He said the incident had already been reported. I asked whether the owner of the purse had been hurt. No, she had not been, although her car too had been ransacked.

I shared with the police officer the joy I had experienced in finding, and being able to retrieve, these items for the owner. Putting myself in the victim's place, I know I would have been devastated had I suffered the kind of loss she had! Soon she would be reunited with her stolen documents. How important it is for each of us to practice the golden rule of Matthew 7:12!

Ofelia A. Pangan

Rachel Weeping for Her Children

"A voice was heard in Ramah, lamentation, weeping,
and great mourning, Rachel weeping for her children,
refusing to be comforted, because they are no more."
—*Matthew 2:18, NKJV*

I watched her wipe the tears as they coursed down her cheeks, one after another. We had claimed the promise in Isaiah 43:6: "I will say to the north, 'Give them up!' And to the south, 'Do not keep them back!' Bring My sons from afar, and My daughters from the ends of the earth" (NKJV).

It had just been a year ago when her seventeen-year-old daughter presented a powerful sermon at our church's youth Week of Prayer. She declared her allegiance to God and was determined to be a model example for Christ among her friends and schoolmates. She was brilliant and strong, yet tender and caring. She had so much to offer. Now eighteen, her focus had begun to shift. She expressed her right to make her own decisions. This was true. But some of her decisions were of great concern to her mother. For example, church attendance and participation were not her daughter's top priorities anymore; she had other interests.

Her mom must have wondered, *Where did I go wrong? What could I have done differently?* So many mothers all around the globe are asking the same age-old questions. The questioning might even have begun with Eve when she had to face the fact that her firstborn son had become a murderer. In Christ's parable of the prodigal son (Luke 15:11–32), the boy's mother is not mentioned. Yet I assume she stood by the door as tears coursed down her cheeks, watching for her younger son to walk back up the road to true freedom.

Where did I go wrong?

Yet in many cases, no great wrong can be attributed to parenting skills. Children sometimes choose a less than desirable path. And there is always hope during the often long wait for answered prayers, despite sleepless nights and many tears. Like the father in the parable, we can keep our eyes on the bend in the road and our trust in God. We can pray that one day we will "kill that fatted calf" to celebrate a wandering child who has come home.

But haven't we all wandered away from God? Yet our Savior has gone to prepare the welcome table for all who choose to come back home to Him. I am excited! How about you?

Sonia Kennedy-Brown

That Old Serpent the Bully—Part 1

And Nahash the Ammonite answered them,
"On this condition I will make a covenant with you,
that I may put out all your right eyes."
—1 Samuel 11:2, NKJV

Nahash the Ammonite menacingly marched his army toward Israel and made siege at Jabesh Gilead. The frightened men of Jabesh Gilead entered into negotiations with this bully. "Make a covenant with us," they pleaded, "and we will serve you" (1 Samuel 11:1, NKJV).

Nahash, whose name means "serpent," responded, "No need for battle skirmishes," he says smoothly. "I'll gladly sign your peace treaty, binding you into our service, but only if," he adds slyly, "I blind all your right eyes."

Blinding the right eye indicates surrender, because the right eye of an archer is needed to shoot an arrow; and the right eye of a soldier directs his right sword arm, while his left eye is protected by his shield. An army's ability to fight is destroyed when warriors lose sight in the right eye. The remaining left eye allows enough sight for conquered fighters to return home as farmers and shepherds and to serve as slaves for the victorious nation.

Enemies of righteousness often use bully tactics. They know people choose the path of least resistance. Goliath knew this when he later taunted the besieged Israelite army: "Save yourselves the trouble of war; just send one man out. He will lose his life, of course, but the rest of you will live and become our servants." Ironically, Goliath's message is echoed unwittingly by Caiaphas: "It was expedient that one man should die for the people" (John 18:14, NKJV).

The Bible tells us, "A worthless person, a wicked man, . . . winks with his eyes" (Proverbs 6:12, 13, NKJV). A wink is a closed (covered) eye, reminiscent of willing submission to right-eyed blindness imposed by the bully. That old serpent the bully still roams the earth seeking whom he may blind in the right eye and take as slaves. Amazingly, today the covering of the right eye, or turning away from the camera to hide the right eye, is a popular photo pose. No one should turn a blind eye to this symbolic image of willing surrender to evil.

When confronting you in spiritual warfare, the bully serpent offers an easy way out of battle. Will you submit to slavery and right-eye blindness, or will you use two-eyed spiritual eyesight to follow Jesus, the One who died to save His people from the serpent's siege?

Rebecca Timon

That Old Serpent the Bully—Part 2

"Now when these things begin to happen,
look up and lift up your heads,
because your redemption draws near."
—Luke 21:28, NKJV

The condition of surrender in the treaty of Nahash the Ammonite opens the eyes of the elders of Jabesh Gilead, and they refuse to willingly submit to right-eye blindness. The elders renegotiate to gain a week for recruiting reinforcements. "If there is no one to save us, we will come out to you" (1 Samuel 11:3, NKJV). Surprisingly, the bully agrees. Messengers are dispatched west across the Jordan River with an urgent appeal from the town caught in the snare of the serpent.

Soon after Saul is chosen as king, he hears the news from Jabesh, the Spirit of God fills him, and he musters thousands of men from every tribe. He sends an encouraging reply to Jabesh Gilead, "Tomorrow, by the time the sun is hot, you shall have help" (1 Samuel 11:9, NKJV).

That evening, the last day of cease-fire, Jabesh delivers a deceptive message indicating surrender to the bully serpent. "Tomorrow we will come out to you, and you may do with us whatever seems good to you" (1 Samuel 11:10, NKJV). The Ammonites feel powerful, confident their bully tactics have effortlessly given them dominion over the frightened people of Jabesh Gilead.

Saul arrived during the darkness of early morning and caught the Ammonites by surprise. Three companies of Israelite men attacked the Ammonites, reminiscent of Gideon's attack on the Midianites years before. In Gideon's battle, confusion caused the Midianites to kill each other in panic. In Saul's battle, confusion caused the Ammonites to scatter in panic. The bully cannot keep his terrified army unified; not even two soldiers are left standing together. God's holy wars cause confusion and self-destruction in the camps of the wicked.

In this story, King Saul is a type of King Jesus, who, with compassionate and heroic action, rescues those who cry for help and arrives with perfect timing to crush the head of the serpent.

When besieged by the bully serpent, fear not. Bullies are cowards who want to look and feel powerful. Never surrender to blind slavery. Instead, call on the Lord God to save you. Turn your eyes upon Jesus, and lift up your heads—your redemption draws near.

Rebecca Timon

Jesus, Save Us

The LORD is my light and salvation; whom shall I fear?
the LORD is the strength of my life; of whom shall I be afraid?
—Psalm 27:1

In 2012 my siblings and I decided to raise some money to build a classroom at the small village school our late father attended when he was young. We set out to do this by running a half marathon and getting friends, family, and even strangers to sponsor each kilometer that we ran. We successfully held the run and raised about US$2,000.

As part of the new classroom preparation, my younger brother and I decided to visit the village and make our intentions known. We rode to the area with some friends who were going there to visit family. They had a lovely one-year-old baby boy. We had a good trip going and met up with my late father's brothers and our cousins and aunts. We discussed with them the idea we had of building the classroom, and they were very happy.

All too soon, it was time for us to return to Lusaka. We started our journey early in the morning because we wanted to be home by late afternoon. When we were about sixty miles (about one hundred kilometers) from our destination, we made a final "pit stop." The driver of the car was anxious to get home, and we were all tired of sitting in the car.

Back on the road, we had not driven very far when we heard a loud bang. The car in which we were riding veered into the other lane, on which traveled oncoming traffic. Headed straight toward us was a bus filled with people.

The driver of our vehicle tried to steer the car away from the bus. Suddenly we were hurtling off the road toward the brush along the roadside. All I could say was, "Jesus, save us!"

The car flipped over and landed on its roof. We were momentarily too shaken to move. Then the crying of the baby moved us all into action. Slowly we crawled out of the mangled car.

Miraculously, no one was seriously hurt. The car itself, though, was a complete wreck. We were so grateful to Jesus for hearing our quick "Jesus save us."

God has assured us that He will answer us when we call. I believe He, our Salvation and Strength, did just that on the day of the accident, and I am alive to tell about it.

I encourage you to call on Jesus today. He will be your strength and salvation too.

Mukatimui Kalima-Munalula

Annoying Scratched Records

He shall deliver thee in six troubles: yea,
in seven there shall no evil touch thee.
—Job 5:19

My dad used to own a turntable record player. He enjoyed playing it, and I enjoyed listening. My favorite record was *Funky Town*, but my least favorite listening moments were when a scratched record played. If the needle, or stylus, got stuck in a groove due to a scratch on the record, the sounds in that groove repeated over and over. It was very annoying and continued until my dad came to the rescue and manually repositioned the needle.

I've often thought that our lives can sometimes be like the repetitions of a scratched record—those times when we're stuck in a bad rut and the same trials just keep repeating themselves. One time, my scratched record was joblessness. I'd been job hunting for more than two years, with no success. During this time, I was accepted for five of the jobs I applied for. But for one reason or another, something always seemed to fall through. I would celebrate getting a job, only to cry a day or two later about losing it due to circumstances beyond my control. My misfortune was stuck on repeat. "Will it end?" I asked. Only silence echoed back.

I've often thought that the life of the biblical character Naomi was like a scratched record. She dealt with loss after loss: her husband and her two sons; then she lost her house, money, and one of her daughters-in-law. Discouragement set in, and hopelessness took over. But one thing Naomi and I have in common was that we never gave up. We trusted in God. Job 5:19 reminded me that God will deliver me from not one, two, or five troubles—but seven (many) troubles. He'll do the same for you.

What's your scratched record? Bad relationships? Financial potholes? Homelessness? Whatever it is, and regardless of how many times it keeps recurring, my God will be your God through it all. He will rescue you. Find the strength to praise God through your scratched record like I did. God is the only One able to lift the "needle" of our lives and reposition it for a blessing.

Until then, stay focused on Him and be patient. He's working things out for your good and for His praise. Just because things don't go your way doesn't mean they're not going God's way. If Naomi and I can survive the scratched record times, you can too.

Amelia Brown-Williams

November 4

Strangely Dim

"When you pass through the waters, I will be with you; and through the rivers, they shall not overflow you. When you walk through the fire, you shall not be burned, nor shall the flame scorch you."
—Isaiah 43:2, NKJV

One of my two roommates was manic depressive, schizophrenic, and an alcoholic. She also abused prescription drugs. She had suffered brain damage in a car accident. Then, when she tried a new med to help her stop smoking, she suffered side effects: hallucinations and rage. She would hide in our bedroom closets or break off ends of light bulbs with kitchen knives. In six weeks' time, she had two court dates and four boyfriends. She rearranged our canned goods and banged hundreds of nails into our walls at all hours of the night. She was intermittently suicidal, and she refused eviction. We felt as if we had unknowingly signed a lease with an evil presence.

At the worst point, my other roommate and I realized our personal safety was being jeopardized and our possessions exposed to theft, damage, or arson. This ongoing crisis made me suddenly evaluate what was truly important in life. If important documents, musical instruments, photographs, souvenirs from trips abroad, childhood artifacts, and carefully selected books in our personal libraries succumbed to theft, intentional vandalism, or arson, how would we react?

What *is* truly important in this life? In high adrenaline moments, there isn't time to ponder philosophical or spiritual concepts in high definition. My roommate and I prayerfully sought the landlord to evict our dangerous roommate. However, we were also concerned for her well-being. It was an unusually snowy and frigid November, so we prayed earnestly that she would have a safe place to go and not end up on the cold streets. We realized that material things are nothing compared to the well-being of people.

The Lord saw us through. Our troubled roommate was eventually evicted but also had a place to go. The fact that our possessions were spared paled in comparison with our gratitude for having survived this ordeal. It was the best Thanksgiving ever! The Lord neither left us nor forsook us. In this battle between light and darkness, the Lamb of God ultimately won.

Never again have worldly possessions had much significance to us. Through it all, we saw more clearly the strength one can have—even under attack—through the Lord Jesus Christ.

Erin Parfet

God Knows His Plans for Us

Many, LORD my God, are the wonders you have done, the things you
planned for us. None can compare with you; were I to speak and tell
of your deeds, they would be too many to declare.
—Psalm 40:5, NIV

The end of the journey for Akunna was in sight. What an arduous journey it had been! Morris and I traveled to Baltimore for this special moment: the defense of her dissertation for a doctoral degree in cellular and molecular physiology at Johns Hopkins University. As we stepped outside of the airport, icy cold winds slapped our faces and snow flurries accompanied us to her apartment. Before going to sleep, we thanked God for safe travel and for helping Akunna reach this significant milestone. We prayed for His blessing on her presentation the following day.

During the night, while we slept, the heavens opened and poured down a superabundance of snow. It was breathtakingly beautiful but unwelcome at such a critical time. An early morning call from a university administrator informed Akunna that the university was closed because of the snow, and Akunna would have to reschedule her defense. Akunna told her that she couldn't because she was scheduled to begin full-time employment the following Monday. My heart sank. In my humanness, I silently questioned God: *Why did You let this happen, knowing how hard and long Akunna worked and persevered?*

Through it all, Akunna remained unperturbed and continued last minute revisions to her presentation. She commented that God is in control. Her advisor, Dr. Sandra Gabelli, promised to try to get the building open. We petitioned God to work it out. Hours later, the building opened and Dr. Gabelli took us to the university. On our way, she commented that if at least seven people attended, including members of the defense committee, Akunna's presentation would be legal.

Silently I pleaded with God to grant the request. After more prayer, the long-awaited moment arrived. Dr. Gabelli introduced Akunna and highly commended her for her outstanding research and tenacious spirit. When Akunna stood up to speak, it seemed like angels stood beside her. God blessed her immeasurably.

"Praise be to the LORD, the God of Israel, from everlasting to everlasting. Amen and Amen" (Psalm 41:13, NIV). It's so sweet to trust in Jesus. He has great plans for you and me.

Shirley C. Iheanacho

Duet

The LORD thy God in the midst of thee is mighty;
he will save, he will rejoice over thee with joy;
he will rest in his love, he will joy over thee with singing.
—*Zephaniah 3:17*

Yesterday when I got the mail, the handwriting on a small envelope caught my attention. I extracted a note card from inside. "Thank you for all the help and support, and for just listening. It has meant so much to me. Like a lifeline for me. Thank you so-o-o much."

My friend who wrote the note is caring for her mother. Since she lives several hundred miles away, there's little I can do to help. But the telephone keeps us in contact. I've been able to pick up on some symptoms and make a few suggestions. And I can listen. I can pray and let my friend know I'm praying. I can share Bible promises for strength and wisdom.

As I read the note, new thoughts about Zephaniah 3:17 came to my mind. Tears welled up. The first time I had read that verse, I was amazed. I'd never pictured God as a singer.

I could hardly believe it. God . . . singing? Besides, I'd never imagined He would rejoice over the likes of me. I reread the context. God's people had rebelled against Him. But some had heeded the prophet Zephaniah's warning. They had repented and were obeying God by faith. They weren't perfect, but they were taking steps in the right direction. God encouraged them with His presence. Then He told them how He was reacting to them and their positive choices—He was rejoicing over them with singing.

Through the years, the promises in Zephaniah 3:17 encouraged me and gave me strength.

Yesterday I read those verses again, and a new thought startled me. God wants to transform me so that His character traits become mine. He wants me to encourage people in their right and good choices. They aren't perfect either, but my job as a Christian is to encourage them and rejoice in the good.

That's when I got the day's mail. And there was that note. A new realization welled up in my heart—and tears in my eyes. In the simplest of ways, I'd been encouraging my friend. I'd been doing what God does. In so doing, I got to sing a duet with God.

Wow! What an awesome privilege! *God, please keep me encouraging the good in Your children. Keep me singing duets with You!*

Helen Heavirland

Fear

Fear not, little flock;
for it is your Father's good pleasure
to give you the kingdom.
—*Luke 12:32*

Christ has told us we should not worry or be afraid but rather trust in Him. The Bible tells us that just before Christ returns there will be a time of trouble such as never has been seen before. Thinking about this evokes fear in many, and, of course, I have thought about this too, wondering what will happen. There have been many dangerous and difficult times in the history of this earth, and more are to come. Yet we are not to fear but trust. How? When we look back on how God has led us in the past, it helps us trust His leading into the unknown future.

When I found out that I was expecting my first child, several of my friends thought it their duty to tell me how painful delivery would be. I was so thrilled to be having a baby that I decided to put their comments out of my mind and enjoy my pregnancy. Why go through the pain before I actually had to? Thankfully, I had an uneventful pregnancy. When the time came to deliver, I still did not allow myself to dwell on the pain—until it became nearly unbearable.

Then I thought I would *never* forget what I was experiencing. In fact, I wondered how the population had ever gotten as large as it had with women having to experience the pain of childbirth. Certainly no one would go through that again voluntarily!

After thirty-six hours of labor and a final push, I heard the most amazing words: "You have a perfect little girl—ten fingers, ten toes." When medical personnel placed the newborn in my arms, I immediately forgot all about what I had just gone through. I had just peered into the most precious face I had ever seen before.

Most people experience times of trouble in their lives—painful times, times of loss, heartache, and illness. Yet God wants us to remember that He is with us. He will never leave us.

And when this life is over and our Savior returns for us, we will look into the *most* precious face we will ever see! All thoughts of the pain we experienced here will leave us; all previous pain will pale in comparison! So when tempted to be fearful, let's remember, now and forevermore, that "The LORD himself goes before you and will be with you; he will never leave you nor forsake you. Do not be afraid; do not be discouraged" (Deuteronomy 31:8, NIV).

Sue Anderson

God's Glory

But we all, with open face beholding as in a glass the glory of the
Lord, are changed into the same image . . . by the Spirit of the Lord.
—*2 Corinthians 3:18*

I n Israel the early and latter rain were seasons to root and then mature crops. Rain is important to us too. But the two rains Israel experienced each year also have a spiritual application. The early rain represented the Day of Pentecost when God's Spirit filled those in the upper room and sent them out as missionaries. The latter rain represents when the Holy Spirit will mature souls for the final and eternal harvest.

We read in Joel 2:28–32 and Acts 2:17–21 that in the last days (the time of spiritual latter rain), God will pour out His Spirit on all flesh, young and old, male and female; they will prophesy and see visions. What does this actually mean?

According to the *Merriam-Webster Dictionary*, *prophesy* means "to speak as if divinely inspired; to give instruction in religious matters; to make a prediction."

The definition of *vision* in the same dictionary is "something seen a dream, trance, or ecstasy; . . . supernatural appearance that conveys a revelation" and "unusual discernment or foresight."

God has promised that if we ask for rain in the time of the latter rain, He will send showers (see Zechariah 10:1).

In Exodus 33:18–23 we find a story in which Moses asks to see God's glory. God says, "OK, but you can't see My face and live." He says he will hide Moses with His hand when passing before him.

In the following chapter, Exodus 34, God declares to Moses—as He passes before him—His character—He is merciful, gracious, long-suffering, abundant in goodness and truth, forgiving, but also rewarding iniquity. God's character is His glory. When we allow God into our hearts, we become like Him. We begin to "glow" with His glory. At the end of time, "servants of God, with their faces lighted up and shining with holy consecration, will hasten from place to place to proclaim the message from heaven."*

Let's open our hearts to receive His rain, His character, and His glory.

Elizabeth Versteegh Odiyar

---

* Ellen White, *The Great Controversy* (Mountain View, CA: Pacific Press®, 1950), 612.

Oh, Mom!

But the fruit of the Spirit is love, joy, peace,
longsuffering, kindness, goodness, faithfulness,
gentleness, self-control. Against such there is no law.
—*Galatians 5:22, 23, NKJV*

And be kind to one another, tenderhearted, forgiving one another,
even as God in Christ forgave you.
—*Ephesians 4:32, NKJV*

O h, Mom! Don't pour your juice out on the table!"
I instantly regretted my harsh tone as I saw the look on my mother's face and the beginning of a tear.

As my mother's dementia worsens, I feel more and more challenged.

Being childless, I never learned the patience of raising children, but I imagine the mistakes of a growing child—while frustrating, if not downright angering at times—bring a certain amount of satisfaction when a parent sees the child learning and then managing new skills. The mistakes of a failing memory, however, bring no such joy.

Yet taking care of my mother, who raised me and loved me as only a mother can, brings its own joys. Caring for her brings the satisfaction of providing a loving home for the woman who first gave me a loving home and family.

And what warm memories I have from those years as a result of her care for me!

These days, I purposefully look for the blessings: For example, the love and smiles that my mother still shows to everyone she meets—those make me proud to be her daughter. As the days and years go by, I am growing into more patience and kindness and acceptance through this task of loving my mother. I know God is developing my character through her declining days. He wants to provide for my mother's special needs at this challenging time in her life, a time that she no longer understands. He wants her to experience happiness.

And He wants to love her . . . through me.

Lord, I am not worthy to take care of this wonderful mother who loved me unconditionally. Please fill me with Your Holy Spirit. May my words and actions show the same love, joy, peace, patience, kindness, gentleness, and self-control toward my mother that she showed to me. Amen.

Suzanne Blaylock

Princesses All!

Behold, you are fair, my love! Behold, you are fair!
—*Song of Solomon 4:1, NKJV*

I love being in the company of friends, enjoying good food and conversation. At other times, I enjoy being in some public setting, feeling a degree of self-confidence, or maybe just feeling comfortable. We were created to enjoy the fellowship of others and to need one another.

As I have gotten older, however, there seems to be an increasing number of occasions when I am quite in my element—my comfort zone—and someone younger, prettier, and more talented than I walks into the room. This disturbs the mental image I have of myself, shaking my self-confidence and making me feel less comfortable.

Funny how that works.

Feelings of inferiority can be overwhelming at times. Those feelings can make us perform less than our best. In the extreme, insecurities can cause some people to become downright hateful. But they are just that—feelings; they're not fact. As daughters of the King we need not feel that way—we are royalty, a race of princesses!

Each of us who becomes a member of the heavenly family has been given gifts (Ephesians 4:7–12). I find it easy to envy someone with a gift I don't have or someone who may be more gifted in an area than I am.

Yet in God's wisdom, He chooses which gifts to give me; my job is to develop them to the best of my ability. He knew right where I would be at this time and what the needs around me would be that I could fill.

He didn't call me to be you, only to be the best of who He made *me* to be. The burden of trying to measure up to someone else is a heavy one. The good news is that God never intended me to bear it!

Did you ever hear the saying, "Everyone is beautiful if someone else likes what they see"? Well, here's more good news: Jesus thinks you are beautiful—beautiful enough to be His bride. When we are arrayed in the wedding garment He provides, He sees only beauty—in each of us. That's because every one of us is special. Our confidence in who we are doesn't have to be shaken by anyone else. We are princesses all!

Sylvia Stark

From a Drug House to the Lord's House

Behold, I will do a new thing; now it shall spring forth; shall ye not know it? I will even make a way in the wilderness, and rivers in the desert.
—Isaiah 43:19

On a dark, rainy October morning, my parents woke me up for a special mission. A few years prior, we had moved from Toronto to Moosonee, a town in rural northern Ontario. The town is so isolated that the nearest paved road is five hours away, or one can take a train to access our town. We had never expected to come here, as we were recent immigrants from the Philippines. But God had an exciting mission for our family—to establish a Christian congregation in this area. We invited believers and guests to worship each Sabbath in our small living room, but we were outgrowing it. So that rainy morning we began to pray for a larger place to worship.

Personally, I had my eye on a gorgeous piece of property, a former inn that overlooked the peaceful Moose River. Another prospective place was a former drug house. The exterior, with white pain chipping off, looked as if it were about to collapse. The interior was full of mold, trash, and traces of illegal substance use. Obscenities had been scrawled on the walls.

We drove to the prospective church sites. Inside the car, at each of the two sites, we earnestly prayed for God's guidance. Personally, I took more time praying for the inn. As it turned out, the inn was appraised at a price we could never have afforded. Therefore, we had to settle for the former drug house. However, it so happened that the house had a complete upper room whose platform at the front end gave the building a church-like appearance. As a result of my father's encounter with a Dr. Juriansz (who was involved with a Christian youth organization dedicated to community service), the doctor soon organized a group of young people from Hamilton to help renovate the old building that would be our church. The former drug house soon looked more radiant and lovely. We had many donations from other churches and individuals varying from a church organ, hymnals, and chairs to even a sink. Truly, the Lord has provided.

Oh, just in case you are wondering how much our congregation paid for the church . . . it was one dollar. That's right. The Lord works in unexpected ways and uses unexpected people to further His work—just as He turned a former drug house into a new church.

Ellen Jane Tejano-Galupo

November 12

I've Fallen, but I Will Rise Again

You, who have shown me great and severe troubles, shall revive me again, and bring me up again from the depths of the earth.
—Psalm 71:20, NKJV

"Hi, it's me again. I am lying here with my face in the dirt because I have fallen and can't get up." Those are the words of a spiritually "old" person, someone who is looking at herself or at other people in the church who are also down, thinking that down is the new up. It's not.

The Bible is a book that recounts many stories of failure. People fall over and over again. Yet the point is not that we fall but that we have a choice to get up again. Those are people who know how to pray, "Bring me up from the depths." I know what it feels like to fail God, to say dumb things that hurt people, to disappoint myself. We all do. We are all in the same boat. But we need to be careful that we don't slip into a spiritual coma, thinking that just sitting in a pew is living the Christian life. There is so much more abundance that God wants for us.

Once I found the word *Nike* in the Bible. It is a Greek word used only once in God's Word (1 John 5:4) and means "victory" or "to finish the race." In Philippians 3:14, Paul wrote, "I press toward the goal for the prize of the upward call of God in Christ Jesus" (NKJV). The prize comes from finishing. It doesn't matter how many times you fall, although it hurts. Falling is no reason to stay down in the depths. Get up!

Where did this idea ever come from that it is OK for spiritually "old" Christians to be cranky, whiny, or cruel? God can help us rise above those depths every time we fall. Where does it say in the Bible that there is no help for one who has fallen? Nowhere!

We have all been through troubles, sore troubles, but God is there to "quicken" us again. God is there to energize when we ask His help to get out of the "depths" and get going again.

People who have been Christians a long time have had much experience in falling and rising again. Younger or newer Christians need to hear about these times in our lives. Others will rejoice in knowing it's possible to rise again. It will give them hope so they too can keep on track with God. They can know that He will help lift them from the depths if they so choose.

The first step to getting up again after a fall is to ask God for His help. Remember that the motto of today's Nike brand is . . . Just do it!

Angie Joseph

Here Below

For this world is not our permanent home;
we are looking forward to a home yet to come.
—*Hebrews 13:14, NLT*

Many people think that last winter was the gloomiest, grayest, most sunless one on record. The darkness was so oppressive I could feel it in my bones. It took an entire summer full of sunshine to drive those bleak days away and chase them into a faint memory.

Now, having been dragged kicking and screaming out of summer into fall, I find myself poised on the cusp of another cheerless winter, bracing myself against being marched unceremoniously into the dark months ahead. It is unforgivably traitorous, but I, someone who truly loves winter and every changing season, actually find myself longing to fly south for the winter with the feckless, departing geese.

In an effort to shore up my spirits against the encroaching gloom, I have begun to employ the usual coping mechanisms: candles, twinkly lights, baking. It's incredible how much bonhomie a little light can provide as it chases away the darkness, and the smell of something comforting as it bakes fills the house with reassurances of nurturing and care.

In the same way my body resists the long, weary days ahead with no sunshine, my soul resists being here below on this tired, dreary, dark planet. Yet every time I slip into a lack of communication with my Maker, I'm amazed at how easily I grow accustomed to it. My mental resistance to the depths of winter in my physical world is far greater than my resistance to the depths of winter in my spiritual world. Days spent basking in the Son fade quickly in the brisk business and stress of everyday life. Winter steals in and settles across my soul before I even know it's there, and it isn't until I feel the pinch that I become aware I have stumbled into a place I don't belong. Ellen White says that "by idle talk, evilspeaking, or neglect of prayer, we may in one day lose the Saviour's presence, and it may take many days of sorrowful search to find Him, and regain the peace that we have lost."* Fortunately, we aren't at the mercy of the weather in our spiritual lives. We can never be parted from the Son, not for a single day, if we will only consent to stay in His presence.

Céleste Perrino-Walker

---

* Ellen G. White, *The Desire of Ages* (Mountain View, CA: Pacific Press®, 1940), 83.

The Heavenly Tutorial

Your words were found, and I ate them, and Your word was to me the
joy and rejoicing of my heart; for I am called by Your name,
O Lord God of hosts.
—Jeremiah 15:16, NKJV

I love to study my Bible. This has not always been the case, however, and there have been years in the past when it took a real effort to find a few spare moments to read a chapter or two, usually with one eye on the clock and less-than-perfect concentration. Even then, God, in His great love, knowing how busy I was with four young children, a multitude of church responsibilities, and long hours of teaching English to supplement my pastor husband's salary, always richly rewarded my pathetic efforts to dig deeper into His Word.

Many years have passed since then, and I am no longer under so much pressure. I can choose how I spend my time. So God started waking me very early in the morning—four o'clock, to be precise—and no amount of effort on my part could recapture that fugitive sleep. He then suggested it was a good opportunity to study His Word, and, of course, He was right! At that time of day, my brain is fresh and ready to absorb information, and there are absolutely no interruptions.

What a change this has brought to my life! The three precious hours until I set off on my morning walk at seven o'clock are never enough. Under the tutelage of God's sweet Spirit, I read at an unhurried pace, though often giddy with excitement at some "new" discovery. The qualifications of my Tutor are unsurpassed, the curriculum so broad and deep that it is inexhaustible. However much I study, I shall never plumb the depths of His wisdom, and every day reveals new secrets of God's intricate workings for the joy and salvation of His fallen children. Add guidelines on how to live a happy, active, and fulfilled life (even at the age of 81) to the privilege of having a Teacher who is always so patient, even when I am slow to understand, despite the best education offered anywhere. And it's *free*!

We are each very different, and the claims on our time vary as much as our ages, work programs, and other responsibilities. However, one thing does not vary, and that is the exhilarating joy of Bible study "addiction." It awaits everyone who sincerely wants to spend more time with God in His Word and who will ask for His help to find suitable opportunities.

Revel Papaioannou

Plans

> "For I know the plans I have for you," declares the LORD,
> "plans to prosper you and not to harm you,
> plans to give you hope and a future."
> —*Jeremiah 29:11, NIV*

If you spend time on Facebook, you may be familiar with Eldad Hagar and Hope for Paws. I've enjoyed learning about Eldad, a rescuer of animals. One can see him in action in numerous videos on the Internet.

The lost, injured, abused, neglected, frightened, confused, and ill—it is Eldad's mission to save these poor creatures. And save them he does, in significant numbers and out of numerous miserable circumstances.

Most of the rescued animals are dogs, and few of them appear to want to be rescued. Their fear is palpable. They run if they can, and hide if they're able. They cower and cry and struggle when being rescued because they're caught and cannot get loose.

With gentle handling, however, and soft, sweet words, often accompanied by kisses on their heads given by Eldad's assistants, the animals always calm some. After the bath, flea treatment, care of the wounds, hearty meal, and safe sleep in a soft bed, almost all of them awaken to their new lives with gratitude and joy. In just a couple of days, these canines are completely different dogs—they run and play and give kisses and come when called. They gain weight and heal. Resisting rescue was not in their best interest. In spite of themselves, though, they were saved. When the struggling stopped and the cooperation commenced, something good—something *very* good—could be done with and for them.

It's like that with us. Jesus wants to save us. He whispers (or shouts), offers (or withholds), chases (or tiptoes). He does whatever it takes to catch us. We run, we fight it; we whimper and cry as we attempt to evade capture.

Once we are caught, our true life, the life we were meant for, begins. We get fed and bathed and treated for our ills and put back on our feet. We find that getting caught is what we really wanted, and needed, all along.

In Jesus we have hope and a future. Without Him . . . not so much.

Carolyn K. Karlstrom

The Sting

This poor man cried out, and the LORD heard him,
and saved him out of all his troubles.
—*Psalm 34:6, NKJV*

I walked right into it!

As I crouched over in disbelief, I thought, *After all of these years of escaping these things, it happens right here—at church?*

I had simply parked my car, opened the door, and stepped out.

However, instead of a peaceful walk to the church food pantry where I was going to assist, I found myself in the midst of a swarm of wasps!

At first, I could not see them, yet I had quickly sensed them close to one of my eyes. At first, I tried to wave them away.

Alas, I was too late!

I felt a terribly sharp pain—a burning sting—shoot into the skin of my face. In high-pitched tones, I cried out.

Suddenly I felt an arm around me, the loving arm of my husband as he held me and, with the other arm, started to wave away the wasps.

My husband, Shawn, had willingly jumped into this swarm of vicious wasps—in the midst of which I was trapped—in order to bring me out. Again and again, Shawn caught the offending wasps in his bare hand, managing to keep them away from me as he brought me to safety. Then he nursed away my pain, all the while ignoring his own. He suffered many more stings than I in order to rescue me from experiencing more pain. By his actions, he saved me from the wasps.

If an imperfect man could love me enough to respond to my cry, how much more is God willing to respond to our cries! Are you crying out today because of some type of pain you are in? Then, cry out to Jesus. He will respond to your cries for help. In fact, He already put Himself in harm's way by coming to this earth and dying in our place in order to rescue us from Satan and the sting of death.

If you find that you have stepped into trouble, cry out to the Lord. He will save you.

Tricia (Wynn) Payne

Allow the Change

Therefore if any man be in Christ, he is a new creature:
old things are passed away; behold, all things are become new.
—*2 Corinthians 5:17*

A few years ago, I sent in a couple of submissions to be considered by a Florida hospital for a devotional book they were to publish. I received a letter from the hospital stating that one of my submissions had made their tentative lineup for the book. The letter further stated that even if my submission was not used for this particular devotional, the hospital would like to reserve the right to use it in the future. If I were in agreement, I should sign the attached permission form.

As I read each statement for the intended use of my work, I was in full agreement with everything until I came to statement number four. If I agreed with that statement, the hospital would have the right to edit, add to, take from, rearrange, alter, modify, revise, translate, reformat, and/or reprocess the materials in any manner determined—at their sole discretion. This caused my spirit of agreement to come to a screeching halt. If I agreed to their terms, they could take my submission and change it around in such a way that it would not resemble anything that I created it to be. As I pondered whether I wanted to submit my work, the Holy Spirit had me look at the situation from the hospital's point of view. Although my work was interesting enough to be used by this entity, my submission in its entirety perhaps didn't represent what was envisioned for the book, and so it must be changed to resemble a product of theirs.

To help make my decision a little easier, the Holy Spirit also reminded me that my goal was to have my submission be part of the devotional. This might mean then that my work would have to be changed. The choice was completely mine.

The invitation to heaven that God extends to each of us is very similar. He invites us to dwell with Him; however, to do so, a change must take place in our lives. We must be willing to allow Him to edit, add to, take from, rearrange, vary, alter, modify, revise, translate, reformat, and/or reprocess our life in any manner He, at His sole discretion, desires. All we have to do is give Him permission to do so. If our goal is to make it to heaven, we must give God permission to change us into His image, which means that we will no longer resemble our original make up.

In the end, we will be grateful we allowed Him to change us.

Carmalita Green

A Father's Love

"I know what I'm doing. I have it all planned out—plans to take care of you, not abandon you, plans to give you the future you hope for."
—*Jeremiah 29:11*, The Message

Unfortunately, not all anniversaries are joyful occasions. As I write, I am approaching the first anniversary of my dear father's passing, which will be a sad time for me. However, as I reflect on my dad's life, I am thankful. My dad was such a blessing to me, and I feel very fortunate to have been raised by such a good man. When I say *good*, I mean that he loved God.

He was a man who made sacrifices in order to provide for me. He was hardworking and often missed out on opportunities that this world could offer because he put God first in everything. My dad loved me unconditionally and taught me, through his example, to love God and develop a relationship with Him for myself. I realize that I have been extremely blessed to have had him as my father. I also know also that my family shares this blessing in having had him as a father-in-law and grandfather. To the end of his life, he continued to have a relationship with God, trusting in Him and never complaining in spite of ill health and the difficulties he faced.

As I experience this anniversary, I will praise God for my dad because he was an example of God's love to me. Contemplating my dad's life, I am reminded that just as he loved me so much, I also have a wonderful heavenly Father who loves me unconditionally. He too is always there for me, and He desires only what is best for me. My Father in heaven is able to save me for eternity and is reaching out in His love and mercy toward me because He wants me to be with Him. He has gone to extreme lengths to rescue me. He sent His own Son to die in my place, and yours too. He doesn't want any of us to perish but rather to have everlasting life with Him.

Whether or not you are, or were, fortunate to also have—or have had—a good dad as I did, you can be certain that you always have a loving heavenly Father who cares for you.

I know that I will be reunited with my earthly father when Jesus returns, for I have given my life to Him.

This is why I can celebrate this anniversary with hope in my heart.

It is my prayer that you and I will place our hands in God's almighty hands today and allow our loving heavenly Father to lead us—all the way home.

Karen Richards

When God Intervenes

God is our refuge and strength,
a very present help in trouble.
—*Psalm 46:1*

efuge refers to a state of being secure from pursuit, trouble, distress, or danger. When the psalmist describes God as a refuge, he intends to convey the idea that God protects, or shelters, the believer from harm, danger, and distressing situations. I suspect that only those who have come face-to-face with imminent troubling situations can appreciate what it truly means to have God as our refuge.

On October 28, 2014, I set off from Accra to visit my son and his family in Fargo, North Dakota. My travel itinerary from Kotoka International Airport in Accra (Ghana) would take me to Heathrow in London (England) to Chicago's O'Hare International Airport (United States of America), and then to Fargo Hector International in North Dakota. Unfortunately, a delay of the Heathrow-to-O'Hare flight threatened to affect my connecting flight to Fargo. After going through the required security checks, I proceeded to gate 16 for my flight to Fargo. A ground hostess informed me that boarding for that flight had closed. I would have to wait six hours for the next flight! I was devastated because my luggage was already on the plane to Fargo. I was also hungry. The airline agent directed me to gate 20 to wait for the next flight, departing in six hours.

I whispered a prayer for the Lord to take care of my situation. I got to gate 20 and, there, an airline agent confirmed that the next flight would be in six hours. After only ten minutes, however, I heard my name mentioned. Curious, I approached the woman at the counter. She informed me that the captain of my original flight to Fargo was looking for me. I introduced myself to a man standing beside her.

"Ma'am," he said, "you are the only passenger left to get on my flight, so I asked that the plane's boarding reopen. I wanted to come look for you." The captain led me back to gate 16, where I obtained a new boarding pass. Then I was ushered onto the plane!

Yes, the Lord intervened, when all hope was lost. God is my refuge and the power that sustains me. He is my ever-present help in time of need. I arrived at Fargo Hector International Airport with my luggage intact and my hunger gone.

Commit your case to God. He is our refuge, a very present help in times of trouble!

Margaret Osei-Agyeman

Tagalong

He leads me beside the still waters. He restores my soul;
He leads me in the paths of righteousness for His name's sake.
—*Psalm 23:2, 3, NKJV*

And I told them of the hand of my God
which had been good upon me.
—*Nehemiah 2:18, NKJV*

My husband and I were strolling in the mall, hand in hand, when a lady stopped us and commented on how nice it was to see an older couple holding hands. This brought up memories of my childhood.

My oldest brother would hold my hand wherever we went. Whenever I got ahead of him, he'd pull me back.

Whenever I lagged behind, he'd pull me forward.

Whenever I wanted to stray from his side, he'd pull me close. Wherever my brother went, I went. I was my brother's tagalong.

I want to be Jesus' tagalong. I want Him to take my hand because He wants me to walk beside Him.

When I go ahead of Him, He gently pulls me back.

Whenever I wander, He pulls me close. When I lag or don't want to follow, He nudges me forward.

What a wonderful God we serve!

My problems come whenever I decide to let go of His hand and try to go forward on my own. Like a loving parent, He watches over me.

When I get lost, He's always there to offer His hand. I must willingly take His hand. He will not force me.

The thought of Jesus taking my hand to lead me brings to mind an old, but well-known, gospel song. The words go like this: "Precious Lord, take my hand, lead me on, help me stand; I am tired, I am weak, I am worn; through the storm, through the night, lead me on to the light: take my hand, precious Lord, lead me home."*

God is offering you His hand of love today.

Will you take it? Will you be His tagalong?

Ruth Cantrell

---

* Thomas A. Dorsey, "Precious Lord, Take My Hand," 1932.

An Almost Grateful Heart

Give thanks in all circumstances;
for this is God's will for you in Christ Jesus.
—*1 Thessalonians 5:18, NIV*

O nce in a Thanksgiving sermon, I shared the following story. A poor man, tired of his miserable life, decided to pray and ask God to resolve his problems. God, in His infinite mercy, answered the request of that man, granting him ten bananas. The man must exchange three bananas for a house, three for food, and three for clothes to replace the tattered rags he wore. The last banana the man was to present to God in gratitude for all that God had done for him. The happy man exchanged three bananas for a house, three for food, and three for clothes. Then he noticed that the "gratitude banana," reserved as a thank offering, was more robust, more beautiful, and more attractive than the others had been. It promised to be much tastier as well.

Seduced by that observation, the man thought, *God owns silver and gold! He is the Creator of everything in heaven and on earth. He will not need this banana.* And the man ate the banana instead of giving it to God to express His gratitude, as he'd been asked to do. He *almost* expressed his thanks but, at the last minute, he did otherwise.

This little story illustrates how selfish we can be with God. God gives us many daily blessings, but so often we fail to appreciate them as we should. We may even "think to thank" but then stay in the realm of "almost," putting our own desires above thanksgiving to God. Luís Fernando Verissimo, a Brazilian writer, states that "nearly" can bring uncertainty and disillusionment because it sadly reminds us of everything that might have been. "Almost" comes close to the mark but doesn't attain it. So I would conclude that the person who *almost* thanked never *really* thanked.

Why do we fervently pray for blessings, yet, when they come, neglect to adequately thank God for them? Paul says that we need to give thanks in everything, for this is God's will for us. Sadly, many of us trip over "almost," leaving "thank You" for later—and it gets lost.

Dear friend, though God owns everything, He still leans down in mercy to receive with joy our thanksgiving for blessings received. Let's not "almost" thank Him. Let's give Him our hearts. Have a grateful heart because an *almost* grateful heart is a heart that never really thanked.

Carmem Virgínia dos Santos Paulo

A Thanksgiving to Remember

Oh, give thanks to the LORD! Call upon His name;
make known His deeds among the peoples!
—*Psalm 105:1, NKJV*

I have many fond holiday memories, but one Thanksgiving stands out in particular. I was serving as a student missionary in India, living in Tamil Nadu, and was spending my first Thanksgiving away from my family and friends.

When I was growing up, my father (who comes from an Italian–Cajun French family) told me stories of how his family ate lasagna, spaghetti, and garlic bread for Thanksgiving when he was a child. While I loved Thanksgiving with family and friends, I often wished we could just eat Italian food for Thanksgiving. As a child, I took our traditional holiday fare for granted. Needless to say, I was homesick that Thanksgiving in India. How I wished I could be at home in New England with my loved ones, eating a *real* Thanksgiving meal with all the fixings! I no longer craved Italian food on this special holiday—I just wanted a real Thanksgiving dinner.

Imagine my surprise when a very large box arrived on my doorstep in Tamil Nadu, India! A former university teacher of mine, Mrs. Jamie Delay, had spent more than US$200 to two-day express mail me that package. I opened the box to find it filled with vegetarian meat, cranberry sauce, instant stuffing, corn, green beans, instant mashed potatoes, gravy, and everything else I had been wishing for! I hadn't told her I was craving a real Thanksgiving dinner. But as a former missionary to Thailand, she knew how homesick I would be on that holiday.

Now every November, I think of that day in India when a lonely student missionary received an amazing gift from a thoughtful, Christ-filled teacher back home in the States. I'll never take another Thanksgiving dinner for granted again!

Galatians 6:10 says, "Therefore, as we have opportunity, let us do good to all, especially to those who are of the household of faith" (NKJV). Mrs. Delay's generosity and selfless act truly embodied this text. Her gift will always serve as an example to me of how we can bless others, especially those who are serving Christ overseas.

I encourage you to send an e-mail or even drop a small care package in the mail to a missionary who is serving overseas. They will be forever grateful that you thought of them!

Amanda N. Gaspard

The Way to Walk

He has shown you, O mortal, what is good.
And what does the LORD require of you?
To act justly and to love mercy
and to walk humbly with your God.
—Micah 6:8, NIV

When one is young and healthy, it is easy to take for granted the ability to walk and run. However, in the event of injury, disability, or age-related disease, the capacity to walk and move freely comes to be recognized as a precious gift. The Bible indicates that God is interested in people's mobility problems. Jesus and His followers healed many who were crippled, lame, or paralytic. According to Isaiah, prominent on the list of blessings that will attend the coming of the Redeemer is that "then will the lame leap like a deer" (Isaiah 35:6, NIV).

Miraculous healings don't seem very common these days, but God has also given wisdom and skill to surgeons and other health-care professionals. After years of increasing pain and limitation due to severe arthritis, my eighty-eight-year-old mother is rejoicing at being able to walk comfortably again following hip replacement surgery.

However, a brief survey of Scripture makes it clear that how we walk spiritually is even more important to God than how we walk physically. In the Bible we can find walking role models—such as Enoch, Noah, and Abraham—who were all described as individuals who walked faithfully. God offers an abundance of both promises and advice for those who also want to walk faithfully. Let me share just a few: "Blessed are those whose ways are blameless, who walk according to the law of the LORD" (Psalm 119:1, NIV). "Those who walk in wisdom are kept safe" (Proverbs 28:26, NIV). In the New Testament, Paul wrote, "Walk in the way of love, just as Christ loved us and gave himself up for us" (Ephesians 5:2, NIV). I also like the promise of 1 John 1:7, which says, "But if we walk in the light, as he is in the light, we have fellowship with one another, and the blood of Jesus, his Son, purifies us from all sin" (NIV). Through John, God also said, "I have no greater joy than to hear that my children are walking in the truth" (3 John 4, NIV).

Perhaps the most wonderful promise of all is that the Lord Himself has undertaken to be our walking companion! "I will walk among you and be your God," He assures us, "and you will be my people" (Leviticus 26:12, NIV).

Jennifer M. Baldwin

My Special Request

"I will give you a new heart and put a new spirit within you; I will take the heart of stone out of your flesh and give you a heart of flesh."
—Ezekiel 36:26, NKJV

I lingered on my knees for a bit longer, waiting for God to answer. My request was deep and reflective. I wanted God to grant me a new heart. I wanted a heart like His heart—a heart of love, patience, and forgiveness. For five years I prayed this prayer and even asked a friend to petition God with me. But the more I prayed and claimed the scripture above, the more Satan tested what was beating in my chest. *Father, is this an impossible request?* I prayed. *Do You hear me? Do You care?* Then, when I was sitting at a funeral, the answer came.

Four years ago, my sister-in-law, Clarissa, informed our family that her youngest brother, Vernon, had just learned he would need an immediate heart transplant if he were to live a normal life. Clarissa asked the family and her many friends to pray that a new heart be found for Vernon. We petitioned God daily, and after being on the transplant list for only a short time, Vernon received a heart. For about a year, things went well. Then other complications developed, and Vernon became ill again and ultimately passed away.

At Vernon's funeral, Clarissa's older brother, Phillip, recounted Vernon's transplant journey. As he eulogized his late brother's life, Phillip explained that someone had to die in order for Vernon to live. At that moment, the light bulb in my head came on. Immediately I understood the answer to my own personal prayer request for a new heart. My heavenly Brother gave up His life. He died of a broken heart in order that I might have a new heart, along with an opportunity for eternal life. It became clear to me that God had given me that new heart. All the trials that were coming my way were merely a test to strengthen the new heart. Is not our God good?

Since that occasion, I have often reflected on Jesus' sacrifice and what it means. The magnitude of His gift to humanity is beyond our comprehension. It will take an eternity to appreciate its greatness. To say Thank You to my Lord and Savior is not nearly enough for all He has done for me. Yet when I see my Jesus face-to-face, I will tell Him how profoundly grateful I am that He chose to grant me a new heart. I will also thank Him for providing me an opportunity for eternal life and for claiming me as one of His own.

Yvonne Curry Smallwood

Out of the Comfort Bubble

"Be strong and of good courage; do not be afraid, nor be dismayed,
for the LORD your God is with you wherever you go."
—Joshua 1:9, NKJV

When was the last time you stepped out of your "comfort bubble"? Have you ever stepped out of your comfort zone?

I stepped *way* outside my comfort zone at church in November 2015. Our pastor wanted to involve members in the church services. So pastoral staff go through the church directory and ask different families to deliver the Scripture reading just before the sermon each week. Yesterday was my turn.

But here's a bit of background. When the church secretary sent me the e-mail with the request that I would take a turn reading the Scripture, I almost said No. That's because I was thinking about how scary it would be—standing up in front of people. But then I remembered that life is about growing and changing . . . and dealing with challenges as they are presented. A vibrant life is about *not* being content with staying in the same place all the time. So I told the church secretary that I would do it.

Just before I read, I said to the congregation, "I'm sure that what I'm about to do is no big deal for you who get up front a lot, or even a little, and are comfortable doing so. However, to the rest of us who are scared by the thought of being up front, this is a big deal! In fact, this is *huge*!" Chuckles rippled thru the congregation, and the ice was broken. I've attended that church for more than twenty years and had never, even once, gotten up front to speak. Quite a few members spoke to me afterwards, thanking me for having the courage to read in public.

Do you have a "comfort bubble" that you're afraid to step out of for Jesus? Queen Esther did when the lives of her people were in jeopardy. But she stepped out. Daniel stepped out of his when he chose to pray by his open window even though it meant a trip to the lions' den. These individuals saved people's lives in stepping out, while also witnessing to God's blessings on the obedient. I hope that what I did that November morning in church will inspire and encourage others to be brave enough to step out of their comfort bubbles as well.

Today how can you step out of your "bubble" in positive ways for Jesus?

Sonia Brock

Grandparents

When I call to remembrance the genuine faith that is in you,
which dwelt first in your grandmother Lois and your mother Eunice,
and I am persuaded is in you also.
—*2 Timothy 1:5, NKJV*

No matter how grandmothers are labeled—Grandma, Granny, Nana, Noni—we are supposed to be special to our grandchildren. When these little ones are born, we are bubbling over with joy, maybe even more excited than when our own children were born.

It means a lot to me to be able to spend time with my grandson. I don't want him to grow up thinking, "My grandmother never did anything with me." I want to be special to my grandchildren—more than just at Christmas and on birthdays when I buy presents for him. I want their memories of me to include the love and time I was able to give them and teach them about Jesus. Every summer, after my son, niece, and nephew turned six years old, they spent those months with my mother. She took them places and made memories.

A lot of grandparents have had to raise their grandchildren for various reasons. Even when they don't have to, they are still an important part of the family support system and can be of great value in sharing their wisdom in regard to child-rearing. They can continually point all family members to God and help them understand that God designed the family to experience love and togetherness. God wants them to understand that His love lasts forever, and one of the best places to find it is in a God-centered family. Ellen White once wrote: "The cause of division and discord in families and in the church is separation from Christ. . . .Thus it is in the Christian life. The closer we come to Christ, the nearer we shall be to one another. God is glorified as His people unite in harmonious action."*

Grandparents, it is time for us to do our part!

Camilla E. Cassell

---

* Ellen G. White, *The Adventist Home* (Washington, DC: Review and Herald®, 1952), 179.

God's Superhighway

For his Spirit joins with our spirit
to affirm that we are God's children.
—*Romans 8:16, NLT*

My husband and I have retired and moved to the country. We're an around-the-house couple. You see, my husband was my chauffeur, and we did some traveling, but now he is legally sightless.

I enjoy electronics, especially small gadgets. I bought my husband a talking clock, called Moshi. If you ask "her" the time, the date, the temperature, or to play sleep sounds, she will talk back to you! However, guess who plays with it? Me!

Our son preached the sermon one Sabbath at our small country church. It was videotaped and put on our church Web site. We naturally wanted some of the family members to view it, so, with my electronic mind, I began copying it via the Internet "superhighway." I forgot, however, to first check how much data (space) I had already used. About that time, my husband decided he wanted to listen to the sermon, so I let him listen on one of my other electronic devices, while I continued to use the superhighway. A few minutes after I finished my project, I noticed I had three new e-mails from my Internet provider, each telling me that I had run over my allotted data usage limit.

I was shocked! I prayed and then got on the phone with Terry, a representative from our Internet provider. I explained my problem as he checked my records. "You're right," he affirmed, "you hardly ever go over like this. So what happened that caused you to go over so much?" I told him I'd been copying our son's sermon. He said, "That is a good enough reason to go over your data usage limit." We started up a conversation about our Lord and Savior, and we stayed on the phone talking for about thirty more minutes. We talked about God's love and grace, my gift of communication, and Terry's gift of music. It wasn't a coincidence that I ran over my data limit, nor coincidental that I got Terry as the representative who received my call. He got my situation straightened out. At the close of our conversation, he thanked me for being a blessing to him, and I thought I was the one who received the blessing!

When we travel down God's superhighway of life, we never know whom we're going to meet along the way or how they will be blessed by the things we say or do.

Elaine J. Johnson

November 28

Message on the Barn

Now may the God of hope fill you with all joy and peace in believing,
that you may abound in hope by the power of the Holy Spirit.
—Romans 15:13, NKJV

We live a short distance from a major interstate highway. Across the countryside, as travelers on the highway can see, are ranches that dot the scenery, making it very picturesque.

One ranch close to the highway especially caught my eye because lettered on two sides of a large white barn were these words in big black letters: "Lost Keeshond." Beneath the first line was a second line stating, "Reward," which was followed by a phone number.

Year after year, that message was left on two sides of the barn, making the notice about the lost dog visible to travelers moving in either direction. Then after about ten years, someone slightly changed the message on the barn. Though the first line remained the same—"Lost Keeshond," the second line was changed from "Reward" to "Ranch," with the earlier phone number painted out. Now the message on the barn read "Lost Keeshond Ranch."

This rancher family was so desperate to find their dear lost keeshond dog that they used every imaginable method to search for it. I don't know whether their dog was ever found, but they certainly did not give up hope for more than ten years. Then they honored their beloved pet by naming their ranch in memory of it. That family made the best of a sad situation and turned it into something positive. What faith they must have had in posting that message on their barn!

Do I have the same kind of faith that is willing to "post" the message of Jesus in a bold way for others to see? Do I use even extraordinary methods to spread the good news of Jesus to travelers along the highway of life? Perhaps we should post a similar message that reads, "Lost Planet! Call JESUS! Our Savior will answer the phone!"

The message on the barn reminds me of our Savior's message to us—that even when we are lost sheep, the Good Shepherd never gives up searching. But wait! There is more!

Just as that family made the best of a bad situation, our *lost* planet will one day turn into a *redeemed* planet, a planet restored by our Creator and Redeemer. Only He can replace a "Lost Planet" notice with a new sign: "Welcome Home!" I'm sure it will be strategically placed along the boulevards of heaven. And what a welcome home celebration that will be!

Ginger Bell

David's Melody

Be strong and take heart, all you who hope in the LORD.
—Psalm 31:24, NIV

My dad, the late Wayne Hooper, who died of cancer in 2007, was well-known as a Christian singer, composer, and music arranger. His musical career was dedicated to creating inspirational music that would lift the soul with the message of Jesus and the assurance of salvation we can have through His grace as we accept His gift and His influence in our lives.

Recently I was browsing through the database that Dad created during his final illness. The database contains nearly 1,500 song titles that Dad had composed or arranged during his life. As I began reading alphabetically in the D's, I came upon this listing: "David's Melody."

Hmm, I wondered, *I don't remember ever knowing or hearing of a song by this title.*

I clicked on the title to see what it could be and was astonished to find a simple, little one-line score. It was a short melody of a few notes in the key of C. The handwritten words of my younger brother appeared just below the melody line: "I believe in Jesus, I know what He can do. I have faith in Jesus, He will carry me through."

Below that simple melody line were my dad's pencil-written notes on two-score lines where he had added four-part harmony—but in the key of D. At the bottom of the page was Dad's handwriting: "David's melody and words at top. Dad's harmonization." My heart melted as I played—on the piano—my little brother's tune from the first line. Then, as I played Dad's two-line composition beneath the childish melody, it became a beautiful song. Brighter. Full of surprising harmonies, hope, joy, and assurance that, indeed, "He *will* carry me through."

I recall David being in the hospital when he was about ten years old. He was there for at least two weeks, undergoing tests and treatment for rheumatic fever. It was around this time that David had written his melody and words. His faith and trust in God had obviously been impacted by the influence and character of our father. My little brother, with his own growing faith and trust in God now, was discovering for himself the musical talent he had inherited.

What Dad did for David's melody, our heavenly Father does for us when we give Him our simple talents to use in service, enhancing them with His master touch, creating something that will witness for Him. Isn't He a wonderful Savior! What talent will *you* give Him today?

Jan Hooper Lind

Protected

Be anxious for nothing, but in everything by prayer and supplication,
with thanksgiving, let your requests be made known to God.
—*Philippians 4:6, NKJV*

The Saffir-Simpson Hurricane Wind Scale categorized Ivan as a long-lasting hurricane. Ivan was the tenth-largest hurricane of all time, causing billions of dollars in damage in some Caribbean islands and part of the United States. The morning following the previous night of terror, we cautiously ventured out into our garden to inspect the obvious and major damage—trees toppled, crops uprooted. Even our precious avocado and lychee trees were gone. And what chance would our small plum tree have in a storm like that? I saw a big sweetsop tree sprawled across the tiny plum. What a sight! Sure that the little tree was totally crushed, I broke off sweetsop limbs in order to reach my precious plum tree. When I reached it, there it was, standing straight and safe! It had survived the fury of one of the most devastating storms in our history.

I marveled at the miracle. Though the little tree had lost a few young plums, it was still safe, standing with most of its "trophies" intact. What protective hands sheltered the little tree from the angry winds? I believe they were the loving hands of our Savior and Protector.

I reflected on the following quote: "The Father's presence encircled Christ, and nothing befell Him but that which infinite love permitted for the blessing of the world. Here was His source of comfort, and it is for us. He who is imbued with the Spirit of Christ abides in Christ. The blow that is aimed at him falls upon the Saviour, who surrounds him with His presence. Whatever comes to him comes from Christ. He has no need to resist evil, for Christ is his defense. Nothing can touch him except by our Lord's permission, and 'all things' that are permitted 'work together for good to them that love God.' Romans 8:28."*

Despite the storm, the miniature plum tree was quite content and protected by the large tree hovering over it. Despite all my anxieties, it was quite happy with its state.

If you are anxious today, ask yourself the question, *Is there anything too hard for the Lord to do?* If He is silent, wait! We are advised to be anxious for nothing.

Dear Lord, when I become anxious about safety, thank You for reminding me that in spite of the worst storm, You are available, and You are protecting me.

Gloria Barnes Gregory

---

* Ellen G. White, *Thoughts From the Mount of Blessing* (Hagerstown, MD: Review and Herald®, 2000), 71.

Yes, I Am Your Father

See how very much our Father loves us,
for he calls us his children, and that is what we are!
—*1 John 3:1, NLT*

When I was eleven years old, my dad and I went on a special trip together. With my fingers safely curled inside his warm hand, we walked side by side on the narrow cobblestone streets of the city of Eger, Hungary. We were on our way to pick up a teenage girl, Maria, from an orphanage.

Dad and I stepped inside the lobby, where a woman in a white lab coat greeted us. "Please have a seat while Maria gets her things ready," she said kindly.

Truthfully, it was quite brave of my parents to add another person to our very simple lives, since both budget and space were tight. My sister had met Maria at a girls' camp, and it was because of her loving persuasion that my parents were convinced to foster Maria.

From the orphanage lobby we saw two narrow hallways with doors on both sides. As we sat and waited, I noticed that one of the doors opened just a crack and a little head popped out. Before long, there was a little head or two looking out every door. A few minutes later, a brave little fellow with dirty blond hair stepped out and began walking toward us. By now it was obvious that all the boys had fixed their eyes on none other than my very own father. The little blond boy's shy voice broke the silence as he turned to my dad and said, "Are you . . . *my* daddy? Did you come to get me?"

Soon others followed, repeating the question with a beam of hope in their eyes that only children possess. "Are you my daddy? Did you come to take me home with you?"

My dad reached out and stroked each little face with a smile, gently shaking his head. The answer was No, an answer they were used to hearing. Dad later told us how his heart was aching because he couldn't be a father to all the little boys. But it was at this moment that I understood the meaning of having a father, a father that I could go home with.

As I grew up, I began to see an even bigger picture of my heavenly Father who, through giving His Son to humanity, adopted each and every human being into His family.

To the question, "Are you my Daddy?" God answers assuredly, "Yes, my child. I *am* . . . your Father. Let's go home."

Ida T. Ronaszegi

December 2

The Bedspread

*My God shall supply all your need
according to his riches in glory by Christ Jesus.*
—*Philippians 4:19*

Every morning during my devotional time, I lay my plans at Jesus' feet to bless or to change according to His will. This has resulted in some quite remarkable occurrences in my life.

About thirty years ago, women's retreats were new events in our area. When the first one was announced, one of my dearest friends enthusiastically urged me to go with her and be her roommate for the weekend. But for registration I needed fifty-three dollars—an amount not in my budget. While my friend busily worked to recruit other church ladies for the retreat, I prayed about my dilemma. I needed a new bedspread to replace the one so badly worn that was on our bed. I'd picked out the spread I wanted in a mail-order catalogue. With shipping, it cost that very amount. I had saved up that amount and was ready to send for the spread. Then the women's retreat came up. Which would be God's will for me— the bedspread or the retreat? I thought about how nice it would be to attend the retreat with my church sisters and room with my best friend. Should I forgo the bedspread and go to the retreat? Obviously I had a lot of praying to do! I must decide soon because reservations needed to be made within the month.

One day, on my way home from work, I passed a well-known thrift shop. On impulse I went in. Wandering about, I happened upon the bedding section. An amazingly familiar-looking bedspread caught my eye. I discovered it to be the exact same model as the spread in the catalogue that I was about to order! I examined it carefully and found it to be in virtually new condition, with a price tag of ten dollars. As I clutched it in my arms and hastened to the checkout counter, I couldn't resist praising God aloud for His marvelous answer to my prayer. Obviously He wanted me to go with my friend to the retreat! "Thank You, thank You, thank You, Lord," I murmured over and over as I hurried to the purchase stand to write a check for my treasure. When I arrived home and broke the news to my friend, we shared in a moment of gratitude and praise. Needless to say, the blessing of that women's retreat is a memory I treasure to this day.

How about you? Do you take God at His word, even in the smallest, least important areas of your life? You can, you know!

Donna Ritchie Casebolt

Let Your Light Shine

"You are the light of the world. . . .
Let your light shine before others,
that they may see your good deeds
and glorify your Father in heaven."
—Matthew 5:14–16, NIV

Just a simple act of faith can go a long way and contribute toward the saving of a soul. We have experienced this reality in our own family.

A doctor working in a Zambian hospital will never know the great impact that his simple act of prayer had on his patients—one of whom was my late grandmother. The impact of his actions has had a positive effect on our family down through my generation.

My grandmother once had a medical condition that called for an urgent and immediate operation. As the doctor came into the operating room, he said, "I have one more thing to do before starting the surgery. I want to pray for you and also pray that this operation will go well."

With that, he bowed his head. "Dear Lord," he prayed, "You are the Great Physician. We commit this woman and this surgery into Your capable hands. In Your name I pray. Amen."

My grandmother, who was not a believer at the time, was so impressed with the doctor's prayer that, in that moment, she decided to become a member of whatever church this doctor attended. She appreciated, and was very impressed, by the faith this doctor had in the power of God. She was convinced that he must belong to a Bible-believing church.

Though my grandmother is no longer with us, my parents, siblings, I, and all of our children are following in the footsteps of Grandmother, who chose, in a time of uncertainty, to believe in God.

I hope that someday I can sincerely thank that doctor who demonstrated his faith to my grandmother—just by a simple act of prayer.

It is important to note that the simple acts of faith we do on behalf of others may go a long way toward bringing them into the kingdom of God. I am sure that doctor will be shocked to see the many stars in his crown because of his long-ago prayer. We will share with him how he changed her life forever and also impacted the rest of the family for generations.

Let's let our lights shine for Jesus!

Grace Phiri Bwalya

December 4

A Mother's Prayer

Then little children were brought to Him
that He might put His hands on them and pray,
but the disciples rebuked them. But Jesus said,
"Let the little children come to Me, and do not forbid them;
for of such is the kingdom of heaven."
—*Matthew 19:13, 14, NKJV*

When I was fourteen years old, my parents sent me to a boarding school to live, work, and attend classes. I was painfully shy and overwhelmed with homesickness.

One cold December evening, I felt so down that I telephoned my mother. At that time, I had to call her through an operator, and it was very expensive. During that conversation, she said four words that have reverberated through my mind, "I'm praying for you."

I could picture her kneeling by her bed in prayer every day, sometimes even more than once a day. Mother went on to assure me that she would always be praying for me every day. I believed her, and I still do.

Through the many trials we face (and we all face many), I carry the comfort of knowing that Mother is praying for me. That statement was the greatest gift she has ever given me. I have clung to it throughout my life.

The New Testament records the story of mothers bringing their children to Jesus for His blessing and His touch. When the disciples rebuked the mothers, telling them Jesus was too busy to bother with children, Jesus said, "Let the little children come to Me, and do not forbid them" (Matthew 19:14, NKJV).

It's a wonderful thing for a mother to bring her children to Jesus, entering His presence through prayer, regardless of the age of the child. We are all children of God.

Let your teenager, twentysomething, or middle-aged son or daughter know you are lifting them up in prayer. You are bringing them to Jesus every day.

As mothers, let us continue daily to bring our children before the Lord, no matter the circumstance or the relationship. Those of us with no biological children still have children in the church—the family of God—for whom we can pray.

All around us are those who need our daily prayers, regardless of age—"for of such is the kingdom of heaven" (Matthew 19:14, NKJV).

Barb Engquist

Hands

And he took the children in his arms,
placed his hands on them and blessed them.
—*Mark 10:16, NIV*

I love to wonder. When I look at everything God has created, my heart sings with a sense of joy, and I feel totally at peace. Outside my window I can see tiny birds, tall silver birch trees, hills, mountains, sunsets, and stars. The sky is always different, and the world is so beautiful.

But sometimes I'm in places where I can't see out of a window or I'm surrounded by concrete and steel. Then I look at my hands. They're always with me, and they always amaze me. I use them all the time, without thinking, and I can forget just how wonderful they are until I have a paper cut or a splinter or I break my wrist or need surgery. With my hands, I write cards, type on my laptop, drive my car, sew, plant seeds, wrap gifts, tidy rooms, touch someone's hand, pour juice, stroke a child's face, or tie a bandage around a knee. Almost everything I enjoy doing depends on my God-created hands. I pray that I'll never lose the ability to use them.

Jesus used His hands every day. He laid healing hands on hurting bodies, broke bread to feed hungry crowds, lifted people up, held them safe, wrote in the dirt, hugged tiny children, washed sore and tired feet, turned water into wine, and touched the untouchables. Then one day, those hands that healed and scattered blessings were roughly bound. Those loving hands that healed and helped were split by cruel nails. But even His bleeding and hurting hands kept on blessing, giving us the gift of forgiveness and pushing open the door to eternal life.

What about your hands? Draw around your hands. Inside the outline of one hand, write down everything your hands can do, such as preparing meals, writing, sweeping the floor, cleaning, ironing, driving, creating, playing, gardening, working, and dressing yourself. Fill the outline of your other hand with all the different things your hands do to bless others: sending a card, making a pie, gathering a bunch of flowers from your garden, pushing a wheelchair, sewing a dress for an African girl, knitting a snug scarf for a homeless person, leaving a generous tip, etc.

Then, pray with your hands. Turn them upside down, as you give all your worries and concerns to God. And then hold them out to receive God's blessings.

How will your hands share God's love today?

Karen Holford

December 6

Life

Trust in the LORD and do good. . . . Seek your happiness in the LORD,
and he will give you your heart's desire.
—*Psalm 37:3, 4, GNT*

What is life? Sometimes I ponder this question. Some say life is what you make of it. This is true because whatever influences you will, through you, influence the world for good or bad. In other words, you reap what you sow.

I think it's safe to say positive thinking contributes to a positive lifestyle, the opposite also being true. Where you put your attention is where you will put your energy. So I ask God to help me focus on Him; He can use me to serve others, whether it's through my work or my play.

I have also learned that in life you need to participate, not just anticipate. When you want something, you must make a serious effort to obtain it or to reach your goal.

Don't be jealous about other people's successes; celebrate them as if they were your own. We all have a power of choice. Let us stop feeling sorry for ourselves.

Our view of success in life is also important. Many people think success is having a business, or a grand job, being married, or driving an expensive car. My analysis of success in life is that it is a state of mind where we are content with whatever God has blessed us with. We need to live the life God created for us. We need to be grateful for what we learn from both good and bad experiences. Then we continue to apply those lessons to our lives. God helps grant us His kind of success when we keep our eyes on Him.

How blessed we are that He gave us the Bible as our manual that shows us how to conduct our lives! Jesus told us that He came to give us life—a very abundant life—and a life full of meaning and purpose. He meant for us to enjoy life. We have purpose when we pattern our lives after Jesus. God's Word and His Holy Spirit will help us define our purpose in life and help us pursue it.

It is my prayer for all of us women that we reach a state of mind where we can live the most abundant life God has created for us. Despite problems or criticism that comes our way, the life we live can be beautiful. I have chosen to enjoy every moment of my life. I hope you have chosen to do the same. May you be blessed and experience God's peace in your life.

Deborah Matshaya

The Famous One

Yet to all who did receive him, to those who believed in his name,
he gave the right to become children of God.
—*John 1:12, NIV*

When I was twenty years old, I told myself a story that went something like this: "I am going to pursue acting, because if I become famous, I can really make an impact for God."

To prepare for this, I had a portfolio of pictures made for myself. I moved with my husband to Southern California and signed up to be an extra in television and movies. I remember how excited I was my first day as an extra on the set of the hit '80s television show *Who's the Boss*, starring Tony Danza and Judith Light. I was able to meet all the cast, and everything went well until Friday morning. The director gathered us extras together and explained there would be two tapings of the show. They would take the best part of each one and edit it to make the final episode. He explained that we would need to be at both back-to-back tapings that evening. The reality began to hit me that the second taping would be after sundown on Friday.

I'd been brought up to regard the Sabbath hours as sacred time to be spent focused on God. I went to the director immediately. "I will need to leave the tapings before the sun goes down so I can observe my holy day," I said.

"Well, I wish you would have told me sooner than this. You might as well leave now because you're of no use to me." I left. This incident made such an impact on me that I decided not to pursue acting after all. All my dreams of becoming famous were squelched.

For many years I struggled trying to find my niche in the world. What career should I pursue? I worked at various jobs before becoming a full-time mom and raising two daughters. As I continued my relationship with Christ, I came to understand that I indeed had become famous! God began to speak to my heart about who I was: *Lee Lee, your fame is that you are My child! Everything you need is found in Me.* And God has led this lavishly loved child of His into ministry. I have even been able to write skits and plays and use my gift of drama to glorify my Savior!

So, in a way, the story I told myself at the age of twenty did come true. Just not in the way I thought it would. You see, God had a much better plan!

Lee Lee Dart

December 8

The Animals We Encounter

Then God commanded, "Let the earth produce all kinds of animal life: domestic and wild, large and small"—and it was done.
—Genesis 1:24, GNT

On the eve of Good Friday in 2015, I arrived home to hear "meow, meow" echoing from a carport full of junk. Surprised, I searched for kittens. Since we did not see or hear any kittens the next day, our fears heightened, especially because of a foul odor. On Sabbath morning, I again heard kittens when I cried, "Meow! Meow!" A faint response led us to two weak kittens with their eyes still closed. With the aid of an improvised milk bottle, they revived. Unfortunately, our effort, love, and care—and the kittens—lasted only a week.

When I first met my husband, Norman, he had a dog. Bagga was a protective, faithful dog, with a beautiful jet-black coat, a bushy tail, and a fierce but intelligent look. After our marriage, Norman introduced me to Bagga: "This is my wife; don't trouble her." The demise of his canine friend almost ten years later left Norman heartbroken, teary, and sad.

Next came Max, a happy puppy with a lovely black coat, white paws, and white chest. Max grew into a faithful, loving, and watchful dog. In the evenings, he greeted Norman at the gate with a dance, some unusual sounds, and a jump in the air. Max was also a good "foster father," dashing across the street when hearing puppies cry. On one such occasion, he was hit by a car. I feared the worst and prayed for his welfare. He survived with the help of a vet. Sadly, Max was subsequently poisoned. This loss also caused grief and pain.

God's creatures, domestic or wild, have marvelous instincts. All over the world, dogs have rescued people from fire, water, and rubble. Likewise, Jesus came to rescue the whole world from everlasting fire. He came to keep us from drowning during the storms of life. He delivers us from the rubble of sin.

As I ponder how the abandoned kittens cried for their mother, I recall Isaiah 49:15, which asks, "Can a mother forget the baby at her breast and have no compassion on the child she has borne? Though she may forget, I will not forget you!" (NIV). In His love for His chosen people, Jesus compared Himself to a mother hen wanting to gather and protect her chicks (Luke 13:34).

Friends, let's learn some valuable spiritual lessons from the animals we encounter.

Bula Rose Haughton Thompson

Angels to the Rescue

"He will call on me, and I will answer him;
I will be with him in trouble, I will deliver him and honor him.
With long life I will satisfy him and show him my salvation."
—*Psalm 91:15, 16, NIV*

I had often heard about angels and how they interact in people's lives. Yet it wasn't until I was seventeen that I had an experience that made me believe in them on a more personal level.

Far from home and penniless, I was just beginning my career as a nursing student, showing up at a Christian college on faith alone. How could I possibly cover the cost of books, uniforms, and life's little necessities like food and proper clothing?

While sitting in the dean's office waiting for him to review my situation, I studied a mural on the wall. It depicted Jesus and the disciples as their boat was being tossed by a storm.

Jesus, Savior, pilot me, I silently pleaded.

Not long after, the dean of the college congratulated me on passing my entrance exam. We discussed my financial plight. I left his office that day with the assurance that, "Where there's a will, there's a way."

So many "angels of mercy" came to my rescue. I was assigned work in the kitchen of a nearby medical care facility. I served delicious food and washed dishes. So, you might be asking, how did I know the food was delicious when I couldn't pay for it? The answer is that my supervisors would save me a plate of leftovers or motion for me to scrape the large pots (for myself) in order to enjoy the last bit of goodness before I washed them.

The campus librarian held back used textbooks and sold them to me for one dollar each. A kind lady from the local relief service supplied me with school uniforms at no charge. I was also informed that an "angel," who wished to remain anonymous, had deposited tuition money into my account. Praise God from whom all blessings flow!

More than fifty years have come and gone since then, and my special angels are probably asleep in Jesus by now. However, some day I hope to hug them tightly and say, "God bless you! Through you, God fulfilled His promise that He would send his angels before me to meet my needs" (see Genesis 24:7).

May the good Lord give each of us compassion to be an angel for someone today!

Jane Wiggins Moore

Eager—To Be Willing, Earnest, and Ready

But we are citizens of heaven, where the Lord Jesus Christ lives.
And we are eagerly waiting for him to return as our Savior.
—*Philippians 3:20, NLT*

By now, as you have read my devotionals this year, you may have realized that I love hymns. I love most religious music, but there's something about hymns that touch my heart deeply. You know, those hymns your grandmother sang or the elderly lady on the church pew behind you sang as she waited for service to begin. Or was it on the radio that you happened across a station playing old hymns? However you heard them, hymns of long ago have words that seem to touch the fiber of my being.

By far, my favorite hymns are those pointing toward Jesus' second coming, hymns that challenge us to stay strong or stand firm in our beliefs until He comes. Hymns that talk about that "golden morning" or counsel us to "watch, ye saints" for His soon return. My mother's favorite hymn was "Face to Face with Christ, My Savior." I would listen to her sing that hymn while cooking or lying in her bed or puttering around in her garden. I would wonder at the words. When I see Jesus come, I will be enraptured and delighted. Nothing else on earth will matter but to see my Jesus face-to-face. The hymn's lyricist wrote that even though we can now "only faintly" see Him, on the day He comes, it will be a "blissful moment" because all pain and grief will be banished. What a day that will be!

The Bible tells us that we should "eagerly wait for the return of our Lord Jesus Christ" (1 Corinthians 1:7, NLT). Paul says, "But we are citizens of heaven, where the Lord Jesus Christ lives. And we are eagerly waiting for him to return as our Savior" (Philippians 3:20, NLT). *Eagerly* means "with earnestness, willingness, and readiness." We must be ready for Jesus to come, not just in words but also in action. Each day we must live to fulfill the gospel call because we are eager to go home.

And so, my sisters, live "looking forward to the day of God and hurrying it along" (2 Peter 3:12, NLT). Why? Because "we are looking forward to the new heavens and new earth he has promised, a world filled with God's righteousness" (verse 13, NLT).

What a glorious day that will be! So let us sing with joy, hope, and strong belief that "when the roll is called up yonder, I'll be there."

Heather-Dawn Small

The Dishwasher

"You shall therefore keep His statutes and His commandments which
I command you today, that it may go well with you and with your
children after you, and that you may prolong your days in the land
which the LORD your God is giving you for all time."
—Deuteronomy 4:40, NKJV

A s we prepared to move, I wondered, *What shall I do with our fairly new dishwasher?*

Straightaway I thought of Lindewe and her husband, a young migrant family from Zimbabwe who were establishing their home in England. I knew she would value the gift but would need clear instructions on how to use it.

My husband installed the dishwasher, while I explained how it operated. "You will need to put some salt in this part and ensure it is kept topped up." Even though Lindewe was very pleased to have the dishwasher, I could see the perplexity on her face as I gave her the instructions. "Yes, it also needs dishwasher tablets and rinse aid," I added, indicating where each should go. After explaining again, I had her demonstrate how to use the dishwasher.

"Follow the instructions, and you can't go wrong," I said, leaving with a smile.

A few days later, I received an anxious telephone call. Lindewe said, "The dishwasher is not working; it's foaming all over the kitchen!" I asked Lindewe what she had put into the dishwasher. "Washing up liquid," was her reply. I burst out laughing. She had not followed the instructions!

At times, we are like that with God. God gives us rules, instructions, and commandments in His Word on how to live and what to do to have a healthy, productive, full, and prosperous life—an abundant life. But because God's Word does not always match up with our understanding of what seems right, logical, or scientific, we choose to do things our own way. Sometimes the consequence of doing our own thing is amusing, and we can laugh about it with family and friends. Other times, the results can be tragic, as pointed out by the wisest man on earth: "There is a way that seems right to a [woman], but its end is the way of death" (Proverbs 14:12, NKJV).

Dear Father, give us the strength and willing heart to always follow Your way because You love us with an everlasting love, and You want only the best for us.

Lucille Fifield

The Last Prayer

*"In my distress I called to the Lord; I called out to my God.
From his temple he heard my voice."*
—2 Samuel 22:7, NIV

My friend's cancer had returned. For the past month, I had called Danis almost every day. On Monday evening, we had such a happy conversation about one of the times she visited me in Albuquerque. We went for a spectacular balloon ride. Danis didn't tell me until that night that she only went because the rest of us were so excited but how happy she was that she had gone. On Tuesday evening, I tried to call Danis, but there was no answer. A few hours later, I got a phone call from Danis' friend, Terresa. She said that Danis had fallen that afternoon and was taken to hospice. There would be no surgery because the cancer had spread so far.

I felt helpless because I now lived in Florida. My biggest regret was that I hadn't prayed with Danis before we finished our last conversation, as was our custom. As I prayed for her and pondered my hopeless situation, I suddenly remembered that Vania, a friend of mine, had recently moved to Amarillo. She didn't know Danis, but I called Vania anyway and asked whether she could visit Danis. She asked me what to say. I told her to let Danis know that I had sent her in my place to pray that she would not have pain. That had been Danis' prayer request. Though a snowstorm was in progress, Vania ventured out to visit my friend on Wednesday.

Later Vania called me and said that Danis understood that she had visited at my request in order to pray for her. Vania had prayed, and she said Danis was in no pain and that she didn't even look ill! The next day, I received a phone call from Terresa as I was traveling home. She said that Danis had died peacefully—and in no pain—on Thursday morning.

Her earthly journey was over, and how thankful I was to Vania that God had impressed on her a sense of urgency. That day, my husband carried in a package for me. It was an early birthday present. Inside was an assortment of gifts, including a little book, *One Minute With God for Women*. After enjoying some of the goodies, I looked at the book and began to read the first devotional. Its title was "Finding Your Voice."

God knows each of our voices when we pray to Him. In this case, He had used someone else's voice to pray that last prayer with Danis.

Rita Kay Stevens

Rain

Rejoice in the LORD your God,
for he has given you the . . .
rains because he is faithful.
—*Joel 2:23, NIV*

As our church youth club packed cars for a weekend camping trip, the children were excited about the adventure awaiting them. We traveled to our destination in a caravan. During our trip, rain started to fall. By the time we reached our campsite, we were in a heavy downpour with lots of lightning and thunder up in the dark, cloudy sky. The children happily set up their tents in spite of the bad weather conditions.

By midnight, the children's tents, sleeping bags, and clothes were soaking wet. The children were cold and miserable. We moved them to a pavilion, but the conditions only got worse. When the camp ranger said we could expect rain for the rest of the weekend, we packed up all the soggy clothes and camp gear and headed home.

Six lovely girls, ages ten through twelve, were riding in my car. I listened to them singing and talking happily about what was going on in their lives. One topic was how they could get their parents to give them what they wanted. They suddenly became aware that I was listening to them. They fiercely begged me not to tell their parents what I had overheard. I assured them I would not tell their parents, as they had probably figured it all out already.

The girls' comments made me think about how we too often try to manipulate God to do what we want. Yet He knows that what we want is not always the best; His way is best.

The girls quickly moved on to the topic of how disappointed they were that the rain had spoiled their weekend of fun and adventure. I couldn't help thinking that just as rain came during that camping trip, we also need God to send a downpour of rain into our lives. We need Him to wash away the drought of sin in our dry, dusty hearts. His words are like refreshing rain for thirsty hearts. He promises that the well of our hearts will never run dry if we fill it up with His holy Words of instruction and promises.

The little tender fruit-bearing plants in our lives "dry out" fast if they are not watered with God's Word and prayer. God will guide and give us renewal if we will trust Him to do so.

Let's keep our hearts healthy and hydrated with His rain.

Carolyn Voss

December 14

Holding On to God

Live creatively, friends. If someone falls . . . ,
forgivingly restore him, saving your critical comments for yourself. . . .
Stoop down and reach out to those who are oppressed.
Share their burdens, and so complete Christ's law.
—*Galatians 6:1, 2,* The Message

We were driving back after visiting our precious granddaughter when we encountered heavy rains. We could barely see the car in front of us and had to slow down significantly to make sure we were still going the right direction. We prayed for our Redeemer's guidance. We asked Him to hold us as we passed through the storm that ended up taking many other lives.

This experience got me to thinking about a lady who is going through relationship issues. Depressed, she does not see any way out because she has no family to confide in and has been carrying the burden on her shoulders. All she is seeing right now is a very foggy road. She does not even know which direction to take. Unfortunately, she is not the only one in this world needing a precious friend to hold her hand as she passes through a life storm.

At one time or another, all of us have gone—or will go—through challenges in our personal lives, times when we will not be able see a way forward or how we are going to sort out our situations. In those times, all looks so dark and gloomy that we don't know what to do or where to go. Sometimes we even forget that it is only by letting God carry us through that storm that we are able to get through these foggy, rainy days.

In the Bible we find stories of many faithful and courageous women. One is Esther. In her time, women were to be seen but not heard. Because of a godly upbringing by her cousin and being chosen by the Persian king to be his queen, Esther had no doubt God had put her where she was for a purpose—to save her people when the situation was so dim that none of them knew what to do. Esther knew, however, that only the faithful Jehovah would help her people. So she and a few others fasted and prayed for several days. God heard and rescued His people.

God has also put you in a place where you can hold someone's hand while you help them through the darkest moments of their lives. This is a responsibility for all of us if we would fulfill His command to love others as ourselves. May the Lord lead you to someone today—maybe someone who is oppressed and needs to be held by you as you continue to hold on to God.

Judith M. Mwansa

Winter Fog

*For now we see through a glass, darkly; but then face to face:
now I know in part; but then shall I know even as also I am known.*
—*1 Corinthians 13:12*

While living for years in California's San Joaquin Valley, I detested its icy, thick, whiteout winter fog. Then, last week I caught a TV news segment about the fog.

REPORTER: Is the current drought why your nut harvest decreased almost fifty percent this year?

PISTACHIO NUT FARMER: Yes. You see, without enough rain and cold moisture in the air, there's been almost no icy fog to speak of. We definitely *need* those long, cold foggy seasons!

No way! I thought. *Do you mean to tell me that that horrible valley-wide, bone-chilling winter fog I hated for all those years actually had a* purpose? Now I was all ears!

REPORTER: What does cold fog, of all things, have to do with your pistachio crops?

PISTACHIO NUT FARMER: Without those days-long fogs, we haven't enough of what we call "chilling hours" to put the trees "to sleep" so the male trees can "wake up" in sync with the female trees for pollination. Winter fog ensures a productive spring and summer *growing* season.

Then I remembered other foggy—and growing—seasons in life. Seasons of uncertainty when we can't see through the fog of today . . . into tomorrow. How we chafe at the unknowns that slow us down and block a clear view of where we're going—or even of where we are!

Know what? I am so glad that God has eyes that *can* see through the fog during those hostile life seasons when He knows that we can't! Paul writes, "We can see and understand only a little about God now, as if we were peering at his reflection in a poor mirror; but someday we are going to see him in his completeness, face-to-face. Now all that I know is hazy and blurred [ah, like fog!], but then I will see everything clearly, just as clearly as God sees into my heart right now" (1 Corinthians 13:12, TLB).

When we are tempted to be discouraged because all we can see and feel around us is an impenetrable, bone-chilling fog—caused by illness, a broken relationship, financial distress, or even the aging process—perhaps it would help if we remembered that God, in our personal "orchards," can still see through that fog to the pistachio trees. And what's happening *there* during those "chilling hours" is how He is preparing *us* for our next productive season of growth.

Carolyn Rathbun Sutton

December 16

Holiday Intruder

The angel of the LORD encamps around those who fear him,
and he delivers them.
—Psalm 34:7, NIV

December 16 is a South African holiday. Many couples choose to get married on that holiday. My friend in east London phoned me to say her son was getting married that day. In thought, I anticipated the excitement that would be going on in that part of the world that day.

It was eleven thirty in the morning as I sat in my study and then heard screeching sounds. I went to the windows to check but could not see anything or anybody around. I returned to the study. After a short while, I heard more noise: the sound of breaking glass. Since I can't see behind the high wall separating my house from the neighbor's, I thought, *They're probably busy over there.*

At noon, midday, I entered my kitchen. That's when I saw a young man looking through my kitchen window! Because my kitchen blind was slightly open, I could see him, but he couldn't see me. I banged on the window through the blinds and shouted hysterically, "What are you doing in here?" He immediately fled, without saying a word.

My yard had been enclosed from top to bottom for my security and safety, so I never expected anyone would be able to enter it. The young man, however, had found a very narrow opening where the razor wire had come to an end. He had somehow wiggled in and slid down from the roof onto my enclosed garden, gaining entry from there.

Because of the positioning of my house, I could not see that side of my yard. So I had looked through all the windows on the *other* side of the house that faced the park. The intruder had smashed a bedroom window that faces the yard. Yet he couldn't gain entrance to my house because of the burglar bar. When I entered the kitchen, he was about to smash my kitchen window. My kitchen door was locked; otherwise, he would have gotten into my house without my knowledge. I never ever expected anyone would get into my secured yard! I shuddered to think of what could have happened.

I thank God and His angels for keeping me safe. "With all my heart I will praise you, O Lord my God. I will give glory to your name forever, for your love for me is very great. You have rescued me from the depths of death" (Psalm 86:12, 13, NLT).

Priscilla E. Adonis

Stupid Situational Sin

I acknowledge my sin unto thee, and mine iniquity have I not hid.
I said, I will confess my transgressions unto the LORD;
and thou forgavest the iniquity of my sin.
—*Psalm 32:5*

When the church was being built at a large Christian college in Michigan, I was a student living in one of the campus residence halls. I enjoyed looking out the windows and watching the progress of the new building. I remember when the trusses for the roof were delivered and laid on the ground. It seemed like ages before the church would be completed.

One day when the structure was nearing completion, I had a little free time and decided to take a walk around the building that would soon be my new church. It was a beautiful spring morning, perfect for a short walk before class and then work.

I was amazed to find that the sidewalks had already been poured on the other side of the new church building. As I absentmindedly stepped onto one, I realized I was beginning to sink! Not only did my feet sink in wet cement, but my heart sank also.

As I quickly moved off the cement, I viewed my footprints. If ever you could actually witness your own sins, this was a visual notice. There before me were my "sin" footprints. My heart melted. I was near tears to think they would remain for everyone to see in years to come.

Just then, I noticed a group of workers troweling the wet cement some distance away. One of the men came over and gently removed my stupid footprints from the sidewalk. I apologized over and over. He was very kind and not angry with me at all—and very forgiving.

Shortly after my careless adventure, I met the son of the kind man. We quickly became friends. After several months of dating, he asked me to marry him. A year later, we were married. That's how the cement worker became my father in law. A sister-in-law later told me that he had encouraged his son to date me, after meeting me, and had even paid for our first date.

What a wonderful family to marry into! What a wonderful family of Jesus that took me in and forgave other sinful footprints as I trod through life.

Thank you, Jesus, for forgiving us our sins (whether stupid or purposeful) as we confess them, acknowledge them, and ask forgiveness. We look forward to living with You throughout eternity.

Avonda White-Krause

December 18

Midnight Sun

"Your sun will never set again."
—Isaiah 60:20, NIV

We studied about the 'midnight sun' in geography class today," said Melissa, skipping along beside me. "Does the sun really shine at midnight in the land of the midnight sun? Does it never set? Have you ever seen it?" Questions tumbled out one after another.

"Matter of fact, I have seen the midnight sun," I replied. "Once. When I was lecturing in Iceland. On the same road trip when my friend, Unnur, and I—like sheep—went astray."

"I remember that story," said Melissa, laughing. "What was it like?"

"Going astray?" I asked innocently.

"No!" said Melissa. "I know *that* story. The *midnight sun!*"

"Oh," I replied, smiling. "It was amazing, actually. One moment we were driving along in a valley, and the next we were on the crest of an Icelandic mountain, and there it was, right in front of us: a huge bloodred ball of fire hovering above the horizon. As we watched, the ball of fire slowly began to sink, down, down, until half of it was buried below the horizon. And then it stopped, almost exactly at the stroke of midnight. And there it stayed."

"You mean it never set?" cried Melissa. "Never disappeared below the horizon?" I nodded. "But that meant there was no night!" said Melissa, an inflection of awe in her voice.

"Pretty much," I replied. "Over the next couple hours, whenever there was a break in the clouds or when we crested another hill, that fiery half-ball seemed to be moving horizontally, west to east. A couple hours later, the sun began to rise up into the sky, changing gradually from fiery bloodred to a glistening globe of gold. It was a magical, once-in-a-lifetime memory."

"Like there'll be no night in the New Jerusalem," mused Melissa. "Now you have an idea of what that will be like."

"You might find a picture of Iceland's midnight sun on the Internet," I suggested, as we turned into our cul-de-sac. Like a flash, Melissa was running up the sidewalk to the front door to access her computer. Following a bit more slowly, it was my turn to muse. *No more night and no more need for sun because the Lord God will give us light* (see Revelation 22:5).

Yes. Now I have an idea of what that might be like.

Arlene R. Taylor

The Invitation

*For the wages of sin is death; but the gift of God
is eternal life through Jesus Christ our Lord.*
—*Romans 6:23*

Crowds gathered in the vestibule. Unmistakable excitement filled the air as expectant concertgoers quickly filled up auditorium seats. Lights dimmed, and the prestigious conductor raised his baton. A hush fell over the concert hall. Soon proficient and melodic voices rose to the occasion. Their performance was exceptional. My heart thrilled as the combined voices in the chorus delighted us with Handel's *Messiah*.

A benevolent neighbor had called and graciously informed us that he had purchased concert tickets as a Christmas gift for my husband and me! You can just imagine our exhilaration as we waited for the night of the scheduled concert. And now the scheduled evening had finally arrived, and no one was disappointed—except our gracious host.

You see, other invited guests for whom our neighbor had also purchased tickets simply failed to show up for the concert. What a wonderful opportunity they missed!

On the way home from the concert, I contemplated what the absentees had missed out on. Yet I realized that is the way some of *us* may have responded to the invitation of Jesus to come to Him for salvation. The Son of God bids us, "Come unto me, all ye that labour and are heavy laden, and I will give you rest. Take my yoke upon you, and learn of me; for I am meek and lowly in heart: and ye shall find rest unto your souls" (Matthew 11:28, 29).

Oh, what a wonderful gift Jesus offers us! He has already paid the price and made all the arrangements. All we have to do is accept His gracious and loving gift.

Yet multitudes of precious souls who say they want what Jesus has to offer will turn their backs on Him for the attractions of this world rather than follow Him into eternity. All will have opportunity to hear of our Savior's life, sacrificial death on the cross for our sins, and miraculous resurrection from the cold, dark tomb. All are invited to know of His ministry in heaven for the precious saints who claim His "ticket" to the Second Coming and trip to His celestial home.

Invite everyone you know to the coming concert of the original and real Messiah, Jesus Christ. Let's not miss this event, for it is sure to thrill one and all!

Cathy Shannon

Strength

"Be not dismayed, for I am your God.
I will strengthen you, yes, I will help you."
—*Isaiah 41:10, NKJV*

I am ready to leave for Nairobi this morning. Bags and many other things are part of this long trip. When I look at my list of tasks that still need to be accomplished, I recognize that I am not powerful enough to do it all by myself. There are times when we come to the point of realizing that trying hard, harder, and our hardest is not enough—times when we need more than physical, emotional, and spiritual strength. We need strength to endure pain and loss in life; we need strength to face fear or make difficult decisions. Many of us need strength to love those who have not loved us—and strength to say No or Yes, in order to have a balanced life.

But in the Word of God we have a message of hope: God is strong. This, for me, is enough. God offers to be our strength. "Do not fear, for I am with you," God says (Isaiah 41:10, NIV). To let God be our strength is to let Him take over our lives so that we can hear the words, "Be still. I am God" (see Psalm 46:10).

As I meditated on Isaiah 41:10, the sentence "I will strengthen you, yes, I will help you" (NKJV) captured my attention. I found myself praying, *Lord, I need the kind of strength only You can give. I need this help, Jesus. Will You please help me?*

Yes, strength is the energy that God gives us to complete a task. It is what helps us endure to the end. What better place to get strength than from God? He is able to provide all the strength we need in order to accomplish what He calls us to do.

Today, as you claim this promise, remember this: Be still. Don't give up. You don't need to understand the entire journey. The only thing you need to know is that if you look to Jesus, He will give you enough strength to move on through this day.

A life in Christ is a life with strength. Why? Because our hope is not in ourselves, but in Him. When we are weak, His strength is ours. Let's live with this assurance and embrace the reality that what God says, He will do it for us. We can live each day united to His strength.

As you look to the day ahead of you, be grateful. You are alive. Provision is available for the journey. You are not alone. "Be not be dismayed, for I am your God. I will strengthen you, yes, I will help you" (Isaiah 41:10, NKJV).

Are you ready for your day? If not, God is. And He has promised to be *your* strength.

Raquel Queiroz da Costa Arrais

Mary—an Example of Faith and Humility

And the angel came in unto her, and said, Hail, thou that art highly
favoured, the Lord is with thee: blessed art thou among women.
—Luke 1:28

To be highly favored by earthly monarchs is one thing, but to be blessed and highly favored and to enjoy the presence and companionship of the Most High God is beyond human comprehension. Such was the enviable position in which Mary, a poor, humble Jewish girl from the obscure city of Nazareth, found herself.

While going about her normal routine one day, Mary's life was interrupted by a heavenly visitant who declared that she was highly favored and blessed. God was with her. The angel further explained that Mary would carry and then give birth to a son who would be the Savior of the world.

Amazed, Mary humbly inquired of the angel how it was possible for her to be pregnant, since she had never engaged in sexual intercourse. After receiving clarification from the angel as to how she, a virgin, could be with child, Mary then submitted to the will of God. I suspect that submitting to God must have been a lifestyle for Mary. Notice that she did not argue with the angel. She did not say, "I am too young. My girlfriends will laugh at me. My family will be disappointed in me. Society will reject me." Or, "My fiancé will put me away for being pregnant out of marriage." God's will transcended Mary's personal concerns. No doubt, the Holy Spirit was accustomed to making His residence in her heart, so it was not difficult for Him to continue accomplishing God's will in and through her. After all, Mary's body was the temple of the Holy Ghost.

Consequently, Mary said to the angel, "Behold the handmaid of the Lord; be it unto me according to thy word" (Luke 1:38). What humility! What faith! What submission to the perfect will of God! She did not fully comprehend the assignment that she was called to fulfill, yet she willingly submitted to God's divine mandate. She was willing to place her fate in His hands.

Today God is seeking for women of faith and humility on whom He can bestow His favor, His blessings, and His divine presence—women He can use to fulfill His purposes. Ours is the blessed privilege to say to God, "Take my life, and let it be consecrated, Lord, to Thee."

Gerene I. Joseph

Light of the World

Ye are the light of the world.
—*Matthew 5:14*

I love light. I love the flashlight's glow in the pitch darkness when the wind howls outside and the power has gone off. I love the mellow outdoor lights that welcome me home even with scary insects fluttering about that I must chase away before I can turn the key in the lock to open the door. Bright lights, colored lights . . . I love them all.

My favorites are the lights of Christmas. Twinkling white lights, wired to look like reindeer munching grass on a field of bright colors. Some lights send a cheery message, brightly spelling out "Merry Christmas" or "Peace on Earth." Other lights appear to have been randomly placed, draped over verandas, roofs, or bushes, with no order or pattern, yet twinkling cheerily.

Recently Christmas lights took on even more significance for me. December 26 found me on a fourteen-hour road trip. Tired and sleepy after about ten hours of riding, I began to doze. I really should have stayed awake to provide company for the drivers in the front seats, but drowsiness took over. That is, until I noticed—really noticed—the lights that we were passing. Everywhere I saw them, both in the large towns and on isolated homesteads. There were gorgeous, formal, Christmas displays, as well as wintry, lighted-letter holiday greetings. And, of course, the randomly placed, but still shining, "artistic" disasters.

Sleep left me as I focused on the lights and absorbed the message they brought to me. So many of the displays, being *Christmas* lights, pointed to Christ, the Light of the world. What a difference His coming has made, not only many years ago in Bethlehem but also during the ages since then, leading up to today! The angels. The star. They lit up the skies of Bethlehem, pointing to the One who would put an end to the dark despair so often experienced by the human race.

Did Christ not say to all who would believe in Him, "Ye are the light of the world" (Matthew 5:14)? That means that some of us are the bright "professional" lights—administrators, directors, and pastors. Some of us shine, not necessarily as leaders but in our lives and words, declaring, "Jesus, the crucified and risen Light of the world, is coming again soon." Others of us may feel like randomly placed lights, yet we are happy to shine quietly for Jesus. Wherever God has placed you, let your light shine on those who walk in darkness. Reflect the true Light of the world.

Annette Walwyn Michael

Good Gifts

"If you, then, though you are evil,
know how to give good gifts to your children,
how much more will your Father in heaven
give good gifts to those who ask him!"
—*Matthew 7:11, NIV*

B irthdays. Valentine's Day. Thanksgiving. Christmas. These occasions always keep me busy wondering what gifts I can get for my family, friends, church family, or colleagues.

When I was a little younger, I would have it all planned. From the very beginning of any given year, I had a list of those for whom I would need to get gifts. Then, when I shopped and saw some good sale items, I would purchase them for gifts to keep for the appropriate occasions. As one gets older, though, giving gifts becomes a little more challenging.

This Christmas is one of those that came just too soon for me. Due to my extensive travel and other responsibilities, I have not really prepared the gifts for my immediate family. So I experienced an "eleventh hour" rush to find gifts. Buying gifts is easy if you know what to buy; it becomes harder when you don't have any idea what to get.

Because I don't have enough time and I am rushing, my mind cannot even think, *What gift can I get for my granddaughters?*

I went to several stores but couldn't find something really meaningful for them. I had started out by going online and getting some ideas as to what to purchase. I found many ideas, but they were not my ideas. I wanted to get things that my granddaughters would treasure. Well, I was in a dilemma. Finally I decided to write a check. That was not my first choice as a gift, but it was the best I could do in that situation.

This experience made me think of the gifts that God has given to us: our families, children, grandchildren, and friends. Most of all, He gave us the most precious gift, His only begotten Son. "This is how God showed his love among us: He sent his one and only Son into the world that we might live through him" (1 John 4:9, NIV). As a Giver of good gifts, God made preparation right from the very beginning! He planned for our Gift well ahead of time!

Indeed, God is truly a Giver of good and precious gifts. Today may we be reminded of His love and treasure the gifts that He has given to us. May we thank Him.

Above all, may we praise Him for the precious gift of His Son!

Jemima Dollosa Orillosa

Crowded in the Stable

So it was, when the angels had gone away from them into heaven,
that the shepherds said to one another, "Let us now go to Bethlehem
and see this thing that has come to pass, which the Lord has made
known to us." And they came with haste and found Mary and
Joseph, and the Babe lying in a manger.
—Luke 2:15, 16, NKJV

The picture of this past Christmas will stay with me for a long time. Or at least I hope it will. I planned to share the Christmas story at my home church and decided to include my nine-year-old niece, Kaleigh, and eight-year-old nephew, Mason. Kaleigh would read the Scripture passages, and Mason would put each figurine in the Nativity scene. We talked about each figurine. I pointed out who Joseph was.

"That doesn't look like Joseph," he responded. I smiled but didn't ask how he knew what Joseph looked like. He was taking this seriously, and I wanted to make sure he understood what to do so he wouldn't be too nervous. I didn't realize how seriously he had taken my instructions. Or how literally. The story moved quickly. Kaleigh was reading the passage about the three wise men, when I finally turned around to see the Nativity scene Mason had created. Mason didn't put things quite the way I thought he would. In my mind, Joseph and Mary go *in* the stable. The shepherds and sheep, as well as the wise men, all go just *outside* the stable. That makes for a pretty picture. Mason's Nativity might not have been as picturesque, but it was so much better.

Mary and Joseph were in the stable by Jesus. So were the shepherds. And all the animals. And all three wise men. It was pretty crowded around that manger. Every figurine huddled tightly to worship the newborn King. I had instructed Mason to put them in the Nativity. And he had! Not sure how he managed to get them all squeezed in. But there they were.

As I later reflected on Mason's Nativity scene, I wondered, What would it be if this was a picture of us today? Each of us crowding in as close to Jesus as we can get, in awe of the miracle before us? Wanting to worship and understand what His birth—and death and resurrection—means for us? I want that. I'm praying for it. That I and others will want to get as close to Jesus as we can. And then that we'll crowd in together to worship. I want to live out Mason's picture.

And I just may set my Nativity up that way each Christmas as a reminder.

Tamyra (Tami) Horst

My Son!

For unto us a Child is born,
unto us a Son is given.
—Isaiah 9:6, NKJV

As I looked into His laughing eyes, it was an unbelievable feeling knowing that my son—my firstborn—was the One chosen to save mankind. How could all this have happened within the past nine months?

Holding the nursing Baby Jesus against my breast, I began reminiscing over the past unimaginable months. I had been so excited about my perfectly planned and romantic Jewish wedding celebration. Then the words from the angel who visited me: "Do not be afraid, Mary, you have found favor with God. You will give birth to a son."

I asked how that could be possible, since I was a virgin. The angel told me not to be afraid. "I am the Lord's servant," I answered in submission to God's will. "May it be to me as you have said." Then the angel left me (based on Luke 1:30, 31, 34, 38).

This was a horrible time for me. I was numb with the thought of being the mother of *the* Immanuel. I was frightened, not knowing when I would feel the first stone thrown at me for being pregnant out of wedlock. I was lonely for Joseph's comforting embrace. How could I be a mother before becoming a wife? I couldn't make sense out of this. And my son, as the Savior of the world . . . how much pain would He go through? How much rejection would He experience? How could I watch all this happen to Him, knowing that . . . ?

The baby, wiggling and crying now on the straw bed that Joseph fixed for Him, brought me back to the reality of the present. No, the smell of the cattle, sheep, and camels around His makeshift crib wasn't what I had envisioned for Him.

As I ran my fingers over the soft tiny fingers, I imagined how many people those hands would touch, making them physically and spiritually whole. Counting His ten toes, I could almost hear His footsteps along the rough, rugged pathways He would walk. Ah, His heart beating so rapidly—how often my heart would be broken realizing that His passionate heart of love would be the one broken for all sinners (including me).

My son! My firstborn son! I loved Him with a mother's love! I accepted Him! My son!

And my Savior! Have you accepted His love this Christmas season?

Mary L. Maxson

December 26

Tsunami!

For as the heavens are high above the earth,
so great is His mercy toward those who fear Him.
—*Psalm 103:11, NKJV*

During the 2004–2005 school year, I served as a student missionary in India. I was beyond excited when my parents and sister told me that they were going to come visit me at Christmastime! I planned an itinerary full of interesting places to see and things to do. Because of their short trip, they wouldn't be able to see the Taj Mahal, so I wanted to take them someplace special in south India instead. I'd heard about the beautiful beaches in Pondicherry, so I planned a trip to the ocean.

My family landed in Chennai, Tamil Nadu, and then traveled with me on a six-hour train ride to the village where I was living. Because Christmas fell on a Sabbath that year, we celebrated the holiday with the children and staff at the orphanage a few days early. My home church in New England had bought dozens of gifts for the children, sending them over with my family. How excited and joyful the children were as they opened their Christmas presents!

Then my father, who is rarely sick, began to feel unwell. I had planned that after our December 25 worship at the orphanage church, we would take a night train to Pondicherry so that we could be at the beach Sunday morning. As my father grew more ill, we reluctantly canceled the trip to Pondicherry. Dad simply was not up to another long train ride.

On Sunday, December 26, a massive earthquake in the Indian Ocean triggered a devastating tsunami. Because news reports largely focused on the destruction in Indonesia and Sri Lanka, people often forget that more than 18,000 people in India also died on that tragic day. My family and I could very well have been among that number had we been at the beach that fateful Sunday morning! By God's grace and divine providence, we were *not* there.

Many times we have our own agendas and forget that God's plans are best. We may never know, this side of heaven, how often our plans have failed so that our lives (physically or spiritually) could be saved.

I thank the Lord for His protection and deliverance throughout my life. Surely "He is my refuge and my fortress: my God; in him will I trust" (Psalm 91:2). Is He your refuge too?

Amanda N. Gaspard

The Better Way

The words of a gossip are like tasty bits of food;
people like to gobble them up.
—Proverbs 26:22, NCV

My husband opened the passenger door, since there was a bit of snow and black ice on the ground. Then he carefully helped me to the employee entrance. I thanked him, and then after a quick kiss, I entered the building as he drove off. As the elevator took me to the third floor, my mind wondered about the people that might have watched us: "Is she that helpless that she can't even get out of the car by herself?" one person walking through the parking lot might have said. Another might ponder, "Whoa, what happened to her? Fifteen years ago she worked out in the gym and looked fabulous. Not now!"

How often is it that we ourselves are muttering thoughts about what we saw or thought we saw? Something that we just have to tell somebody about! Those words we speak—whether spoken in love or because we gossip for the pure joy of it—could cut deeply into someone's heart. Is it our business to surmise and add our personal perspective on someone else's circumstances? Not one of us ever knows the real story about someone else, only what we perceive, which is not always truth! Maybe there's some truth in it. Maybe not. Until we come to know a person and have a relationship that grows from mere acquaintance to good friend, we are simply guessing. Words we utter, either to someone's face or behind that person's back, cannot be taken back and can have a devastating and long-lasting effect on them or those who love them.

Many times, words fall loosely from our lips in jest, out of ignorance, or because we really do want to say something hurtful. And I ask, Is that the way a Christian should be in conversation?

Jesus spoke many words with, to, and about countless people—words of encouragement, words of affirmation, words of life! In all that He did, He knew the life circumstances of the person and showed His care in what He uttered publicly. Even with those who had done wrong things that, unfortunately, took them down rough and rugged pathways, He offered a better way through His words of encouragement and hope.

Dear ones, with the love of Jesus—the best Friend any of us could ever have—and by His example, let us lift up someone else by the words we speak. He has shown us the better way!

Iris L. Kitching

"And He Shall Hear My Voice"

Evening and morning and at noon I will pray,
and cry aloud, and He shall hear my voice.
—*Psalm 55:17, NKJV*

This past holiday season, I was reminded of the power of women of prayer. We were gathered together as a family in worship on the first day of the new year. One by one, we started sharing the reasons for which we were especially grateful to have God in our lives. As I listened to the moving, heartfelt praises, I realized that much of what we shared were direct answers to the prayers of my late grandmother. As a child, I watched my grandma frequently kneel down for her prayers at home. She prayed first thing after she got up in the morning. Then after reading her Bible in bed, she would kneel for what seemed to me a never-ending time in prayer. Though not understanding, I was impressed by the whispered mumblings, often mixed with sighs and tears.

To my pleasant surprise, however, she would always get up from prayer with a smile, greet me with a warm hug, and go about her duties with joy, humming a tune, always with kind and loving words to share. Every time we would leave the house or come back from running an errand, we would kneel down again and ask—or thank—God for His protection. At noon, she would invite us kids to come and kneel with her to pray. Sometimes we would rather be playing. She would then go alone, kneel, and pray. The same routine happened later in the evening. Back then, I wondered whether all that praying was a bit excessive—sometimes I felt reluctant to join her.

I listened to my family members' list of praises—one for returning to God, another for understanding God's love after Bible studies with my grandpa, another for walking after a serious spinal injury, others for the godly influence of our grandparents, others were thankful for having received and accepted the call to ministry—I realized that Grandma's prayers were perhaps the reason why we were all together worshiping God in thanksgiving. Those memories renewed in me the desire to follow my grandma's example and set aside more time—at least three times a day—to kneel and pray.

I don't know what burdens you may have in your life today as a mother, grandmother, wife, or single woman, but I invite you to consider adding more prayer time into your daily routine. God's promise is true, and you can tell the world like David: "He shall hear my voice!" (Psalm 55:17, NKJV).

Katia Garcia Reinert

Where Is Your Faith?

"If you then, being evil, know how to give good gifts to your children, how much more will your heavenly Father give the Holy Spirit to those who ask Him!"
—Luke 11:13, NKJV

While my husband, Verne, and I were serving as missionaries in the Palau Islands, our church appointed me as Women's Ministries director for the Micronesia Island area—an area comprising more than 2,100 island nations dotted over 3,000 square miles of the South Pacific Ocean. Wherever I traveled, women kept asking, "Can we have a women's retreat? We've never had one." Yet how could hundreds of women, with barely enough resources to provide for their own families, afford to fly to Guam and stay four days in a hotel for a women's retreat?

Oh, Lord God, I pleaded, *where could we ever find funding for all these wonderful island sisters?* In response, I heard, *Where is your faith?* I was impressed to send out e-mails requesting retreat "scholarships." Then, our newly organized retreat committee began to fast and pray. During that time, God impressed me to ask a dear friend in Oregon to be our keynote speaker, though we couldn't pay her airfare or lodging. She assured me that God would provide.

He did! Just three weeks after Christmas, planeloads of women from the far corners of the South Pacific landed at Guam's largest airport. Many had sold their own clothes and possessions and eaten only one meal a day in order to save for their airfare and hotel expenses. As the various island groups—wearing matching, colorful floor-length dresses—filed into the first evening's meeting, the very air was charged with anticipation. The queen of Palau and her daughter were present, as well as another honored guest, the popular lady governor of Guam.

A hush fell over the great ballroom as I rose to welcome more than five hundred dear sisters from all the island groups. Never have I ever experienced such Holy Spirit power as I felt that evening! In response to our weeks of prayer and fasting, God was ready to pour out *His* supreme blessing. Our speaker spoke on "holiness to the Lord." The presentation brought both tears and shouts of "praise the Lord!" During those four days, the outpouring of God's Spirit surprised and refreshed us—friendships were mended and healings experienced! Most of all . . . revival came!

What is God calling you to do for which your faith "feels" small right now? Start with prayer. Fast. In His time and through His resources, He will make a way—with untold blessings.

Patty L. Hyland

The Power of a Woman's Prayer

Do not be anxious about anything, but in every situation,
by prayer and petition, with thanksgiving, present your requests
to God. And the peace of God, which transcends all understanding,
will guard your hearts and your minds in Christ Jesus.
—*Philippians 4:6, 7, NIV*

D o you ever feel that God does not hear your prayers? Do you become impatient because you don't see immediate results to your prayers? Robert, along with two sisters, was raised in a conservative Christian household in the early 1900s. His parents taught them of God's love. When Robert became a teenager, however, he hung out with friends who drank, smoke, gambled, and partied nightly. Yet Robert's mother continued to pray for him, especially through his hospitalization following a horrific motorcycle accident. Eventually Robert married a girl who loved partying as much as he did. His mother continued to pray.

One day, a Christian book salesman came to his door while he was at work and sold his wife a copy of Ellen White's *The Desire of Ages*, a book about the life of Christ. While reading the book, Robert's wife gave her heart to the Lord. Angered, Robert tried to keep her from attending church. Yet his mother continued to pray for them both until she passed away.

When three children were born into Robert's home, his wife raised them to love the Lord. When Robert refused to pay for their Christian education, his wife got a job and paid their tuition. She, along with Robert's two sisters, continued to pray for this man. Robert's two sons became ministers, and his daughter grew up to become very active in the church. While his family attended church, Robert stayed home to watch TV, do yard work, or play poker with his friends.

One Friday night, Robert—now more than seventy years old—agreed to accompany his wife to church because he was concerned for her safety while traveling alone after dark. That evening, the words of a visiting evangelist touched and softened Robert's heart. He was soon baptized by both of his sons! Although Robert, my grandfather, died of a massive heart attack one year later, he remained faithful in his new commitment right up to the end and died in the arms of Jesus.

Too often we are tempted to give up praying when we don't see immediate answers to our prayers. Though God's answers may not come quickly or in ways we expect, we can trust that He hears and will give us peace as we wait.

Terri Lutz

All Things New!

"Behold, I make all things new."
—Revelation 21:5, NKJV

In New York City on December 31, I looked in awe at a giant shredder set up on a street corner in Times Square (Manhattan) in commemoration of Good Riddance Day.

The shredder was part of a tradition that offered individuals an opportunity to say "good riddance!" to all the unpleasantness of the preceding year. On this bitterly cold day, people of differing races and creeds—male and female, young and old—lined up holding bank statements, credit cards and reports, eviction notices, and medical reports and bills. I saw one girl hobbling along on a pair of crutches. She held a sheet of construction paper on which were written the words, "Good Riddance to My Crutches!" This throng of hundreds was waiting to have unpleasant parts of their lives shredded and gone. I marveled at this amazing sight!

Yet many families had struggled through the past year with broken hearts and marriages, health and financial concerns, straying children, and escalating fears. Hope seemed all but lost. People were grabbing at this opportunity to start anew, even if for only a moment. With this symbolic shredding experience, they hoped to erase every bad memory of the past year. They hoped to eliminate the source of their brokenness and embrace the hope of a new beginning.

Isn't this "shredder" experience just what our heavenly Father offers us when He asks us to surrender our lives into *His* keeping? He offers us new hope, a new beginning. He promises to one day vanquish our hurt and pain, erase our fears, and destroy all that afflicts us. Isn't it worth the effort to plunge the broken things in your life into the healing blood of Jesus, His Son?

God says, "See, I will create new heavens and a new earth. The former things will not be remembered, nor will they come to mind" (Isaiah 65:17, NIV). Our Father promises He "will wipe away every tear from [our] eyes; there shall be no more death, nor sorrow, nor crying. There shall be no more pain, for the former things have passed away" (Revelation 21:4, NKJV). He offers us a clear promise of hope when He says, "Behold, I make all things new" (verse 5).

Dearest Father, I choose to believe Your promise to make all things new. I give You everything that is broken in my life today. I thank You for the hope of a new beginning. In Jesus' name I pray. Amen!

Shanter H. Alexander

2018 Author Biographies

Tabitha Abel is an avid outdoors person and involved in outreach, teaching, and music ministries in her church in Chiloquin, Oregon, United States of America. A semiretired health professional, Dr. T. is also a freelance writer and Christian speaker. Find her at TabithaAbel.webs.com. **Apr. 10, July 1**

Betty J. Adams is a retired teacher in California, United States of America. She has been married for more than sixty-one years and has five children, seven grandchildren, and three great-grandchildren. She has written for her church newsletter and *Guide*, and works for her church community services ministry. She enjoys gardening, scrapbooking, and her grandchildren. **June 4**

Priscilla E. Adonis writes from Cape Town, South Africa. She likes writing, card making, and working in the flower garden. She has two daughters and two grandsons that live in the United States of America. As a widow, she thanks God daily for keeping her safe and for His blessings on her. **June 14, Dec. 16**

Harryette Aitken loves to travel and has coordinated group tours to the Middle East and Europe. She and her pastor husband, John, live in southern California, United States of America, where she assists her husband in ministry. She's served her church in many capacities, her last position being a development director for a North American Division ministry. Her greatest joy in life is being a grandmother to two precious boys, John III and James. **Feb. 27, July 7**

Shanter H. Alexander is a licensed psychologist and certified autism specialist. She lives in Berrien Springs, Michigan, United States of America, and enjoys travel, public speaking, cooking, and long walks in the beauty of nature. **Jan. 13, Dec. 31**

Dorett Alleyne lives in Palm Bay, Florida, United States of America, with her husband, and they are parents of three wonderful young adults. She is a senior laboratory technologist who loves to sing, cook, organize and plan, watch old movies, and play puzzle games. She is currently a member of the praise team, the choir, and a female quartet in her church. Her prayer is to become more like Christ each day and to be a more effective instrument for Him. **May 6**

Deniece G. Anderson is a registered nurse living in Atlanta, Georgia, United States of America. Her motto is, "If I can help somebody as I pass along, then my living shall not be in vain." **Mar. 13**

Sue Anderson retired from the United States Department of Agriculture, Forest Service. She's been married to Chuck for fifty-two years. Living in the Pacific Northwest of the United States of America, they have two married daughters, a granddaughter, two grandsons, and two great-grandsons. She enjoys writing and spending time with family and friends. **July 20, Nov. 7**

Ellen Diniz de Andrade is a native of Brazil. She practices medicine. She likes to read, study, and run. She also enjoys being out in nature and with family and friends. **May 13**

Simonette Appleton has two sons, two daughters-in-law, and a brand-new granddaughter,

Naomi Simonette. Her husband recently retired from the United States Army. They attend the Killeen New Hope Seventh-day Adventist Church in Texas, United States of America, where she is treasurer. She teaches full time. During the summer, she engages in her passions of reading and traveling. She is a brand-new writer. **Feb. 1**

Patsy Arrabito is a film producer living in Angwin, California, United States of America. Her loves in life are her children and grandchildren, travel, and gardening. She is waiting eagerly and hopefully for Jesus to come. **Jan. 5**

Raquel Queiroz da Costa Arrais is a minister's wife who developed her ministry as an educator for twenty years. Currently she works as associate director of the General Conference Women's Ministries department. She has two adult sons, two daughters-in-law, and three adored grandchildren. Her greatest pleasures are being with people, singing and/or playing the piano, and traveling. **Feb. 3, July 24, Oct. 13, Dec. 20**

Jean Arthur is an attorney living in Silver Spring, Maryland, United States of America. When not at work, she is in her very large fruit and vegetable garden; at home baking, reading, or knitting; traveling around the world; or running, bicycling, or boxing. **June 21**

June Ayers is employed in a regulatory branch of the Texas Department of State Health Services in the United States of America. In her challenges to be instrumental in assisting citizens to comply with rules, God has impressed her to always be firm but cordial, and patient but persistent, until the law is fulfilled. Her husband, son, and three granddaughters have been very supportive of her profession and are the joy of her life. **Apr. 21, Sept. 3**

Edna Bacate-Domingo, PhD, MSN, RN, lives in Loma Linda, California, United States of America. She is an associate professor and serves as elder, Sabbath School teacher, and superintendent in her church. She has three adult daughters and is blessed with one granddaughter. **Mar. 17**

Yvita Antonette Villalona Bacchus is a graphic designer and violinist. She works in the Music and Communications departments of her local church in the Dominican Republic. She is grateful for the opportunity to bless and be blessed. **Oct. 1**

Carla Baker lives in Maryland, United States of America, and is director of Women's Ministries at the North American Division of Seventh-day Adventists. She enjoys walking, cooking, reading, and spending time with her three grandchildren. **Aug. 16**

Jennifer M. Baldwin writes from Australia, where she works in Risk Management at Sydney Adventist Hospital. She enjoys family time, church involvement, Scrabble, crossword puzzles, and researching her family history. She has been contributing to the devotional book series for more than eighteen years. **Nov. 23**

Beatrice Banks is a retired principal and teacher in Pooler, Georgia, United States of America. She served the South Atlantic Conference for thirty-nine years and eight years on the board of education. She loves gardening, desktop publishing, traveling, the classroom, and home decorating. Her poetry has been sold in bookstores. **Mar. 9**

Sylvia Wright Barnes is from Jamaica. **June 9**

Dottie Barnett is retired and lives in a beautiful country setting in southeast Tennessee, United States of America. For more than fifty years, she has been involved in children and adult Sabbath School leadership. She has written a devotional blog for the past several years called *Whispers of His Wisdom*. She loves working with plants and flowers, mowing her large lawn, photography, and camping with her family. **Sept. 9**

Gyl Moon Bateman and her husband have three sons and live in Michigan, United States of America. She is a registered nurse, and her hobbies are reading, music, cats, visiting friends and relatives, and cooking. She is an active Blue Star Mother, since her son served in the army. **Apr. 23**

Dana Bassett M. Bean is an educator from Bermuda who loves God, food, the color orange, photography, writing, and children, and still enjoys granola. She works for the Lord as church clerk, Sabbath School teacher in cradle roll, and Adventurer leader. **Mar. 18, Aug. 18**

Dawna Beausoleil is a retired teacher who lives with her husband, John, in a retirement community in London, Ontario, Canada. She praises God for the wonderful care with which He has blessed them. **May 23**

Candy L. Bedford lives in Port Charlotte, Florida, United States of America, and serves God as the school treasurer for the Port Charlotte Adventist School, assistant treasurer for her church, and an involved helper in other ministries. She has her first published work available, a fiction work entitled *The Secret Deceptions of Love and Lies*, based on snippets of her own life. **Apr. 29**

Ginger Bell resides in Colorado, United States of America, with her pastor husband. Their two grown children and families live close by and are a delight! Ginger is active in Women's Ministries on the local and conference levels. Her hobbies include gardening, crafts, antiquing, and being in the beautiful Rocky Mountains. **Nov. 28**

Sylvia Giles Bennett lives in Suffolk, Virginia, United States of America, with Richard, her husband of thirty-four years. She is the mother of two adult children, David and Samantha, and grandmother to four adoring grandchildren: Kennedy, Derrius, Davion, and Donte. A member of the Windsor Seventh-day Adventist Church, she enjoys reading, writing, and caring for the elderly. **July 12, Sept. 19**

Annie B. Best is a retired teacher in Washington, DC, United States of America, a widow, mother of two adult children, and grandmother to three grandchildren. She enjoys reading and listening to music. Being a leader in the cradle roll and kindergarten departments of her church years ago inspired her to compose a song published in *Let's Sing Sabbath Songs*. **July 26**

Suzanne Blaylock is a practicing physician in Muscle Shoals, Alabama, United States of America. She enjoys providing services for her community as part of her service to God. **July 8, Nov. 9**

Julie Bocock-Bliss and her husband are active members of the Honolulu Japanese Seventh-day Adventist Church in Manoa, Honolulu, Hawaii, United States of America. She loves reading, traveling, and crafts. **Apr. 3**

Denise C. Braswell lives in New Jersey, United States of America, and worships in the city of Philadelphia. She is an active church member, serving as an assistant clerk and singing in the choir. Denise enjoys reading and traveling and looks forward to the many ways God will reveal Himself in her life as she studies His Word and grows closer to Him. **Mar. 21**

Sonia Brock lives in Palmer, Alaska, United States of America, on a little more than nine acres in a small cabin she built herself. Her dog is her faithful companion. She has been privileged for twenty-three years to drive a school bus in the rugged but beautiful forty-ninth state. She finds service to her church a joy and privilege, whether it's mowing the churchyard in the summertime or greeting at the front door on Sabbaths. **Nov. 25**

Vivian Brown, a retired educator, lives in Madison, Alabama, United States of America, with her husband. They both are members of the Oakwood University Church. Her life's passion is sharing God's love with family and others. Her six grandchildren bring so much joy to her. Her ultimate goal is to be ready, with her family, to meet her Lord and Savior when He comes. **July 5**

Amelia Brown-Williams is a Jamaican living in New York, United States of America. A freelance writer and blogger, she writes for The Bottom Line Ministry. **Nov. 3**

Dorothy Butler writes from the Portland, Oregon, area in the United States of America. **Oct. 6**

Grace Phiri Bwalya is fifty-three years old and married with four grown children. She lives in Ndola, Copperbelt Province, Zambia. A Women's Ministries and Children's Ministries leader and church kindergarten teacher, she also holds neighborhood Bible story lessons for community children. She also loves to encourage entrepreneurship among young women. **Dec. 3**

Elizabeth Ida Cain is an administrator at one of the leading farming companies in Jamaica, where she resides. She is a professional florist who enjoys teaching the art and finds spiritual blessings in writing devotionals for this wonderful devotional book project. She is looking forward to completing a master's degree in education very soon. **Feb. 9**

Laura A. Canning lives in Berkshire, England. God has gifted her with the art of writing. She enjoys country life, photography, gardening, and her pets. **July 10, Oct. 19**

Ruth Cantrell is a retired teacher and counselor from the Detroit Public Schools Community District, United States of America. She has two adult sons and resides with her husband in Belleville, Michigan. She enjoys women's ministry, children's ministry, prayer ministry, reading stories, music, organizing programs, and encouraging others. **Nov. 20**

Dorothy Wainwright Carey lives in Ocala, Florida, United States of America, and believes in living each day to the fullest. She considers her greatest accomplishments to be her better-than-good forty-eight-year marriage, her one fine son, and her twenty-year-old grandson, whom she'd love to tell you about. **July 29, Sept. 24**

Donna Ritchie Casebolt is a volunteer writer and editor at Gospel Outreach in College Place, Washington, United States of America, where she lives with her husband, Don. She is the mother of two sons and two daughters, grandmother of two granddaughters, and great-grandmother to an adorable great-grandson. Widowed in August 2011 after sixty-one years of marriage, she met and married her second "soul mate" in 2014. **Dec. 2**

Camilla E. Cassell, a retired postal worker of forty years, attends Berea Temple Seventh-day Adventist Church in Pennsylvania, United States of America. Aaron and Abena, her children, along with four grandsons and one great-granddaughter, make up her family. She was privileged to witness the birth of Amari, her second grandson. She enjoys gardening, crafts, writing, designing greeting cards, and listening to music. **Nov. 26**

Bezaida (Betzy) Castro was born in the Dominican Republic. Until recently, she served the Southwest Region Conference as Hispanic Women's Ministries leader and coordinator for five states in the United States of America. An international preacher and motivational speaker, she also serves the Houston Maranatha Church (Texas) as assistant clerk and family life director. She is a happy wife and mother of two. **Mar. 5, July 15**

Suhana Chikatla, born in India, has two master's and one doctorate degree. She volunteers in children's, youth, and social leadership positions at her Hanceville, Alabama, church in the United States of America. She is on the executive council for the Gulf States Conference Women's Ministries department. She and her husband, Royce Sutton, have a beautiful one-year-old daughter, Rehana. **July 6**

Caroline Chola lives in Pretoria, South Africa. She is currently the Children's Ministries and Women's Ministries director of the Southern Africa Indian Ocean Division. She is married to Habson, and they have five adult boys and two grandchildren. She enjoys gardening. Her passion is to see women discover their potential and use it to the glory of God. **Apr. 17**

Rosenita Christo formerly taught at the college level. She and her husband, Gordon, wrote *For Better or For Worse*, an adult Bible study guide. She loves singing and writing and is the choir leader at her church in India. **Feb. 15**

Rosemarie Clardy enjoys being a stay-at-home mom in North Carolina, United States of America. Her husband plans to retire soon, which will be a new venture for both of them. She is involved in small groups, learning how to knit and crochet, and getting back to artwork, which was her passion when younger. She would also like to foster animals. **July 13**

Rose Coleman, a first-time contributor, writes from Jamaica, where she is a primary school teacher. An ardent lover of children, she serves her church as a children's department leader. She is also married, the mother of four young adults. **July 17**

Aminata Coote is currently serving as the Women's Ministries director in her local church in Montego Bay, Jamaica, where she lives. She's the wife of one man and has one son, both of whom keep her on her toes. She created the Web site Hebrews12Endurance.com, which focuses on the types of endurance featured in Hebrews 12:1. She dreams of becoming a writer. **May 2**

Maria Raimunda Lopes Costa resides in the city of Bacabal, Maranhão, Brazil. She is a teacher, a writer, and a poet. She is involved in missionary work and is an avid reader of the women's devotional series. She has a published book: *Vivências (Experiences)*. Her hobbies are walking and good reading. **July 9**

Patricia Cove, writing from Ontario, Canada, is a semiretired teacher, church elder, volunteer chaplain, freelance writer, gardener, and lover of outdoor pursuits. She and her husband of fifty-nine years treasure their children and the freedom to share their love of Jesus to all who will listen. **June 6**

Celia Mejia Cruz is a retired pastor's wife, church elder, mother of five adult children, and grandmother of eight grandchildren. She is an editor and writer, living in Tennessee. Her interests include her family, her dogs, and giving Bible studies. **Feb. 5, June 28**

Martha (Marty) Cunnington lives with her husband in the lovely small town of

Armstrong, British Columbia, Canada, in the sunny Okanagan Valley. They have two grown children. Marty helps in several departments at her local church. She has a special love for animals and the outdoors. **Mar. 6**

Nahomie Daubé is originally from Guadeloupe. She is currently pursuing her studies in counseling psychology at the University of the Southern Caribbean, Trinidad and Tobago. **Apr. 16**

Lee Lee Dart is a pastor at the Adventure Seventh-day Adventist Church in Windsor, Colorado, United States of America. She is passionate about being a conduit of God's love to others. She is a wife and mother of two daughters. She enjoys traveling, art, and partnering with organizations that help widows and orphans all over the world. **Mar. 3, Dec. 7**

Jean Dozier Davey and her husband, Steven, live in the beautiful mountains of North Carolina, United States of America. She retired in 2003 from a career as a computer programmer. She enjoys spending time with family, cooking, reading, walking in Pisgah Forest, sewing, photography, and encouraging others. **Aug. 3, Oct. 7**

Avery Davis lives in England. She has a passion for women's ministries and loves to write. She considers it a privilege to be able to record and share these stories and thanks God for the support of her husband and children. **Apr. 25**

Rebecca Davis serves as a pastor with the South Atlantic Conference of Seventh-day Adventists in the United States of America. She is the first woman to serve as a senior pastor in her conference. Her churches include Canaan Heights, located in Thomson, Georgia; and Washington Seventh-day Adventist Church, located in Washington, Georgia. **Feb. 17**

Leonie Donald thanks God every day for the beauty of Queen Charlotte Sound, New Zealand, where she lives. She enjoys long walks, "devours" books, and admits to spending more time in her garden than doing housework. She and her husband of more than forty-seven years attend the Blenheim Seventh-day Adventist Church. **May 17**

Louise Driver is the wife of a retired pastor who still preaches almost every Sabbath in the state of Idaho, United States of America. Her sister, three sons, and their families live nearby. She enjoys gardening, reading, and traveling. **May 3**

Clody Flores Dumaliang is from Los Angeles, California, United States of America. She is a behavioral health therapist, social worker, and educator. Clody is married to Bonn, her grade school classmate, and they have a daughter, Victoria. **Mar. 26**

Mary E. Dunkin is a daughter, sister, aunt, cousin, friend, caregiver, home economist, Pathfinder, teacher, seamstress, concierge, business owner, writer, and God's daughter. She is most proud of being God's daughter and eagerly waits for Him to come back. Until then, she'll keep working. Her home is in New Mexico, United States of America. **Jan. 18, Aug. 13**

Missilene B. Edwards, of Hogansville, Georgia, United States of America, is a retired registered nurse who was widowed in 2011. Mother of Steve and Carolyn and grandmother of Qwynn, Chelsea, and Sade, she has served the church in many capacities, including Women's Ministries leader and church clerk. She delights in crocheting hats, scarves, and lap throws for hospice, shelters, and needy children. **July 14, Sept. 5**

Charity I. Ekeke is the single parent of four well-adjusted, self-directed young adults. She has worked in different aspects and positions of health care. Living in Torrance, California, United States of America, she currently gives critical care part-time, while also pursuing the path of being a recording artist. Her debut album, released in October 2016, contains songs about the challenges women face and is entitled *She*. **Oct. 24**

Barb Engquist lives in Lincoln, Nebraska, United States of America. She is active in Adventurer and Pathfinder clubs. She enjoys spending time with her family, reading, creating mini gardens, and being outdoors. **Oct. 25, Dec. 4**

Donna Engu lives in the beautiful Cook Islands with her husband. They have three children and two grandsons. As she spends time studying the Bible, she prays for God to impress her as to whom she should pass on the message in order to share the blessings. **June 10, Sept. 23**

Ruby H. Enniss-Alleyne writes from Guyana and is in love with youth, athletics, and working in the treasury office at the Guyana Conference of Seventh-day Adventists. She serves as youth elder and Family Ministries leader at her home church, Mount Carmel. She lost her spouse, Ashton, in January 2011. She enjoys her three adult children, her daughter-in-law, and her adorable grandson, Alaric. **Aug. 2**

Renee Farmer resides in Canada with her husband, whom she adores, and their baby. She is an educator, and her passions include traveling, learning, playing the piano, and the arts. **Aug. 25**

Mona Fellers is a pharmacy liaison helping people with mental illness. She is Women's Ministries leader in her church. She lives in Colorado, United States of America, with her husband and has two lovely daughters and one grandson. She loves animals, birds, and serving the Lord. **Jan. 16, Oct. 14**

Briana Fewell-Johnson is a gifted, home-schooled, thirteen-year-old seventh grader. She loves church and strives to be the best person she can be. She is learning to play guitar and piano. She has taught herself sign language and is learning Korean and Spanish. An excellent speaker, writer, and actress, her hobby is designing and making her own clothes. She lives in North Carolina, United States of America. **Oct. 10**

Carol Joy Fider, a retired educator, writes from Mandeville, Jamaica. She serves her church as a local elder, education director, and Sabbath School teacher. The yearning of her heart is to go with Jesus when He gathers the saints of all the ages. She and her husband, Ezra, have two adult daughters. **June 29**

Lucille Fifield, though born in England, spends time with her husband, Arthur, in Jamaica. She is a registered nurse and health visitor with a master of science degree in public health and a master of business administration degree. She is also managing partner of an agricultural and food processing equipment enterprise. She has three adult children and enjoys farming, sewing, working with teenage mothers, and medical missionary ministry. **June 27, Dec. 11**

Edith Fitch wrote from Lacombe, Alberta, Canada, before she passed away in 2016. She retired in 1993, after forty-one years of teaching. Life ran smoothly until 2013, when she was diagnosed with an inoperable malignant thymoma. She strove to meet each crisis courageously. No matter what, she thanked God for the blessings between the struggles. **Mar. 15, July 2, Sept. 22**

Janice Fleming-Williams is a school teacher and certified family life educator. She is Family Ministries leader at her church and works for her local school. She and her husband live on Saint Thomas, United States Virgin Islands, and have two adult sons. Her favorite pastime is reading. **Mar. 19**

Edith C. Fraser is a retired university professor in social work, and currently lives in Alabama in the United States of America. She was in education for more than thirty years and speaks nationally and internationally about issues for women, families, and spiritual growth. She has been married for more than forty-five years and has two adult children and two grandchildren. **July 19, Sept. 27**

Kathleen Freeman, a retired intensive care registered nurse, loves working in children's ministries and presenting several workshops on the topic. She also coordinates a church prayer quilt ministry for people in crisis, making quilts for underprivileged kids, veterans, and women's shelters. She and her husband consider their three children, their spouses, and six grandchildren to be a very special blessing. **June 15**

Gloribeth T. Gancedo was born in Panama and first became acquainted with Adventism through Radio Mia. The program was *La Voz de la Esperanza*. She was baptized in 1983. She studied business administration and worked for the United States Army, stationed in Panama, before her retirement. She is a member of the Castella Seventh-day Adventist Church in Panama City, Panama. **June 23**

Amanda N. Gaspard is an environmental health specialist at the San Bernardino County Department of Public Health in California, United States of America. She is a Sabbath School teacher, pianist, and song service coordinator at Advent HOPE in Loma Linda, California. Her hobbies include traveling, reading, collecting coins, and snorkeling. **Nov. 22, Dec. 26**

Marybeth Gessele is a hospice caregiver living in Gaston, Oregon, United States of America, with her husband. She enjoys preserving food from their garden and orchard. Making and donating baby quilts to a foster care organization is a rewarding outreach for her. **Apr. 20**

Yan Siew Ghiang is a Singaporean Seventh-day Adventist Christian with no income ceiling as a temporary home caregiver. The hawker center (an open air market) is her evangelism network. She loves to read, write, and do indoor exercises. **Mar. 16, Aug. 22**

Evelyn Glass and Darrell live on their family farm in northwestern Minnesota, United States of America. Their greatest joy in life is spending time with their children, grandchildren, and their spouses. She keeps busy writing, serving her church, and quilting. Life is good. **Apr. 24**

Ruth Middaugh Goodsite is a retired nurse who lives in Florida, United States of America. She has two grown children. She enjoys puttering in her yard, reading, helping at church, and walking her dog. **Apr. 7**

Alexis A. Goring, a freelance writer and photographer with a background in teaching, resides on the East Coast of the United States of America. Working as a freelance writer has provided her opportunity to interview Pulitzer Prize winner Max Desfor, pastor and musician Wintley Phipps, and lieutenant governor Anthony Brown, and to meet Jasmine Star, wedding photographer. Her grandmother (Annie B. Best) and mother (Cynthia Best-Goring) have also been published in these devotional books. **July 23, Aug. 1**

Carmalita Green lives in Montgomery, Alabama, United States of America, were she works as a nutritionist for the state program that provides a special supplemental nutrition program for women, infants, and children (WIC). She is also very active in the women's ministry of Bethany Seventh-day Adventist Church. **Nov. 17**

Glenda-mae Greene, a retired university educator, writes from her wheelchair in Palm Bay, Florida, United States of America. She enjoys meeting people and sharing in the narrative of their lives. She is a member of her church's disability ministries team. **Feb. 24**

Gloria Barnes Gregory is inspired by nature and her precious granddaughters. She seeks to motivate others to make positive life choices. Currently she and her husband, Milton, serve at the Victory Church in New York, United States of America. **Nov. 30**

Meibel Mello Guedes was one of the pioneers of Women's Ministries and AFAM (Shepherdess Organization) in Brazil. Today she is dedicated to writing books and articles and lecturing on church events and educational institutions. She coordinates a graduate course on family therapy and counseling. She lives in Curitiba, Paraná, Brazil. **Aug. 10, Sept. 20**

Bertha Hall has been an educator for thirty years. She is married to a pastor, Curtis. They live in Tennessee, United States of America, and look forward to seeing Jesus in peace. **Aug. 30**

Dora Hallock lives in beautiful New England, United States of America. She is a clinical nurse specialist in oncology. She is also a pastor's wife, mother of a lovely daughter, and mother-in-law to the husband of the wonderful couple who parents their amazing grandchildren! Her hobbies include walking the beach, sailing, photography, and praying with friends. **July 22**

Diantha Hall-Smith is a daughter of God. She is a wife to a devoted Christian husband who serves in the United States Air Force. A mother of two beautiful children, she was born in New York City, United States of America, and has had the honor and privilege to have lived and visited other interesting places, domestically and globally. She enjoys writing, traveling, and spending time with her family. **Feb. 21, Sept. 8**

Marsha Hammond-Brummel is a teacher living in Claremont, New Hampshire, United States of America, and wrote about her experience on a snow day from school. From May through October, she can often be found at the historic Washington, New Hampshire, Seventh-day Adventist Church and Sabbath Trail, where she helps her husband, Ken, welcome guests to the site. **Mar. 2**

Marian Hart-Gay lives in Florida, United States of America, with her husband, David. She is a mother, grandmother, and great-grandmother. Knitting and volunteer mission trips are two activities she enjoys. **July 25, Sept. 6**

Anita Livingston Hayward is a lawyer living in New Jersey, United States of America. Before coming to the United States, she worked for the Southern Asia Division of Seventh-day Adventists as a law officer and advocate. She is registered as an advocate in the supreme court of India. **May 8**

Beverly D. Hazzard is a daughter of medical missionaries. A retired nurse administrator, she lives in Canada and is mother of two and grandma to five. She enjoys time with family, her dogs, traveling, sailing, and mission trips. She is a church elder and school board chair. **May 15**

Helen Heavirland is an author, speaker, and encourager who lives in Oregon, United States of America. She has written numerous articles and four books, including *My God Is Bigger*. For more information or inspiration, go to HelenHeavirland.com. **June 12, Nov. 6**

Judy M. Helm lives in Evergreen, Colorado, United States of America, part of the foothills west of Denver, with her husband, Wilton. She has taught in Adventist elementary schools for fourteen years in Alaska and Colorado. She is currently a registered nurse involved in home health nursing. She enjoys her grandchildren, hiking, camping, traveling, and gardening. **Sept. 29**

Muriel Heppel enjoys the quietness of country living in the lovely Robson Valley situated between the Rocky and Cariboo Mountains in British Columbia, Canada. She also enjoys the the wildlife that comes onto her property, entertaining friends, playing Scrabble, and doing church and community service work. **May 24, Sept. 30**

Denise Dick Herr taught English at Burman University in Lacombe, Alberta, Canada. She enjoys travel and is excited to explore the new adventure of retirement. **June 24, Sept. 18**

Rosemary Byrd Hickman lives in Florida, United States of America, with Ray, her husband of forty-seven years. They have three daughters and a son. They have been blessed with six granddaughters and eight grandsons. Their quiver is full. She is currently the church clerk at North Lake and also enjoys plants, quilts, baking, reading, and living. **May 5**

Patricia Hines is originally from the Caribbean, has lived in Orlando, Florida, United States of America, and recently moved to Sebring, Florida. She is a teacher who enjoys music and writing. **Jan. 20, Aug. 19**

Denise Hochstrasser is Women's Ministries director for the Inter-European Division of Seventh-day Adventists and lives in Switzerland. Her vision: That all people have the same possibilities in life and can accept a calling without restriction. **Jan. 1**

Roxy Hoehn is retired in Topeka, Kansas, United States of America, after many wonderful experiences, such as being the Women's Ministries director for the Kansas-Nebraska Conference of Seventh-day Adventists for many years. Retirement is fun, but she misses the great women and teen girls she learned to love. **Jan. 9**

Karen Holford is the Family Ministries director for the Trans-European Division. She enjoys writing, creative worship, sewing, teaching recycled crafts, and playing with her grandchildren. **Apr. 6, Oct. 12, Dec. 5**

Tamyra (Tami) Horst writes from Paradise, Pennsylvania, United States of America, where she lives with Tim, her husband of more than thirty years. Author, speaker, and the Women's Ministries and Communication director for the Pennsylvania Conference of Seventh-day Adventists, she loves being a mom to her two young adult sons, being a friend to an amazing group of women, enjoying quiet with a great book and a cup of chai, and sharing adventures with those she loves. **June 1, Dec. 24**

Jacqueline Hope HoShing-Clarke has been an educator since 1979, serving as principal, assistant principal, and teacher. She is currently chair of the Teacher Education Department of Northern Caribbean University in Jamaica. She is married and has two adult children. Jackie enjoys writing, gardening, and—most of all—spending time with her grandson. **Mar. 22, Oct. 28**

Cheryl Howson is an interior designer born in Pune, India. She is married and lives in Colombo, Sri Lanka, a beautiful island throughout which she has traveled more than most locals. Her husband is the youngest church elder on record at the Bethel Chapel church, where she is in charge of the choir and enjoys writing plays for the youth and choir to perform. **Apr. 26**

Patty L. Hyland is a retired teacher, her final position being an instructor at Rogue Community College in Grants Pass, Oregon, United States of America. She and her pastor husband, Verne, served as missionaries for fourteen years in Sri Lanka and on the island of Palau in Micronesia. At present, she is a chaplain at Three Rivers Community Hospital in Grants Pass. **Oct. 11, Dec. 29**

Shirley C. Iheanacho lives in Alabama in the United States of America and where she regularly participates in Maranatha overseas mission projects, ministers to the sick and shut-in, serves as an elder and speaker, and encourages women to write. **Feb. 26, July 28, Nov. 5**

Amanda Amy Isles is a young woman residing on the island of Dominica, where the Lord has blessed her with a wonderful job as accounts clerk. She is active in her church and hopes to reach other young women by sharing her experiences of God's goodness with her devotional submissions. **Apr. 11, Sept. 16**

Joan D. L. Jaensch lives with her, husband, Murray, in Murray Bridge, South Australia. They have two married sons, two granddaughters, two grandsons, one great-grandson, and one great-granddaughter. Gardening and potted plants are her hobbies. **May 31, Aug. 29**

Greta Michelle Joachim-Fox-Dyett is a wife, mother, artist, potter, writer, and teacher. Most of all, she is a child of the Most High God. At the time of writing this devotional, she was getting her second degree in fine arts and living in Trinidad and Tobago. **Mar. 31**

Elaine J. Johnson is retired from thirty-three years working in day care and preschool (fourteen and a half at Building Blocks and Children's Corner, fifteen and a half with Catholic Charities, and the remainder at home through the county). She has been married for more than fifty years and has four children, seventeen grandchildren, and fourteen great-grandchildren. She lives in Alabama in the United States of America where she pursues her three passions of reading, writing, and computering. **Nov. 27**

Erna Johnson was born and raised in Iceland. She's part of the Discipleship Ministries team in the South Pacific Division and is married to Eddy, a pastor. They have served in the church around the world. She speaks Icelandic, English, and French. They have two adult children, and she loves being a grandmother. Her passion is helping women reach their potential in Jesus. **Mar. 1**

Angie Joseph is a pastor's wife, codirector of lay evangelism in the Iowa-Missouri Conference of Seventh-day Adventists in the United States of America, a speaker at women's retreats, and a Bible instructor. **Mar. 20, Nov. 12**

Gerene I. Joseph is married to Elder Sylvester Joseph. They have two children, Sylene and Sylvester Jr. She was director of Children's Ministries and Women's Ministries of the North Caribbean Conference for six years and is now that conference's director of Education. This writer of poems and musician (piano) is also a certified lay preacher and has conducted one campaign. **Feb. 23, Aug. 20, Dec. 21**

Nadine A. Joseph, a longtime writer of devotionals and other inspirational writing, spends much of her time making presentations to youth and women, encouraging them to grow in a faith relationship with God. She is currently based in Brooklyn, New York, United States of America, where she is working with a ministry, SanareLife. **Jan. 23, Sept. 15**

Mukatimui Kalima-Munalula is a medical doctor training as an obstetrician and gynecologist in Lusaka, Zambia. She is married to Themba and blessed with three children and a nephew. She serves as deaconess at Lusaka Central Adventist Church. Her hobbies include trying out new recipes and running for charity. **Sept. 13, Nov. 2**

Carolyn K. Karlstrom is a Bible worker for her home church in the Pacific Northwest of the United States of America. She gives Bible studies, teaches, and preaches. She is also a freelance writer; her articles have appeared in a variety of magazines. She is married to Rick, and they have a sweet black cat named Minuet. **Aug. 7, Nov. 15**

Sonia Kennedy-Brown lives in Ontario, Canada, and is a retired nurse and teacher. She is presently working on her biography. She loves to read, dabble in writing poetry, and witness for God. **May 9, Oct. 30**

Edith Kiggundu, PhD, is a visiting assistant professor in the Faculty of Education at Memorial University of Newfoundland, Canada. She is a Ugandan but now lives in Canada with her husband, Fred, and their three children. She serves as a Sabbath School superintendent, adult Bible lesson teacher, and prayer ministry leader. A prayer warrior, she enjoys singing and studying the Word of God. **Mar. 4, July 27**

Iris L. Kitching enjoys creative endeavors, spoken word poetry performances, and writing for children. She has worked at the General Conference of Seventh-day Adventists in Maryland, United States of America, for more than twenty years, first in Women's Ministries and then in Presidential. She and her husband, Will, appreciate the joys of spending time with family and friends. **June 18, Oct. 26, Dec. 27**

Kênia Kopitar is Brazilian but now lives in Florida, United States of America. She enjoys gardening, writing, reading, teaching music and piano, and taking care of animals. Her greatest desire is to meet God and her loved ones at Jesus' second coming. **May 11**

Betty Kossick is a freelance writer who has been part of seventy-seven books. She has authored three of her own: *Beyond the Locked Door, Heart Ballads,* and *The Manor.* For more information, e-mail her at bkwrites4u@hotmail.com. **June 7**

Patricia Mulraney Kovalski lives in Collegedale, Tennessee, United States of America. She loves to travel and enjoys visits with her family in Michigan, United States. She has many hobbies and has been doing English teas for family and friends since 1997. **May 21, Aug. 31**

Mabel Kwei, a retired university and college lecturer, did missionary work in Africa for many years with her pastor husband and their three children. Now living in New Jersey, United States of America, she reads a lot and loves to paint, write, and spend time with little children. **Feb. 19, Aug. 15**

Janet Lankheet, a mother of four, was a news reporter before entering editorial work for the church and traveling worldwide as a minister. She lives in Michigan, United States of America, and is a local church elder. Her delights are her husband, Roger (fun to live with); her grand-girls; her CKCS (Cavalier King Charles spaniel) puppy; her betta fish; and her violets and orchids. **Apr. 4**

Wilma Kirk Lee, a licensed clinical social worker, currently directs the Center for Family Wholeness (CFW), located in Houston, Texas, United States of America. Her husband (of five decades), W. S. Lee, serves as codirector of Family Ministries of the Southwest Region Conference of Seventh-day Adventists. She holds a bachelor of social work degree and a master of social work degree. **Feb. 7, Feb. 8**

Loida Gulaja Lehmann spent ten years selling religious books in the Philippines before going to Germany and getting married. She and her husband are active church members and are both involved in radio, jail, and laymen's ministries in the Philippines. Her hobbies are traveling, nature walks, writing, and photography. **Mar. 27, June 19**

Joan M. Leslie is a native of Kingston, Jamaica. She is currently a grade one teacher in New York, United States of America. She takes great pleasure in reading, traveling, and crocheting. **May 18**

Jan Hooper Lind enjoys being involved with music at the Coeur d'Alene, Idaho, Seventh-day Adventist Church in the United States of America. She is married, a mom to five adults and a grandmother to five grandchildren. She is a retired registered nurse and loves to knit. **Nov. 29**

Sharon Long (Brown) retired in 2015 from a thirty-four-year social work career. She is an associate certified coach and is excited to serve God in Edmonton, Alberta, Canada, and abroad. **Jan. 3, Aug. 27**

Lynn Mfuru Lukwaro was born and raised in Tanzania. She and her husband, Gureni, live in Sharjah, United Arab Emirates, with their two beautiful daughters. They serve the Lord in their church. Lynn enjoys traveling, stories, nature walks, teaching, and reading. **May 10**

Terri Lutz, a registered nurse, lives in central California, United States of America, with her husband, Dan. They are actively involved in church ministries and sharing the love of Jesus through mission work in developing countries. **June 13, Dec. 30**

Rhona Grace Magpayo enjoys going on mission trips with her husband, Jun. A photo enthusiast, she loves traveling the world and capturing sunsets with her camera. **Feb. 14**

Fe C. Magpusao is married to a pastor. She is a church school teacher and a mother of two kids. She lives in the Philippines and loves to travel to new places, hike, read, listen to Christian music, and experience adventure. **May 19**

Debbie Maloba is the Women's Ministries and Children's Ministries director for the East-Central Africa Division of Seventh-day Adventists. She and her husband, Jim, have been blessed with five children who graciously adjusted to their new life in Nairobi, Kenya. She loves to train women in leadership and to make ministry proposals. **May 7**

Zeny Marcelo, before her recent death, lived with her husband in California, United States of America, though they had spent the last ten years as self-supporting missionaries to the Philippines, where they were involved with the Adventist World Aviation Foundation. The mother of four children and grandmother to six, she enjoyed playing the piano, quilting, and floral design. **July 4**

Tamara Marquez de Smith writes from Florida, United States of America, where she lives with her husband and two daughters, Lillian and Cassandra. A native New Yorker who misses home, she is looking for new opportunities to use her talents for God. **June 20**

Gail Masondo is a wife, mother of two adult children (Shellie and Jonathan), women and children's advocate, songwriter, chaplain, Life in Recovery coach, and international speaker. She has authored *Now This Feels Like Home*. A New York native, Gail now resides in Johannesburg, South Africa, with her musician husband, Victor Sibusiso Masondo. **May 12**

Deborah Matshaya writes from South Africa, where she a teacher. She enjoys gospel music and has contributed many times to this devotional book series. **Feb. 12, Dec. 6**

Mary L. Maxson, a southern lady transplanted from Memphis, Tennessee, to Paradise, California, in the United States of America, is a former missionary to Argentina and Uruguay (where she spoke Spanish with a southern accent). She served at the *Adventist Review* and Adventist World Radio, and is a former Women's Ministries director for the North American Division of Seventh-day Adventists. Now God has her nurturing His flock as associate pastor of the Paradise Adventist Church. **Mar. 10, Dec. 25**

Retha McCarty is retired and lives in Missouri, United States of America. She enjoys reading, crafts, poetry, crocheting, and bird-watching. She has made numerous quilt tops for the Bags of Love ministry. She has been a church treasurer since 1977 and publishes a church newsletter each month. She is also the author of a poetry book, *Rainbow of Rhymes*. **May 16**

Vidella McClellan is retired and lives in beautiful British Columbia, Canada. She is married, mother of three, grandmother of seven, and great-grandmother of one—along with four stepchildren, seven step-grandchildren, and two great-grandchildren. She loves gardening, cats, and helping in the church and community. Her current hobbies are crosswords, sudoku, Scrabble, and crafts. **Apr. 2**

Theresa M. McDonald was born in and grew up in Jamaica, then emigrated to the United States of America, where she worked in early childhood education as teacher, administrator, and provider consultant. She holds a doctor of health sciences degree and is a former assistant professor at Northern Caribbean University in Jamaica. She anxiously awaits the soon return of her best Friend, Jesus. **June 8**

Arlene West McFarland is a marriage and family therapist in north Alabama, United States of America. She is currently the organist and cradle roll leader in a small church. She is twenty-three years into her second marriage and enjoys five children and seven grandchildren. **Mar. 14, Aug. 6**

Raschelle Mclean-Jones is an elementary teacher in Haines City, Florida, United States of America. She has two sons, Aaron and Josiah, who love basketball. She is married to a devoted, loving man, John Jones. She loves to cook, sing in the choir, and write. **Apr. 30**

Jenel A. N. Campbell McPherson writes from Baritca, Guyana. She is the wife of a pastor, Mark, and they have a baby boy. Her passion is for young people, with a special emphasis on nurturing young women. She has served in many capacities in her church. **Apr. 22, Sept. 17**

Judelia Medard-Santiesteban is from an island in the Caribbean named Saint Lucia. She is a high school teacher and involved in women's and youth ministries. She is learning to lean on Jesus. **Apr. 15**

Sylvia Mendez, from Victoria in Australia, attends the Wantirna Seventh-day Adventist Church. She is currently studying ministry and theology and loves talking with women about the healing power of Jesus in their lives. She reminds them they are fearfully and wonderfully made in the image of God. **Jan. 30**

Cindy Mercer is a pastor's wife who lives in Morganton, North Carolina, United States of America, where she works part-time as a registered nurse. She is passionate about prayer and personal Bible studies and enjoys the opportunity to speak at prayer retreats and women's events. **Apr. 28**

Annette Walwyn Michael writes from Saint Croix in the United States Virgin Islands. She is a retired English teacher and a published writer of Caribbean literature. She has three adult daughters, three sons-in-law, and seven grandchildren, who are beautiful additions to her family. Her husband, Reginald, is a busy retired pastor. **Mar. 29, Aug. 24, Dec. 22**

Quilvie G. Mills is a retired community college professor. She and her husband are members of the Port Saint Lucie church in Florida, United States of America, where she serves as a musician and Bible class teacher. She enjoys traveling, music, gardening, word games, reading, and teaching piano. **Oct. 20**

Ruth Minoza-Gunida is a mother of three and active in her church. She writes from Ghana. **Mar. 11**

D. Reneé Mobley, PhD, is trained in clinical pastoral education and has owned a Christian counseling practice for more than ten years. A member of the National Christian Counselors Association, she trains and facilitates workshops, seminars, and conferences. She is mother of two adult women, mother-in-law of the greatest son-in-law in the world, and grandmother to three grand-dogs. **Jan. 24, Sept. 12**

Marcia Mollenkopf, a retired teacher, lives in Klamath Falls, Oregon, United States of America. She enjoys church involvement and has served in both adult and children's divisions. Her hobbies include reading, writing, and music. She has been blessed to have a growing postcard ministry. **Jan. 6**

Jane Wiggins Moore is a retired registered nurse, teacher, and secretary who lives in Tennessee, United States of America. She has held many church offices through the years, but her favorite is Community Services leader. Widowed after thirty-six wonderful years with the love of her life, husband John Moore, her family inspires and reminds her to "be thou faithful unto death, and I will give thee a crown of life" (Revelation 2:10). **June 22, Dec. 9**

Lila Farrell Morgan writes from North Carolina, United States of America. She is a widow, mother, grandmother, and great-grandmother of one. She enjoys reading, walking, baking, table games, observing nature, and keeping in touch with family and friends. **Mar. 30**

Valerie Hamel Morikone works for the Mountain View Conference office in West Virginia, United States of America, and leads out in the Communication and Women's Ministries departments. She loves to read, cook and bake, and do Internet research. **May 30**

Nilva de F. Oliveira da Boa Morte lives in the state of Mato Grosso, Brazil, with her husband, Jucinei Claudio C. da Boa Morte. She teaches art, works in the state health department, and is the secretary at her church. She enjoys reading, painting, and witnessing about what Christ has done in her life. **Jan. 4**

Bonnie Moyers lives with her husband and two cats in Staunton, Virginia, United States of America. She has two adult children and three granddaughters. She is a musician for Methodist and Presbyterian churches on Sundays and in her own church on Sabbaths. She writes freelance, and her writings have been published in numerous magazines and books. **Oct. 4**

Judith M. Mwansa recently returned to her native Zambia with Pardon, her husband, to Rusangu University after years of church work in the United States of America, the last ten being at the General Conference of Seventh-day Adventists. While there, she worked at the Women's Ministries department, assisting with the production of these devotional books. She has adult children and a granddaughter, and she enjoys music, traveling, and spending time with family and friends. **May 14, Dec. 14**

Jannett Maurine Myrie is currently employed at Florida Hospital. She serves as Women's Ministries director and Sabbath School superintendent in her church. A proud mother of one son, her hobbies include reading, cooking, going on cruises, and serving overseas as a medical missionary. **Jan. 14**

Anne Elaine Nelson is a retired elementary teacher in Michigan who authored the book *Puzzled Parents*. She is a widow with four children and eleven grandchildren. She is active in church work as Women's Ministries leader and assistant superintendent for Sabbath School. She enjoys music, crafts, photography, and creating memories with her grandchildren. **Mar. 8, Aug. 14**

Samantha Nelson is a pastor's wife who loves serving alongside her husband, Steve. She is also the CEO of The Hope of Survivors, a nonprofit organization dedicated to assisting victims of clergy sexual abuse and providing educational seminars to clergy of all faiths. She and Steve live in Wyoming, United States of America, and love traveling, hiking in the mountains, and enjoying the beauty of God's creation. **Oct. 17, Oct. 18**

Stacey A. Nicely, a certified and licensed counselor, was born and raised in Jamaica. She studied and worked at Northern Caribbean University before moving to Berrien Springs, Michigan, United States of America. She holds a master's degree in community counseling and is pursuing a doctorate in counseling psychology at Andrews University. She is the testing coordinator at the Andrews counseling and testing center. **Jan. 8**

Lynn Nicolay lives on the western slopes of Colorado in the United States of America and is a mother of three adult children, grandmother of four grandchildren, and wife who has been blessed to share her life with her husband, Don. **Oct. 16**

Linda Nottingham lives in Florida, United States of America, and teaches an adult Bible study class at her church. She is semiretired but serves as a mentor to women business owners. She was also a 2012 Honoree of the Florida Commission on the Status of Women. **May 20**

Margaret Obiocha has been married to her husband, Fyneboy, for more than forty-seven years. They are now retired. She served her local church as Sabbath School teacher, deaconess, and treasurer. She and her husband are involved in church projects to help poor village churches in eastern Nigeria. She enjoys supervising her grandchildren with their schoolwork. **Jan. 7, Oct. 2**

Elizabeth Versteegh Odiyar of Kelowna, British Columbia, Canada, has managed the family chimney sweep business since 1985. She has married twin sons, a daughter, and adorable "gifts" named Jadon and Leah! She loves creativity and keeps busy with cooking, sewing, painting, writing, crafting, technology, church activities, mission, and road trips. She is still a Pathfinder at heart. **Feb. 13, Nov. 8**

Pauline Gesare Okemwa was born in Kisii District, Kenya, in 1973. She attended Kajiado A.I.C. Primary and then Sironga Girls High School. Married in 1990, she has three children: one girl and two boys. Her husband is a pastor in the South Kenya Conference. A self-supporting student, she is in her sixth year of studies at the University of Eastern Africa, Baraton, Kenya. **Jan. 22, Aug. 12**

Jemima Dollosa Orillosa, originally from the Philippines, works in the Secretariat at the General Conference of Seventh-day Adventists in Maryland. Married to Danny, she loves to witness for Christ and is involved in prayer, visitation, and overseas ministry (she takes a group each year on an overseas mission project). Her favorite thing to do is to babysit her granddaughters, Aryia and Amelia. **Dec. 23**

Charlotte Osei-Agyeman has served for twenty years as a women's ministries director. She has two children, is a retired civil servant, and writes from Ghana. **Nov. 19**

Sharon Oster is a retired teacher assistant living in Evans, Colorado, United States of America, with her retired pastor husband. She enjoys automobile day trips in the nearby Rocky Mountains. She and her husband have three children and seven grandchildren. **Oct. 23**

Hannele Ottschofski lives in Germany. A speaker for the Hope Channel, she organizes women's events and has compiled several women's devotionals, besides publishing her own book, *My Father's Shirt*. **Jan. 17, Aug. 9, Oct. 5**

Ofelia A. Pangan lives in Clovis, California, United States of America, with her husband, Abel. They both love gardening, helping with the Hmong brethren, being with their loved ones, and helping in their church. They are blessed with three children and in-laws and ten grandchildren. **Oct. 29**

Anelia Panova serves as a church elder in the country of Bulgaria. **June 11**

Revel Papaioannou helps her pastor husband to care for the biblical church of Berea, Greece. Teaching, preaching, visiting, church maintenance, and gardening, as well as hiking, keep them busy. Their large family of twenty-two brings them much joy. She volunteers part time at the local library. **Mar. 7, Nov. 14**

Erin Parfet resides in the beautiful Golden Isles of Georgia, United States of America, but is active, long distance, in church congregations in Loveland, Colorado, and New Port Richey, Florida. Outside of work and church, she enjoys snorkeling, skydiving, piano, viola, and photography. **Nov. 4**

Jodi Eulene Owens Patterson (Dodson) is a composer and writer. She volunteers for a variety of projects. She is blessed to be one of the composers for the Scripture Singer App, which is also available online. **Feb. 11, Sept. 21**

Carmem Virgínia dos Santos Paulo graduated with a degree in languages and literature and is a specialist in linguistics and teaching. She is a health and socioeducational agent. In her free time, she likes to read, sing, and speak of God's love to others. At church, she is the youth director and the associate music director. She writes from Brazil. **May 4, Oct. 8, Nov. 21**

Tricia (Wynn) Payne resides in Indianapolis, Indiana, United States of America, with her husband. She serves as a pastor in the Lake Region Conference of Seventh-day Adventists. **Nov. 16**

Evelyn Gabutero Pelayo, originally from Odiongan, Romblon, Philippines, works as a teacher and assistant librarian at Zurcher Adventist University in Madagascar. She and her husband, Roger, have two sons, Roger Jr. and R. D. Gem. They also have two granddaughters, Kai Sofia and Anya Rei. Their family has a passion for helping orphans and their churches in any way that they can. **May 1**

Kathy Pepper is a pastor's wife living in Pittsburgh, Pennsylvania, United States of America. She and her husband, Stewart, have a son, two daughters, a daughter-in-law, a son-in-law, and were blessed with their first grandchild in February 2017. Kathy enjoys working with her husband and graphic designing, and she uses this creativity in their ministry. **Apr. 8**

Céleste Perrino-Walker is a much published Vermont author in the United States of America. News about her most recent books and upcoming releases can be found on her website, cperrinowalker.com. **Feb. 20, June 30, Nov. 13**

Diane Pestes, author of *Prayer That Moves Mountains* (DianePestes.com), served for ten years in Women's Ministries at the Oregon Conference of Seventh-day Adventists in the United States of America, where she coordinated events, training, mentoring, speaking, and prayer for and/or with people. Her priority is being a servant and friend of God whenever she speaks at evangelistic series, prayer conferences, retreats, or prisons. She loves memorizing Scripture. **Sept. 25**

Margo Peterson writes from Eagan, Minnesota, United States of America, where she works as a program assistant in a special education school district. She has three children. She is a tutor in reading and math. Besides studying at school, she works with the young people at her church; spends time reading, traveling, and walking; and enjoys time with her family. **July 21**

Birdie Poddar is a retiree who comes from northeast India and settled in south India. She has two adult children, a girl and a boy, and five grandchildren. She enjoys gardening, keeping house, cooking, baking, telling stories, writing articles, and composing poems. She has a handcrafted card ministry for those who need comfort and encouragement and to glorify God's name. **Feb. 6, May 29**

Prudence LaBeach Pollard, PhD, MPH, RD, SPHR, is vice president for Research and Employee Services at Oakwood University in Huntsville, Alabama, United States of America. She is also interim director of the dietetic program and professor of management. She has authored the book *Raise a Leader, God's Way* (available at AdventistBookCenter. com or as an eBook at Amazon.com). **Sept. 1, Sept. 2**

Evelyn Porteza-Tabingo is a retired cardiac nurse living in Oceanside, California, United States of America. She and her husband have served as missionaries. She enjoys reading, writing, gardening, music, traveling, and spending time with her four grandchildren. **Jan. 10, Aug. 17**

Beverly Campbell Pottle has worked as an administrative assistant in Kenya, Lebanon, Cyprus, and at Andrews University in Berrien Springs, Michigan, United States of America. Now retired, she enjoys writing, walking, genealogy, birding, and traveling with her husband. **May 28**

Beatrice Tauber Prior, PsyD, is a clinical psychologist with more than twenty years experience in the field. She is passionate about her family, friends, and walking the pathway of healing with her clients. **Jan. 25, Aug. 8**

Nadine Parker Proctor has been married to Lynden Proctor for almost fifty years. They have two married children and four granddaughters. She has a scrapbook business in her home and works with women's ministries. Her hobbies are photography, scrapbooking, and snow skiing. **Jan. 11**

Katia Garcia Reinert, MSN, PhD, is the author of *Ten Choices for a Full Life*. Originally from Brazil, this family nurse practitioner and public health clinical nurse specialist practices internal medicine in Hyattsville, Maryland, United States of America. She is also associate director of Health Ministries at the North American Division of Seventh-day Adventists. She enjoys bicycling, hiking, traveling, and exploring nature's wonders. **Sept. 10, Sept. 11, Dec. 28**

Darlenejoan McKibbin Rhine, born in Nebraska, raised in California, and educated in Tennessee in the United States of America, has now retired from the *Los Angeles Times* to the "soggy" state of Washington. She is a widow with one son. She has a BA in journalism and belongs to the North Cascade Seventh-day Adventist Church and supports the Anacortes Adventist Fellowship company. **Apr. 5**

Karen Richards, who writes from England, is a teacher in a reception class for children aged four and five. She has been married for thirty years and has two adult daughters. She loves writing and believes that God wants her to use this gift to encourage and bless other women in their relationship with Him. **Jan. 27, Nov. 18**

Marli Elizete Ritter-Hein was born in the city of Sao Paulo, Brazil, married an Argentinean doctor more than forty years ago, and worked with him as a missionary in Nepal and now Paraguay. The mother of two young adults, she is a teacher by profession, and she loves music that points to heaven. She also enjoys nature, flower arrangements, visiting family, interior decorating, and coordinating her church's music ministry. **Feb. 18, July 3**

Taniesha Robertson-Brown is a teacher who enjoys reading, writing, and ministering to people. She hopes to someday commit herself to full-time ministry. She appreciates the company and support of her husband, Courtney. She is a previous contributor and also author of the book *Godly Families in an Ungodly World*. **Jan. 2, Aug. 23**

Charlotte Robinson has spent most of her life working and helping her husband raise three children. She has been published in *Our Little Friend*, *Primary Treasure*, *Guide*, and *Insight*. After living seventeen years with her parents near Ozark Academy, she moved to nearby Decatur, Arkansas, United States of America, when she married. She now lives on her late mother's property, where she lived as a child. **July 18**

Terry Wilson Robinson lives with her husband, Harry, in the Blue Ridge Mountains of North Carolina, United States of America. Her greatest joy is assisting him in teaching Revelation seminars. **Apr. 9**

Dixil L. Rodríguez is a university professor and volunteer chaplain who lives in Argyle, north Texas, United States of America. **Feb. 28, May 22, Aug. 11**

Ida T. Ronaszegi, MFA, is a writer and professor of English as a second language (ESL) at

Savannah College of Art and Design Language Studio in South Carolina, United States of America. Her work has appeared in *Adventist Review*, *Susie*, *Trazzler*, and *Document* (an academic journal). She serves as an elder in her church and has a passion for women's ministries. She and Arpad, her husband, have three grown children. **Oct. 22, Dec. 1**

Terry Roselmond-Moore is a native of Barbados, a tiny Caribbean island, but has lived most of her life in the United States of America. She is a nurse executive with Kettering Health Network in the metro Dayton, Ohio, area; a proud mother of her daughter, Taryn Lynch; and the Pathfinder and Adventurer Club leader of the New Life Aviators' Pathfinder Club in Dayton, Ohio. Heaven is her destination. **Jan. 19**

Zlata Sabo lives with her husband, Joseph, in Ocala, Florida, United States of America. She is a retired music teacher and enjoys traveling and photography. In her free time, she likes to read and write; she has had several articles and poems published. **June 3, Oct. 3**

Teresa A. Sales, a retired journalist/editor, lives in Colorado, United States of America, with her minister husband, Don, who is also a writer. Since retiring, she has taught creative writing to junior high students, an age she enjoys. The couple has also served eight churches as the interim pastor couple and continues to be active in area churches. **Oct. 15**

Darlene Grunke Sanders, a retired teacher, currently serves on four scholarship committees and two boards (National Alliance on Mental Illness and Daughters of Norway) and also enjoys participating in the book clubs of sister churches of all faiths. Her free time is shared between the local garden club, her walking group, and functioning as secretary of her local community association. **May 27**

Deborah Sanders lives in Alberta, Canada, with her husband, Ron, and her son, Sonny. In 1990 God blessed her with a successful writing and prayer outreach ministry, Dimensions of Love. In 2013 she selected the best stories and compiled a book of sacred memories entitled *Saints-in-Training*, a book she hopes Sonny can use to continue his witness for Jesus. **Mar. 23, Aug. 26**

Jennifer Jill Schwirzer resides with her husband, Michael, in Philadelphia, Pennsylvania, United States of America, where she conducts a private counseling practice and a speaking, writing, and music ministry. They have two daughters, Allison and Kimberly. Her latest book is *13 Weeks to Peace*, available through Pacific Press® Publishing Association. **Jan. 21, June 26**

Omobonike Adeola Sessou is the Women's Ministries and Children's Ministries director at the West-Central Africa Division of Seventh-day Adventists in Abidjan, Côte d'Ivoire. She is married to Pastor Sessou, and they are blessed with three children. Her hobbies include teaching, counseling, making new friends, and visiting with people. **Jan. 26, Oct. 9**

Cathy Shannon resides in Pikeville, Tennessee, United States of America, with her husband, Dale, in a rustic mountain home that they built together. She is an art and life skills teacher and Women's Ministries leader at her church. She has published a cookbook and loves to sew, quilt, write short devotionals, and create art. **Dec. 19**

Rose Neff Sikora and her husband, Norman, live happily on their hobby farm in the beautiful mountains of North Carolina, United States of America. She is retired from a forty-five-year career as a registered nurse and volunteers at Park Ridge Health. She enjoys walking, writing, and helping others. She has one adult daughter, Julie, and three lovely grandchildren. She desires that her writing will bless others. **Mar. 25**

Slavka Simeonova is a retired pastor's wife living in Bulgaria. **Aug. 4, Aug. 5**

Ella Louise Smith Simmons is a vice president at the General Conference of Seventh-day Adventists in Maryland, United States of America, and the first woman to hold this position. A veteran educator, she has served as provost, academic vice president, and professor in church and public sector universities. She is married to Nord, and they have two children, three grandchildren, and one great-grandson. **Apr. 18**

Heather-Dawn Small is director for Women's Ministries at the General Conference of Seventh-day Adventists. She has been Children's Ministries and Women's Ministries director for the Caribbean Union Conference, located in Trinidad and Tobago. She is the wife of Pastor Joseph Small and the mother of Dalonne and Jerard. She loves air travel, reading, and scrapbooking. **Jan. 12, Apr. 13, Sept. 14, Dec. 10**

Yvonne Curry Smallwood enjoys life's simple pleasures—a colorful sunrise, a crisp autumn day, and time with family members. Her stories have appeared in several publications. She writes from Maryland. **May 25, Nov. 24**

Peggy Miles Snow retired first from the Adventist Health System and then as administrator of skilled nursing facilities in three states. She now lives in Florida, United States of America, at a retirement facility and is involved in many activities, as well as continuing to share her faith. She has four children, four grandchildren, and four great-grandchildren. **Feb. 2, Oct. 21**

Sylvia Stark is an artist who lives in Tennessee, United States of America. Her artwork is displayed in several states and in South America. Sylvia enjoys being in the outdoors, hiking, camping, backpacking, and enjoying the work of the Master Artist. She has been published in *Guide.* **Nov. 10**

Ardis Dick Stenbakken, now living in Colorado, United States of America, edited these devotional books for seventeen years. Retired as director of Women's Ministries at the General Conference of Seventh-day Adventists, she and her husband, Dick, love spending time with their two children and their spouses and four grandchildren. She is still hoping to find time to once again pursue some hobbies. **Feb. 16, June 16, Sept. 28**

Rita Kay Stevens is a church administrator's wife living in New Mexico, United States of America. She works as a medical technologist in a local hospital. She is a liaison for Women's Ministries and sponsor for the ministers' wives in the Texico Conference of Seventh-day Adventists. She is the mother of two grown sons and is thankful for a daughter-in-law, grandson, and granddaughter. **Dec. 12**

Emiliya Stoykova, Women's Ministries director in Bulgaria for eight years, works as an assistant pastor with her husband (also a pastor and prayer coordinator for the Bulgarian Union). They are blessed with three adult children, one son-in-law, and two wonderful granddaughters. Emiliya enjoys reading, walking in nature, and mentoring women, teenagers, and children. **June 25**

Naomi Striemer lives in Franklin, Tennessee, United States of America, with her husband, Jordan, and dog, Bella. She is a best-selling author, a chart-topping Christian singer and songwriter, and a sought-after speaker who tours around the world singing and speaking. In her spare time she enjoys baking, board games, and the outdoors. **Jan. 31, May 26**

Carolyn Rathbun Sutton and her husband, Jim, are volunteer field representatives for Adventist World Radio. From their home in Alabama, United States of America, she edited this year's General Conference Women's Ministries devotional book, the proceeds of which go to support higher education for women globally. **Mar. 28, Oct. 27, Dec. 15**

Loraine F. Sweetland, a retired widow, lives alone in Tennessee, United States of America, and awaits the soon return of her Lord and Savior, Jesus. **Feb. 10**

Frieda Tanner is a retired nurse and moved to Eugene, Oregon, United States of America, more than twenty-four years ago to be near her daughter and family. She spends most of her time making nice Sabbath School items for children all over the world. So far, her items have gone to ninety countries. Frieda is more than ninety-six years old. **June 5**

Charmaine N. Williams Tate is a woman whose rich history of trial, restoration, and renewal has set the foundation for her passion to inspire others to live for God. A native of Jamaica now living in Toronto, Canada, she is a mother, wife, friend, confidante, singer, writer, and Christian motivational speaker. She embraces each day as an opportunity to make a difference. **Mar. 12**

Arlene R. Taylor recently retired from health care after decades of working with Adventist Health facilities. Still living in the Napa Valley of northern California, United States of America, she devotes her time and energy to brain function research, writing, and speaking. **Feb. 25, Sept. 26, Dec. 18**

Ellen Jane Tejano-Galupo is a university student in Ottawa, Ontario, Canada. Originally from the Philippines, she immigrated to Canada in 2006 with her family. They then moved to Moosonee, Ontario, answering God's calling to become His missionaries in rural Ontario. Ellen loves to write, enjoys volunteering at a local hospital, and has served as Sabbath School teacher and campus ministry leader. **Sept. 4, Nov. 11**

Rose Joseph Thomas is an educator with the Florida Conference of Seventh-day Adventists in the United States of America. She's married to her best friend, Walden, and they have two children: Samuel Joseph and Crystal Rose. **Jan. 29, July 30**

Bula Rose Haughton Thompson serves as Women's Ministries director for the Goshen church in the West Jamaica Conference of Seventh-day Adventists. A dental assistant for thirty-seven years, she is now retired but still works and studies part-time. Her hobbies are sewing, singing, reading, and meeting people. Norman, her husband, lectures in the Department of Humanities at Northern Caribbean University in Jamaica. **Dec. 8**

Miriam L. Thompson lives on a blueberry farm in Pugwash, Nova Scotia, Canada. She has two adult children and one grandchild. Her favorite activities are reading, quilting, and enjoying the outdoors. **July 11**

Rebecca Timon recently transitioned into two new roles: grandmother and editorial assistant, working with this Women's Ministries devotional book, at the General Conference of Seventh-day Adventists. She leads a Bible study and belongs to several more. Her mission is to encourage others to fall in love with Jesus and His Word. **Oct. 31, Nov. 1**

Carolyn Voss, PhD, is a widow and a retired nurse educator. Her hobbies are sewing, quilting, crafts, walking, golfing, and studying God's Word. **Feb. 4, Dec. 13**

Kalisha A. Waldon resides in Sunrise, Florida, United States of America. She is a product of Adventist Christian education and served as a principal and/or teacher for eleven years. She is presently a doctoral candidate and adjunct professor. **Apr. 19**

Dolores Klinsky Walker is discovering joy in "enhanced adulthood." Limited physical activity provides time for her to ponder God's ways, to write, and to pass God's love on to others. She is married. She and her husband have three children. Dolores writes from Walla Walla, Washington, United States of America. **July 16**

Anna May Radke Waters, a retired administrative secretary from Columbia Adventist Academy, has served as an ordained church elder and greeter. At the top of her long list of hobbies are her eight grandchildren and husband with whom she likes to travel and make memories. She also enjoys doing Bible studies on the Internet and answering prayer requests for Bibleinfo.com. **Jan. 28, Aug. 28**

Elizabeth Darby Watson, PhD, MSW, is an associate professor of social work in North Carolina, United States of America. A freelance author, her talents include creative writing, motivational speaking, and children's ministry. She is an intelligent, assertive, professional, and successful single parent, the mother of three adult children (and their spouses), and grandmother to five wonderful grandchildren. **Feb. 22**

Lyn Welk-Sandy, Mother, Nana, and Great-Nana from South Australia, enjoys nature and caravanning Australia with her husband, Keith. Grief counseling, photography, playing the pipe organ, and hand chiming are her favorite activities. **Apr. 1, June 17, Sept. 7**

Penny Estes Wheeler, a displaced Texan, loves travel almost as much as her kids and grandkids. She considers her visits to Israel and Australia "trips of a lifetime," and she'd go again in a heartbeat. But more of the world beckons. **Aug. 21**

Avonda White-Krause is a retired special education teacher who is married with four children, nine grandchildren, and eleven great-grandchildren. She loves being with people, reading, traveling, and crocheting. **Dec. 17**

Vera Wiebe, who lives in Alberta, Canada, has been a women's ministries leader for nine years. She enjoys playing the piano, cooking, sewing, and knitting. She and her pastor husband, Ken, have two sons and four grandchildren. **Mar. 24**

Patrice E. Williams-Gordon is a Jamaican motivational speaker and seminar presenter who enjoys writing, speaking, reading, and a good laugh. She shares ministry with her husband, Pastor Danhugh Gordon, who currently serves in Nassau, Bahamas. Mother of Ashli and Rhondi, she is excited about reaching anyone for Jesus. **June 2**

Rachel Williams-Smith is a wife, mother, writer, and speaker. She has a bachelor's degree in language arts, a master's degree in professional writing, and a doctorate in communication. She chairs the Department of Communication at Andrews University. Her book, *Born Yesterday*, was published by the Pacific Press Publishing Association. **Jan. 15, July 31**

Sylvia Jackson Wilson, retired after twenty years as Women's Ministries director of the South Atlantic Conference of Seventh-day Adventists, spent thirty-four years teaching in Adventist schools. A recipient of the North American Division Excellence in Teaching Award, she now owns Prince of Peace Christian Academy in Greensboro, North Carolina, United States of America. **Apr. 14**

Nena A. Wirth is a diet and nutrition consultant with a practice at her Eat to Live Learning Centre in Ontario, Canada. She is the author of four books and is passionate about helping others improve the quality of their lives. She serves as Health Ministries leader at her church and also provides nutrition seminars for various groups. **Apr. 12**

Jeanne B. Woolsey currently serves as church clerk at Waynesville Seventh-day Adventist Church in Waynesville, Missouri, United States of America. Before retirement, her primary work was in health-care positions. She enjoys writing. **Apr. 27**